THE PIAZZA.

Venice,

FROM

Napoleon to Radetzky,

VENICE;

THE CITY OF THE SEA,

FROM THE INVASION BY NAPOLEON IN 1797 TO THE CAPITULATION TO RADETZKY IN 1849; WITH A CONTEMPORANEOUS VIEW OF THE PENINSULA.

BY EDMUND FLAGG,

LATE CONSUL OF THE UNITED STATES AT THE PORT OF VENICE—AUTHOR OF "THE FAR WEST," "THE HOWARD QUEEN," ETC, ETC.

EVERYTHING about Venice is extraordinary. Her history is like a dream—her aspect like a romance.—BYRON.

WITH A MAP AND EMBELLISHMENTS.

IN TWO VOLUMES.

VOL. I.

NEW YORK:

CHARLES SCRIBNER, 145 NASSAU STREET.

1853.

C. W. BENEDICT,
STEREOTYPER AND PRINTER,
12 Spruce Street, N. Y.

Dedicatory Epistle.

TO

GEORGE D. PRENTICE, ESQ.,

OF LOUISVILLE.

PERMIT me, dear Prentice, to honor these volumes with your name. The humblest of Western writers might, perhaps, claim this as a right of the most distinguished, though nothing were due to a long and faithful friendship. But there is a claim yet more undeniable. If to " perpetrate a book " be that crime which the Preacher would seem to intimate, when he says—" Oh, that mine enemy would write a book !"—then, for the perpetration of the present book, it is a question, whether you may not be arraigned, as hardly less criminal, than the actual perpetrator !—whether, to all intents and meanings, you may not be deemed, at least a *particeps criminis !*—an accomplice not only " before the fact," but " in the fact," and " after the fact ;" since, very surely, but for your suggestion these volumes would never have been commenced, and but with your encouragement they might never have been completed. Nay, more, but for certain flattering words from your pen, years ago, when, for the first time, the writer found himself anonymously "in print," in all the glories of actual type, in the columns of the "Louisville Journal," he would, in all probability, never at all, heretofore, nor at present, have intruded in the line of letters. And, more yet—but for your own suggestion, with express disavowal of all political claim, the writer would, in all probability, never have been honored with that position which has enabled him to prepare the present work.

You perceive then, dear Prentice, that it is clearly impossible you should avoid acceptance of the responsibility now imposed; and, if you can not find it in your good nature to assume nearer relationship to an adventurer about seeking its fortunes, you will, at least, most benevolently, accept the office of godfather; thus adding one more to the many obligations of,

Most faithfully yours,

EDMUND FLAGG.

NEW YORK, July 4th, 1853.

ILLUSTRATIONS—VOL. I.

ILLUSTRATIONS—VOL. II.

PREFACE.

THESE volumes do not aspire to the dignity of History. Should they supply a deficiency in the Literature of the day, and afford the future historian a digest of material, they will have subserved their purpose.

That a comprehensive view of Venice as she once was and as she now is, together with a sketch of her invasion by Napoleon and her fall in '97 after fourteen centuries of flourishing existence, has long been a desideratum, every tourist in North Italy is aware; while it is certainly remarkable, that, among the numberless volumes of "Revolution Literature" since '48–49, not one has appeared to record in detail the heroic struggle of the "City of the Sea." Had such a work in any language appeared, the present would never, probably, have had existence; although, doubtless, an American pen can always render events in another land more comprehensible to an American reader, than could even a native of that land himself. Thus Botta, for example, has presented the Italian a far more lucid view of the American Revolution, than could, perhaps, the most graphic and impartial of American historians.

Facts being the object of this work, every available source of information has been called on for its quota—the history—the archive—the review; the pamphlet—the newspaper—the placard. To the accomplished historian of the Italian Republics, and to the excellent Itinerary of Lecomte, the writer has been chiefly indebted in his Introduction. The works of Thiers, Scott, Botta, Spalding, and others, have been freely consulted and carefully collated, in absence of original archives, in Part First; while, to the little volumes of Debrunner, Garrano, and Contarini, and to the larger ones of Mariotti, Pepé, and Stiles, as, also, to foreign reviews, to journals of the day and to the writer's own contributions to their columns during official residence abroad, he has been greatly indebted, in Part Second. No labor has been spared to render the work reliable as a reference.

Despite all efforts, however, errors will, doubtless, have occurred; though the suggestion may, perhaps, be pardoned, that, considering deficiency of reliable material and the conflicting character of much possessed, it is almost as noticeable that errors are so few as that they are so many.

New York, July 4th, 1853.

CONTENTS OF VOL. I.

INTRODUCTION.

VENICE PAST AND PRESENT.

PART FIRST.

VENICE IN '96-97. HER FALL.

CHAPTER I.

ALLIANCE.

CHAPTER II.

THE VERONESE EASTER.

CHAPTER III.

VENGEANCE.

CHAPTER IV.

"SPOLIATION."

CHAPTER V.

CAMPO FORMIO.

CHAPTER VI.

"PERFIDY."

CHAPTER VII.

LOMBARDO-VENETO.

CHAPTER VIII.

INTERVENTION.

CHAPTER IX.

"YOUNG ITALY."

PART SECOND.

VENICE IN '48–49. HER RISE.

CHAPTER I.

RETROSPECTION.

CHAPTER II.

REVOLUTION !

CHAPTER III.

BLOOD !

CHAPTER IV.

MARINOVICH.

CHAPTER V.

EVACUATION.

CHAPTER VI.

"THE HOLY WAR."

CHAPTER VII.

DIPLOMACY.

CHAPTER VIII.

"LA SPADA D'ITALIA."

NOTE.—Correctness, or even uniformity, in the spelling of foreign words, and especially of proper names, seems by no means an easy task in an English book. Subjoined are those which appear to have suffered most in these volumes:—Acqua, Pescheria, Mocenigo, Morosini, Cappello, Conaro, Ticino, Vincenzo, Valeggio, Custoza, Lago, Galateo, Radetzky, Wimpffen, Schwartzenberg, Alessandria, Mussulmans, Bevilacqua, Baudin, Appenines, trabaccolo, canaletto, ricochet, liaison, gendarmes.

Introduction.

VENICE PAST AND PRESENT.

There is a glorious city in the sea!—
The sea is in the broad, the narrow streets,
Ebbing and flowing; and the salt sea-weed
Clings to the marble of her palaces.

ROGERS.

INTRODUCTION.

VENICE PAST AND PRESENT.

IMPERIAL VENICE! The Ocean Queen! The throne of a thousand years! The mistress of an hundred isles! Venice, with her prisons and her palaces—her ducal domes and her dusky dungeons—her Rialto Bridge and her Bridge of Sighs! Venice, with her *Piombi* and her *Pozzi*—her leaden roofs and her mystic "wells"—her racks and her "Question"—her bronze steeds and her Giant's Staircase—her Strangling-chamber and the Winged Lion of St. Mark! Venice, with her monks and masqueraders—her courtiers and courtezans—her sbirri and signory—her bravoes and beggars—her fanatics and familiars—her Improvisatori and Gondolieri—her Doges, her spies, her terrible "Ten!" The home of Tasso, and Shylock, and the Moor! The city of the gliding gondola and the moonlight serenade—of snowy plume and sable mantilla—of the crimson *tabarro* and graceful *zendale*—of the guitar and the stiletto! The city of crime and chivalry—of gloom and gaiety—of mystery and mimicry—of canals and causeways—of piety and poetry—of religion and romance! The city of the Ridotto and the Regatta—of the Lagune and the Lido—of the Carnival, the Bucentauro, and the "espoused Adriatic!" The mart of Europe for the opulence of India! Genoa's rival—Italy's emporium—Rome's last refuge from "the scourge of God!" Christendom's citadel against the Greek and the Goth, the Saracen and the Frank! The sea-city of freedom! The lazar-house of despotism! "Gehenna of the waters!" VENICE! What a flood of associations throng the memory at mention of her name! VENICE IN THE SIXTEENTH CENTURY!

It is years since the above florid sentences were first written; and it was years afterwards before the writer had seen the Venice he then so ambitiously strove to represent. Venice in her prime—"Venice in the sixteenth Century"—Venice three hundred years ago—they purport to portray; and, though the traits were drawn from history and fancy, many of them are scarce less true of her as she is, in the middle of the nineteenth century, than as she was, in the middle of the sixteenth. Venice, in many respects, is the most changeless capital of Europe. Her scenes and localities it is impossible should change, until, indeed, she fulfil the ancient and favorite prevision, and

"Sinks, like a sea-weed, into whence she rose."

Venice is, also, so dream-like—so like a dream—so like "the stuff of which dreams are made," that, with a few general outlines in the mind gained from Canaletto,* it is not difficult to dream out a pretty correct panorama of her visionary charms.

* Antonio Canal, or Canaletto, as he has been named, owed, to a great extent, that graphic power of his views of Venice, which has rendered him famous the world over, to the use of the *camera*. Names are common to Italian artists, based on place of nativity, peculiarity of genius, or on other like circumstances. Battaglia was called *Tempesta* for his skill in representing storms. Bambini owed his name to his genius for painting infants. Padovanino, Veronese, Bassano, Pordenone and Vicentino owed their *soubriquets*

"Venice," says Byron, "is one of those places which I know before I see them."

"I feel as I gaze around me," says Mrs. Jameson, "as if I had seen Venice in my dreams; as if it were itself the vision of a dream."

"You should go to Venice," says Willis, "to know how like a dream reality may be."

And yet, after all, the Venice of reality never resembles the Venice of vision; and of no city in the world is the remark of the celebrated Volney more true: "It is vain that we attempt to prepare ourselves, by the perusal of books, for a more intimate acquaintance with the customs and manners of nations; for, the effect of narratives on the mind will always be very different from that of objects on the senses." Venice is so utterly unlike every other city in the world, that no symbols or comparisons are afforded by what is known of others for its description, or even its idea. No city but itself can be its parallel, or its comparison. "There is but one Venice in all the world." Amsterdam, and Rotterdam, and Copenhagen are intersected by canals spanned by bridges; and Stockholm occupies seven rocky islands and two peninsulas. But here all likeness ceases. Who would think of comparing the Flemish, or the Swedish, or the Danish capital with the City of the Sea, any more than their respective inhabitants? Everything, therefore, is strange, peculiar, remarkable in Venice; and the writer who takes up his pen to attempt to convey an idea of it to distant friends, finds himself, at once, "all at sea" in the multiplicity of novel objects which crowd upon his mind, each claiming attention; while the confusion and bewilderment caused by this throng of unusual scenes renders

to the names of the places of their nativity; Cuticello to a wound in the hand; Sebastian del Piombo to his office of exciseman of lead under Clement VII.; Tintoretto to the trade of his father, a dyer; Giorgione, because very tall, his name being Giorgio; Zingaro because a wanderer—whom like Quentin Metsys, *love* transferred from the forge to the easel.

him quite unable to do justice to any. He knows not where to begin; and it is not until he has fixed on a starting point—it is not until he has decided to take the city in detail—to analyze it, as it were, and to delineate its objects of interest in classes, that he finds himself making the least progress in conveying an idea of Venice. To present a *coup d'œil* of the sea-city, therefore, or to attempt it, and then to sketch the elements of which it is composed, would seem the only mode of doing her anything like justice; yet, even that mode would be a hopeless one. In fact, Venice is indescribable!

Most persons know more of the Ocean-Queen as she was fourteen centuries ago, than as she is in the present; more of her history for fourteen hundred years, than during the half hundred years last past. The reason seems obvious. The annals of Venice, since her fall, have found no chronicler. That Venice was founded early in the fifth century, by a body of Italians fleeing before Attila, to ninety small islands formed at the head of the Adriatic by the *debris* of the rivers flowing from the Appenines and the Alps; that, protected by the locality and their poverty, and supported by fishing and salt-making, magnificent Venice, rising like Aphrodite from the sea, in a few centuries almost verified the line of the poet Sannavar—

"Men built Rome—the gods Venice!"

that the zenith of her grandeur was reached at the close of the fifteenth century, one thousand years from her origin, and that then, the discoveries of Columbus and Gama struck a blow at her commerce from which she could never recover—all this is known by every child who has faithfully studied his school geography and his Compendium of History.

About the year 400 of the Christian era, Consuis were sent from

Padua to govern the Port of Rivo Alto,* the central isle of the future Queen of the Adriatic. In the library of the Camaldolites at the Convent of St. Michael, where is now the cemetery of Venice, is to be seen a decree of the Senate of Padua in 421, ordering the fugitives, who were scattered upon the isles of the Lagune, to unite on that of the Rialto, for the purpose of founding a city and constructing a fleet. Seventy-three years later, the other islands becoming settled and peopled, a Tribune for each was chosen by the inhabitants. This continued from 473 to 503, a period of thirty years, when a single Tribune for all the islands was substituted, which *regime* lasted for seventy-one years. In 574, the number of chief magistrates was increased to ten, so continuing for one hundred and thirty years, until 604, when it was again increased to a dozen, and so continued for ninety-three years, until 697. But the Tribunes became tyrants and the system was abolished. A solemn assembly was convened at Heraclea, one of the islands of the Venitian Archipelago, by the Patriarch Gradus, and a Duke, or Doge, was chosen to govern all the islands of the Lagune consolidated into a State. Then began the Doges, Anafesto of Heraclea, being the first. He and his successor reigned quietly, but the third Doge, Urseo, was massacred by the people, and the government was again given to magistrates annually elected, called "Masters of the Militia." This lasted until 742, when Ziani, the fifth of these officers in succession, was deposed and deprived of sight, and Deodato Urseo, son of the last Doge, and the third of the *Masters*, was elected Prince. But, in 755, after a troubled reign of thirteen years he, also, was deposed and deprived of sight. Then follows for a period of 1043 the long line of Doges, whose *Dantesque* portraits look down from the walls of the Ducal Palace, be-

* Meaning—"Deep stream"—whence Rialto, by elision.

ginning with the ninth, Obelerio, in 804, and closing with the last, Manini, who abdicated in 1798.* The number of families which furnished Doges was remarkably small. The office was in the Contarini family eight times and in the Moncenigo seven. In the year 1612, when the celebrated Angelo Emo was elected, amid furious popular commotions, the *Dogat* had, for a period of more than two centuries, been continuously held by only nineteen patrician families! During the first five hundred years a very large number of the Doges were deposed and deprived of sight, massacred by the people, or banished. Indeed, of the first fifty Doges, one-third were violently dethroned. A large number, also, abdicated; and three of them, Participazio, in 932, Urseolo, in 978, and Malipieri, in 1192, "implored peace" in the shades of a cloister. In the Ducal Palace, only one hundred and fifteen of the one hundred and twenty Doges have portraits; and, after that of Manini, are vacant pannels for thirteen more. In the frame which the portrait of the fifty-seventh Doge should fill, hangs a black veil bearing the words—*Hic est locus Marini Falieri decapitati pro criminibus.*†

Thus—from the fifth to the sixth century, Venice was ruled by Consuls; from the sixth to the eighth, by Tribunes; and from the eighth to the nineteenth, by Doges, Anafesto, the first Doge, being elected in 697, and Manini, the last Doge, abdicating in 1798.

* The striking profile resemblance of the Doges of Venice, as shown in their portraits in the Ducal Palace, and in their busts upon their tombs, to those of the celebrated Dante, has been more than once noticed. The sharp and aquiline features of the Italian poet, with their severe yet serene expression, who that has ever seen them on the canvass, or in the marble, can forget? The same *Dantesque* face is that of the Doges of Venice.

† After the treason of Faliero, every representation of him was destroyed by order of the Senate. Even his portrait in the picture of the conquest of Zara in the Ducal Palace was effaced, and a soldier substituted for the victorious general. There is, however, said to exist one portrait of him at Treviso, which has always been kept very secret and very sacred, in a family of which he was a friend. An apocryphal portrait of this Doge is, also, shown in the Museum of Sanquirico, at Venice.

The island of the Rialto, which was, at first, the capital of the Lagune, was soon superseded by that of Malamocco, at the extremity of the Lido; and, though once destroyed by inundation and once by conflagration, Malamocco continued the capital, until, early in the ninth century, Pepin, the father of Charlemagne, King of Lombardy, having taken the neighboring isles of Chioggia and Pelestrina, advanced his galleys thitherward with hostile intent. Powerless to resist, the inhabitants sought safety in the shallows of the friendly Lagune, where the pursuing galleys were stranded and burned; and, once more concentrating themselves on the central isle of the Rialto, the spot became the settled seat of future power. The smaller islands, some of them solid and even granitic in soil, but most of them scarcely firm enough to uphold the weary sea-bird pausing in his flight, were united to the capital and to each other by bridges; the intervening canals were deepened; churches and palaces were erected; and the mighty march of Venice began.

For a period of more than three centuries the power of the Doge was nearly absolute. He made peace or war, commanded the army and navy, selected his counsellors, appointed officers, condemned or pardoned the accused, and often designated his successor. In the ninth century commenced curtailment of his powers, and it continued from year to year, and age to age, until hardly a shadow remained. By his oath of office he engaged to seek no augmentation of power; to keep secret affairs of state; to read no letter from abroad, save in presence of his councillors; to send no despatch; to give audience to no ambassador; to return no response to any demand; to receive no gifts; to possess no property without the *Dogado;* to erect or repair no monument; never to leave Venice without permission; never to receive in private generals of the republic; and to permit no member of his family to exercise governmental, ecclesiastical or commercial influence within Venice or without. His sons were compelled to reside in Venice, and to have no connection with foreign states or princes. His wife, the *Dogaressa*, was entitled to no coronation, as at first, and was forbidden to entertain foreign ministers. Each month the councillors of the Doge read to him his oath anew, and also a decree, that, after his death, his body would, for three days, be exposed in public, that all demands upon him might be satisfied by his family. He was limited in the amount of largess he should give the people on his election; in the amount he should give for charity; in the amount he should expend in certain fetes; while his household was reduced to an usher, a master of ceremonies, a few priests and fifty guards. In the grand council he had but a single vote and no voice. He presided on an *estrade* of five steps on an elevated seat; all rose as he entered or left; papers were presented him on the bended knee. His costume was of purple brocade set off with ermine, the jewelled *beretta* covering his head. He was generally a very old man, one who had never married, or who was widowed and childless. Personally, his power was nothing. There were rules for his household, his table, the employment of his time. For eight hundred years, a power never but once abused, was constantly curtailed; yet, despite all precautions, the conspiracy of Faliero had well nigh overturned the republic. Before the thirteenth century, the Doges fought bravely at the head of armies; but subsequently there were but three instances, and Morosini, the *Peloponesiaque*, was the last. The state would not trust her sovereign. He was no longer a warrior or a ruler; he was only "a marvel and a show." To no one, indeed, more eminently than to the aged dotard who filled the ducal chair of Venice, could be applied the words of Machiavelli in his *Prince*, with reference to a certain potentate of his day: "Powerless for good and passionless for evil, he was but a crowned puppet." One would suppose the place anything but desirable; yet, only one person ever refused "the horned bonnet" during the whole existence of the Ducal office.

The prerogatives of this potentate have thus been grouped: "He was a king in parade—a senator in power—a prisoner in the Lagune—a citizen beyond it; the coin bore his name, but not his head; decrees bore his title, but not his signature; he opened despatches addressed to him only before his council; he presided in assemblies, but could only propose measures and never decide them; he nominated the clergy and created Knights of St. Mark; he was exempt from sumptuary laws; his relatives could receive no office; he could not abdicate, but could be deposed; his salary was two thousand ducats each year; he was subject to the inquisition of the "Ten;" his family, after his decease, was liable for his acts."

At first, the Doge was elected directly by the people; but, subsequently, by the Grand Council—which was, itself, elected annually by the people—and by a most complicated balloting with gilt balls, to preclude collusion. In 1297, the celebrated decree called, *La Serrata del consiglio*"—"The closing of the Council," was carried; and only the descendants of those who had previously sat in that body could henceforth have seats; and it is a somewhat noticeable fact, that it was five centuries, to a day, from the time Venice assumed the form of an hereditary aristocracy (1297), when the senate could no longer be chosen from the masses, but only from among those, who, for four years, had already been senators—to her final fall, in 1797. Thus was established "that hereditary aristocracy—so prudent, so jealous, so ambitious—which Europe regarded with astonishment; immovable in principle, unshaken in power; uniting some of the most odious practices of despotism with the name of liberty;

suspicious and perfidious in politics; sanguinary in revenge; indulgent to the subject; sumptuous in the public service, yet economical in the administration of finances; equitable and impartial in the administration of justice; knowing well how to give prosperity to the arts, agriculture and commerce; beloved by the people who obeyed it, while it made the nobles who partook its power tremble."* Twelve years later the oligarchy was completed by the creation of the "Ten"—at first a mere committee of safety, and for a few days only—to suppress the conspiracy of Tieopolo; but, continued in existence from day to day, and week to week, till it became the grand state inquisition of Venice, with a power above all law, all authority, and all appeal! It seemed to possess the very attributes of the Deity himself; for it was everywhere, knew everything, and could do everything. And yet, its members were unknown; they sat in secret, and judged, and doomed, and executed. They issued no written orders. The proudest senator, the most successful general, the Doge himself, nay, even the members of the Ten were not inviolable. Efforts were made to check and crush it, but they all recoiled; while from its bosom sprang another tribunal yet more terrible—the Council of Three. Thus fortified, those who had assailed it, one after the other, disappeared! The people when they referred to it spake no words, but pointed upward; yet, though they feared, they seldom suffered by it. The nobility supplied victims to the "Ten;" the people were its children. It was inflexible and incorruptible. Traitors to the state it strangled in its dungeons and suspended by the feet between the columns of the Piazetta; while to maintain the salutary terror, when victims were deficient, corpses from the hospitals were thus suspended.

In many points the Ten of Venice recalls the *Vehme Gericht*, or

* Sismondi.

Secret Tribunal, of Germany, which originated in the thirteenth century, and had become so formidable in the fourteenth, that the Princes of the Empire united to suppress it. Its members were called Free Judges, Sages, or Seers, and were very numerous, including most of the prominent personages of the time. They were unknown, however, save to each other; and their meetings were held in secret, at night, in the crypts of ruined churches or castles. Its avowed purpose was to protect the innocent and feeble, and to punish the crimes of those too powerful for law to reach. The Free Judges were bound by oath to deliver up, or to slay their dearest friends or relatives, if found guilty. The doom of one sentenced was inevitable; it was as sure as fate. Like the Ten of Venice, the Vehme Gericht of Westphalia was everywhere—everywhere! The victim received three warnings, and soon after was found hanged by a willow withe to a tree, or stabbed to the heart, a dagger bearing the words "Secret Tribunal" remaining in the wound. Sometimes the accused was cited before the judges, who were in mask, and tried; but oftener he was assassinated without citation, conviction, or even warning. Its original design was good; and, like the Venetian Ten, it doubtless accomplished good. Like the Ten, however, it became, a fearful engine of hate and wrong.

And yet despite all its terrors, Venice owed much to her Ten. Perhaps, to this terrible tribunal she owed, that she outlived all the other Italian Republics. The Ten protected the weak against the strong, the feeble against the powerful, the poor against the rich, the low against the high, the people against the nobles; and, in return, it was sustained by the people against the same nobles, its deadliest foes. Its police was the most perfect the world ever saw. The offender, the robber, the assassin, it pursued with the celerity and the certainty of death—the secrecy and cruelty of the grave. It suffered no obtrusion upon its dread prerogatives; its jealous monopoly of blood none questioned; its single charter to torture and to slay, none dared dispute or doubt. Its "Lions' Mouths," ever open, invited the secret denunciations of patriotism, or perfidy, or hate, or revenge; its inquisitors, its agents, its familiars, its sbirri were ubiquitous; and, at no hour of the day, or of the night, was there, in all Venice, a sanctuary too sacred for its power and its pursuit. Denunciation, suspicion, arrest, torture, conviction, disappearance, followed each other with fearful speed; yet was all shrouded in a cloud as impenetrable as that which veils another world. Faithfully was observed the oath which constituted the pass-word to the chamber of council. "*Jura, perjura, secretum prodere noli*"—Swear, forswear, and reveal not the secret, said the porter at the door: "*Jura*"—I swear—was the deep response of the masked inquisitor as he crossed the threshold. Spies were everywhere. The Lion's Mouth was everywhere; at the landing of the Giant's staircase, at the portals of the ducal palace, at the entrance to the chamber of the Ten, a lion's mouth of marble with yawning jaws, for every department of state, for every crime, for all comers, against all persons, for written or for oral communications, anonymous or signed; and below each was inscribed—"Denounce! denounce!"* Once denounced, the victim is seized; once seized, he is sentenced; once sentenced, all is over. Nothing is seen, heard, suspected of his fate. He *disappears!* A man is suddenly missing to his family. Where is he? They dare not ask. The *Pozzi*, the *Piombi*, the *Ponte de' Sospiri*, the *Rio Orfano*, alone can tell. At midnight one hears a splash. He stops, he listens, he hears no more, all is still; he hurries on, breathless with terror, with quaking heart and footsteps.†

* "*Denunzie Segrete.*" All were destroyed in 1797.

† Hugo.

> "The thunderbolt
> Falls heavy, and the hand by which 't is launch'd
> Is veiled in clouds."*

To the *people*, Venice was the city of fetes and festivals—the city of the opera, the gondola, the moonlight serenade; the city of love and *liaison*, of masquerade and carnival for half the year: to the *nobles*, it was the city of mystery and dread. A weird spectre called "The State," unseen, unheard, flung its icy shadow over everything. A tribunal of blood arose!

> "A strange, mysterious power was there
> Moving throughout—subtle, invisible,
> And universal, as the air they breathed;
> A power that never slumber'd, never pardon'd
> All eye, all ear,—no where and every where;
> Most potent when least thought of—nothing dropt
> In secret, when the heart was on the lips,
> Nothing in feverish sleep—but instantly
> Observed and judged—a power, that if but glanced at
> In casual converse, be it where it might,
> The speaker lower'd at once his eyes, his voice,
> And pointed upward as to God in Heaven.
> But, let him in the midnight air indulge
> A word, a thought against the laws of Venice,
> And in that hour he vanish'd from the earth!"†

In 1315, the *Libro d'Oro*, or Golden Book, a register of all who had sat in the Great Council, was opened; and, three years later, the council itself was opened to every descendant of an ancient councillor who was twenty-five years old. The "Council of Ten," whose chief duty was to watch the Grand Council, consisted, despite its name, of *seventeen* persons—the Doge, ten councillors of the black robe—*I Neri*—and six of the red—*I Rossi*. Then there was a Council of Forty—*Quarantia*—and the Council of Three; the latter

* "*Il conte di Carmagnola*," by Alessandro Manzoni.—*Act V., Scene II.*
† Rogers.

consisting of one councillor of the red robe and two of the black, selected from the Ten for a period of six months, by lot; so that they were utterly unknown, except to each other. Ten slips of paper were placed in an urn—seven being blank. Each of the Decemviri drew a slip. On reaching his home, if he found the slip was not blank, he repaired, masked, at a pre-appointed time, to a pre-appointed place, and was there met by two other masks. The three constituted the council. They could meet and act anywhere, everywhere—in the Piazza—on the Lagune—in a church—at a *fete;* and two constituted a quorum. There were, in all, seven councils at Venice. The first was *Il Consiglio Grande*, in which all the nobles, numbering at one time two thousand five hundred, but at the fall of the Republic, only twelve hundred,* had a seat, a vote, and a voice; the second was *Il Consiglio dei Pregadi*, consisting of three hundred and ten nobles; the third, *La Quarantia*, consisting of forty; the fourth, *La Signoria*, consisting of the Doge and six councillors; the fifth, *Il Consiglio Proprio*, consisting of twenty nobles, which, united with the *Signoria*, gave audience to ambassadors; the sixth, *Il Consiglio dei Dieci*, composed of ten counsellors, which had charge of criminal matters, and the seventh, *Il Consiglio dei Tre*, consisting of those members of the *Dieci*, whose control in the state was without limit and without appeal—even more so, if possible, than that of the Ten.

The system was now complete, and, for five hundred years, terror was the spirit that ruled Venice. And yet, despite her despotic rule, the City of the Sea advanced in opulence, in power, in prosperity, beyond all precedent, beyond all parallel, and almost beyond all belief. Manufactures of velvet, silk, glass, gold, etc., supplied her

* Whether the extraordinary diminution in the numbers of the Venetian nobility from two thousand five hundred to twelve hundred, more than one-half, in a single century, is attributable to luxury, celibacy, or the plague, either or all, seems undecided.

staples of export. Her glass fabrics, especially, found their way all over the known world—even to China, farther India, and the extreme East. Marco Polo, the great traveller, who had witnessed the fondness of the savages for colored stones and gems, suggested to his countrymen, on his return in the 13th century, the fabrication of similar ornaments of glass; and, for many years, Venice, from this source, maintained a lucrative trade. Glass was not invented by the Venetians, as has, by some, been supposed; for it was known to the Arabs, the Greeks, the Chinese, in the earliest ages, and even to the Egyptians, three thousand years ago, as indicated by the decorations of a mummy at the Armenian Convent of San Lazzaro. But, as early as the 12th century, Venice had glass furnaces near the Rialto Bridge, which, at the close of the 13th, were removed to Murano, on account of the numerous conflagrations they caused; and, henceforth, that island, by decree of the Senate, was devoted exclusively to that manufacture.

But the great source of wealth to Venice was her maritime and commercial advantage, arising from location. Midway between the East and the West—between Europe and Asia, she was the factor and the carrier of the civilized world; while her port was the mart for merchants of every tribe, and kindred, and tongue. That she encouraged, and had cause to encourage, foreign merchants to frequent her marts, is proven by the vast edifices erected for their special use, of which the *Fondaco de' Tedeschi* and the *Fondaco de' Turchi*, near the Rialto, remain to this day. In the 14th century, she is said to have had ships of two thousand tons burthen, bearing freights valued, sometimes, at two millions of francs; while in the 15th, she had three hundred and thirty war vessels and forty thousand seamen, in addition to her merchant marine! This seems incredible, but it is well authenticated. As late as her fall, in 1797, she had three hundred merchant vessels and eight thousand sailors.

In her career of conquest and glory, Venice had no rival. From her Archipelago of a hundred islets in a shallow Lagune, she found herself, in the course of a few centuries, mistress of half the Eastern world. She had provinces on both shores of the Adriatic, and islands, numberless and rich, in the Ægean sea, even as far as the Dardanelles; while her leonine standard rolled out its purple folds over Candia, Cyprus, and the Morea. For centuries she claimed the Adriatic as her own, even as the bridegroom claims the bride; and, every year, on the day of the feast of Ascension, with surpassing pomp, in the presence of all her nobles and people, and all the ambassadors of foreign lands, who by their presence recognized the act, she renewed that claim, by dropping a nuptial ring into the bosom of the deep, repeating the formula—*Desponsamus te, mare, in signum veri perpetuique dominii.* Nor was that "perpetual dominion" a mere affair of words. For centuries, Venice held the Adriatic as if it were a citadel; and woe! unto those who affected to despise her claim! Her galleys were the keys to that stronghold, and her Captain of the Gulf the only warder.

In 1630, for example, the Spanish envoy at Venice desired permission for a Neapolitan ship-of-war to enter the Adriatic, for the purpose of carrying from Naples to Trieste the Infanta Maria, who was to wed the king of Hungary, son of the Emperor. The Senate refused, and sent a fleet to repulse the Neapolitan squadron, should it attempt to enter the Gulf; proffering, at the same time, one of its own ships to the Infanta for the voyage. The court of Madrid at first declined the offer, alleging that the ships of Venice were all infected with the plague; but it was finally forced to concede, and Venetian obstinacy and pride had their triumph.

But the Adriatic nuptials of the Doge of Venice were not the only nuptials indicative of her power. Monarchs were proud to wed her fair daughters. Constance Morosini became Queen of Servia; Thomasine Morosini, Queen of Hungary*; Catharine Conaro, Queen of Cyprus, and Bianca Cappello, Archduchess of Tuscany. It was in this day of her power and prime, that the Winged Lion of St. Mark was a significant symbol of the glory of Venice; and with poetical propriety, has he been portrayed as resting his flanks on Lombardy, with his tail flung up towards the Alps, with his mane shadowing the Lagune, with Venice under his heart, with one paw grasping the shores of Dalmatia, and the other upraised to sweep every hostile sail from the Adriatic; whilst his haughty head is turned threateningly towards the Orient, and his rolling eyeballs survey his conquered isles of the Ægean. And if, in power and prosperity, Venice had no rival, neither had she a rival in the astuteness of her policy, domestic or foreign, or in the wisdom and firmness of its administration. Her republic, at any rate, outlived all its sister republics of Italy. That of Genoa lasted but six centuries; that of Florence, but four; while that of the Adriatic was prolonged to fourteen. Even when the whole Peninsula was at the feet of the Emperor, Chas. V., after 1530, Venice was independent and powerful. If her people had not liberty, they had order, law, and a species of justice. The government cost them nothing. Their taxes were light and equally imposed, and they were economically expended for the glory of the country. "*Giustizia in palazzo, e pane in piazza*"† was the motto of the State, and it

* In the Morosini palace at Venice, are beheld the portraits of four Doges of that illustrious house, as well as those of the Queens of Hungary and Servia, and that of Augustino Morosini, Abboss of San Zaccaria, who presented the original *beretta*, or bonnet of the Ducal office.

† "Justice in the palace and bread in the Piazza." Apologists for Venice designate her cruelties as of the age and country. In 1308, the Visconti, Lords of Lombardy, issued an

seems to have been seldom disregarded, so far, at least, as the *people* were concerned. And, in return for this protection, the children of St. Mark would, at any time, give their lives for St. Mark's cause.

The only factions and parties ever permitted to exist in Venice were among the lower classes; and these factions were not only permitted by the State, but, from motives of profound policy, were encouraged. They occupied opposite extremes of the city. One party had the isle of San Nicolo for its capital, while its limit was the Rialto. Its members were called *Nicollotti.* The other party had its nucleus at the island of Castello, and its limit at the Piazza, and its members were called *Castellani.* Between the Piazza and the Rialto was neutral ground, and the parties were divided by the Grand Canal; while the bridge of San Barnaba was the principal battle ground—the *Ponte di Pugni.* The Nicollotti were the democrats—the Castellani the aristocrats. Red was the color of the latter—black of the former; and the only badges were cap and sash. The *Arsenalotti,* or, men of the Arsenal, lived in the *Sestiere,* or ward, of Castello, and it was their privilege to *chair* the newly elected Doge around the Piazza: but the Nicollotti had a Doge of their own called the *Gastaldo,* and a banner of their own, bearing the image of their patron Saint. Every species of gymnastic and aquatic sport was encouraged among these men to cultivate their hardihood; and *Mardi Gras,* the last day of Carnival, was specially devoted to their exhibitions of skill. On that day the "tributary bull and twelve hogs" of the Patriarch of Aquilea were chased around the Piazza by the rival factions, and the heads of the animals were stricken off, by single blows of immense two-handled swords, yet extant in the Museum of Sanquirico. The Arab feat

edict prolonging capital punishment to forty days' duration, and designating the member to be mutilated, one after the other, before the *coup de grace!*

of "Human Pyramids"—men standing on the shoulders of others to the height of eight stories, was also, a favorite one: and sometimes a man at the base stood on the steel beaks of two gondolas in the water, and sustained three men above him—a feat of power and equipoise seemingly impossible. The Regatta was another sport of the two factions, particularly encouraged. Indeed, it was the national amusement of Venice. Even the women of Pelestrina, an island some leagues from Venice, at one time contended with the men for the prize. The course was more than three miles in extent, commencing near the Public Gardens, doubling a *paletto* planted at the mouth of the Cannaregio and closing at an *estrade* erected between the Balbi and Foscari palaces, where were distributed the prizes. The first was a small flag of purple silk, the second one of blue, the third of green, and the last of yellow, bearing embroidered on it a—pig! Each banner was accompanied by a purse of gold. For centuries the Regatta continued the national sport of Venice, and was gotten up with great splendor on occasions of royal visits. Even the young nobles prided themselves on their skill in wielding the oar and guiding the gondola, as much as would others, on *terra firma*, on their equestrianism.

The *Arsenalotti*, or workmen of the Arsenal, were always considered the most reliable sons of Venice. "*Viva San Marco!*" was their rallying cry from the earliest era. The guards of the council, of the palace, of the treasury, and of the mint, were selected from among them. They were also, the firemen of the city; and often, as soldiers and seamen, defended their beloved Venice. It was they, also, who bore the newly elected Doge around the square of St. Mark, while he distributed *largess*. Among their privileges was a naval school, at which their sons were gratuitously educated, until, at the age of eighteen, they entered the corporation. In the sixteenth century, they numbered 16,000; in the eighteenth, 3000; and at the fall of the Republic, 2,500. Under the French rule the number was increased to 4.000, while under that of Austria it has varied from one to two thousand,--some three or four hundred, usually, being—galley slaves! In 1574, when Henry III. of Poland, in his route to assume the crown of France, visited Venice, the *Arsenalotti* gave him a feast, and put together and armed a galley, in one of their docks, before his eyes, whilst he ate!

The briefest catalogue of events which have rendered celebrated the name of Venice, would demand a volume. The defeat of Barbarossa—the conquest of Constantinople—the acquisition of Candia—the sea-victories over Genoa and Pisa—the treason of Marino Faliero—the triumphs of Carlo Zeno—the war of the Chioggia—the cruel fates of the Carrara, and Carmagnola, and the two Foscari—the marriage of Catharine Conaro and the acquisition of Cyprus—the League of Cambray and the King of France on the Lagune—wars with the Ottoman and the victory of Lepanto—the loss of Candia and the concession of the Morea—such is a brief abstract of more prominent events, which, to a mind familiar with the chronicles of Venice, cannot fail to call up a throng of like associations. Nor are these the only associations of interest with the name of Venice. Here Galileo, in 1609, on a visit, while Professor in the university of Padua, invented the telescope; and, having with it studied the stars from the tall summit of the campanile of St. Mark, more than three hundred feet high, presented it to the Doge Donato. Here, too, at a subsequent period, Sirturi constructed an instrument of the same description; and, while using it in the tower, was interrupted by the people from below, who, for hours, examined it with the utmost curiosity, to the astronomer's exceeding annoyance. Here Loyola, in 1536, organized, with his friends, the order of Jesus; and hence repairing to Rome, sought and gained the sanction of Paul III., to his enterprise. Here were born or lived, or died, Titian and Tintoretto, Vittoria and Canova, Sansovino and Palladio, Giorgione and Tasso,* Goldoni and Cardinal Bembo, Paolo Sarpi and Marco Polo; and the dwellings they inhabited are yet pointed out. The palace—once a church, then a convent, next a hospital, and now an Austrian barrack—appropriated by the Senate to Petrarch, during his visit to Venice, is likewise shown, as are also, a few of the books—the nucleus of the Library of St. Mark, now embracing 70,000 volumes—which he then presented to the State.† Here lived Lucretia Conaro, a Doctor of Laws; Mariana Martinez, the vocalist and composer; Carriera Rosalba, the painter of portraits, and Marietta Robusti, daughter of Tintoretto, who, with well-nigh the genius of her illustrious father, sacrificed ambition to love—declined invitations to the Spanish and the Imperial courts—became the bride of a jeweller—lived in obscurity—died early, and was buried—no one knows where!

At Venice, the first book printed in Italy was issued from the press. It was the "Familiar Epistles of Cicero," printed by Jean de Spire, in 1469. Next year, Janson established his presses at

* Tasso was the son of a Venetian. His father was a poet, and brought him, at the age of ten, to Venice, for his education. Tasso and Ariosto are the poets of the gondoliers.

† *La Marciana*, or the Library of St. Mark, was founded by the gift of Petrarch, in 1364, and was enriched a century later by Cardinal Bessarion, Patriarch of Constantinople, followed by Wieland, Cosmo de Medicis and numerous others. Bessarion was appointed Historiographer of the Republic, an office then founded and ever after maintained by the State, and filled principally by Patricians. But few of Petrarch's books remain at Venice. His celebrated Virgil with its impassioned note to Laura, went to Paris in '97, and is now in the Ambrosian Library at Milan. About the middle of the sixteenth century, the superb edifice on the Piazetta, called the "Library of St. Mark," was erected, and received the books; but in 1812 they were removed to the Ducal Palace, where they now are. The Library consists of 70,000 volumes and 5,000 manuscripts.

Venice, and made great improvements in type. The first editions of the Bible,* and of the classics were issued at Venice; and more books in the Hebrew language are estimated to have been printed there, than in all the rest of Christendom together! There dwelt the famous Aldini, whose name is classical. The first of the name was Aldus-Manucius, who was succeeded in the business of publishing and printing by his son Paolo, and his grandson, Aldus. At the opening of the seventeenth century, the first newspaper in the world appeared at Venice, which was sold for the coin called a *Gazetta*, and thus took a name. Strange that the great "palladium of liberty" should have originated under the most jealous despotism that ever existed! At Venice, too, appeared the first Bill of Exchange, the first Bank of Deposite and Discount, and the earliest miracles in the manufacture of glass. Artillery, too, was first invented, it is said, by the Venetians; and the species of *bombard* invented and employed by Vittorio Pisani against the Genoese, in the war of the Chioggia, as early as 1380, is yet to be seen at the foot of his statue, at the Arsenal. The engine could be discharged but once a day, and it threw a stone of more than an hundred pounds weight. Doria, the Genoese general, was crushed by one and died. It was a Venetian, also, Francis delle Barche, who invented a *balista* which threw masses of rock of three thousand pounds weight; but, one day, at the siege of Zara, while superintending its repairs, he was hurled by it—instead of a stone—a shapeless corpse, over the walls of the hostile city! In like manner the Spanish monk—some say a monk of Venice—who invented gunpowder, was destroyed by his own invention; and the benevolent Dr. Guillotine, of Paris, was one of the earliest victims of his death-dealing machine; while the

* The first Italian Bible was printed at Venice, 1471, followed by forty other editions in other cities of Italy. The first Protestant edition appeared at Geneva, 1562.

wise and good De Marigni, minister of Philip IV. of France, was the first to hang on his new gibbet at Montfaucon!

At the close of the fifteenth century, or the commencement of the sixteenth, Venice had "reached the highest point of all her greatness." The discoveries of Columbus and Gama seemed not, however, at once, to affect her prosperity. Indeed, for a century later, she appeared hardly to retrograde, even if she did not advance. But, if she was nearly thirteen hundred years attaining her prime, she was a whole century dying. "For a thousand years," it has been forcibly said, "she fought for life; for three hundred years she invited death; the battle was rewarded, and the call was heard." In 1669, Venice, with an expenditure of one hundred and twenty-six millions of ducats, had fought the Ottoman twenty-five years; and Candia, after sixty-nine assaults, eighty sorties, the explosion of one thousand and forty-six mines and three hundred counter-mines, capitulated in ruins! No wonder, that even to this day, in Venice, a "War of Candia" means "War to the knife, and knife to the hilt." Thirty years later, however, the Morea, won by the prowess of Morosini, was, by the Péace of Carlowitz, ceded to her to supply its place.* The War of the Succession occupied the first thirteen years of the ensuing century; but Venice took no part. The cause and origin of that conflict may be briefly stated. When the Emperor Charles VI., of Austria, died, October 21st, 1740, he gave his crown to his daughter, Maria Theresa, Queen of Hungary and Bo-

* In 1687, when Morosini drove the infidels from the Morea, Athens was bombarded for six days by Konigsmarck, a Swedish general, when a shell chancing to explode in the Parthenon, which had been converted into a magazine, the magnificent pile was demolished, burying in its ruins the statue of Minerva, the master-piece of Phidias Morosini was loaded with honors, on his return to Venice—was immortalized by the title of the *Peloponesiaque*, and was shortly after chosen Doge. Among the trophies of this triumph were the lions of the Arsenal, more than two thousand years old.

hemia, who had married Francis of Lorraine, Grand Duke of Tuscany. Spain, Bavaria, Saxony, Poland, Sardinia, and France presented claims to the same throne; and the long and bloody War of the Succession began. The Elector of Bavaria became temporarily Emperor; but, by the prowess of the Hungarians, Maria Theresa recovered her rights, and Francis I., of Lorraine was elected emperor in the ancient Kaisersaal of Frankfort, where stand the busts of forty-four emperors besides. Venice was urged to join the league against Austria; and her weight might have turned the scale. It is certain, at any rate, that, but for the active aid of Hungary, and the forbearance of Venice, the proud house of Hapsburg-Lorraine, now the merciless despot of both, would never have even begun to exist! With the peace of Passarowitz, which ensued in 1719, the wrongs of Venice through Austria, may be said to have commenced; the Morea was returned to the Turk.

Henceforth, for the space of eighty years, the Republic made neither war nor peace. She declared timid neutrality in all the succeeding contests, and was insulted with impunity, by all the belligerents, on her own sea, and in her own territory; and that, too, while boasting two and a half millions of people,* 14,000 troops, arms for 50,000 more, and a dozen men-of-war. From all accounts, her dissolution — almost her decomposition—had already commenced. She was ruled by a distracted oligarchy—her nobility, in extreme poverty, sold their suffrages in the Grand Council; the families from which were selected the "Ten," made all others tremble and obey; the State was viewed as a prey for spoil—justice was venal—the finances were exhausted—the fortifications were in ruins —the ranks of the army embraced not half the number on its rolls

* In 1722, Venice had two and a half millions of inhabitants, and in 1788 three millions.

—the debt, in time of peace, was increasing—manufactures were in decay—the provinces were infested by brigands—the city was torn by factions, which the Senate encouraged, in order to weaken the force of both—immorality was promoted to enervate the people—the government, cruel and jealous, was sustained by spies—no question or investigation of public affairs was tolerated—the accused were deprived of all defence before the tribunals—prosecutions began with torture, and ended with strangulation: secresy was the sole safeguard; no limit to the right of judicial penalty by the dagger, poison, cord, sack, or axe, was recognized, save the will and boldness of the inquisitors; and thus, the very name of Republic became execrated and execrable. It is, however, noticed as a strange inconsistency in the policy of Venice, by the same historian* who has thus detailed her atrocities, that, while she crushed liberty at home, she succored those who upheld it abroad. Thus, she countenanced Henry VIII. of England, in his conflict with the Pope and the Catholic powers: she was the ally of the Dutch in their struggle for their rights, a century later: she sided with German Protestantism during the thirty years' war, and gave aid and comfort to Bethlem Gabor and Ragotski in Hungary; while, nearly at the same time, she supported the Prince of Piedmont against Philip III. of Spain, and the Protestant Grisons of Savoy against the Catholics. She also declared for Henry IV. against the League, when, in 1589, upon the assassination of Henry III. by the fanatic monk, Clement, he left the throne of Navarre for that of France, opposed by Savoy and Spain, and excommunicated by the Pope. She went so far even as to lend him money, and ordered his bonds for the same to be destroyed in his presence. Henry was not insenible to this kindness. He subsequently presented the Republic with a

* Sismondi.

suit of armor he had worn, which is yet to be seen at the Arsenal, and also his sword of service at Ivry, which disappeared in the invasion of '97. And when he married Marie de Medicis, his name, at his desire, was inscribed in the *Libro d'Oro* as a patrician of Venice, the ballot showing 1420 votes in his favor to only twenty opposed. Venice was almost always the friend of France; but more than half a century before these events, she declared for Charles V. against Francis I. The Emperor being, at first, unsuccessful, however, Venice obeyed interest and inclination, and brought back her adhesion to her old friends. But she seemed to bring only misfortune. At Pavia, on the 24th of February, 1525, Francis lost his army, his liberty—"everything but honor." The Duke of Brunswick then approached the frontiers of Venice, and dispatched a challenge to single combat to her aged Doge, Andrea Gritti, even as Francis had challenged Charles; and, centuries before, even as Pompey had challenged Cæsar; and, centuries afterwards, even as Sir Sydney Smith challenged Napoleon. The challenge was very ridiculous, Gritti being an octogenarian: yet, the fiery old Doge was with difficulty restrained from accepting the *cartel*. The result of all was the total rout of the Duke—even as Pompey and Francis had been routed before, albeit Sir Sydney was *not* routed afterwards.

But, we approach the last days of the Venetian Republic. As her power diminished abroad and her prosperity at home, in direct ratio increased despotism in the government and corruption among the people. "Venice became the Sybaris of the modern world." Her license became horrible—incredible! Nuns and monks in masks, mingled at balls, countenanced by the Pope's Nuncio himself. Every noble had his *casino*—his *boudoir* of gallantry on the Place St. Mark. Gaming was universal, incessant and ruinous, and was promoted by the Senate because a profitable monopoly—one of its own body always presiding unmasked over each board or bank. Revenge and cowardice went hand in hand; and the Bravo's stiletto was ever bare and ever bloody. Tho honor of wives and daughters became a marketable commodity; and the vile contracts legally made and authenticated were formally recorded. There was no punishment for adultery, no obstacle to divorce. Iago's denunciation of his fair countrywomen—

—"they do let heaven see the pranks
They dare not show their husbands; their best conscience
Is—not to leave undone, but keep unknown"—

was untrue—only because too lenient. Innumerable courtezans, once exiled the capital by edict, were now recalled by edict, and palaces and revenues appropriated to their use; while they, in acknowledgment, became spies of the State. Luxury and pleasure formed the staple of existence in Venice. "Scarcely did the sun rise upon the Lagune uncelebrated by the pomp of some religious or political festival; the whole year was one continued holiday, in which amusement appeared to be the professed and serious occupation, the grand and universal object of existence among the inhabitants. Besides the numerous fixed and customary ceremonials, occasions for extraordinary joy were greedily sought in the accession of a new Doge, the election of a Procurator, or the entrance of a foreign Ambassador; and the annual recurrence of the Carnival seldom attracted fewer than fifty thousand strangers from all parts of Europe to mingle in the sports of St. Mark's."*

The Carnival of Venice was little more than a public masquerade prolonged for days and weeks, the grand scene and saloon of which was the Place St. Mark. Here, in mask and domino, individuals,

* Smedley.

ranks, conditions, positions, even sexes, were all confounded. The scenes which transpired and the practices which prevailed, amid the multitudinous sports and the inextricable crowds and confusion of the occasion, may be imagined. For centuries the mask was in universal use in Venice. It served to level somewhat the marked distinction between the nobility and people. In the Ducal halls, the nobles, in black mask and domino, with huge wigs, joined in the dance, and the custom was acquiesced in even by the legate of the Pope. The mask was by law and usage, for six months in the year, inviolable; and monks and nuns, beneath its protection, indulged in fetes, spectacles and pageants. Politics, pleasure, intrigue—the friendly mask favored all alike; and, like the mantle of charity, covered numberless sins. And then the gondola—"the mysterious and discreet spirit of the Lagune and canals"—invariably black all over, in accordance with an edict of the 15th century, ostensibly to repress extravagance, but really to favor political intrigue, and which really did favor the intrigue of love—the gondola, with its windowed, curtained, blinded *Felzè*—

> "Just like a coffin clapped in a canoe,
> Where none can make out what you say or do.
> But not to them do woeful things belong,
> For sometimes they contain a deal of fun."

What with the mask and the gondola, what wonder that Venice was for ages the city of mystery, and romance, and license!

The celebrated Addison, who visited Venice at the opening of the last century, confirms the statements of cotemporary and subsequent writers, relative to the boundless corruption at that time. Speaking of the Venetian Senate, he says: "The preservation of the republic is that to which all other considerations submit. To encourage idleness and luxury in the nobility, to cherish ignorance and licentiousness in the clergy, to keep alive a continual faction in the common people, to connive at the viciousness and debauchery of convents, to breed dissensions among the nobles of the *terra firma*, to treat a brave man with scorn and infamy, in short, to stick at nothing for the public interest, are represented as the refined parts of the Venetian wisdom. They generally thrust the females of their families into convents, the better to secure their estates. This makes the Venetian nuns famous for the liberties they allow themselves. They have operas within their own walls, and often go out of their bounds to meet their admirers, or they are very much misrepresented. They have many of them their lovers, that converse with them daily at the grate; and are free to admit the visits of a stranger. There is, indeed, one of the Conaros, that, not long ago refused to see any under a prince. The Carnival of Venice is everywhere talked of. The great diversion of the place at that time, as well as on all other high occasions, is masking. The Venetians, who are naturally grave, love to give in to the follies and entertainment of such seasons, when disguised in a false personage. These disguises give occasion to abundance of love adventures; for there is something more intriguing in the amours of Venice than in those of other countries; and I question not that the secret history of a Carnival would make a collection of very diverting novels." Addison states, also, that trade was far from flourishing; that the duties on merchandise were heavy, though a free port was talked of in order to meet the rivalry of Leghorn;* that the mer-

* In 1735, Trieste was declared a free port by the Emperor. The Pope then declared Ancona a free port, and it became indispensable to the welfare of Venice, that the Doge, Pisani, should declare the port of Venice partially free.

chants who had grown rich by trade had bought nobility and given it up; that the manufactures of cloth, glass and silk, once the best in Europe, were now excelled; that the tenacity of old laws was excessively prejudicial to commerce; that the decay of Venice was admitted by her citizens; that the Arsenal was well supplied and arranged; but that its arms and furniture, though extraordinary a hundred years before, were then generally useless, the suits of armor being almost as numerous as the guns, the fire-arms being fitted with old-fashioned locks, and the numberless swords being unwieldy and antique; albeit the Venetians pretended they could, in case of necessity, fit out thirty men-of war, a hundred galleys, and ten *galeasses!**

The state of affairs at Venice at the close of the 18th century, could hardly, under any circumstances, have lasted long. But the French Revolution came, and Europe quaked to its centre. To Venice it was the decree of destiny. Another Hannibal—a second Attila, rushed down the Alps, and swept away, like chaff of the threshing-floor, the power of the House of Hapsburg, which, for three centuries, had ruled the Milanese. The guilty city—cowardly as corrupt—shrank back into her usual timid neutrality. But it was too late! Her doom was decreed; her sentence was sealed; her fate was recorded. She fell; and without a struggle to elicit sympathy, or to inspire regret.

The fall of Venice in 1797; her spoliation by the French; her delivery to Austria, under the treaty of Campo Formio; her re-delivery to France, under the treaty of Presburg; her recovery by the Empire, under the treaties of Paris and Vienna; the long wars on the continent of Europe and the long blockade of the Adriatic,

* "Remarks on several parts of Italy, etc., in 1701, 1702, 1703, by the late Right Hon. Joseph Addison, Esq., London, 1745."

had, of course, independently of other vicissitudes, a most disastrous effect on her commerce, her industry, her general prosperity. The single fact, that, by the Census of 1778, her population was one hundred and fifty thousand, and by that of 1816, was but one hundred and three thousand, speaks volumes. No wonder, that, at the commencement of the year 1815, and during the twenty years which succeeded, she presented "a most deplorable aspect of decay and desolation;" and no wonder that the lugubrious descriptions of that desolation, so numerous and so unanimous, from the pens of writers by whom she was visited, have left an impression respecting her on the minds of all, which, despite her recent comparative regeneration, have not been effaced, and, probably, never will be. To none of these writers, however, nor to all of them combined, indeed, does the Ocean-Queen owe so much her fame for "romantic desolation," as to the Venetian poems of Lord Byron—"Marino Faliero"—"The Two Foscari"—the fourth canto of "Childe Harold"—the "Ode to Venice"—"Beppo," etc., together with their accompanying notes. These poems every one has read, and the impression produced on the mind and imagination is almost ineffaceable. The traveller therefore, at the present day, when about to visit Venice, expects to behold her a ruin. He expects to find in her a Tyre, a Tadmor, a Palmyra of the ocean; for he has seen her compared to each and to all of them, to say nothing of Babylon, and Nineveh, and Carthage, and Alexandria, and Thebes, and Memphis, and Constantinople, and Athens, and Rome. He expects to see her, as depicted, more poetically than truthfully, by a recent writer—"A ghost upon the sands of the sea, so weak, so quiet, so bereft of all but her loveliness, that one might well doubt, as he watched her faint reflection in the mirage of the Lagune, which was the city and which the shadow;" and like him, perchance, he thinks, that fain would he "endeavor to trace the lines of this image before it is forever lost, and to record, so far as he may, the warning which seems uttered by every one of the fast-gaining waves, that beat, like passing bells, against the stones of Venice."* He expects to find her, as portrayed by every writer he has ever read—a tomb of the dead Past—a mausoleum of buried centuries—a wreck on the ocean-sands of time—a scene of desolateness unchanging—of solitude unrelieved—of silence unbroken, save by the dull and infrequent plash into her stagnant waves of the marble of her crumbling palaces. He expects, in fine, to behold the doomed city in full fulfillment of old Faliero's terrific malediction—

"Sinking into the slime from which she rose."

He is disappointed! He finds Venice *no* ruin—no Tadmor of the ocean—no Tyre—no Palmyra; and he sighs, perchance, to discover, that the touching and mournful romance of desolation, with which her picture had been shrouded, owed more to the genius and the fancy of her poetic portrayers than to any reality of fact.

Venice is no tomb, no monument of the past; no city of the dead, no catacomb of silence, and solitude, and despair. The fair bride of the sea presents not now, perchance, the bright and lovely vision of centuries since, when wedded by the Ducal ring and the Papal benediction. Change—change has been busy with her, as with all else of earth. The fresh flush of youth has fled her cheek—threads of silver have besprinkled her night-black tresses; sor-

* Ruskin. "Since the first dominion of man was asserted over the ocean," he adds, "three thrones, of mark beyond all others, have been set upon its sands: the thrones of Tyre, Venice, and England. Of the the first of these great powers, only the memory remains; of the second, the ruin; the third, which inherits their greatness, if it forget their example, may be led through prouder eminence to less pitied destruction."

Dickens says of Venice—"It seemed a very wreck found drifting out at sea." Very poetical—and very preposterous.

row, and humiliation, and bereavement have left their sure, sad traces on her still stately and beautiful brow; and the smile which, once, all light and joyousness, illumined her sweet face, though it yet lingers and pláys like a halo of the past, is as sad and as mournful as a broken heart. Such is the Ocean-Queen; but she is *not*—no, she is not that old, and withered, and toothless, and wrinkled, and horrible hag, which some would paint her! She is not the "weird sister of a blasted heath!" She is not the foul witch of prophetic evocation! Or, if she be, indeed, a "witch," she is rather "the Witch of the Alps," or "the Spirit of the Sea," whom the lapse of ages renders only more lovely! She is rather the Niobe of grief than the Nemesis of desolation. Once a blushing, and brilliant, and blooming bride, she now reclines a bereaved, yet still beautiful matron, at the base of the throne on which, centuries ago, she sat in state; and, with a mournful smile, looks out on the waves of the blue Adriatic, which for long ages owed and owned no allegiance save her own: and she still is, as she has been, and will ever be—"*La bella! Venezia la bella!*"

That a city more than fourteen hundred years old, and many of whose structures date back their origin to her earliest history, should exhibit marks of decay, is not to be wondered at. That the façades of some of her massive edifices should be time-stained—that her colonnades and arches should be sunken—that the gorgeous sculpture which flings its flowers so gracefully over her walls should be moss-grown—that the medallia of porphyry and serpentine by which their fronts are blazoned, should be somewhat shattered—that her "roof-terraces wreathed with Arabian imagery of golden balls suspended on the leaves of lilies," should be blackened, and that "the salt sea-weed" should "cling to the marble of her palaces" rising from the waves—all this was inevitable, and *is* the fact. But it is not true, that these matchless and massive mansions "have been degraded to the most ignoble and debased of purposes," and that "the rich and costly decorations of their architecture are crumbling piecemeal, and, day by day, are filling up with their *debris* the waters which undermine their base."

Shorn, though she may be—this Syren of the waters—of many of her glories, and bowing, as it were, her guilty but beautiful brow beneath those chastisements of Nineveh and Babylon, so fervently invoked on her centuries ago, by the Florentine monk of St. Dominic, Savonarola, or those deeper woes, still more ancient, attributed to her false Doge; and, though "the barbarian hath verily come down as an hungry lion," and she verily "hath been bought and sold, and become an appanage to those who despise her;" yet, those dread maledictions have much still to attain before they shall have been fully fulfilled. Her palaces have not yet "crumbled to the shore;" she has not yet "sunk into the slime of her own canals."

Venice, as has been already stated, is built on the sands, brought down from the Rhœtian Alps by several small rivers, which being repelled at the *embouchure* by the billows of the Adriatic, have been fashioned into shoals and islands of various sizes, and, large and small, are from seventy to one hundred in number. To form foundations for the ponderous structures which have been erected upon these islands, capable of resisting, for centuries, the action of the waves, and sustaining the enormous masses of incumbent marble—immense quantities—whole forests, indeed, of piles—mostly of larch, but some of cedar, and some even of oak and ebony, it is said—were forced into the depths of the alluvion, to the number, in some instances it is recorded, of millions of piles for a single edifice. The instrument made use of to accomplish this vast undertaking was, as is seen by the ancient model yet preserved in the Arsenal, the simple pile-driver of the present day. The basis—the foundation thus formed, was almost as firm as the everlasting hills, but not quite; and it is not, therefore, strange, that in some of the more aged and ponderous of the public or private structures of Venice, the lapse of time, the ceaseless washing of waters, and the enormous pressure of the superincumbent masses of marble, have produced obvious effects. Thus, the tesselated pavement of St. Mark's Minster, which is more than ten centuries old, has a surface as undulatory as the waves of the sea; hardly one of its five hundred porphyry, serpentine, and marble columns, is perfectly upright; and the fractures in its massive walls and mosaic domes, are quite innumerable. Even its lofty *Campanile*, or bell-tower, more than three hundred feet high, and nearly as old as itself, has a palpable leaning towards the Basilica; while each one of the sixty *Campanili*, with which the city bristles, seems much in the same predicament. Not one is perfectly "plumb," and those of *San Giorgio de Greci* and old *San Pietro di Castello*, are veritable leaning towers of Pisa. But these structures never fall—never. Such a thing, common enough as it may be in some new cities of the New World on *terra firma*, is never heard of in old and sea-girt Venice. The massiveness of the masonry, the tenacity of the cement, which, by age, becomes of adamantine hardness, and the frequent use of huge iron cramps, utterly preclude the idea. The edifices of Venice, even the humblest, seem constructed for eternity—not time. Sites for building being limited in extent, the very best use of the space granted, has been made; and, while their marble walls have been made to combine the solidity and cyclopean proportions of Egyptian architecture with the ornament of the Arabian, the legal right of the proprietor of the soil, in all ages and all the world over, to sink his foundations to the centre of the earth, and raise his superstructure to the clouds—*ab terra, ad cœlum*—seems to have been by no means forgotten. In some instances, the base of the edifice is said to have involved an expenditure greater than even the edifice itself! The structures are generally of vast height, and some of those in the Cannaregio, would compare favorably for number of stories with those in Edinburgh itself. Many also are irregular in proportion and incomplete in plan. The reason seems obvious. Land was precious. A palace, which was destined for centuries of futurity, was founded with extreme care, and embraced in its plan adjoining land, which was to be, but which, often, never was, obtained. Neighbors, also, engaged to erect a double-palace together; but they fell out, or failed in means, and only one fulfilled, or could fulfill, his compact. Most of the palaces rise directly from the water on one side, —even if, on all sides, the foundations are not washed; and in gliding through the smaller canals, the action of the waves, for ages, is perceived plainly written in grooves and furrows. The facades of some of the palaces on the *Canalazzo*, or Grand Canal, were once ornamented with frescoes; but the frosts and storms of centuries have peeled off the paint and stucco in many places, and left only grotesque exhibitions of artistic anatomy, in trunkless heads, or headless trunks, in *torsos* without limbs—expanded arms without legs, and sprawling legs without corresponding arms. This is particularly observable on the front of a palace called the *Fondaco de' Tedeschi*, now the *Dogana*, or Custom House, near the Rialto, which was frescoed more than three centuries ago, by the pencils of Titian and Giorgione. The edifice was erected by the State for the accommodation of German merchants at Venice, in 1506;* but, though its walls are seemingly as solid as on the day it was completed, the half-effaced frescoes give it an air of dilapidation. Ano-

* A similar structure, for the Turks, stands near the Rialto, as already mentioned.

ther circumstance which tends to lend the same aspect to some of the most gorgeous structures in Venice, is the fact, that, whenever a grain or two of sand, lodged by the wind in a crevice of the marble walls, or in a depression or inequality of the florid and sculptural architecture, affords the smallest seed opportunity to take root, there springs a wall-flower or a sea-weed; and the dank leaves wave mournfully in the breeze on the facades of the most costly piles. In some of the less frequented *campi*, or open places, in the city, adjoining churches, the grass, also, springs greenly in the crevices of the pavement; although it is often cut up, and with scrupulous care, by order of the Municipal authorities.

If to all these *indicia* of "desolation and decay," in the City of the Sea, it is added, that the marble walls of nearly every structure in Venice are black with years—that some of the most ancient palaces have been appropriated to more useful public or private purposes, than merely to stand from age to age, as a splendid spectacle; and that some of the narrower and less frequented of the canals are not, at all times, the most agreeable thoroughfares—every circumstance that could be recalled has been enumerated, which might afford possible cause for the doleful tales of tourists, as touching the ruinous aspect of much-abused Venice—always excepting, indeed, the passion for the "picturesque,"—which picturesque seems as much an object of search now, as in the days of Doctor Syntax; and which, where it ought to be found and cannot be, is fancied or invented, as much now as then. Because Venice is the oldest capital of Europe—because she has fallen from her high estate, "stooping to be the slave of slaves"—because "the Hebrew is in her palaces," and the "Hun in her high places," and the "Greek walks o'er her mart and smiles on it for his"—because all the histories and geographies of the half century last past have copied the one from the other, that she is "*a ruin*"—therefore, it seems fixed, that she, verily, *is* a ruin, and of right should be a ruin, and a ruin only! Because that melancholy bard, Byron, some forty years ago, sang of the "empty halls, thin streets and foreign aspects," which had "flung a desolate cloud o'er Venice's lovely walls;" and his friends, Moore and Shelley, about the same time, cursed her in good poetic terms—the former describing her fall "as awful as if ocean's wave swept o'er her," and his friend—improving on the figure—declaring that she would be—

"A *less* drear ruin *then* than now
With her conquest-branded brow"—

and, finally, the trio being followed up by their mutual friend Rogers, deploring her palace-fronts "shattered by time," and "the salt sea-weed clinging to their marble"—*therefore*, she *is*, and she must be, forever, "a ruin," and only "a ruin" even to the end of time; and the "desolate Venice" of 1820, can but be a still more desolate Venice in 1850! In the days of those famous bards, the poetical idea was indulged, and it seems to have been entertained with much "unction," that Venice was doomed to be whelmed, ere long, by the waves of her own Adriatic; that, though she had stood for some fourteen hundred years steadfastly enough, and the waters, at the very worst, had never risen on her more than three inches in the century—she was, yet, very speedily, destined to fulfill the curse, and "sink into the waves!" Byron opens on her thus, to this end, in his "Ode"—

"Oh, Venice! Venice! when thy marble walls
Are level with the waters, there shall be
A cry of nations o'er thy sunken halls,
A loud lament along the sweeping sea."

Shelley repeats the sentiment—

> ' Seagirt city ! thou hast been
> Ocean's child and then his queen.
> Now has come a darker day,
> And thou soon must be his prey."

Finally, Tom Moore, indulging the same idea, "feels the moral vengeance *sweet*, and *smiles*" over the anticipated "wreck !" And these *poesies* have been viewed by later poets, to say nothing of tourists, as veritable prophecies; and there seems, moreover, to have been no little indignant feeling expended against the poor "Queen," because she yet presumes to "hold her head above water," and persists in not being "whelmed," and don't make haste and "sink" and have done with it !—that she don't become a Tyre, or a Sidon, at once, and fulfill her own "inevitable doom," and their own poetical predictions !*

As touching this notion of the *sinking* of Venice, once so popular, it seems to owe its suggestion to the fact, that, by the pillars of the *Broglio*, the Patrician's Promenade, in the lower gallery of the Ducal Palace, the pavement of the Piazetta seems to have been elevated some fifteen inches, in the course of the five centuries since the palace was built.† But, whether this elevation has become

* Even the Roman poets, centuries ago, seemed fond of predicting the fall of Venice as well as that of the "Eternal City"—

> "Nec tu semper eris, quæ septem amplecteris arces,
> Nec tu, quæ mediis æmula surgis aquis."

† In 1810, by excavations of the French engineers, three inches of the pillars of the *Broglio* were found buried, as also, twelve inches of the pedestal, resting on the old brick pavement, which covered both piazza and piazzetta until 1406. In 1792, the pavement was again elevated a foot, the rise of the sea compelling. If these French engineers, to say nothing of the literary Jeremiahs and poetical Volneys have "writ their annals true," in less than a thousand years, the Square of St. Mark will be inundated at every tide; and a thousand years later, should the sea have claimed her own, the story of Venice may be deemed so wonderful, as to be hardly less fabulous than is the story of Troy deemed now! Well—"Venice is a daughter of the sea, and, like Palmyra, may perish by it."

necessary because of a proportionate elevation of the surface, or of the bed, of the Lagune, is not easy to say. The latter idea would seem to have obtained a century and a half ago, by the following extract from Addison's "Remarks," on his visit in 1701:—"Our voyage-writers will needs have this city in great danger of being left, within an age or two, on the *terra firma;* and represent it in such a manner, as if the sea was insensibly sinking from it, and retiring into its channel!" But Addison's apprehensions were put at rest, by his asking several persons, and among them Father Coronelli, the State Geographer, respecting the truth of the statements. They all assured him, that the sea rose as high as ever, and that Venice would never be an inland town so long as her canals were kept clear. This prevision quieted, it was a whole century before the "voyage-writers" took up the more poetical idea, suggested no doubt by the guiltiness of the place, that Venice was to share the fate of the Cities of the Plain—was to be whelmed beneath the waves of a Dead Sea, if not burned by fire and brimstone—and, instead of being an inland town, was not even to be an island town, but a subterranean town altogether!

But this is folly. Give even Venice her due. The day has been when the old city was prouder in power, and splendor, and opulence than she now is; and the day has been when she was humbler; and the day may be when she will be prouder than now—or than ever. "The day of her destiny" may, indeed, be over; "the star of her fate" may, indeed, have "declined;" but, that she is a *wreck*, or a *ruin*, in any offensive, or humiliating signification of those terms, is not true. It is not true that Venice is desolate and deserted, and sits upon the islands of her Lagune, like Tyre upon her rocks, where fishermen dry their nets; or, like Tadmor, beneath her columns, amid the sands of the desert, where the

Bedouin seeks the shade. The arcades of the Square of St. Mark, and the Cafés of Florian, and Suttil, and Quadri, nightly swarm with brilliant throngs; and not less than two hundred American travellers, alone, passed through the city, in 1851, within as many months. It is not true that the trade, and commerce, and industry of Venice are prostrate and stagnant. More than five hundred vessels every year enter her port, exclusive of coasters and packets. The railroad which connects her with the Peninsula pours into her the opulence of rich Lombardy, like life-blood through an artery; while the restoration of her Free-Port franchise has filled her harbor with vessels of all classes* and nations, and not a day passes without numerous entrances and clearances at her *Dogana del Mare.* It is not true that Venice has been despoiled by her tyrant, Austria, and that "her richest gems of art are in the galleries of Vienna." This is simply preposterous. Vienna has literally nothing of this description belonging to Venice, or which ever did belong to Venice. Indeed, her oppressor, instead of despoiling her of her "gems," is proud of her attractions, and deems herself, and most fitly, the richest gem in his own stolen diadem. Nor has Paris any thing belonging to Venice. Every master-piece was returned by Canova, in 1815, or recompensed by other *chefs d'œuvre;* and Venice is yet, what for ages she has been, "a museum of monuments, and a monument of museums;" and, instead of being "literally a ruin," is only a ruin in literature. It is not true that Venice, in the vivid imagery of the public newspapers, was "laid in ruins" by the bombardment of August, '49; albeit, the assault continued, without cessation, for twenty-four days and twenty-four nights, and 60,000 shot and shells were thrown within her limits. But most of these

† The stupendous dikes at the port of Malamocco have deepened the channel to eighteen feet.

projectiles dropped into the Lagune, or the canals; and the only evidence of the bombardment now visible is an occasional rent in a *plafond* of Tintoretto, or Salviati; or a ragged aperture in the richly gilded stucco, or ancient fresco, of the vaulted dome of some exposed and lofty church; or a pile of cannon-balls, here and there, in some palace-court, on the Canalazzo, or Cannaregio,* laid up for future generations as mementoes of the Siege of '49. It is not true as lovers of the desolate picturesque would fain have it believed, that many of the most spacious, antique, and once gorgeous palaces of Venice have been dismantled and demolished, by their princely but poverty-stricken proprietors, for the sake of the sale of the costly material for building—for the Istrian and Oriental marble, the porphyry, the serpentine, and the precious medallia which the demolition would furnish:—albeit, there was a time, in her day of deepest desolation, some thirty or forty years ago, while the primitive poetical Jeremiahs were wailing over her their wildest woes—when her desperate and degenerate nobles, unable to gratify their propensity for gaming on the two Austrian *Lire*† per diem allowed them by their Imperial pensions, were tempted to dispose of their hereditary palaces to Hebrew speculators, who found it very lucrative business to take them to pieces, and to sell, and, sometimes, to export their rare material, for the structure of other edifices elsewhere; and, had St. Mark's Basilica, itself, or the Ducal Palace, fallen into the clutches of these harpies, it would have shared a like fate. But this sacrilege was stopped by Imperial authority almost as soon as it began. Nor is it true, that numerous splendid palaces of the proudest Patrician families of ancient Venice, have been degraded to the basest uses: albeit, the vast Morosini Palace *is* now the

* Canal Royal.

† An Austrian *Lira* is sixteen cents.

General Census office, the Grimani Palace is the Post-office, the Foscari Palace is an Austrian Barrack, the Corner Palace is a Legislative chamber, the Farsetti Palace a City Hall, the Moecenigo, Giustiniani and Grassi Palaces are Hotels; while another splendid palace of the same great Grassi family is the Exchange of a company of merchants, the Pesaro Palace was, until lately, an Armenian College, and a neighboring edifice, said to have been given by the Republic, three centuries ago, to her fair daughter Catarina Conaro, Queen of Cyprus, is now a *Mont de Pietè*—a Pawnbroker establishment and Savings Bank for the poor. Moreover, the beautiful Trevisian Palace, or Palazzo Cappello, on the Rio Canonica, behind the Cathedral,* is now the abode of a French mantua-maker; and the mansion of Marino Faliero at the Campo S. S. Apostoli, is that of an equally noted boot-maker! And, if the lovers of the dilapidated picturesque can find a more appropriate and profitable use for these vast structures, than that to which many of them have been applied, the practical utility of the age would no doubt feel grateful for the suggestion.

Besides, these facts, if they indicate any thing, indicate the magnificence of Venice, quite as much as her decay. When mantua-makers and boot-makers can afford to drive their useful vocations in palaces—why—palaces must be somewhat numerous thereabouts—that's certain: or, if an honest boot-maker can find no "single-story frame," in a city wherein to plant his bench, he must needs put up with a

* It was not from this palace that Bianca Cappello eloped with the Florentine adventurer, Bonaventuri, on the night of the 28th of November, 1563, but from a much humbler mansion, situated on a narrow canal branching from the Canalazzo on the left—near the Ponte Storto, and not far from the house of Giorgione, at the Campo di San Sylvestro—Lady Bulwer to the contrary, in her novel, "Bianca Cappello," nevertheless. The Palazzo Trevisano, one of the richest palaces in the Lombard style, or in any other style, in Venice, was purchased by Bianca, when Grand Duchess of Tuscany, in 1673, and presented to her imperious brother, Victor.

palace—that of a celebrated Doge even, if he can get no other, no matter how anxious he may be to observe the motto of his craft—"*Ne sutor ultra crepidam.*" The fact is, old Venice, unlike more modern capitals, London and Paris, not excepted, was "*finished*" long ago: so that her present dwellers are forced to accept the splendid mansions of the past, and adapt them to the changes of the present. No palaces, now-a-day, are erected in the Island City, and but few structures of any kind: and all, for the very good reason, that there are palaces and structures enough already, and that there is neither space nor necessity to construct more.

But, if it is not true, however poetical—that Venice is "sinking rapidly" into the waves or sands of the Lagune, neither is it true, though rather less poetical, that the waves or sands of the Lagune are rising to whelm her. In both these particulars, as already intimated, she seems to-day wonderfully as she is said to have seemed some ten centuries ago, or some fourteen centuries ago, as to that. Nor is it true, that the smaller of her canals—*Canaletti*—are rapidly filling up with the rubbish of her decaying dwellings; nor that, during the sultriness of summer, they emit a noisome atmosphere, or a pestilential miasma. "On the contrary, just the reverse,"—at least, so far as the miasma is concerned. These smaller canals, called *Rii*, or *Canaletti*—are about a hundred and fifty in number, bestrid by about three hundred bridges. These bridges, by the bye, in Addison's time, had, it seems, no parapets, which deficiency the worthy man thinks would have been "a great inconvenience to a city less *sober* than Venice!" But, despite the moist air and moderate clime, her nobles, it appears, "conversed too little with strangers, and were too distrustful of them," to acquire habits of intemperance! The canals of Venice vary in width from the three hundred yards of the Canalazzo, to some three yards of its lesser sisters; and, from a depth of a dozen feet, to that of as many inches. Twice in twenty-four hours the tide ebbs and flows, from one inch to six, and with considerable current, sweeping through all the arteries of the city, and carrying off all impurities to the sea. Besides, every month or two comes a violent Sirocco, and pours the salt waves of the Adriatic in billows all over the city, submerging even the pavement of St. Mark's Place to the depth of several inches, and giving every *canaletto* and *calle* (lane) a thorough cleansing. Moreover, there is a species of machine called *Cava Fanghi*, a sort of dredging machine driven by steam—constantly at work deepening and cleaning the canals; while municipal ordinance is especially severe against pouring into them rubbish, or incumbering them with obstructions. The result of all these cares and precautions is exactly what they contemplate; and Venice is the neatest capital in Europe. The graphic authoress of "Consuelo" is correct when she says, that "the snowy flag-stones of Venice are the cleanest in the world." It is really surprising, indeed, how the Venetians manage to keep the narrow and tortuous *calla* and *canalletti* of their "peopled labyrinth," so thronged with a poor and immense population, so clean. That some of the narrowest, and shallowest, and least-frequented canals, in some unfrequented *sestieri* of the city, crowded by the lower classes, are not always very savory in the odors with which they address the nostrils, especially upon a damp and sultry dog-day, when the tide is out, is most true; and it would be most incredible were it not most true; but, that such facts make up the rule and not the exception, is utterly incorrect; while there is hardly a city in Christendom which does not present a larger number of filthy streets than does Venice of canals. Paris, London, Rome, Naples, Florence, Vienna, Berlin, New York, New Orleans, Boston, St. Louis—every one of them is less unexceptionable in this regard than

Venice. Addison more than a century and a half ago, remarked—"the streets of Venice are paved and always kept very neat;" while, at the same era, beasts of burthen were wont to get *stalled* in the thoroughfares of Paris and London!

There is about all sea-ports a marine, a saline atmosphere, the smell of which is peculiar—and to some persons, peculiarly unpleasant; although to others just the reverse. Such an atmosphere has Venice, and to it, probably, does she owe her high reputation for salubrity—a reputation she has enjoyed from her earliest origin. That she deserves this reputation may be inferred from a fact made known by her vital statistics compared with those of Paris, which city is considered one of the healthiest in Europe. At Paris, there is one sexagenarian for every two hundred inhabitants, and one octogenarian for every nine hundred: at Venice, there is a person sixty years old in every hundred and sixteen, and one eighty years old in every four hundred and ninety-one. The clime and site are considered peculiarly favorable to valetudinarians, and to persons advanced in years, while general health is remarkable, and centenarians numerous. The probable cause of all this is that very circumstance, which by some might be viewed as a fruitful source of disease—the humidity of the atmosphere. But the water which surrounds Venice is always pure and salt; and emanations from the sea are never noxious. The air is constantly charged with vapors, it is true; but those vapors are saline; and while they relax the animal fibre by moisture, they stimulate it by the chemical properties with which they are impregnated. Thus, vital action is maintained in a manner the most suitable, and the celebrated axiom of Brown, that "life is sustained by excitation," is happily fulfilled. It is a singular fact, however, that the atmosphere of Venice is far less humid than that of Padua, or Milan. The most common complaints are of a nervous character, which are aggravated, from time to time, by the Sirocco; but even the Venetians themselves, exaggerate the disagreeable influences of this wind, and do not seem to reflect, that, though it may bring lassitude, it does not bring dust—that curse of every inland town—while at the same time it dispels all noxious vapors. That the medical men of Europe regard the clime and site of Venice conducive to health, may be inferred from the fact, that they order there their chronic patients from all parts of the continent—in summer for the benefit of the baths—in winter for the benefit of the equable temperature. There is said to be a peculiar virtue in the slime and ooze of the waters of the Lagune, for some of the most afflicting of maladies, while the saline atmosphere is especially beneficial in cases of phthisis and scrofula. On the whole, therefore, the words of the celebrated physican, Grimaud de Caux, in his essay on "*Venice and her Laguna*," read to the Ninth Congress of learned Italians—*Scienziati Italiani*—are not without significance: "*Quelle ville en effet pourrait on comparer sous ce rapport à Venise, même en Italie? Venise est agréable à habiter en tout tems, &c.*" It is true Venice, by her close connection with the Orient, was, some centuries ago, liable to visitations from the plague; but what city of all Italy or, of all Europe, was not equally, if not more subject to these ravages, until Venice defended herself, and the peninsula, and the continent, with the Lazaretto? During the fearful plague of 1348, for example, Venice, within six months, lost one-half of her patricians; but Florence lost 100,000 of her inhabitants; Naples, 60,000; Genoa, 40,000; Sienna, 80,000, and the continent of Europe generally, three-fifths, at least, of all its population! It is also true, that the ravages of cholera in Venice, during her Siege of the summer of '49, were fearful; but there were abundant causes for this, as will be seen, independently of clime or site. The only wonder is that her population had not been decimated.*

The climate of Venice, as to temperature, is an agreeable medium between Boston and St. Louis, being warmer than that of the former, and cooler than that of the latter, but more equable than that of either. The latitude, however, is about that of Quebec—that of Venice being 45°, that of Quebec being 46°, while that of Boston is 42°, and that of St. Louis 38°. The months of June, July, and August, the months of summer at Venice, are, it is true, sultry, especially during the middle of the day, when the sun is so withering in its intensity, that no one willingly exposes himself to its rays; but even then, the narrow *calles* and canals, shaded by the tall structures on either side, are delightfully cool, as are, also, the marble depths of the massive palaces. But no sooner has the sun gone down behind the Friulian Mountains, than a fresh breeze comes careering in from the Adriatic, and the atmosphere of the evening and night are perfectly charming. In spring and autumn, the climate of Venice is delightful, while the winter has all that mildness and equability which characterises the season in places surrounded by the sea.

The city is most luxuriously, and profusely, and cheaply, supplied from *terra firma*—especially from the fertile Veronese, and from the neighboring islands, with fruits and provisions of every description, which the climate can afford; and no market in the world, probably, presents such abundance and variety of fish, as the Lagune pours daily into the *Peschiera* of the Rialto. It would really be worth the while of the *ichthyophist*, not less than the *ichthyophagist*—the

* Milan was more severely scourged by the plague than Venice; while the cholera, on its first visit south of the Alps, in 1830, spared Venice more than any other city of the peninsula.

student of natural history not less than the epicure—to "walk the wards" of the great *Peschiera* of Venice. He would certainly form the individual acquaintance of some inhabitants of the deep, of whose peculiar proportions,—of whose very existence, indeed, he knew nothing before, save from the plates of the Cyclopædia. The surpassing beauty of some of the fish of the Lagune, especially in hue, is noticeable, while the flavor and *texture* are so superior, that the *regime ichthyologique* of Venice, is renowned the world over. The roach, sturgeon, turbot, tunny, mullet, sardine, and sole, are among the most noted. Styria supplies beef; Chioggia and Rovigo, veal; Padua and Citadella, mutton; while the marshes of the Lagune, near Mestre and Fusina, afford exhaustless stores of wild fowl and game. The wine of the country, which is drank as freely as water, is the *vin ordinaire*, the best being of the vintage of Conegliano and Vicenza. Of foreign wines, the Cyprus is esteemed as highly at Venice, as is the *Lachrymæ Christi* at Naples. Champagne, Sauterne, and Voslauer, are also in common use. Oysters, in their season, are excellent; and, among the numerous muscles which are eaten, the most abundant and common is the *pidocchio*, which, despite its name (louse!), is a common and popular dish, in all forms and with all classes. As a general thing, as touching comestibles and the like, while the fish, fruits, provisions, butter and cream of Venice, have a reputation notoriously good, the meats and wines have a reputation notoriously bad. The Restaurants, likewise, are few and indifferent, while the Cafés are numerous and unequalled. As for house-rent, or rather palace-rent, it is very reasonable; and all manner of dry and fancy goods are more so than even at Paris or Vienna: gloves, for instance, being about two dollars the dozen.

On the whole, therefore, to a person with an annual income of a few thousand dollars, with or without wife or family—to a person whose tastes and pursuits are literary or scientific, and who cares nothing for politics—to a person fond of pleasure, amusements, the Opera and the arts, and especially to one who is an invalid, and who can appreciate the *dolce far niente*—the "sweet nothing-to-do" of Italian life—but above all, to one "a-weary of the world," disappointed, chagrined, sick at heart and in soul—there is not a spot in all Italy—in all the world, perhaps, which can present such attractions for a few years' residence, as "Beautiful Venice."

The idea that Venice is a silent city, with a sparse population, which is sometimes entertained in connexion with the romantic idea of her desolation and decay, is erroneous enough. With the single exception of Naples, the City of the Sea is, for its limits, the most populous city in Italy, and, despite the absence of wheels or hoofs, the most noisy. The gondoliers, the hucksters, the story-tellers, the sellers of *Melonaro* (water-melon), of *Zucca* (pumpkin), and of fish and fruits, to say nothing of *Aqua* (water), keep up a ceaseless yell from morning until night, and almost from night until morning; which yell is mitigated to the ear only by the change and the changes of the almost as ceaseless pealing of church bells. There are also few cities, even of Italy, which present such an aspect of unvarying gaiety and liveliness, as Venice; and a stranger, though direct from Rome, Florence, or Milan, entering St. Mark's Square, almost any summer evening, would be certain that a *Festa* was at its height, judging from the multitudes of well-dressed people of all nations, kindreds, tongues and tribes, and in almost every costume, which throng the pavement and arcades; and, in the midst of all, the Austrian band "discoursing most eloquent music." The voice of song, however, and the tones of instruments are going up from the canals, and cafés, the *campi* and *calli*, of Venice, all day long, and nearly all night long, too, as to that. It must have been very different thirty odd years ago, if we are to credit Childe Harold, for he says—

"In Venice Tasso's echoes are no more,
And silent rows the songless gondolier:
Her palaces are crumbling to the shore,
And music meets not always now the ear."

True, that the loves and wars of Rinaldo and Armida, of Tancred and Clorinda, are heard no more, or very seldom, on the canals of Venice; but the choruses and ariettas of Bellini, Rossini, Donizetti, and Verdi, which the gondoliers have caught beneath the windows of the Fenice, the San Samuele, or the San Benedetto, are sung with equal gusto and power, and, doubtless, with far more taste. The gondoliers have also their own *barcarolla* and *canzonette*, some of which have appropriate words, and all, charming airs. Among the most celebrated of these is the famous "*La Biondina in Gondoletta*," composed by Lamberti—the Moore—the Morris of Venice—the heroine of which is said to have been no less a personage than the accomplished and lovely Countess Benzoni, a friend of Lord Byron who died some ten or twelve years since. "*Un Ziro in Gondola*," "*La Marina*," "*La Brava Catina*," and "*Canzonetta della Frittola*," may also be named, as among the most common and most popular.

Some idea of the theme and burthen of the songs of the Venetian gondoliers may be gathered from the subjoined hasty, and rather free, translations. The songs themselves may, possibly, be deemed rather *free*, also: but, if so, what would be said of some other songs, very popular on the canals of Venice! The celebrated "*Biondina in Gondoletta*" done literally into prose—the flower bereft of the perfume—runs somewhat thus:

THE BIONDINA * in gondola last night I conveyed,
Tranquil and happy, the fair girl slept—
She slept on my arm, and sometimes awoke,
But the rocking barque re-lulled her to rest.

The moon in heaven was half hidden by clouds
The Lagune was calm, and the breeze was free—
A gentle zephyr played with her hair,
And, lifting her kerchief ———

But, really, this must stop, though there are three more verses. It is to be hoped, that the fair and accomplished Countess Benzoni felt complimented, by the inscription of this most celebrated of songs! In the original it is very *expressive*, and affords a somewhat striking comment on the taste of Venetian society, to say nothing of the propriety, morality, &c. As illustrative of these, its insertion entire might, possibly, be pardoned, despite its objectionable tone. No translation, however, could convey an idea of its poetical claims. In the soft Venetian dialect † it is deemed exceedingly beautiful. It is certainly a very famous lyric, to say the least of it.

The following opening lines of Tasso's "*Gerusalemme Liberata*," a poem translated from the Italian of Tuscany into the Italian of Venice—dialects so different, that the Florentine can, at first, hardly

* The Blonde.

† "The dialect of Venice," says Madame de Stäel, "is as soft and as light as a zephyr. One cannot conceive those who resisted the famous League of Cambray, speaking a language so flexible." In the Councils of Venice, speakers were obliged to speak Venetian. The Tuscan was tolerated only in the exordium. Rousseau, when secretary of the French Legation at Venice, in the last century, is said to have devoted much attention to the Venetian dialect, and made quite a collection of the Songs of the Gondoliers, which he published with their respective airs. Byron says of this dialect—

"I love the language, that soft bastard Latin,
That melts like kisses from a female mouth."

The dialect of Venice is that of Florence, with an elision of consonants--taking away in force what is imparted in softness. "The Venetian is to the Tuscan what the Portuguese is to the Castilian."

comprehend the Venetian—by Mondini, and called "*Il Tasso alla Barcarola*"— constitute one of the most popular of the modern "*Canti d'Gondolieri Veneziani.*"

I SING the army and the pious knight,
That the great sepulchre of Christ did free:
Much did he toil in heart, in mind, in might,
Much in the glorious conquest suffered he.

After a brief pause, another voice responds with a second stanza, to the same air, somewhat as follows:

In vain to him did earth oppose her rage—
In vain to arms did Turks and Lybians fly;
In vain did comrades fierce their quarrels wage—
Favored of Heaven and blest by powers on high.

Another song very popular on the canals—"*Un Ziro in Gondola*"—or, "An Evening in a Gondola," was composed by Madame Dudevant, the celebrated George Sand, who resided for some months at Venice, in 1834, and there wrote the well-known Venetian romances—"*Leone-Leoni,*" "*La Derniere Aldini,*" "*Les Maîtres Mosaïstes,*" "*L'Uscoque,*" and others. A free rendering of the words of her song is subjoined:—

AWAY with sad thoughts and come—come with me,
Away in the gondole to the deep blue sea.
We leave the canals and the islands behind;
We fly o'er the wave with the speed of the wind.
All golden and cloudless the sun goes down,
And over the Lido uprises the moon.
Her pale light expands on the silvery wave,
A mirror as pure as a woman in love.
The zephyr of evening plays with your hair;
How gently it kisses your forehead so fair!
You are lovely, and youthful, and fresh as a flower—
Tears, apace, come to all—but now is love's hour.
The Venus of Greece in a sea-shell once seen
Was thee, in thy gondola, fairest, I ween.

Another of the gondolier songs runs something thus :—

Oh, come to the gondola, angel bright!
We'll away o'er the beautiful sea:
By the Felze's* soft shade we'll be hidden from sight,
And how happy—how happy we'll be!

We'll shut out the daylight's gay, glittering glare,
No eye shall our blessedness see;
But alone, heart to heart, banish sorrow and care,
While I whisper of love, girl, to thee.

Ay, of love—while the ardor of youth is our own;
For years chill the heart-pulse with frost;
To be happy on earth we must list to love's tone—
Of its rapture bereft life is lost.

The arietta of "*La Donna è mobilè*," from "*Rigoletta*," Verdi's last opera, was very popular on the canals, as well as with the bands of the Austrian garrison in St. Mark's square, two summers since. The plot of the opera is that of Victor Hugo's "*Le Roi s'Amuse*";† and the dramatist attributes the words of the song—("*Souvent femme varie*," *etc.*)—to no less a personage than Francis of France. If this be sooth, his departed, good-natured Majesty may, possibly, pardon the following :—

Woman is changeable—fickle as fair,
A beautiful feather tossed by the air;
Her lips are as fluent as her heart is mute;
She is ever a tempting, deceiving fruit.

A deceiver is she, if deceiver e'er were,
Oh! woe to the heart that is given to her!
But we love her—we love her—our bosom's dear dove,
And he never was happy who never knew love.

There is also a ballad from the opera of "The Brides of Venice,"

* *Felze*—the canopy or cabin of the gondola. The pronunciation is *Felzè*. Vowels are never mute in Italian. Thus *Campanilè*, *Fenicè*, *barcarollè*, *etc., etc.*

† The Drama was forbidden at Paris in 1830, and the opera at Naples, in 1853, by government.

by Jules Benedict, which was sung in this country by Jenny Lind at her Concerts, which is sometimes heard in the saloons, or on the canals of the sea-girt city, commencing thus:—

By the sad sea-waves,
 I listen, while they moan
A lament, o'er the graves
 Of hope and pleasure gone.

But the songs of Venice are not all of them sentimental. Some are vastly comic in tone. "*La Canzonetta della Frittola*," or "The Song of the Fritter," presents, perhaps, a fair sample. It runs somewhat thus:—

Peter, Peter, here's a fritter,
Which I wish to give to you:
Many would have gladly munched it,
But I said for him I'll keep it—
To my old one I will give it,
And my old one—you are he.

Nay—but stop—we first must parley,
Swear you'll ne'er be false to me!
Swear—but in your eyes I read it—
Here's your fritter, come and eat it—
Don't stand staring, come and eat it,
For my old one—you are he.

The voices of the gondoliers are more remarkable for strength than for sweetness—for power than for melody; yet, at night, in the open air, at a distance, on the Lagune, the Giudecca, or the Grand Canal, singly or accompanied by half a dozen other voices, nothing can be more delightful than the song of the Venetian gondolier. "Idle and alone in his barque, awaiting his company, or his fare, he abbreviates the night and breaks the silence of the Lagune. Solitary in the heart of a crowded city, he sends his voice over the tranquil mirror; and the sleepy canals, the calm of the heaven, the splendor of the moon, the shadows of the lofty palaces prolonged on the water, the distant moaning of the Adriatic, the noiseless gliding of the sable gondolas, which move like spirits hither and thither—no rattling of wheels, no echo of footsteps, only the fitful and unfrequent plash of an oar—all these circumstances impart an indescribable charm to these world-renowned melodies."* The wives and children of the fishermen of the Adriatic, are said, at night fall, to go down to the sea-shore of the Chioggia, Malamocco, Pelestrina, and the Lido, and shout their well-known and not unmusical songs, until each can distinguish in the distance, through the twilight, over the waves, the husband's and father's peculiar response. A like custom is said to prevail in the Tyrol.

But no where is the "Gondolier's Song" so indescribably charming as on the Grand Canal of a moonlight midsummer night. This is the great *salon musicale* of Venice; and, upon principles of acoustics, is admirably calculated to heighten harmonious effect. The silence of the night, the gondola gliding noiselessly over a waveless surface which acts like an harmonic mirror on the voice; the façades of marble palaces on either side with their overhanging balconies, their open portals, their endless halls and galleries, and their leafy gardens beyond, augmenting without echo, the intensity of the sounds, all concur to aid effect. At midnight you stand on the *Pergolo* of the Palazzo Buzinello, opposite the *Posta*, the ancient Palazzo Grimani. You hear the accord of distant voices rising on the still night. A choir of gondoliers in their barques are slowly ascending from the Molo, half a mile below, and singing "*La Biondina*," as they advance. The voices are full and round, the harmony perfect—air, tenor, bass, counter—every part is complete. The moon is riding high over the slumbering city in a cloudless sky—the

* Goethe, perhaps Chateaubriand, quoted from memory.

marble piles are throwing their deep shadows over the slumbering canal; the *trabaccoli*, lying at anchor, seem slumbering, too. Nearer—nearer—nearer—by a *crescendo* which no art can match, the barque and the *barcarola* approach: louder and louder rise the notes on the ear, until, at length, beneath your balcony, the song has attained its *fortissimo*. It passes—the rougher sounds soften—they lessen—they lessen, as the barque ascends. At length it is beneath the Rialto-arch, which, for a moment, with its echoes, augments and rounds the air. It passes on—it turns the winding of the stream—it dies away—it is dead—it is gone! You hear no more; but you listen still; you listen—hushed—entranced—your very soul absorbed in the departed harmony. You draw a long breath—you speak to the friend at your side—your voice sounds to you harsh—you relapse into silence; and for hours after, those sweet melodies play like a rapture around your heart. And your thoughts, your dreaming fancies—they are far, far away—away from fair Venice, away from sunny Italy, away from the grand Old World, away over the wide, wild ocean—away—at your home! Who that has listened to the moonlight, midnight serenade of the Venetian gondolier, can, while his life lasts, forget?

Venice has been called "the City of Song," and not without reason. The time has been, and, perchance, even yet is, when her mark of approbation upon a *cantatrice*, or an opera, was as indispensable, as is the die of the mint upon the ingot of gold to give it currency. For her *Fenice* all the great composers of ancient and modern times, Rossini, Zingarelli, Donizetti, Persiani, Perotti, Verdi,* have written; and all the most wonderful vocalists, Malibran, Pasta, Catalini, Grisi, Tadolini, Rubini, have sung. From

* It is announced that Verdi is at present engaged in writing an opera for the Fenice on the famous French drama called the *Dame aux Camélias*, by Alexandre Dumas Jr.

1791, wnen the house was erected, until 1819, no production was presented on the Fenice stage unless written expressly for it. In December 1836, the house was burnt to the ground; but, in May 1837, true to its name of Phœnix, it had risen from its ashes, more beautiful than ever; and it was well said, that the theatre of the Phœnix had become the Phœnix of theatres. With the exception of the San Carlo at Naples, and the La Scala at Milan, the Fenice is the largest theatre in the world, as well as one of the most magnificent. Byron, in 1816 says—"The Fenice theatre is the finest I have ever seen; it beats our theatres all hollow in beauty and scenery, and those of Milan and Brescia bow before it." Yet the Fenice of 1816 was less splendid than that of 1850. During the three winter months the Fenice is the grand saloon of Venice, where the fair Venetian receives her friends and admirers in preference to the parlors of her own palace. The drop-scene by Busato, represents Dandolo refusing the imperial crown of Constantinople. The predominent colors of the house, are gold on white. The circles, or galleries, are five in number, one over the other; and the *loges*, stalls, or boxes, like those of most other theatres on the continent, are veritable boxes, or separate apartments, for six or eight people each, with a door opening on the lobby, and a front opening towards the scene; and in which the inmates can neither see nor be seen so well as where all is open, as with us. But the boxes of Italian theatres are not visited generally for the sake of being seen; often the reverse, rather.

The dimensions of the Fenice externally, are 254 French feet, by 158; parterre, 55 by 58; proscenium, 13 by 45; scene, 61 by 85. The breadth of scene of the San Carlo is 80 feet, and that of La Scala 121.

Besides the Fenice, there are four other theatres at Venice—the San Benedetto, the Apollo, the San Samuele, and the Malibran, all of which are in full blast during some nine months out of the twelve. The Malibran is the People's Theatre, and owes its name to the benevolence of the great *cantatrice*, who gave it a few gratuitous nights in 1835, when it had been almost ruined by her long and brilliant engagement of that year at the Fenice. A *loge*, or box at the Fenice, for the season costs 1000 *Zwanzigers*, about $167; a season ticket about $10, and a single admittance for a single person, from fifty cents to two dollars, according to locality. The terms of the minor theatres are less. The theatres at Venice, as, indeed, all over Italy, are the grand resort for conversation, social intercourse, and intrigue—quite as much so, as for the operatic, dramatic, or *balletic* entertainments offered.

The question is often asked by the stranger at Venice—"How do all these people manage to live?" He beholds no extensive manufactures, no heavy mercantile or manufacturing operations, no commercial uproar; and it is a mystery to him how the swarming multitudes around him manage to get a subsistence. Nor is the mystery easy to solve, nor the question to answer.

It may be safely assumed, however, at the very outset, that a Venetian will manage to live, and manage to live very well, too, where an American or an Englishman could manage only to starve. The glass works at Murano, together with the numerous work-shops at Venice pertaining to the manufacture, give employment to some four or five thousand persons, and subsistence, probably, to some eight or ten thousand more. The daily wages vary from two zwanzigers to six; while the chief workmen receive twelve, being equivalent to two dollars. The value of the articles turned out from Murano in a year—chiefly *beads!*—is estimated at eight millions of francs. Murano makes beads for the world! The North American savage, as well as the savage of South Africa, looks to the Sea-city for the choicest decorations for his person!

Then the manufactures of gold and silver stuffs, silks, lace, and velvets; of soap, earthenware, tobacco, candles, &c. &c., employ some thousands more. Book-printing and boat-building employ others, while immense numbers live on the Adriatic and the Lagune, drawing a sustenance and support from the exhaustless riches of the deep. The Sardine fishery, outside the Lido, is of considerable importance. Visitors, also, leave not a few Napoleons in the book-stores, and print-shops, as well as at the hotels, and with the gondoliers; likewise at the shops of the goldsmiths of the Piazza and the Rialto, who are as famous now for their *bijouterie* as they were centuries ago.

But, above all, as a means of support, Venice is the resort and residence of many persons of wealth, and is a favorite capital of the Austrian empire, the seat of a Vice-regal court during the winter months, and the scene of liberal expenditures. Here, too, is the site of the banking and discount business of commercial Trieste. Every disposition, likewise, is manifested by her citizens and her rulers to efface the outrages of time and the devastation of revolutions. On all sides reigns intelligent activity. The quays are repaired, the bridges rebuilt and enlarged, the temples and monuments restored, the streets and squares illuminated, the palaces and mansions accommodated to modern taste in comfort and luxury; and, well and truly has it been said by a distinguished writer—"*Venise n'est pas ce qu'on vous la représente dans les guides: le Phénix—car il n'y a qu'une Venise au monde—le Phénix sera bientot sorti de ses cendres.*"

First impressions of places, as of persons, are generally lasting.

Enter Paris of a sunny day in June, by the *barriere* of the Arch of Triumph, and your first impression of the capital of Europe will be very different from that you would have on entering it by the Faubourg St. Marçeau, or the gate of St. Denis, in the midst of a dismal autumnal rain. So of London, so of Naples, so of Rome, so of Venice. Enter Venice in the dusk of a damp October evening, after some thirty hours of constant travelling, night and day, by *vetturino* or railroad, from Bologna or Milan. The tide is out—huge banks of mud and sand heave up their shapeless masses from the bed of the Lagune; a cold mist bounds the horizon along the shore of the Adriatic, and, sweeping over the intervening marshes, chills you to the very bone, during the ten minutes the cars are rolling over the bridge, as you strive to get a first view of that "beautiful Venice" you have read about all your life, and of which you expect so much. But, through the gathering mists and deepening shades of night, you perceive nothing save a few indistinct masses of irregular architecture, towers, and domes, and roofs; and, thoroughly vexed, and disappointed, and chilled, you draw up the glass, and wrap yourself more closely in your cloak. The cars stop—you are hurried out—all is confusion—luggage and passports must be examined—you are carried hither and thither by the popular billows—you are squeezed almost to death—you get thoroughly out of temper. There is, certainly, no "romance" in all *this*. It is, on the contrary, rather real, and rather disagreeably real. Well, this at length over, next you run the gauntlet of porters, gondoliers, and *valets de place*. You can comprehend not a syllable of this Babel; but you can say—albeit with horrible mispronunciation—*Albergo Reale Danieli*—the name of the hotel to which you have been advised to repair. Then you are packed, with a dozen or two of other people of all nations and languages, into a huge, mis-shapen ark, covered in closely on every side, called familiarly an "omnibus;" and very like an omnibus it is, and would be still more like an omnibus, were it on wheels, instead of on water; but, just as unlike the gondola of your fancy, or of reality, as one floating thing can be unlike another; just as unlike it, indeed, as is the Venice of your sad experience unlike the Venice of your glad dreams. You commence your voyage of some two miles. You cut across a broad sheet of water—you plunge into a perfect Egypt of darkness and labyrinth of walls—horrible marine and other smells assail your olfactories—you whirl round a sharp corner—you dart under a low bridge—you hear not a sound, save the warning cry of the gondoliers in some unknown tongue,* from time to time, to avoid collision with the long, low, black, funereal, hearse-like barques, which, like spectres, shoot past you. At length you pass under a dark and lofty bridge between two vast structures, —it is the Bridge of Sighs—under another bridge—it is the Bridge of St. Mark—up a dark passage—and suddenly, stop. Then you step out on the slimy and slippery stone steps, and enter the cold, damp court of the "Danieli." You demand a chamber. After considerable delay, you are led up stairs innumerable, and through passages inextricable, and find yourself, at length, in a vast apartment, the ceiling covered with frescoes, the walls sheeted with pier-glass, the floor apparently paved with a mosaic of marble. The furniture, also, is of the most ancient, but most gorgeous description, and heavy tapestry droops along the walls. But you would give it all—all for a good blazing fire in the huge porcelain stove, and a warm warming-pan between your sheets. You are too sleepy, and too vexed, and too thoroughly tired-out and disappointed, however, to wait for all this; and so you abruptly dismiss the chattering valet, and, with teeth chattering from chilliness quite as fast as his from

* Turkish or Armenian, it is said, but not Italian or Venetian.

civility, leap into damp sheets, and dream of Greenland or Kamschatka, or of any place on the foot-stool, save—"Beautiful Venice!"

But, change the picture. You leave Trieste some sunny June morning in the elegant packet steamer "*Venezia.*" The Adriatic is blue as heaven and smooth as a mirror. In a few hours, you descry a long, low bank along the western horizon. You approach—domes and towers rise glittering beyond it, as if from the sea—you wonder at the vast fortifications that defend the port—the massive sea-walls that protect the *littorale*—the stupendous dikes that improve the harbor. You enter the port of Malamocco. You turn a point almost at right angles, and Venice—world-renowned Venice—"*Venezia la Bella*"—with her towers and spires—her domes, palaces, churches, and wonderful memories, is before you. If it is sunset, you look away over the roseate Lagune, and—

"A sea
Of glory streams along the Alpine height,
Of blue Friuli's mountains."

But, if it is "high noon," as it probably will be, a flood of sunny illumination is poured over the enchanted scene. The tide is in—the Lagune is a tranquil mirror—the waves sparkle—green islands and white sails fleck the surface. You pass the Armenian convent with its oriental minaret; the lonely isle of the Lazaretto; the quiet asylum for the insane on the eyot of San Servolo; the leafy beauties of the public gardens at the extremity of Castello. On your left rise the domes and towers of San Giorgio Maggiore; on your right the *Riva degli Schiavoni* with its gorgeous piles, terminated by the Ducal Palace; while in front spreads out the open expanse of the Giudecca and the Grand Canal, with their long avenues of palaces and churches; and, to close the vista, the lordly *Reden-*

tore swells majestically in the distance. At length your steamer drops her anchor in front of the columns of the Piazetta. She is instantly surrounded with gondolas; the Zecca and the Royal Gardens—the Palaces of the Republic and the Empire—the domes of the *Salutè* and the Cathedral—the towering Campanile of St. Mark, and the gorgeous Clocktower, are all before you: you are, at last, in Venice! And then, if it so be, that you cannot say with Mrs. Jameson,*—"I can conceive nothing more beautiful, more singular, more astonishing than the first appearance of Venice;" or with Mrs. Radcliffe†—"Nothing can exceed the admiration on the first view of Venice, with her islets, palaces, and towers rising out of the sea, whose clear surface reflects the tremulous picture in all its colors, as if they had been called up from the ocean by the wand of the enchanter, rather than reared by mortal hands—" why—is not the fair inference this—that you lack the taste of the one, or the genius of the other, as well as the power of appreciation of both? Might not, indeed, either of those ladies, or the many like them, say to you in the words of Rosalind—"I will scarce think you have swam in a gondola"? Be this as it may, however, and whatever the character or intensity of the first impression of Venice, is it not pretty plain, that the traveller will regard her very differently if he approach her on the bright mid-day in June, instead of on the chill October evening?

Few tourists, especially if they be American, remain long enough at Venice, or indeed, at any other city, save, perhaps, Paris, to get more than one impression of it; and if that impression chance to be unfavorable, why, the case for them is hopeless. The traveller arrives at Venice on the chill October evening, we will suppose,

* "Diary of an Ennuyèe."

† "Mysteries of Udolpho."

and threads rapidly only those narrow canals in which the city appears most time-worn, on his route from the *Strada Ferrara* to the Danieli, the Europa, the Luna, the Italia, the Brettagnia, or the Hotel de Ville; and then, after rushing about, with electric celerity, a few hours of the following day, to visit the Ducal Palace, St. Mark's Cathedral, the Academy of Fine Arts, and the Manfrini galleries, he is off at midnight on the steamer for Trieste, and says "farewell forever" to the city of the Doges. Under these circumstances, it is not very marvellous that he should send home a very lachrymose sheet about Venice; nor that he should imagine his own "desolation" to pertain to her.

Now, if instead of all this, the traveller could only manage to reach Venice on a bright June day, by way of the sea; and if then, he could only be content to pass a quiet month, or even a quiet week, in the dreamy, delicious old place; if he would wander alone and leisurely through glorious St. Mark's, and study its marvellous mosaics, its unique architecture, its whole ages of history, and its spoils of nations; if he would meditate, for only a day, in the palace of the Doges, with its endless halls, glittering with gilding, gorgeous with carving, and illuminated with the historic canvass of Tintoretto, Bassano, Palma Vecchio, and Veronese—with its vast and valuable array of volumes, its countless council chambers, hoary with years and dim with the memories of guilt—with its *piombi*, and its *pozzi*, and its Bridge of Sighs; if he would wander slowly and thoughtfully through only a few of the sixty ancient and venerable churches of Venice—the *Frari* and the *Saints John and Paul*, with their magnificent monuments of Senators and Doges—the *Salute* and the *Redentore*, with their memorials of the plague—the *Scalzi* and the *Jesuits*, wonderful in sculpture, and glorious in painting; if he would visit some few of the hundreds of marble palaces which rise like the giants of oriental fiction along the Canalazzo, the Cannaregio, or the Rio Canonica—the Manfrini, with its galleries of *chefs-d'œuvre* of art—the vast and opulent Vendramini, now owned and occupied by the Duchess of Berri—the Mocenigo, where Byron wrote some of his most inspired poetry, and where his bed, and his chair, and his desk, and his apartments, and even his *night-cap*, are yet shown;—the Barbarigo, where Titian lived, and painted,—the Trevisano with its memories of the haughty Cappellos—the *Ca' Doro*, belonging now, with half a dozen other palaces, to the once-renowned Taglioni, or rather, to her lover*—the Pisani, with its *souvenir* of Paul Veronese, "The Family of Darius"—the gorgeous Foscari, where, as guests of the Republic, have sojourned Francis and Henry of France, the King and Queen of Poland, the Emperor Frederick, and Casamir, of Hungary—now a Bohemian *caserma*—the palace of Catharine Canaro, Queen of Cyprus, now a Pawnbroking Bank—the humble mansions of Enrico Dandolo and Marino Faliero, "the glory and the shame" of Venice; not to mention the Balbi palace, the home of the great geographer, from whose windows and balconies Napoleon and Josephine so often witnessed the aquatic sports, the regettas and *frescas* of the City of the Sea; nor the Giustiniani palace, now occupied by Schiavoni, the artist, but in which the great Chateaubriand, so unjust to Venice, sojourned while her guest, on his pilgrimage to Jerusalem; nor the *Ca' del Duca*, so illustrative of the jealousy of the Venetian "Ten," presenting the basement only of a magnificent palace, commenced with its permission, by the Duke of Modena, three centuries ago, and then suddenly forbidden; nor the Fondaco de' Turchi, once the mart of the Ottoman, then the property of the Duke of Ferrara, until the "Ten" compelled him to sell, and now the favorite haunt of wall-flower

* Now her son-in-law, the Russian Prince Troubetskoi.

and weed; nor the Palazzi Grimani and Contarini,* and Rezzonico and Pesaro, and the palace of Cardinal Bembo, where once lived the lover of Lucretia Borgia, Duchess of Ferrara, before he had received the red hat of his station from Pope Paul III;† could the traveller devote a few hours to the matchless museums of Martinengo, Sanquirico, Valmarana‡, and Correr, and a few more to a glance at the dwellings of Titian, and Tintoretto, and Giorgione, of Canova, Vittoria, Sansovino, and Carlo Goldoni; could he pass a day amid the artistic treasures of the *Academia*, where is Titian's "Assumption," next to Raphael's "Transfiguration" at Rome, the first painting in the world; and half as long with Schiavoni's fair Venetians of his own time, whose voluptuous charms would fire the

* The palaces of the Contarini are five in number, as, also, those of the Giustiniani; the palaces of the Grimani are three, as also those of the Mocenigo family. Four palaces bear the Conaro name, and two the Cappello. The Cozzi palace, or the Palazzo d'Espagna, long belonged to Spain; and, as the abode of her Embassy, was a sanctuary for offenders against the civil laws, as was, also, the Embassy of France. The Consulate of France is now at the palace Cavalli; and the double-headed black eagle of Russia expands his baleful wings over the exquisite medallia which decorate the facade of the Rezzonico; while the stars and stripes of the "Great Republic," during the stormy scenes of '48-49, floated over the beautiful Palazzino Gambara, close beside the Academy, conspicuous for its gardens and shrubbery.

† Bembo's *liason* with Lucretia Borgia commenced in 1503, and continued three years; but they corresponded until 1517. Subsequently he married Morosina, a Venetian lady of extreme beauty, who died a dozen years later, after becoming the mother of a numerous progeny. In 1539, Bembo was made a cardinal by Pope Paul III. His tomb at Rome was erected by his son Torquato. In a church at Padua, where he long resided, is seen his bust, executed according to the directions of his friends, Titian and Sansovino. Bembo's *liason* with the Borgia antedated his cardinalate thirty years. He was also an admirer of the Queen of Cyprus, who must have been worthy of admiration, if her portrait by Titian, in all the splendor of oriental costume, at the Manfrini gallery, speaks true: and, at her Paradise of Asola, immortalized her in a volume called "Asolini," extremely admired for a century later. Tasso, it may be remarked, immortalized the virtue of Bianca Cappello, and Ariosto that of Lucretia Borgia!

‡ At the Palazzo Valmarina is to be found every work on Venice ever written, and every production ever presented on the Venetian stage!

blood of an anchorite; could he pass a morning at the Arsenal, with its savage weapons, and its yet more savage instruments of torture—its trophies, its standards, its armor, its early artillery, its models and monuments, its statues and steamers; and an evening at Murano* with its miracles of glass work, at St. Christopher with its silent tombs, at the Armenian convent with the memories of Byron, at the Lido with its sublime view of the blue Adriatic and the snowy Alps, at deserted Torcello with its "chair of Attila" and its moss-grown *dome;* and many—many evenings upon the glassy Lagune with its constellation of smiling, sleeping isles; could he gaze upon the setting sun from the summit of the lofty bell-tower of the Basalica, hundreds of feet high, consecrated by the starry studies of the great Tuscan, and behold the broad disk go down the cloudless sky of Italy behind the Tyrol, while the Euganean Hills, and the blue Friulian Mountains, and the dim Adriatic, and the distant *terra firma*, and the mirrored Lagune, and the countless domes, spires, palaces of insulated Venice at his feet were steeped in a deluge of purple effulgence; could he, hour after hour, by night and by day, with company and without company, muse and meditate, and wander and ponder, in the magnificent Square of St. Mark, with its endless Arcades, its tesselated pavements—with "its arches and pillars of ponderous construction and great strength, but as fragile to the eye as garlands of hoar frost or gossamer,—its cloisters and galleries, so light they might have been the work of fairy hands, yet so strong that centuries have battered them in vain;" with its ancient palaces, its snowy and sacred doves, its twin columns, its

* Here were manufactured those immense mirrors which were the marvel of the Middle Ages, and those crystal glasses which poison shivered to atoms, as well as those pearls of glass more precious than pearls of the sea, and those *verroteries* of many colors, the staining of which was, for centuries, and is, even now, a secret.

bronze steeds, its triumphal masts, (bearing now, alas! only the eagles of the conqueror,) its mystic Clock-tower, its antique lions, and its mighty multitudes of all nations in all costumes, speaking all languages, promenading to the matchless music of martial bands; and, " more than this, than these, than all," with its world of solemn memories, and hoary legends, and dim traditions—its historic chronicles of wondrous scenes, and wondrous men, and vast events, so thickly thronging the mind, that—

> "Not a stone
> In the broad pavement, but to him who has
> An eye, an ear, for the inanimate world,
> Tells of past ages"—

—could the pilgrim to old Venice somewhat in this wise perform his pleasant pilgrimage—could he somewhat in this manner behold all this, or only the moiety of all this, or even a lesser portion yet of all this; and then, " with many a longing, lingering look behind," bid farewell to her fairy image, some sunny morning, when on his railway-route to Verona, as her fast-fading charms sank like a vision into the waves—the world would hear less of her " desolation," and his " first impressions" would be far more favorable, and far more valuable, too, than now they usually are. And if, in addition, he could be so happy as to be blest with a full moon while at Venice, to light him on his excursions, in the luxurious gondola, among the isles of the Lagune and the palaces of the Grand Canal; and could he *time* his visit so fortunately as to be present at one or more of the splendid *Festas* so numberless in the Venetian calendar, and at which more of the characteristics of Venice may be witnessed in a single night, than during weeks of ordinary days; and could he be favored with a gondolier serenade, or with the novel spectacle of a *Fresca*—a *Corso di barche*—a gondola-promenade; and could he be lucky enough to lose himself a few times amid the labarynthine web of those tangled and intricate lanes and foot-paths called streets, hemmed in by towering structures, and intersected at every dozen yards by equally narrow and labarynthine canals bestrid by bridges, —could he be favored with this *addenda* to the original programme—why, he would then leave the old city still better qualified to convey some faint idea of Venice *as she is;* and with information respecting her which should entitle his opinion to some respect. And yet notwithstanding, nothing has been said of the famed Rialto Bridge, nor of those old Arcades hard by, "where merchants most *did* congregate," and where the Christian "spat on the Jewish gaberdine;" nor of that dark old edifice where was founded the first bank in the world, and whence issued the first bill of exchange; nor of the *Campo di Marte* where the Austrian field-officers do daily exercise the only horses to be seen in the city, except four or five of bronze, and as many of monumental marble; nor of the beautiful *Ponte Sulla Laguna*, that iron link, which connects the Venice of the past with the peninsula of the present; nor of the Viceroy's Palace; nor of the Royal Gardens and the Public Gardens of Napoleon; nor of the gilded *Bucentauro* and state barges at the Arsenal; nor of the bronze giants, that, with ponderous sledges, beat out the hours on the Titanic bell of the clock-tower of St. Mark; nor of the Winged Lion of St. Mark himself; nor of many, many another strange and splendid object—many another scene or spectacle, which contributes to render Venice the most remarkable city in the world.

Nor is the writer singular in this admiration of Venice. Were he *not* her admirer—her lover—he *would* be singular indeed; for, of all those who have visited or written of her, in the long lapse of ages—and their name is literally legion, not one is there who is known to him to have expressed a sentiment dissimilar to his own. Centuries ago, the Roman poets, Martial and Altinus, celebrated her charms in classic verse, and compared her delights with those of Baiae and Pozzuoli, that Elysium of imperial luxury; while, by another bard, she is immortalized thus—

> " Venetia stands with endless beauties crowned,
> And, as a world, within herself is found.
> Hail Queen of Italy! for years to come,
> The mighty rival of immortal Rome!
> Ausonia's brightest ornament! by thee
> She sits a sovereign, unenslaved and free." *

" Venice is very entertaining to the traveller," wrote Addison, more than a century and a half ago. " It looks at a distance as if half-floated by a deluge."

" I was sorry to leave Venice," says William Beckford, in 1780.

" How I regret to leave Venice!" echoes Mrs. Jameson, in 1840.

"And so it is over! and thus end our Venice days!" sighs Schroeder, in his " Shores of the Mediterranean." " How thought clings to her as reluctantly we embark!"

" Thus parted I from Venice," writes Dana; " but there can be no farewell to scenes like these."

" Venice! farewell, forever!" exclaims the lamented Wilbur Fisk. "I leave thee with mournful pleasure. As I recede, thine image is with me still, sitting like a dethroned princess on the waters, dignified, and courtly even in decline. But the vision fades in distance and sinks into the waves."

" Of all the places the tourist visits," says Robert M. Walsh, " none leaves an impression more vivid than the city which 'sits throned on its hundred isles.' And when the moon appears, and

* *Quis Venetæ miracula proferat urbis, &c.*—ZANAZARIUS.

her beams begin to glitter upon the Saracenic turrets of St. Mark, and play amid the venerable arches of the Ducal Palace, and dance upon the shining waters of the Adriatic, truly is enchantment the proper epithet for the scene."

"Not Florence," writes another American tourist, "in the beautiful and classic vale of Arno, nor smiling Naples, with its unrivalled bay, nor Rome itself, with all its solemn grandeur, distinct and vivid as they all are in my recollection, has power to lessen the charm which memory throws around that unique and most lovely city, whose moonlight scenery still mingles with the most delicious of my waking dreams."

"It was with unmingled pleasure," writes the poetical Willis, in 1831, "that I again saw the towers and palaces of Venice rising from the sea. There is nothing like—nothing equal to Venice. She is the city of the imagination—the realization of romance—the queen of splendor, and softness, and luxury. Allow all her decay—feel all her degradation—see the 'Huns in her palaces,' and the 'Greek upon her mart,' and after all, she is alone in the world for beauty, and spoiled as she has been by successive conquerors, almost for riches, too. *Abroad in a summer's moonlight in Venice*—is a line that might never be written but as the scene of a play. * * * It was melancholy to leave Venice. Oh, how magnificently looked she in that light, rising behind us from the sea, all her superb towers and palaces, turrets and spires, fused in gold; and the waters about her, like a mirror of stained glass, without a ripple."

"Venice! Queen of the Adriatic! City of the heart!" writes the practical Greeley, twenty years later, in 1851, "how can I ever forget thee? Brief—too brief, was my halt amid thy glorious structures; but such eras are measured, not by hours, but by sensations, and my first day in Venice must ever hold its place among most cherished recollections of my life. Fallen Queen of the Adriatic! a long and mournful adieu!"

And here is a poetical tribute from the pen of the accomplished lady of the American *Chargé* at Turin, who visited Venice nearly at the same time:—

"Still in death, in decay, thou art Venice the Grand!
Embosomed in waters, impearled by the stars;
And now, in this moonlight, how calm dost thou stand,
While no discord the scene of thy peacefulness mars.
'Tis enchantment!—I dream! In a cradle I glide,
Embedded as softly in velvet and down
As if lulled in Love's lap, while around and beside,
Old temples and turrets majestically frown!"

"The mystic figures of the past grappling our spirits, lead them away," writes Ik. Marvel—"willing and rejoicing captives through the long vista of the ages that are gone. Carry is in a trance; wrapt by the witchery of the scene into a dream. This is her Venice; nor have all the visions that played upon her fancy, been equal to the enchanting presence of this hour of approach."

"Venice is the centre of pleasure," wrote Lady Montague to her husband a hundred years ago; "less noisy but more refined than Paris."

"The mere sight of Venice wakes a host of memories," exclaims Corinne; "her dialect is as soft as her zephyrs."

"Next to the East, Venice has ever been the greenest isle of my imagination," epistolizes Byron to Moore, in sober prose.* "She pleases me as much as I expected, and I expected much. I do not even regret her evident decay, though I do regret her vanished costume."

* For Lord Byron's *poetical* opinion of Venice see his poetical works *passim*, especially "Marino Faliero," "The Two Foscari," "Beppo," and the opening of the fourth canto of "Childe Harold."

"Underneath day's azure eyes
Ocean's nursling, Venice lies;
Column, tower, and dome, and spire,
Shine like obelisks of fire.
Pointing, with inconstant motion
From the altar of dark ocean
To the sapphire-tinted skies,
As the flames of sacrifice."

Thus wrote Shelley; while the glowing picture of "the glorious City in the Sea," of his friend Rogers, is, perhaps, too trite for quotation. To Venice—to Italy—this poet, like all others, sighs adieu:—

"And now farewell, perhaps
Forever! yet methinks I could not go,
I could not leave it, were it mine to say—
Farewell forever!"

"My eye was unwearied," writes Schiller, "beholding the delightful prospect; but my *sensations*, oh, how different from those on first beholding this enchanting city!"

"Nothing can exceed the admiration at the first view of Venice," says Mrs. Radcliffe. "I cried with delight," says Mrs. Bullard.

"Venice," writes Williams, "is unrivalled for beauty."

"Venice, the strangely-floating city! the Queen of the Adriatic! the richly-adorned bride of the mighty sea! the magnificent Venice lay like a dead swan on the waters!" Thus exclaims the "Improvisatore" of the Swedish Andersen, who, alone of all writers, expresses disappointment at Venice. But he had imagined too much: he had even "imagined St. Mark's tower to be much loftier"—albeit the angel on its pinnacle is three hundred and fifty feet from the flags of the Piazza! But hear that remarkable woman, the authoress of "Consuelo":—

"Venice! thou who seemest born rather of the spirit than created by the hand of man, and designed as the passing sojourn of pure souls, as a foretaste, on this earth of heaven; whose fairy structures seem the habitation of the departed, and round whose architectural glories the air of magic still lingers; whose colonnades in airy lightness seem quivering in the evening air; whose piercing pinnacles intermingle in beautiful confusion with the masts of floating ships; whose angels and saints seem just to have alighted on thy spires to feel with trembling wings the cool sea-breeze: thou city that seemest, not like other cities, to rest on the dull and heavy earth, but to float like a swan upon the waters—rejoice—rejoice—rejoice! A new destiny is before thee!—a new greatness, glorious as the past!"

And this prophecy was written long years before the 22d day of March, 1848!

And here is the tribute of another daughter of genius, equally enthusiastic, if not equally eloquent, the tribute of Felicia Hemans:—

"Venice, exult! and, o'er thy moonlit seas,
Swell with gay strains each Adriatic breeze!
What though long fled those years of martial fame,
That shed romantic lustre o'er thy name,
Though to the winds thy streamers idly play,
And the wild waves another queen obey;
Though quenched the spirit of thine ancient race,
And power and freedom scarce have left a trace,
Yet still shall Art her splendors round thee cast,
And gild the wreck of years forever past."

"The glory of the day which broke upon me in this dream," writes Dickens in his exquisite "Italian Dream"—"its freshness, its motion, its buoyancy, its sparkles of the sun in the water, its clear blue sky and rustling air, no waking words can tell. * * * I have, many and many a time, thought since of this strange dream upon the water, half wondering if it lie there yet, and if its name be VENICE."

"Venice, with her towers and domes," writes the delightful authoress of "The Diary of an Ennuyee"—"indistinctly glittered in the sunset and distance, like a gorgeous exhalation on the bosom of the ocean. Farewell, then, Venice! I could not have believed it possible, that it would have brought tears to my eyes, to leave a place merely for its own sake, unendeared by the presence of any one beloved."

"Venice! dear, dear Venice!" apostrophizes the Countess of Blessington—"shall I ever see thee again? Alas! I fear I have breathed thy balmy air, glided over thy noiseless waters, and listened to the mournful cry of thy Gondolieri for the last time! It makes me sad to think so; for, dearly do I love thee, Venice, and rarely have hours passed so happily as during the brief period I dwelt in thy luxurious atmosphere."

But the writer had no purpose of imposing on his good-natured, long-suffering reader, a whole "Dictionary of Quotations"—albeit, the views expressed are more valuable, perchance, than would be his own, and, beyond all peradventure, are more graphically presented. He designed but to quote a few distinguished names in confirmation of the views he had himself advanced; and to this end turned rapidly over the leaves of his note-book, to catch here and there a random sentence, that he might offer a Venetian "brick," as it were, from the "Babel" of its multitudinous, confused, and blotted pages. And there, in addition to the well-known names already quoted, he finds those of Tasso and Dante, of Petrarch and Milton, of Alfieri and Sismondi, of Victor Hugo and Casamir Delavigne, of Lamartine and Chateaubriand, of Scott and Moore, of Thiers, and Allison, and Daru—of Cooper, Ruskin, Rose, Read, Valery, Nodier, Royer, Lecomte, and Lady Bulwer; and a host beside, each of whom, at some period, has written of Venice, or made with her a brief abode; and each of whom expresses for her the same deep and mournful, yet enthusiastic, admiration.

But of all those who have sought at Venice a retreat from the great world—who have sought an asylum for heart or mind, there is none whose name is so intimately associated with hers as that of Lord Byron—at least during the present century. Byron lived at Venice three years, and, at one time, resolved to die there, and be buried at the Lido. In the autumn of 1816, he left Diodati, near Geneva, crossed the Simplon to Milan, and, after a brief sojourn at that capital, proceeded to Venice, where he took lodgings on the 10th of November, with a cloth-merchant, Signor S., at a house on the *Frezzeria*, since occupied by the distinguished advocate, Baron Avesani, whose name occurs in the events of '48–49. The merchant's wife, named Marianna, was young and beautiful. So was Byron; and, as the feelings of neither of them were pre-engaged, and, as neither of them was troubled with conscientious scruples, the result, unhappily, was inevitable. This *liaison* lasted about six months, and the poet says his love was "fathomless"—as, indeed, was with him generally the case, about every six months, with a new object. At length, a terrible scene, originating in the lady's jealousy of a sister, revealed all to the husband. No daggers were used, however.*

One day, moreover, a Venetian jeweler offered to sell his lordship a certain *parure* of diamonds, which he had himself recently presented his lady-love! It was at this time that the poet studied the Armenian language, for some months, at the Convent of San Lazzaro; but the lady, he says, was "less obdurate than the language."

* The tradition of Stilctoes," says Lecomte, "has passed away at Venice; bravoes live only in the romance and the melodrama; and the only wound the stranger need fear, is that immedicable one which he receives from some dark Venetian eye!"

His lordship managed, however, to translate into "choice" Armenian Paul's Epistles to the Corinthians; and aided his teacher, Paschal Aucher, one of the ninety monks then at the Convent, in preparing for press an Armenian and English Grammar.

In April he went to Rome, visiting Ferrara and Florence, *en route*, and returned to Venice in May. From Rome he writes, "I am delighted with Rome, but I must go back to Lombardy, because I am wretched at being away from Marianna." He was absent from her just one month! In June, he went with the lady to his *villaggiatura*, at La Mira, near the Brenta, a few miles on the mainland, and not far from Venice. Here he met with Margarita Cogni, a very magnificent and very ignorant *contadina*—also married. Between Marianna and Margarita stormy scenes soon arose; and when, on Byron's return to Venice, in October, he established himself in one of Palazzi Moncenigo, Margarita followed and established herself under the same roof, thus completing her triumph over her rival. Subsequently, Marianna went with her husband to Naples, where, some years ago, she was yet living. But Margarita's triumph was of brief duration. She was too *tempestuous* even for Byron. In a paroxysm of jealousy, at a Carnival masquerade, she tore the mask from the face of Madame Contarini, a noble lady who was leaning on the noble poet's arm, and perpetrated other outrages similarly atrocious! "She was a fine animal, but quite untameable," writes her lover, who gives a detailed account of the amour. And so, with much ado, and with the aid of the *police*, he got her back to her husband! Ten years ago she was yet alive, and residing on the mainland some miles from Venice. She was a widow, about fifty years old, with thick black hair sprinkled with gray—with brilliant eyes, and the remains of great beauty.

After parting with the "Fornaretta," the poet's amours seem to have been shamefully promiscuous; and, by those now living, who knew his mode of life, the scenes witnessed by the Moncenigo palace are said to have been worthy only of his own Sardanapalus.

An article in Blackwood's Magazine for August, 1819, supposed to have been written by John Wilson, its editor, in a slashing review of "Don Juan," alludes to Venice as "the lurking place of his (Byron's) selfish and polluted exile." The poet in his rejoinder says—"How far the capital city of a government which survived the vicissitudes of thirteen hundred years, and might still have existed, but for the treachery of Bonaparte and the iniquity of his imitators, a city which was the emporium of Europe, when London and Edinburgh were dens of barbarians—may be termed a "lurking-place" I leave to those who have seen or heard of Venice to decide. How far my exile has been "polluted," it is not for me to say; but that it has been '*selfish*,' I deny." The poet then cites his acts of benevolence and charity, which were, in fact, quite numberless.

At this time he was enchanted with Venice, and especially with her women. "There is a *naïveté* about them," he writes, "which is very winning, and the romance of the place is a mighty adjunct. Here have I pitched my staff, and here do I purpose to reside for the remainder of my life."

Again, of the city he says—"There can be nothing more poetical in its aspect than the city of Venice. Does this depend upon the sea, or the canals?—

"The dirt and sea-weed whence proud Venice rose!"

Is it the canal which runs between the palace and the prison, or the "Bridge of Sighs" which connects them, that renders it poetical? Is it the "Canal Grande," or the Rialto which arches it, the churches which tower over it, and the gondolas which glide over the waters, that render this city more poetical than Rome itself?"

And of the women :—

"I like the women, too, forgive my folly,
From the rich peasant cheek of ruddy brown,
And large black eyes, that flash on you a volley
Of rays that say a thousand things at once,
To the high dame's brow more melancholy,
But clear, and with a wild and liquid glance,
Heart on her lips and soul within her eyes,
Soft as her clime and sunny as her skies."

Byron's health suffered from his dissipation at Venice, especially during the Carnival, although he strove to obviate the effects by leading an active life, swimming, boxing, boating, and taking a daily gallop of miles on the beach of the Lido. His works completed at this time were "Manfred," "Beppo," "Mazeppa," "Ode to Venice," the fourth canto of "Childe Harold," and the first canto of "Don Juan."

It was in the autumn of 1818, at a *conversazione* at the palace of Madame Albrizzi,* that Byron first met Teresa, Countess Guiccioli, then on a visit to Venice with her husband, an old and wealthy nobleman of Ravenna. She was the daughter of Count Gamba, a Romagnese noble of high rank, though broken fortunes; and, at the age of sixteen, fresh from a convent, was immolated on

* The Countess Albrizzi, authoress of the "Ritratti," or portraits of the celebrities of her day, was a highly accomplished and very lovely lady, the De Stael, the Aspasia of Venice, thirty years since. Divorced from the Chevalier Marini, her first husband she became the wife of Count Albrizzi, an Inquisitor of State, albeit, a very "mild-mannered man." Byron refused, for some reason, to sit to her for his literary portrait, and deserted her saloons for those of the Countess Benzoni. The Palazzo Albrizzi, a splendid structure of the 16th century, in the Campo Albrizzi, at San Apollinare, was recently the residence of the Count Carlo Albrizzi, nephew of the Countess.

the altar of mammon. She was now about twenty, and one of the loveliest *biondinas* north of the Po. Byron was ten years her senior, and as remarkable for beauty as herself, although his style was the exact reverse. A mutual and intense passion sprang up between the pair on their very first interview. In April, 1819, she returned with her husband to Ravenna. Byron visited her in June, and in October all three returned again to Venice. At this time Byron had a visit from his friend, Moore. The rencontre seems to have been a jovial one. "We were very merry and very tipsy," writes Byron. "Moore *hated* Venice, by-the-way, and swore it was a sad place."

In November, the Countess returned to Ravenna with her husband; and Byron, after a severe illness and several passionate letters of "farewell," left Venice for the last time and hurried after her. At Ravenna, he continued constantly to reside, from December 1819, to November 1821, a period of nearly two years. In July 1820, Pope Pius VII. granted the Countess a decree of separation from her husband, at her request. The scandal was very great, and repeated attempts were made on Byron's life.

In his journal, Byron says, "The Countess, in despite of all I said and did to prevent it, *would* separate from her husband." The poet's annual income at this time was about $20,000, independently of receipts from his publisher, Murray, of some $10,000 per annum, besides. He was exceedingly benevolent, and was greatly beloved at Ravenna; while his own attachment for the place was very strong.

In the summer of 1820, during the disturbances in Italy, originating with the revolution at Naples, the father and brother of the Countess, together with Byron, being suspected, and not without cause, of being *carbonari*, the two former were, in July of the following year, banished the Papal States. Repairing to Pisa, Byron joined them in November. While at Pisa, Byron suffered two severe bereavements ; his friend Shelley perished in a tempest in the Gulf of Spezzia, and his natural daughter, Allegra, about four years of age, died of a fever in a convent near Ravenna. The latter loss drove the poet almost mad for a time. Her mother was English, and had, at his desire, sent her to him at Venice, in September, 1819. By a codicil to his will, a month or two later, he left her $25,000, to be paid her on her attaining her twenty-first year, or on the day of her marriage—provided she did not marry with a native of Great Britain.

In September, 1822, the Gamba family, with Byron, repaired to Genoa. Here the poet met the Countess of Blessington, and here he remained until the 13th of July 1823, when, accompanied by the brother of the Countess, he sailed for Greece. It was in vain the Guiccioli besought him to permit her to go with him. At Genoa he addressed a letter to Mr. Church, the American Consul at that port, at that time, asking advice, which concludes thus : "An American has a better right than any other to suggest to other nations the mode of obtaining that liberty which is the glory of his own."

The sequel all the world knows. Embarked in the cause of down-trodden Greece, the noble poet was seized by an inflammatory fever at Missolonghi, which, on the 19th of April, 1824, at the age of thirty-seven, terminated his life. The Countess was profoundly impressed by this sad event. For some years she dwelt with her family in Italy. Afterwards she took up residence in Paris, and occupied herself with the translation into Italian of portions of the poems of her illustrious lover. Her influence over Byron was, at one time, very great—greater, perhaps, than any other woman ever attained. It was at her request he wrote "The Vision of Dante," and discontinued "Don Juan" before completing his plan of the poem. By the Countess of Blessington, Leigh Hunt, John Galt, Willis, and others, however, he is said to have "treated her shamefully." She has always, nevertheless, seemed to retain respect for his memory; and, although greatly sought, because of her beauty and accomplishments, and the *prestige* attached to her name, long remained true to him. She speaks and writes fluently the English, French, and Italian languages; and, though now upwards of fifty, would be taken, it is said, for a woman of thirty-five. The latest notice of her which has appeared is embraced in the subjoined paragraph from a letter of the Parisian correspondent of the "New York Herald," under date of June 24, 1852, by which, it seems, she has at length again become a wife:—"Madame, the Marchioness of Boissy, formerly Countess Guiccioli, the *egerie* of Lord Byron, has just published a very remarkable translation of 'Lamartine's Meditations' in the Italian language." The Marquis de Boissy, her husband, who was a liberal Peer under Louis Philippe, and has been recently made a Senator under the new Empire, is said to be distinguished only for eccentricity and immense wealth.

Returning from this prolonged digression, and resuming our general view of the City of the Sea—there are two objects of interest, already glanced at, which, in a special manner, claim our attention—the Place St. Mark, and the Ducal Palace which shadows it.

THE PLACE ST. MARK!—the heart of Venice!—the forum—the garden—the grand hall of the Dogal city! The general rendezvous for business, or for pleasure—the place where one meets whom one seeks—where one hopes to meet whom one loves! And then, its historic and traditionary *prestige*—the wonderful scenes it has witnessed—the gorgeous fetes and solemnities of which it has been the theatre! It was here, eleven centuries ago, that blind old Dandolo received the crusader-chiefs of France—Montfort, Montferrat, Montmorency and Baudoin—here that Barbarossa bowed his neck to the sandal of the aged Pontiff; here that the splendid nuptials of Francis Foscari—so soon, alas! to die an exile!*—were celebrated by a tournament witnessed by thirty thousand people, and continuing, with other pageants for ten successive days; here that Petrarch assisted at the gorgeous fetes for the conquest of Candia, and exclaimed—"I know not that the world hath the equal of this Place"; here that the conspiracies of Tiepolo and Faliero were crushed, upon the only two occasions, in the long period of fourteen hundred years, when Venetian fought Venetian on the Place St. Mark. It was around this square that the newly-elected Doge was wont to be borne in his chair of state, on the shoulders of the *Arsenalotti*, scattering largess in his course; and around the same square, on the *Mardi Gras* of each year, for several centuries, that "the bull and twelve hogs," in memory of the unique ransom of the Patriarch of Aquilea and his twelve Canons, were fiercely chased, and, finally, "with a single blow from two-handed swords, four feet long and four inches broad," were slain! Around this same Square, also, proceeded—and still proceeds—once every year, in pompous procession, the priestly pageant of the *Corpus Domini*, with lanterns and flambeaux, and torches and candles; and here, for centuries, was held the famous *Fiera Franca*, or Free Fair, to which flocked the merchants of all Europe, when, during a certain period of eight days, in every year, a city of shops filled with rarest and most costly commodities, rose on the pavement of St. Mark, the lanes and streets of which are yet beheld traced out

* In less than four years after these nuptials, this same populace, in this same Square, loaded Foscari with curses, and demanded his banishment!

by lines of tesselated stones. Here, too, is the theatre of the *Tombola*, that characteristic Lottery of Italy, which draws into the Piazza, *en masse*, the whole population of the Dogado; and here the home of the white pigeons of St. Mark, once supported by the State, but now by a special legacy of a devout old patrician, and which, when the hour of twelve is beaten out on the huge bell of the Clock-tower by the bronze giants, pour down in clouds upon the northwest angle of the Place for their accustomed food.* In modern times, this ancient Square has been the scene of more than one splendid spectacle, not the least imposing of which was that which signalized the visit of the Emperor Ferdinand, some fifteen years ago, when returning from his Coronation at Milan, when the vast area blazed with illumination—when the balconies, entablatures, cornices, friezes, and all the caprices of architecture of the palaces and Cathedral, were traced in lines of irised light—when the lofty Campanile heaved up its mighty mass, wedge-like, into the dark sky, as if a blazing beacon from a sea of fire; and dome and spire, and pinnacle of the Saracenic, yet sacred architecture of St. Mark, was outlined in flame! It was at the base of the Tree of Liberty planted in the centre of this Square, that the insignia of the ancient Republic were consumed on the 4th of June, 1797; and here, fifty years later, on the 22d of March, 1848, that ancient Republic was declared anew!

Verily, many wonderful scenes hath witnessed this same Square of St. Mark! And, then, its *surroundings*—the old and new palaces of the Procurators—the *Fabbrica Nuova*, erected by Napoleon in 1810, on the site of a church—the Cathedral of St. Mark with its Campanile—the Piazzetta, with its columns, its Ducal Palace,

* These white, or rather gray, pigeons, were sacred from touch, even during the horrors of famine, in 1849.

its Library, its *Zecca**—the Clock-tower—the Cophtic pillars—the Broglio—the Stone of Shame—but the simple enumeration would occupy a page.

The Place St. Mark of Venice recalls to the traveller the Place Palais Royal of Paris; both being surrounded by palaces with arcades. But here the similarity ceases—the garden of the latter being only a naked pavement in the former. The *enceinte* of St. Mark, on three sides, is formed by the old and new palaces of the Procurators and the palace of Napoleon. The so-called "Royal Palace" of the present rule, in which dwell the two Governors of Venice, as well as the Viceroy of the Lombardo-Veneto in the winter, and in which are entertained the Emperor and princes of the blood, when guests at Venice, embraces the whole range of edifice, even from the old palace of the Procurators to the Zecca. The old Procurator Palace, which bounds the Square on the north, and is terminated by the Clock-tower, is now private property, and is said, not many years since, to have fallen, by descent into the possession of a young girl, who subsequently married a Russian noble. The dial of the Clock-tower—or *Torre del' Orologio*—is divided into twenty-four hours, according to the Italian mode of computing time, and displays, also, the signs of the zodaic and the phases of the moon, in brilliant hues of azure and gold. During the six weeks of Epiphany and Ascension, and likewise at other religious seasons, the figures of three Moorish monarchs, upon the striking of

* In the *dogat* of Giovanni Dandolo, 1285, with the permission of the Pope and the Emperor, the gold *zecchina*, or sequin, worth about $2 50, was first struck at Venice, the coin bearing upon it the name and the image of the Doge, at first seated on his throne, but subsequently standing, and finally, represented on his knees receiving from St. Mark the banner of the Republic. As early as the ninth century, coin was struck, and in the year 938, a *Zecca*, or Mint, was established on the site of the present, deriving its name from the *zecchina*.

each hour, issue from a little door in a balcony above the dial; and, taking off their crowns before the gilded image of the Virgin, as they move in procession before her, pass out at another door on the opposite side. This hardly equals the wonders of the celebrated clock of the cathedral of Strasburgh, to be sure; yet it is, nevertheless, deemed sufficiently wonderful by the *flaneurs* of Venice. On the uncovered platform, or roof of the low tower, two colossal figures of bronze strike the hours, with huge sledges, on a stationary bell equally huge, one closely succeeding the other. A few years since, a thunderbolt damaged the mechanism of these figures to the amount of some nine thousand ducats. On the façade of the tower, above the dial and the gallery of the Madonna, is emblazoned the winged Lion of St. Mark with his gospel, gold on azure, in imposing show.

The Campanile, or bell-tower, of St. Mark, is a quadrangular mass of brick, about forty feet square at the base, with a pyramidal pinacle surmounted by the gilded colossal figure of an angel with outspread wings, at an elevation of nearly three hundred and fifty feet* above the pavement. In the north of Europe, the bell towers of the churches are generally two in number, ponderously massive, and attached to the main edifice. But, south of the Alps, the Campanile†—"the voice of the temple"—stands almost invariably some few rods distant from the church itself; and the Campanile of St. Mark presents no exception to the general rule. So long ago as the year of grace, 1008, a tower for the bells of St. Mark was commenced at the south-east angle of the Cathedral, where now stand the Cophtic columns of Acre; but the earth sank beneath the enormous pressure, before the tower was half completed, and, with

* Or, only three hundred and twenty-three according to Murray.

† Paul of *Campania* invented bells, it is said,

exceeding care, a firm foundation was laid on the spot where it now stands. It was not entirely completed until 1510. At its base is seen that exquisite gem of art, the Logietta of Sansovino—once a guard-house of the Ducal Palace during the sessions of the Grand Council, when no one was permitted to pass bearing arms—but now a public auction room, and also, a lottery office, where once every month, the wheel of fortune is whirled by agents of the State! The upper gallery of the Campanile is circled by a colonnade of verd-antique and oriental marble. The tower is ascended without fatigue in about ten minutes, by means of an inclined plane, to the platform, where hang the five heavy bells, about two hundred and ninety feet from the ground, and thence some fifty feet higher, to the upper gallery, by means of stairs. Napoleon is said to have ascended the inclined plane to the belfrey on the back of a mule! The feat would have been of far easier performance, certainly, than the passage of the Great St. Bernard he is represented by artists to have performed on the back of a fiery charger, albeit, the former feat is hardly more probable than the latter: and, as he is *known* to have rode over the Alpine pinnacle on the back of a donkey—like other people—therefore, he, probably, ascended the Campanile of St. Mark, and enjoyed the matchless view from the summit, like other people, also. Byron, on the 14th of April, 1817, writes:—"To-day, I have been up to the battlements of the highest tower in Venice, and seen it, and its view, in all the glory of a clear Italian sky."

The Cophtic columns, to which allusion has been made, stand detached from the Cathedral, but near it, on the south side. They are of marble, two in number, and were carried off from the portal of the Temple of St. Sabra, at Acre, after a fierce fight, between the allied forces of Venice and Genoa, for the spoil. They are covered with Cophtic hieroglyphics, and monograms, Egyptian or Persian, quite untranslatable, and incomprehensible, if not undecipherable to archeologists. Even the famous David Weber found the Cophtic pillars too hard for him, as appears from a letter in the *Inscrizzioni Veneziane* of Chevalier Cicogna—a work, by the by, which embraces all the insciptions, devices, legends, epitaphs, monograms, &c., to be found in the churches or palaces of Venice, or her isles, whether lapidary or delineatory, sacred or profane, and whatever the language or character, with notes and comments historic, archeologic, philologic, &c. This great work was begun in 1824, and was designed to comprise ten volumes, though but half a dozen have appeared; and these were published at the author's own expense, although, like most authors, he was a very poor man. The only words guessed out by Weber, on the Cophtic pillars, were *Deo Summo, Auxiliatori,* and *Deo Supremo, Maximo*—the peculiar significance, or the application of which, remaining quite as recondite as ever.

Near the pillars at the corner of the Minster, stands "The Stone of Shame," so called—which is said to have once been the pedestal of a statue of a Chief of Acre, decapitated for crime. His statue was hurled from its base, and his sentence of death was read from the throne of his renown. At Venice it probably had a similar use anciently; although it is said, also, to have been a place from which bankrupts declared their insolvency, in like manner as from the "Bankrupt's Stone," or the "Hunchback," in the old Rialto Square. Above this block of marble, on the balustrade of the gallery of the church, stands a porphyry head of the unhappy Carmagnola; while, imbedded in the wall at an opposite angle of the church, stand four figures of the same material, stolen, like the Cophtic pillars, from Acre, in the twelfth century, and which have tormented the *archelogues* almost as much as the aforesaid pillars themselves. Some declare that they represent Harmodius and Aristogeiton, the patriotic assassins of Hipparchus, tyrant of Athens; while others insist that they are effigies of the brothers Anemuria, foes of Alexius Comnenus, sovereign of the Greek Empire. The astute Lecomte suggests, however, that the assassins were only two in number, and the brothers only three; while the grotesque red effigies are four!

It is close beside these curious statues that opens the grand portal to the court of the Ducal Palace—the *Porta della Carta*, celebrated as one of the most perfect works of art in Venice, and owing its singular name—"Gate of the Paper"—to the fact, that, upon its heavy leaves and lintels were anciently affixed all edicts of civil magistrates. It stands between the Basilica and the Palace, and was constructed in 1439, at the expense of the Doge Francis Foscari, by Bartolomeo, the same architect who erected the gorgeous Foscari Palace. It is through this gate that is approached the abode of the Doges.

With the exterior façades of the Ducal Palace of Venice—veneered and tesselated with a mosaic of alternate plates of red and white marble, and diversified with columns, arches, ogives, and sculptured windows of *composite* architecture—every one is familiar. There is not an edifice in all the world, probably, of which all the world knows more, as to its external aspect, thanks to the brush and the burin of the artist, than the Palace of the Doges. Waiving all description, therefore, of this famous edifice, and merely remarking, that the lower gallery was called the *Broglio*, and was appropriated to the Patricians, even as the Rialto was appropriated to the merchants, and that the corner column is deemed by architects a miracle of static art, while, among the columns of the upper colonnade, are two composed of the red *brocatelle* of Verona, from between which the sentences of the condemned, and the edicts and proclamations of the Senate, were wont to be read to the people, during the days of the Republic, by a masked Inquisitor of State,*—we enter the Palace Court. Passing the celebrated public cisterns on our right, and the almost equally celebrated statues of Adam and Eve over our heads, we ascend the Giants' Staircase, so called, not for its colossal dimensions, but because of the colossal dimensions of the statues of Mars and Neptune which look down from its landing. It was upon this landing that the newly elected Doge received the *beretta* of his office; and, then, having heard mass in the Basilica, and made the tour of the Piazza on the shoulders of the *Arsenalotti*, scattering largess the while, he retired quietly to his future abode within: and it was upon this landing, that, on the morning of the 25th day of October, 1457, the aged Foscari fainted with anguish, when forced to abandon a palace, which, for more than thirty years, had been his home: but it was *not* upon this landing, according to Lecomte, that Faliero was beheaded; nor did his head "roll down the Giants' Staircase," despite the tragedies of Byron and Delavigne; for the very good reason, that neither staircase nor landing had any existence until more than a century after the event, Faliero having been executed in the middle of the fourteenth century, and the staircase having been constructed in the middle of the fifteenth.

Passing the "Lions' Mouths" at the head of the staircase, and the marble tablet in the wall, commemorative of the visit of Henry III. of France, in 1574, we traverse the long colonnade and ascend the Staircase of Gold—very gorgeous no doubt, but a misnomer

* It was between these columns that the Chief of the Ten appeared, and, brandishing the sword red with the blood of old Faliero, exclaimed to the crowds in the Piazzetta below—*E stata fata giustizia al traditor della patria*—"Justice has been done on the traitor to his country."

hardly less deceptive than that of the staircase just mounted—and, at length we are within the *Palazzo Ducale.* We pass through the Library of St. Mark, and, entering the immense Hall of the Grand Council, our eyes are dazzled with its splendor. With awe-struck and wondering gaze, we look upon the gorgeous canvass which covers its walls and ceiling, and on the long line of Doges which seem to frown on the intruder; and deeply do we ponder the scenes it has beheld. Regardless of a thousand other scenes, and the events of an earlier era, we reflect, that it was in this hall the brave old Admiral, Victor Pisani, was falsely condemned; and that here he was brought from his dungeon, to receive the supreme command in defence of Venice, amid the imminent perils of the War of the Chioggia. It was here, too, three hundred years later, that the great Morisini, at the acme of his fame and service, was arraigned at the bar of his country, for the surrender of Candia; and here, triumphantly acquitted, was he subsequently laden with honors, and declared her Doge. In this same hall were witnessed also, the splendid fetes attending that rare event, the coronation of a *Dogaressa*—a daughter of the same illustrious house of Morosini, wife of Marino Grimani, whose lordly pile yet throws its shadow over the Grand Canal, being crowned. In this hall, likewise, on two occasions—in the thirteenth and again in the fourteenth century—was gravely discussed the removal of the government of Venice—first to Constantinople, and last to Candia—the first proposition being negatived by only a single ballot; and here, at the close of the eighteenth century, after a stormy struggle of three days and three nights, this mighty Republic of fourteen centuries pitiably fell!

The space around the walls of this hall, formerly occupied by seats for the patricians, is now claimed by presses of books, pertaining to the Library of St. Mark; and among the many literary curiosities, is to be seen a singular map of the world drawn by Fra Mauro, a monk of the order of the Camaldolites, at the convent on the island of St. Michael, in the year 1460, on which map the Cape of Good Hope is clearly and correctly laid down, although it was not doubled by Vasco di Gama on his first voyage to India, until nearly forty years later, 1497, nor discovered by Diaz for nearly thirty, 1486. In 1459, Alphonse of Portugal obtained a copy of the map from the author; and, guided by that, the Portugese discovered a new route to the Indies! Thus was the liberality of Venice fatal to herself. In 1804, England sent a distinguished engineer to request of Austria a copy of this remarkable map.

Leaving the Hall of the Grand Council, a narrow passage leads us into the Hall of the Ballot, where the Venetian Senate, with gilded balls, decided the fate of men and nations, as well as that of their own Republic. And, in this connection, it is a fact worthy of mention, that, however jealously closed, and vigilantly guarded, against all obtruders, might be the Council Chambers of Venice, at all other times, yet, when the Senators entered the Hall of Scrutiny to cast their votes, even on the most secret and momentous questions, the doors were thrown wide, and even strangers in masks might watch the ballotings undisturbed! There were three urns of different colors: *white* for the affirmative, *green* for the negative, and *red* for neutral. The ballotings always took place in this *Sala dello Scrutinio;* and in this hall did Henry III. of France, once cast a gilded ball in the election of a Procurator, and in this hall was Henry IV. elected a Patrician of Venice.

Passing through the *Bussola* or ante-chamber of the Council of Ten, at the portal of which once yawned a "Lion's Mouth," to receive denunciations, we enter the hall itself, of that dark and terrible tribunal. But nothing here of the dark or the terrible is to be seen.* We glance around amazed—almost disappointed. We surely looked not for this! Voluptuous paintings from the brushes of Veronese and Aliensè, adorn the walls and ceiling, while the floor is beautifully tesselated with squares of white and black marble—the gorgeous decorations of the chamber presenting a startling contrast to its dread purposes and associations, and to the dark scenes it has witnessed. It was in this hall, on the night of the 15th of April, 1355, that the aged Faliero was doomed to die. At the same hour, and while a terrific tempest was raging over Venice, and the roar of the Adriatic mingled with that of the thunder, his two accomplices, Calendario, architect of the Palace, and Bertuccio, Chief of the Arsenal, here sentenced, were strangled in the dungeons below, and then suspended by the feet between the columns of the Piazetta—being the first of nearly five hundred, who, in the same manner, expiated the same treason!† It was in this chamber, too, that Francis Basson, the gallant Carmagnola, on the night of the 5th of May, 1432, was doomed to die for imputed treason, after having been deprived of food three days, and tortured in his dungeon by the application of plates of red hot iron to his feet,—the ordinary torture by dislocation of the arms being spared, because those arms had served well the Republic; and, before the dawn, gagged and blindfolded, his head fell beneath three blows of the

* The only exception to this remark, is a small, but horrible, painting—horrible in every sense of the term—representing infliction of the *question*, in all its hideous forms. The picture seems appropriate enough to the place, however, and only shows more glaringly, perhaps, the inappropriateness of the other pictures. If this horrid painting has any business here, the others, certainly, have not; and *vice versa*, whether subject or execution is considered.

† In like manner, May 14, 1618, was quelled "The conspiracy of Cueva," on which is founded Otway's "Venice Preserved."

axe, between the fatal columns! In the ante-chamber of this same hall, the same Carmagnola is immortalized by the brush of Aliensè, as the hero of Bergamo; in like manner, as, in a neighboring hall, Faliero had been immortalized by the brush of Tintoretto, as the conqueror of Zara.

Here, too, was condemned Carrara, the Tyrant of Padua, charged with having conspired to poison the cisterns of Venice—subsequently strangled in his dungeon with his two sons; while their accomplices were torn by wild horses, on the morning of the 10th of May, 1372. The fearful dooms of Carmagnola and the Carrara, enticed as they were from abroad within the sphere of the sweep of the vengeful arm of Venice, impresses one not more with the perfidy, than with the power, of her terrible Ten. Within the territory of the Republic, that power was every where—every where—even unto the most insignificant isle of the far-off Ægean; while, within *Venetia Prima*, or the *Dogado*,* which occupied, or closely circled, the Lagune, it was omnipotent and omnipresent. Even at the present day, after the lapse of long centuries, on that distant and dreary eyot of the Archipelago, "St. Francis of the Desert," possessed only by an abandoned convent and a few aged trees—is beheld, the Winged Lion, on a marble tablet, in a garden wall, expanding his wings over a decree of the Ten, that, upon this deserted spot, was solemnly inhibited "all gambling, duelling, sacrilege, and blasphemy!"

From the Chamber of the Ten we pass to the Cabinet of the yet more terrible Three, where in a *bureau* sat the Inquisitors concealed, whilst they listened to the answers of witness or accused, as elicited by their Secretary, who, without, questioned and recorded. From this chamber, a secret door and staircase conducts to the

* All territory *without* the *Dogado*, was comprised in *Venetia Secunda*.

piombi above, or the *pozzi* below, and to the fearful Bridge of Sighs.

The *Piombi*, or *Leads*, of Venice, consist of a dozen chambers lying under the *leaden* roof of the Ducal Palace. They are light and airy, however, and seem not entirely deserving of all those horrors with which they have been clad by history and romance. The *Pozzi*, or *Pits*, consist of some twenty dungeons, in two stages, one above the other, in the basement of the palace—none of them, however, being below the level of the canaletto which washes the foundation—the inconsistent, incoherent, and highly incorrect account of them given by Sir John Hobhouse, in his notes to the fourth canto of Childe Harold, to the contrary, nevertheless. These dungeons are said to have been no worse than those of the age all over Europe; and they had not been in common use for more than two centuries before the fall of the Republic. In the sixteenth century, the New Prison was completed, by Antonio da Ponte, together with the Bridge of Sighs—the celebrated *Ponte de' Sospiri*—which for the sake of convenience in conducting prisoners from the tribunals to the dungeons, had been thrown across the Rio Canonica, thus connecting the prison with the palace. The construction of this new prison, sufficiently capacious to accommodate four hundred persons, is said to have rendered quite useless the leads and wells of the Ducal Palace; and it was declared by the English philanthropist, John Howard, when he visited Venice in the last century, the best arranged prison, in view of health and humanity, he had ever entered. For all this, however, it must have been rather warm under the leads of that Ducal Palace, of a sultry July noon; and rather cool in the dungeons below, close beside the frozen canal, of a freezing December night; while one can hardly suppose—albeit, the aforesaid leads and dungeons were *not*, "for more than two centuries in common use"—that Casanova, who, in 1787, wrote a history of his imprisonment in the *Piombi* of Venice, or Silvio Pellico, who, forty years later, narrated the touching tale of his "Prisons," were the only persons who in modern times experienced their comforts.

But, whatever, the associations of the tourist when standing "in Venice on the Bridge of Sighs," the view presented to his eye from the window looking out on the Canal of St. Mark is truly magnificent. At his feet glide the cold, dark waters of the canaletto, spanned by the *Ponte della Paglia*—or, "Bridge of Hay"—the spot having been once the Hay Market of the city for the farmers of the Isles in their boats:* before him expands the harbor, spotted with vessels and exhibiting all the animation of an Italian seaport; while away in the distance, as far as his eye can compass, stretches the broad expanse of the Canal Giudecca, with the dim Adriatic beyond.

From the Council Chamber of the Ten, passing through narrow corridors and several anterooms, you enter the Hall of the Ambassadors, gorgeous like all its predecessors, with *chefs d'œuvre* of art—so gorgeous, indeed, that it is related, that an Envoy of Genoa was so impressed by the splendor of the Hall, and the imposing aspect of the Doge and Council, that he could only articulate *Serenissimo Duca!* when presented, and then retire! The result, unhappily, was the reluming more fiercely than ever the flames of war between the Adriatic and Mediterranean Republics. The Council for the reception of Ambassadors consisted of the Doge and his six counsellors, together with the Ten State Inquisitors and the ten Grand Sages, comprising, in all, twenty-seven persons. But the

* Cows are almost the only quadrupeds ever seen in Venice; and their life is one of perpetual imprisonment.

magnificence of the Hall was not confined to the walls and ceiling; for even the floor, or rather the pavement, is a rich mosaic of precious gems! There prevails at Venice a peculiar species of flooring called *terazzo*, composed of mortar and pulverized brick, with pebbles of various colors interspersed. The whole is then beaten smooth, and, when dry and hard, is polished by rubbing with pumice-stone and linseed-oil. But in the *terazzo* of the Hall of the Ambassadors in the Ducal Palace, the *pebbles* used are of porphyry, malachite, agate, amethyst, cornelian, lapis-lazuli, "and other precious gems"! Imagine the effect—to say nothing of the expense!

Unfolding a door, you pass from the Hall of the Ambassadors to the Hall of the Senate, which is larger than either of the other apartments, the Hall of the Grand Council only excepted, and is in no respect inferior to the rest in magnificence. It may be remarked of the paintings in this Hall, and in the Ducal Palace generally, that, sadly as all paintings have suffered at Venice from the saline humidity of the atmosphere, they have here suffered least. The brilliancy of coloring which distinguishes the Venetian school has been sought in superiority of material, peculiarity of touch of the brush, and loveliness of the climate. The *brilliancy* of the painters, however, best explains, perhaps, the brilliancy of the paintings. Oil painting, which was invented by the brothers Van Eyck of Antwerp, about the middle of the fifteenth century, was brought to Venice, soon after, by Antonello of Messina, who was assassinated by Andrea del Castagno, for refusing to reveal to him the secret—which secret, by-the-by, had by himself, been obtained by fraud. The *Academia* was founded on the site of a convent in 1807, and churches, palaces, and religious houses contributed its treasures. It has been well called a "Museum of *Venetian* Art," for it contains little else than Venetian pictures.

The Venetian Senate, or the Council of the Pregadi, consisted of three hundred and ten members, embracing in the number the Ten, the Three, the Council, or rather the Councils, of Forty—Civil and Criminal; the Colleges of Fifteen and Twenty-five, the Procurators, the Avvogadors, and the ten Grand Sages of War and Peace—presided over by the Doge, with his six counsellors, his secretaries, and chancellors. The Doge and his counsellors, the ten Inquisitors, and the ten Grand Sages, who constituted the Council for the reception of Ambassadors, numbering twenty-seven persons, occupied the broad *estrade* of the magnificent chamber. War, peace, treaties, the preparation of *projets* of laws, and the nomination of envoys, generals, and other high officers were among the subjects discussed by this august body. It was in this Hall that the Emperor Frederick III. was received, returning with his bride from his coronation at Rome; and a splendid service of crystal from Murano having been presented him, his court jester, at a hint from his master, fell against and crushed it to atoms. "Had it been of gold, it would not have been crushed!" cried the coarse and covetous German! Foscari, the Doge, replied not, but, at once, by his order, the table was covered with another of the manufactures of Venice—coin from her Zecca! It was in this Hall, by a vote of one hundred and forty-four ballots to forty-three, that the exiled Louis XVIII. was, at the request of the French Directory, in 1795, desired to leave Verona, which he had made an asylum for nearly a year; and here, three centuries before, in 1506, ambassadors from Nuremberg, a free Imperial city of Franconia, now subject to Bavaria, received the laws of Venice from the Doge Loredano, which event is immortalized by the brush of Veronese.

The chambers, ante-chambers, cabinets and halls which have been named, are, of course, by no means all, which go to make up that vast and splendid edifice, the Ducal Palace of Venice. Those only interesting from historic or artistic associations, have been entered; and the Chapel, situated in the rear of the Hall of the Senate, is the last apartment which will be named. Here is a fresco by Titian, the only one in Venice—representing St. Christopher; here the State Inquisitors are said to have held their most secret sessions; here the Dictator, Daniel Manin, was accustomed to meet, in private conclave, his counsellors, during the troubled times of '48–9; and, lastly, here, on the right of the altar, after opening a small door, is discovered a narrow staircase which leads down to another door—which leads—no one knows whither—for it has never been opened; though it probably leads to the sacristy of the Basilica of St. Mark—even as another narrow staircase leads to the dungeons: for, at Venice, in the sentiment, if not in the language of an imaginative writer, the sanctuary of temporal and of divine justice are side by side—one punishing the body, the other the soul. Tribunal, prison, fortress, town-house ducal-dwelling, palace; Doge and family for the dwelling—Senate and Procurators for the town-house—soldiers and sbirri for the fortress—the Ten and Three for the tribunal—gaolers for the prisons, and all for the fetes of the palace. By this terrible centralization, a Doge who ruled and entertained, was once accused, judged, condemned, and executed all within these walls! Their history lives in the paintings they bear; and Faliero, Calendario, Carmagnola, had only to raise their eyes, to see how Venice rewarded worth and punished crime.*

In the long lapse of a thousand years, the Ducal Palace at Venice has experienced fully its share of Time's changes. Commenced in the year 820, it was destroyed in a popular commotion, almost

* Lecomte.

as soon as completed. Rebuilt by the Doge Orseolo, in 976, it was swept away in 1102 by one of those fearful conflagrations, so frequent in the island-city when she was built of wood, making her a veritable "volcano of the sea." Rebuilt a second time by the Doge Ordelafo Faliero, progenitor of the unhappy Doge Marino, in 1102—it was again a victim to the flames in 1354. Its reconstruction was at once commenced for a third time, by Calendario, under the direction of the Doge Faliero; but the Doge, who ordered, and the architect on whose plan it was re-built, both perished beneath its shadow—the Doge beheaded in its court-yard—the architect strangled in its dungeons and suspended before its windows. Completed in 1428, under the *dogat* of the unhappy Francis Foscari, it was again partly burned in 1477, under the *dogat* of Andrea Vendramini. Again repaired, it again suffered by fire in 1574, and yet again in 1577, when, for the last time, its repairs were completed in 1590, under the *dogat* of Pasquale Cicogna, who erected the Rialto Bridge of stone. Thus, the old edifice has been once demolished by a mob; twice totally destroyed by fire, and three times partially so. Its reconstruction and repair, however, has always been conducted on the original plan; and the fact, that the two last windows on the right, as you look up from the *Molo*, are somewhat unlike the others in shape, size, and locality, arises from another fact, that they alone were spared in the later conflagrations. The edifice, as it now stands, is nearly two and a half centuries old.

In the commencement of this introductory and general view of the City of the Sea, it was suggested, that the only mode which could hope for any degree of success, in attempting to convey an idea of a capital so unique as Venice, was to take the city in detail—to analyze the place, as it were, and to view its prominent objects of interest in classes. Two of the classes into which these great features of Venice divide themselves are the PALACES and the CHURCHES. To the former, the glance already given engrosses all the space which can be spared, in a *coup d'œil* so rapid; but, the historic, artistic, and moral interest of the latter class, even at the hazard of prolonging these introductory remarks to an unreasonable length, demands consideration more detailed. Venice without her churches!—as well Venice without her canals! The churches of Venice, indeed, when we consider the circumstances of their origin, the events which they have witnessed, the monuments and inscriptions which they contain, and the singular alliance existing between the religion and the government of the old Republic, throughout all its long career, may be deemed to embody more of its history, than any, or than all, of its other edifices, however historic—the Ducal Palace, with its leads and dungeons, and council chambers, not excepted!

The earliest policy of Venice, undoubtedly, was, to plant a parochial church on every one of her larger islands, and then to surround each parish church with a host of satellites. To some writers this has afforded proof of the deep religious tone pervading the Venetians from the earliest ages; and a recent writer goes so far as to assert, that the decline of the political prosperity of Venice was coincident with that of "the domestic and individual religion, which so wonderfully characterized the lives of her citizens." That her opulent nobles contributed liberally to the construction of churches and convents, is undoubtedly true; but, whether prompted most by religion, superstition, or some other less worthy emotion, is not easy to decide. As early as the ninth century, the Doge Participazio erected, at his own expense, the first receptacle for the relics of St. Mark, and the Doge Tradenigo and son erected St. Paul; while, as late as the nineteenth century, the church of San Maurizio, begun by the patrician Zaguri, as a substitute for that of San Geminiano, twice desecrated by demolition to enlarge the Place St. Mark—was completed by the patrician Diedo. But, for Venice as a State, neither the writer above referred to, nor any other writer, has been preposterous enough to claim the influence of religious obligation—if we except, perhaps, the French historian, Philippe de Commynes, who, describing his entry into Venice as Ambassador, in 1495, says: "To be short, it is the most triumphant city that I ever saw, and where the commonwealth is best governed, and God most devoutly served; and I verily think, that God prospereth them because of the reverence they bear to the service of the Church." It is, nevertheless, very true, that never did the commercial interests or peculiar state-policy of Venice come in conflict with the wishes of the Papal See, but that the former eventually triumphed. Despite the thunders of Innocent III., as early as the twelfth century, Venetians diverted the armies of the Fourth Crusade from the plains of Palestine to the walls of Zara and Constantinople; while the double interdict of Clement V., a hundred years later, was long powerless to tear Ferrara from the rapacious grasp of the Lion of St. Mark.* Very true, a few years later, when the Winged Lion was gorged with his prey, Francesco Dandolo, the Envoy of Venice, prostrated himself in a penitential garb, with an iron collar around his neck, at the Pontiff's feet, and there remained, with sighs, and prayers, and tears, until he had extorted a reluctant assent to the removal of the curse; and, equally true is it, that, at an earlier period of Venetian history, the cause of the fugitive, Alexander III. was espoused by Venice against all the power of Barbarossa, and that the Emperor was brought to the feet of the Pope in the

* In 1308, and again in 1309, Pope Clement V., infamously celebrated for the abolition of the Order of the Templars, excommunicated Venice for the seizure of Ferrara; but in 1313, Ferrara was regained, and the interdict was removed.

vestibule of St. Mark. But it is plain, that, in all this, Venice consulted her own selfish interests, and those only, and but aimed to subserve them, and them alone, under a pretence of religious obligation. Moreover, while Venice bowed most humbly at the feet of the successor of St. Peter, as a spiritual head, when it was her secular interest so to do, never did she admit within her borders the slightest exercise or recognition of his temporal authority; and even the Inquisition of the Holy Office was always in utter subservience to her terrible "Ten."

In 1557, Felix Peretti, subsequently Pope Sixtus V., chief of the Holy Office at Venice, was repeatedly forced to flee the abhorrence of her citizens; and, after a fiery ordeal of three years, cheerfully obeyed his recall to Rome. In 1483, Pope Sixtus IV., in support of the House of Estè, launched his anathema against Venice; but Venice triumphed, and the curse was revoked by Innocent VIII. In 1523, Clement VII. wrote to the Doge Grimani, that, sooner than the *protegè* of Venice, Cæsar d'Estè, natural son of Alphonso II., should mount the throne of Ferrara, he would sell the last chalice of the Church, and himself die in the ditch of Ferrara, holy host in hand!* History records, that the voluntary submission of the aspiring prince to the wishes of the bellicose pontiff, hushed this menace of war, and spared the Church and Christendom the scandal of the fulfillment of Clement's terrible threat. In 1606, Paul V. protested against the election to the *dogat* of Leonardo Donato, who had been seven times Envoy of Venice to Rome, and was Paul's inveterate foe; yet, Donato was made Doge, despite the Papal protest; and again Rome's impotent thunders pealed over the City of the Sea!

* This reminds one of Pope Julius II, who threw the keys of St. Peter into the Tiber, requiring, he said, only the sword. He thus "took the sword"—and he "perished by the word," in fulfillment of Divine declaration.

But, whatever the religious character of the Ocean Queen, it is very certain, that very few Catholic cities have ever erected a larger number of sacred edifices than she. As late as the middle of the last century she numbered over a hundred, while she had a priest for every fifty-four of her hundred and fifty thousand inhabitants. At the same time, even Spain had a proportion of but one priest to every seventy-four inhabitants, and France only one to every hundred and fifty. In the year 1827, Venice had a priest to each two hundred and sixteen inhabitants, thanks to the purgation of Napoleon twenty years before; and the number, great as it now is, has, doubtless, yet further decreased. It still remains, however, vastly disproportioned to the aggregate of her population,* as also do the churches, although many of the latter have been diverted to secular uses. You are jostled by ecclesiastics of various grades, in their broad-brimmed hats and black coats, and by mendicant-monks of various orders, in their rope-girdled serge, and "sandal-shoon," with their bare heads and shaven crowns, at every corner, and in every cafe of Venice; while every island has its church, and the pealing of bells from their forest of campanili is literally unceasing and deafening, from morning dawn until deep in the night. Indeed, at midnight, one is often roused from sleep by the pealing of bells. Every day in the calendar is sacred to some Catholic saint; almost every day, also, is claimed by some church for its own peculiar feasts and fasts, and you can at no hour enter a church when some one of its shrines is not illuminated, or when all of its chapels are destitute of worshippers.

Of the mendicant-monks seen at Venice, many belong to convents

* At Rome, the disproportion is still greater, there being a priest to every fifty inhabitants—the population being 150,000, priests 3,000, nuns 2,000, value of church property in the Popedom, $100,000,000, and income, $5,000,000, according to Gavazzi.

on the islands of the Lagune, and more especially to the convent on the small island of St. Michael. It once belonged to the order of *Camaldolites*, but it is now possessed by the Franciscans, who every morning go over to Venice to beg. The cloisters are a favorite burial-place of the rich of the city. Here is Bernini's tomb of Cardinal Dolfini, who fell dead in the chapel, in 1822, while preaching to the monks. The edifice has a remarkable echo. The Camaldolites—also called Camaldulians, or Camaldunians, were a religious order, established at the commencement of the twelfth century, in the valley of Camaldoli, among the Appenines, by St. Romuald, a Benedictine of Ravenna. They were, at first, hermits, residing in separate cells, but, subsequently, lived together as monks in convents. They devoted themselves to fasting and penance, rarely spoke, never cut their beards, and wore white garments. At the close of the eighteenth century, when the order was suppressed, there existed in Europe five fraternities, one of which was at St. Michael. There were, also, about a dozen convents for Camaldolite nuns, at the same time.

Exclusive of the Basilica of St. Mark, Venice now numbers some seventy churches maintaining regular service, more than sixty of which prefer decided claims to historic and artistic interest. The number of parishes and parochial churches is about thirty. It is only since the recent period of 1817, that St. Mark has been the cathedral church of Venice. In earlier ages, the vast and ancient, but obscure church of St. Peter, situated on the island of that name, at the eastern extremity of the city, in the *Sestiere di Castello*, was the patriarchal edifice; while that of St. Mark was only a chapel attached to the Ducal Palace. This fact—so remarkable, when it is considered that, in every other capital of Europe, the most prominent church is the cathedral, and always has been so—may serve to confirm the idea which has been advanced respecting "that most curious phenomenon in all Venetian history—the vitality of religion in private life and its deadness in public policy."

The church of *San Pietro di Castello* is now chiefly noticeable for its antiquity, its vast size, its splendid clock, its lofty campanile, which leans a little more to one side than any of its sister campanili, and its antique marble chair, which served the apostle in the church of Antioch, as some say; or, which was the throne of some Moslem monarch, in the belief of others! The latter idea seems corroborated by the fact, that the old chair bears inscribed upon it a couple of verses from the Koran. It was from this old church the "Brides of Venice" were carried off by the Istriote corsairs, in the tenth century, according to some authorities. Others lay the scene of the event at a little church on the site of the present edifice of *Santa Maria Formosa.* By decree of the Senate, twelve maidens of beauty and virtue, selected from poor but honest families, were annually doweried by the State; and, decked for the occasion from the treasury of St. Mark, had their nuptials celebrated in the presence of the Doge and all his court, with great pomp, at this church. In similar manner, with much ceremony, at Rome, on the day of the Annunciation, nine months before Christmas, the Pope, even now, bestows dowries on a dozen girls about to marry. It was on one of these occasions that the corsairs of Trieste landed from their boats, seized the "beauty and booty" and fled, but were shortly overtaken by the bereaved bridegrooms, and the spoil and the prisoners were regained. For centuries the custom was handed down and the event celebrated. The church of *San Pietro* was rebuilt in 1621.

The Cathedral Church of St. Mark fills up the eastern side of the quadrangle of the celebrated Square to which it has given a name:

and, gorgeous though it be in barbaric decorations, and in Greek, Gothic, Arabic and Byzantine architecture, Corinne is correct when she says—"it resembles rather a Mahometan Mosque than a Christian temple." Its western façade presents a perfect mass of domes, spires, statues, arches, columns, the whole illuminated by nine immense mosaics over the three entrances, each as brilliant now in its golden, crimson, purple hues, as when executed two hundred years ago—

> "Still glowing with the richest hues of art,
> As though the wealth within, up-gushing, had run o'er."

The first and third of these mosaics represent the removal of the remains of St. Mark from Alexandria, and their arrival at Venice; while the fifth, which is four and a half centuries old, gives a view of the primitive church upon the present site.

In the gallery above are those famous travellers, the four Bronze Steeds of Lysippus; and, in the pavement of the vestibule below, a cube of porphyry indicates the spot where the proud old Pontiff, Alexander, planted his sandaled foot on the stubborn neck of the imperial Barbarossa.* The external gates are of bronze, one of them nearly six hundred years old, and the three inner ones admit-

* In 1159, on the death of Adrien IV., two Cardinals, Roland and Octavien, were, by division in the Conclave, each declared Pope, and assumed the titles, severally, of Alexander III., and Victor IV. At the installation of Roland, Octavien tore the scarlet cape from his rival's shoulders, and, in his haste, put it inside-out on his own! He was then installed in the Vatican by his party, as Victor IV. Alexander fled to St. Angelo, and thence from Rome. Frederick Barbarossa declared for Victor; and Alexander, having excommunicated both, fled to France, and, finally, to Venice. Victor died and was succeeded by Paschal III., who, also, dying, was succeeded by Calixtus III. Venice assumed the cause of Alexander, defeated Barbarossa by sea and land, took prisoner his son Otho, forced him to come to Venice and sign a treaty of peace, July 23d, 1177, and placed the fugitive Pope on his throne, after an exile of twenty years—Calixtus fleeing at his approach. As a recompense, Alexander presented Venice, through her Doge Ziani, with the insignia of the lighted candle, the umbrella, sword, trumpets, and flags, to be borne in processions before her Prince. It is from this event, also, that the Winged Lion as the device of Venice takes date.

ting to the church from the vestibule, are inlaid with silver, two being of Venetian workmanship and about seven centuries old, the third having been stolen from the Mosque of St. Sophia, at Constantinople, in the year 1203. The vault of the vestibule is one continuous superficies of mosaic, illustrative, chiefly, of scenes in the Old Testament. Some of these mosaics date back to the eleventh century, and have little claim to notice, save their antiquity. They tell the whole story of the creation, temptation and fall of man, and that of the deluge and the lives of the patriarchs. One of them, which may be cited as a sample of all, represents the Deity, in the guise of an aged man, taking the rib from the side of the sleeping Adam to make of it a woman! Some of the mosaics of the vestibule, however, by the celebrated brothers Zucatti, in the sixteenth century, from cartoons of Titian, are beautiful and sublime. On entering the nave of the Basilica, the eye is dazzled, and the mind bewildered by the gorgeous spectacle presented—"a grand and dreamy structure, of immense proportions, golden with old mosaics, redolent of perfumes, dim with the smoke of incense, costly in treasure of precious stones and metals glittering through iron bars, holy with the bodies of deceased saints, rainbow-hued with windows of stained glass, dark with carved woods and colored marbles, obscure in its vast heights and lengthened distances, shining with silver lamps and winking lights, unreal, fantastic, solemn, inconceivable, throughout." Beneath the feet, the undulatory pavement is of marble, curiously tesselated, and the entire roof, with its countless arches and its five vast domes, is one blaze of mosaic; while around the edifice are beheld some five hundred columns of porphyry, serpentine, alabaster, and rarest marbles covered with choicest carvings and sculpture. The ponderous shafts which support the domes, are of richest oriental marble. There are, also, several tombs of Doges, a large number of statues, and many exquisite specimens of carved oak to be seen and admired. The interior is but dimly lighted by the splendid rose-window at the northern extremity of the transept, aided by a few small apertures in the domes. Opposite the rose-window is a singular mosaic, called "The Genealogical Tree of the Virgin." The roots of the tree are in the body of Adam, prostrate on his back, and on each of its branches sits a patriarch with his staff, or a prophet with his harp; while on the topmost branch, stands the Virgin herself, emerging from a blossom and bearing the child! The subject and design are identical with those which illuminate one of the immense windows of the Cathedral of Cologne.

The form of the Minster of St. Mark's is a Greek cross. Upon its site was commenced the first settlement of *Rivo Alto*, in the fifth century, and the first sacred structure on the spot was a chapel to St. Theodore, the earliest Patron Saint of the Island city. In the year 828, this edifice was demolished, and a more splendid one erected by the Doge Participazio, at his own expense, to receive the remains of St. Mark, then first brought from Alexandria. In the year 976 this second church was burned to the ground, and the third and present edifice was not completed until a hundred years later: nor was it until after the conquest of Constantinople, and of numerous other cities, that the acmè of its splendor was attained. St. Mark's, indeed, seems to have been made the receptacle of all the plunderings of the Venetians for ages, without any reference to their incongruity with the place, or the order of their arrangement. Here stands a costly column stolen from one city, there a sculptural door from another; while over the portal are the stolen bronze horses, and at the northern entrance are the hieroglyphic pillars ravished from the Temple of St. Sybla, at Acre, and the famous porphyry knights from the same conquered place. During the whole century St. Mark's was in course of construction, every Venetian galley trading to the East, was required to bring back some article of spoil to contribute to this great work. Yet, not St. Mark's alone, but almost every other church or public structure in Venice, was decorated with plunder. The very body of the Patron Saint himself, was stolen by the crafty Venetians from Alexandria! The tradition is this:—A certain ruler of Alexandria erecting a palace, and not having the fear of St. Mark before his eyes, despoiled the Apostle's church of its most precious marbles, to the extreme indignation of the priests, to whose care his remains had been entrusted, which priests, to save which remains from the menaced profanation, sold them to certain "super-subtle" Venetian sea-captains who chanced to be in port—or, as some say, to Bono, Tribune of Malamocco, and Rustico, Tribune of Torcello, in seaman's guise. To conceal the barter from the populace, to whom the saint—at whose shrine miracles were daily performed—was deservedly dear, the priests substituted the remains of Santa Claudia—a *woman*—in the Evangelist's cerements! But so powerful became the odor of sanctity in this transaction, and so all-pervading, that the people came flocking to the temple with demands to be suffered personally to inspect the relics of their saint. The cerements were exhibited to them inviolate—for the slit by which the transfer had been made was behind! The remains were then deposited in a basket, and, to obviate search by the Musselmen, were covered with their especial abhorrence—*pork*—and thus conveyed on board the Venetian galley, where, for still further safety, they were enveloped in her mainsail which was secured aloft to the yard! By this notable device they escaped discovery in the strict search of all outward-bound vessels, then as now—and put to sea. On the voyage a storm arose, when, lo!

the saint's spirit appeared amid the tempest, and "gave the captain orders to furl his sails and lay-to," which manœuvre, wonderful to tell, "saved the ship," as also the precious freight!

Arrived at Venice, the relics were welcomed with the utmost pious pomp and holy joy. The celebrated church was erected for their worthy reception; and henceforth, for a thousand years, St. Mark was the patron of Venice—his golden lion was blazoned on her purple *gonfalon*, and his name was her war-cry. All these marvels transpired in the year of grace 827, and the whole story is related in gorgeous mosaic on the western front of the Minster, as before mentioned—the mainsail, Musselmen, pork-basket, and Tribunes, all as large as life! Unhappily, some two hundred years after these events, the Emperor Henry III., pious soul, made an express pilgrimage from the heart of Germany to the saint's shrine to worship the relics; when, lo! to the holy horror of all concerned, when the reliquary, in which they had been deposited, was examined—they were no more there! The lamentations by which the island-capital was filled at this intelligence are, of course, indescribable. At length, early one morning, when the sacristan opened the church, a wonderful illumination surrounded one of the ponderous pillars which aid to support the principal dome; and, from an aperture in the massive marble, protruded a naked arm! In terror ran the sacristan to the archdeacon, and the archdeacon ran to the archbishop, and the archbishop ran to the Doge; and the Doge, with the archbishop, the archdeacon, the sacristan, and all the dignitaries of church and state ran to the enchanted pillar, when the hand of the naked and protruding arm dropped a ring into the archbishop's bosom, and the pillar, widely expanding, an iron coffin, containing the precious remains, was revealed! They were then, for safe-keeping, committed to the Doge, and by him to his successor. But, ere long, the sarcophagus containing them again disappeared. So lately as 1811, however, it was discovered in a secret crypt of the subterranean chapel under the church, which, for nearly three centuries, had been unvisited, because of inundations from the canals, and where it had been so closely concealed by the Doge Vitale Faliero as again to have been lost! A festa commemorating the miracle of the column was instituted, and is annually celebrated on the 24th of July. Another festa commemorating the second discovery, is also observed, as well as a third, on the anniversary of the day the relics first reached Venice. They now repose in safety, as is supposed, beneath the high altar, and under a marble tablet inscribed with the saint's name; although superstition will have it, that the talismanic bones were stolen by Napoleon in '97, before he could cross the Lagune! As to St. Mark's ring, it seems to have experienced as many vicissitudes as his body, and was, at length, most sacrilegiously stolen, and thus lost forever. Tradition recites of it that, one stormy night, the Apostle employed a poor fisherman to take him passenger in his gondola to the Lido; when, by miraculous might, he sank a whole galley of demons rushing up the Lagune to whelm Venice in the waves; and then giving the fisherman a ring in payment of his fare, bade him present it next morning to the Doge amid his dignitaries; and, in proof that it was the veritable ring of St. Mark, the signet of the saint would be missing from the treasury! And so it turned out, and the old fisherman got a pension for life and his heirs after him, for his trouble. This presentation of the ring by the fisherman to the Doge is the subject of a celebrated painting of Paris Bordone, in the Academy.* But all the

* It is also said to represent the restoration to the Doge of the nuptial ring with which he had wedded the Adriatic, dropped into the sea at the entrance of the port of Lido, near the fort of St. Andrew, and regained by the fisherman. Cooper, in his graphic and truthful novel, the "Bravo," which has its scene at Venice in the 18th century, associates

incidents of St. Mark's history have been similarly immortalized. The legends of this saint which tradition and chronicle have transmitted are quite numberless. His peculiar affection for Venice, and the peculiar affection of Venice for him, is said to date as far back for origin as a visit he made the marshy islands of the Lagune during his earthly pilgrimage, and a prediction he then made of its future glory!

But so much space has been devoted to the ancient Basilica, that nothing can be said of its precious treasury so often robbed; nor of its gorgeous baptistry, with its sculptured font; nor of its sacristy with its firmament of mosaic; nor of its chapel of Cardinal Zeno with a noble monument to a noble man; nor of the humble tomb of the descendant of "blind old Dandolo," the first historian of Venice, and her last Doge deposited within the walls of St. Mark; nor of the Oratory of the Cross, supported by most costly columns, and crowned with the vastest agate in the world—as large as a human head; nor of the wondrous *Pala d'oro*, with its priceless gems;* nor of the splendid portal of Sansovino, to which he is *said* to have devoted thirty years of toil; nor of the mass of rock on

a similar incident with his old fisherman of the Lagune, Antonio. From 1520 to 1796 no less than 276 ducal rings were dropped into the Adriatic; of all which number, the recovery of but one is chronicled, and that from the maw of a fish.

* This splendid specimen of Grecian art, as curious as it is splendid—this *Pala d'oro*—this Oriental *Icon*—was brought by Orseolo from Constantinople, as spoil. in 976. It was however, enriched in 1105, 1209, and 1345; and repaired as late as 1843. The designs are from the Old and New Testaments and the life of St. Mark, with Greek, Latin, and barbaric inscriptions, intermingled. It is composed of pearls, amethysts, onyxes, topazes, sapphires, emeralds, rubies, opals, turquoises, cornelians, chrysolites, adamants, aqua-marines, enamel, &c., and is deemed as it may well be, of inestimable value. It is covered by an oil painting, the work of Venetian artists in 1354. At the church of San Salvatore is to be seen a similar *Icon*, or metallic picture, on occasion of great fetes. The *Pala d'oro* has always been respected by invaders—even by Napoleon. He seized the unbridled steeds at the portal, but crossed not the threshold of St. Mark's.

which was beheaded John the Baptist, still stainea with his blood; nor of the antique stone chair of St. Mark; nor of the gorgeous Baldacchino, supported by its sculptured columns; nor of the reliquary full of priceless treasures, among which is a *leg* of St. Pietro Orseolo, presented by Louis XV.; nor of the exquisite *marqueteries* of wood; nor of many—many another most marvellous thing, which frequent pilgrimages only, and alone, to the ancient Minster, enables one to behold.

The Basilica of St. Mark has been well styled "a museum of mosaic." Every where is mosaic. The whole interior of the temple is draped with this tapestry of stone—these paintings of marble. It spreads itself along the walls it leaps into the arches, it bends in the domes, it folds itself in the angles, it drops between the pilasters and pillars, and even flows down over the pavement, in designs as numerous as caprice can multiply, and as symbolic as oriental fiction can invent. Figures or landscapes, groups or individuals, animals real or apocryphal, scenes pagan or Christian, objects sacred or profane—the mosaic is every where, tracing its brilliant lines with myriads of colored particles, each one seemingly a gem of price; here a saint from the cartoon of Titian—there a scene from the design of Palma—yonder a glimpse of the glories of Paradise, and close beside it the red flames of Hell; and all this accomplished by means of fragments of colored glass embedded in a ground of gold, rendering the whole work so inestimable in value, that, with hardly an image, the temple was long since styled *La chiesa aurea*—the church of gold!* And then, the priceless opulence of marble under every possible form of column, cornice, pilaster, pillar, plate, tablet,

* "Who would dream," says that graphic writer, Lecomte, in a description of St. Mark's Church which has suggested much on the subject here presented—"Who would dream, that a picture as brilliant as that of a master, and ten times as durable, could be produced by little fragments of colored gla ;?"

balustrade, staircase, altar—the product of oriental quarries—the spoils of Greece and Byzantium, of Palestine, Asia Minor, and Syria. Jaspar, porphyry, alabaster, serpentine, verd-antique—granite, veined and spotted, white and black, gray and variegated—all bound together, and consolidated by the crimson *brocatelle* of Verona, every where wrought into *marqueterie* or *vermiculato*—the mosaic of marble. Mosque, temple, church—with the proportions of the fane of Jupiter Capitolinus at Rome, and the domes and decorations of St. Sophia at Byzantium—with its Greek, Gothic, Saracenic architecture—with its useless columns, its balustrades without object, statues without niches, animals without name, bas-reliefs inexplicable, inscriptions indecipherable, legends incomprehensible: Moorish minarets assuming the form of the Christian cross—Byzantine columns crowned with Corinthian capitals—all inconsistent, incoherent, fantastic—all indicating a perfect *embarras du riches*—a profuse opulence of spoil, which sought only to enrich, and which has resulted in an order and style, to which the word *composite* can alone hope to do justice! And thus, by the re-union from all parts of the world of things most precious, has been completed a monument *bizarre*, doubtless, yet *unique*—novel as well as rich to excess—in splendor incomparable, and which, whether museum or minster, temple or palace, would alone suffice as an artistic illustration of this Adriatic Rome—were she not already, by reason of other magnificent piles, one of the most renowned cities in the world, and, without any exception, the most original. The Basilica of St. Mark is the history of Venice in marble, where every event is immortalized by a column, a bas-relief, a relique—by a statue, a legend, an inscription, a tomb; and it offers a theme for thought, not more to him who meditates and prays, than to him who analyzes and studies; to the architect, the sculptor, the painter, not more than to the antiquarian, the poet, and the historian. For centuries, as already mentioned, every vessel that entered the Lagune brought its tribute to St. Mark: every conquest contributed a colonnade of jaspar and serpentine—every treaty a collection of bas-reliefs and balustrades—every ransom a relique—every siege a statue; and, while the sons of St. Mark, as soldiers and seamen, brought booty from the ends of the earth to enrich his shrine, those who tarried at home exerted all the powers of transcendent genius—Zucatto combining with Titian—to render it glorious with the new-found arts of *marqueterie* and mosaic.* Even the huge columns of the Piazetta were designed to enrich St. Mark's when brought from Naxos by Michieli; but it was found impossible to render them available, and for fifty years they lay on the *Molo* forgotten; and even Ferdinand of Austria, as lately as 1838, when returning from his coronation at Milan, did not forget to deposit here his crown and sceptre, having already deposited his royal mantle at Monza, with the iron crown he had just assumed—the crown of Agilulpha, and Napoleon, and Charlemagne.

Next to the patriarchal Church of Venice, that of *Santa Maria della Salute* is most admired. It is a grand and imposing structure. It rises at the entrance of the Canalazzo, and its lofty and lordly double-dome is beheld far out in the Adriatic, the first object in approaching Venice from the sea. It was commenced in 1631, as a votive monument of the plague of the preceding year, which swept off 60,000 of the people of Venice. This devoted city has been visited five times in its history by this awful scourge—in 1348, when three-fifths of the population of Europe are supposed to have succumbed to its ravages—in 1413, in 1478, in 1575; and, last, in 1630. At the height of the mortality and terror produced by this

* Lecomte.

latest visitation, the Doge Contarini and the Patriarch Tiepolo recorded a solemn vow, to erect a temple in honor of the Virgin immediately upon the cessation of the pestilence. Wonderful to relate, on that very day the plague ceased, and, on the Feast of the Annunciation, on the 25th of March of the ensuing year, the anniversary of the founding of the city, the first stone of the votive church to "Holy Mary of the Salvation" was laid with great pomp by the Doge, attended by all the Senate in procession. The inscription, "*Unde origo inde salus*," on the pavement, commemorates the coincidence in the founding of the city and the church, and the cessation of the plague. The event added a new fête, of course, to the Venetian calendar. It was called "*La Sagra.*" Every year, on the anniversary of the event, High Mass is said in the church with exceeding pomp, and some years it is celebrated by the people with great rejoicing. This was especially the case in March of 1848, immediately upon the expulsion of the Austrians.

The architect of the Salute was Longhena, who laid its massive foundations on a substratum of 1,200,000 piles; and, despite its vast disproportion of ornament, it is a most stately and magnificent edifice. Its form is octagonal; its dome is supported by eight ponderous pillars; it possesses one hundred and twenty-five statues. It has six secondary altars, all, like the grand altar, oppressed with ornaments. It is opulent in marbles, candelabra, bronzes, sculptures, and *chefs d'œuvre* of Titian and Tintoretto. In the oratory of the adjoining convent is the tomb of the celebrated architect Sansovino, who was a wanderer all his life, and whose remains have been wandering from one church to another ever since his death.

The church *Del Redentore* which uplifts its stately shape almost alone on the island of the *Giudecca*—or *Zuecca*—so called because anciently the quarter appropriated to the Jews, and previously called

Spinalonga, because supposed to resemble a *thorn*, owes its origin to like cause with the Salute. At the time of the visitation of the plague in 1575, the Doge Moncenigo and the Patriarch Trevisano recorded a joint vow, similar to that of Contarini and Tiepolo, a hundred years later in imitation, and with similar result. The scourge at once ceased its ravages; and, before the year had closed, Palladio had been charged to rear the church *Del Santissimo Redentore*—"The church of the Most Holy Redemer"—in fulfillment of a vow so potent and so providential. On the 3d day of May, 1578, the Doge and the Patriarch, with appropriate pomp, laid the first stone. This event added a festa to the Venetian calendar similar to that of the Salute—similarly named *La Sagra;* and, on the 19th of July, 1851, it was celebrated with unwonted splendor in connection with the restoration by Austria of the privilege of a free port. The form of the Redentore is a Latin cross; its façade is vastly majestic in distant view; it has four altars, all surcharged with ornament, and about a dozen fine paintings by Veronese, Tintoretto, Bassano, and Palma.

The church of *San Giorgio Maggiore*—"St. George the Great," a very popular saint at Venice—on the island of the same name, directly opposite the Piazetta, and one of the most prominent objects in approaching the city from the Adriatic, with its dome and towering campanile, was commenced by Palladio in 1566, as a rival to his famous *chef d'œuvre*, the Redentore; but was not completed until forty years later, and by an inferior artist. Its façade of Istrian marble, adorned with columns and statues, has a splendid effect when illumined by the gold and purple of the setting sun and viewed from the *Molo* or Piazetta. Its dome is one of the grandest, and its campanile one of the loftiest, in Venice. Its form is a Latin cross, and its interior its decorated by columns, statues, bronzes, and pictures by masters. Its eleven altars are laden with ornament, especially the high altar, which is completely incrusted with marbles and bronzes. The choir is splendid with decoration, and the stalls of oak elaborately sculptured. This imposing pile is honored with the remains and monuments of three of the most illustrious Doges that ever wore the *beretta* of the Ocean Queen. The first monument is that of Dominico Michieli, the conqueror of Jaffa, Tyre, Ascalon, and Jerusalem, and "The Terror of the Greeks," who died in 1128. It was this hero who brought home from the Archipelago the two famous granite columns, gray and red, which stand in the Piazetta, bearing on their summits the Lion of St. Mark and the statue of his predecessor in the protectorate of Venice—St. Theodore, standing on a crocodile. A second monument is that of the Doge Leonardo Donato, distinguished for his noble defiance of the spiritual despotism and secular assumption of that haughty, Pontiff Paul V., despite all the anathemas of Rome, who died in 1612; while the third is that of Marc' Antonio Memmo, who dispersed and routed the formidable piratic bands of the Uscoques of Dalmatia, which, for a hundred years, had been the terror of the Adriatic. He died in 1615. Here, too, are monuments of the Procurator Veniero, who died in 1667, and Vincenzio Morosini, who died in 1538, besides portraits of numerous Venetian senators by Tintoretto. Over one of the doors is seen, also, the pleasant portrait of Pope Pius VII. It was in this church that he was crowned, after his election by a conclave of cardinals convened at Venice in the month of March, 1800. The church itself is said to owe its earliest origin to a singular cause. The island where it stands was once covered with cypresses, and inhabited by Benedictine monks. A ferocious mastiff belonging to the society tore in pieces a young son of the Doge Pietro Ziani in 1205; who, in his fury, ordered the church and the convent of the monks to be at once levelled with the soil. As his wrath and grief became assuaged, however, by the lapse of time, his piety awoke; and, as a self-inflicted penance for his sacrilege, he erected on the spot a church to St. George the Great. In 1566, this church having fallen into decay, the present edifice was commenced by Palladio on the old foundation.

The church of the *Frari*, or *Santa Maria Gloriosa de' Frari*, was erected about six hundred years ago, and is celebrated for its numerous and sumptuous mausolea. Of these, there are about a dozen, several of which are equestrian, erected to the memory of doges, generals, and senators of the Republic. But there is one humble tomb which attracts more attention than all of these. At the base of the second altar, on the right as you enter, you see a simple slab in the pavement, which indicates by its inscription, that beneath repose the ashes of the immortal Titian. He was one of the last victims of the plague of 1575. He died August 27th, 1576—at his own house, which is still to be seen, *Campo·Rotto* 5526, and not at the Palazzo Barbarigo, where he long lived and painted—at the advanced age of ninety-nine years, almost with the brush in his hand.* The unfinished painting of "Christ at the

* The great masters at Venice most of them attained very great age. Sansovino died at 93; Vittoria at 82; Tintoretto at 83; Bellini at 80; Veronese at 60; Canova at 65; while Goldoni, "the Italian Moliere," died at 86. Giorgione died of grief at 33—the same age as Raphael—for the loss of a mistress, who eloped with Pietro Luzio, one of his pupils, who subsequently fell, a soldier, at Zara. The mistress of Titian, immortalized by his brush, was Violante, daughter of the elder Palma. The great master was at one time wealthy, and entertained nobles at his table; but he became impoverished by a natural son, who seems, nevertheless, to have been a very *un*natural one, who was a priest—and he died destitute. To complete the picture, upon his death, his house was entered by thieves and thoroughly sacked, the customary vigilance of the police having been paralyzed by the pestilence.

Tomb," on which, at the time, he was engaged, is to be seen at the Academy. His remains, by order of the Senate, were not consumed by quick lime, as were those of other victims of the pestilence, but were deposited in the Frari church, where they have ever since remained. At the close of the last century, Canova was engaged to furnish a design for a monument to the great master, and did so gratuitously; but the execution of the work was prevented by the fall of the Republic. Some years since, a monument was ordered by the late Emperor of Austria, Ferdinand, at his own expense, and is now in slow progress. The monument designed by Canova for Titian stands over the remains of Canova himself, at the altar directly opposite, across the nave. The elevation presents a section of a lofty pyramid of Carrara marble, with bronze doors opening into a tomb, with allegorical figures of Art, Genius, etc., in funereal procession—not in very good taste, as a whole. It was erected in 1827, by a subscription of the sculptor's admirers in all Europe, at a cost of $20,000. This same monument, originally designed for Titian, but erected over its designer, was by himself modified to be a monument to the Archduchess Christina of Austria, and stands to her memory in the Church of the Augustines at Vienna.

Only the heart of Canova is beneath his tomb at the Frari. His right hand is preserved in an urn at the Academy, while the classic temple, devised by himself, at the little village of Passagnano, at the foot of the Alps, where he was born, received his body, on the 25th of October, 1825. His tomb bears but two words: *Hic Canova.* He died at Venice, October 13th, 1822, at the age of sixty five years. His works number about one hundred and sixty pieces, one of the most noted of which—his colossal Washington was possessed by the Capitol of North Carolina. In 1792, the Venetian Senate awarded the artist a pension of two hundred ducats and a gold medal, for his monument to the celebrated Admiral Emo, at the Arsenal, although the work had been gratuitous. In '97, Napoleon confirmed the pension, and Austria did the same in 1815, on condition that the sculptor should superintend the Austrian students of art at Rome, a city he had then selected for his abode. Subsequently, Pius VII. made him Marquis of Ischia, the revenues amounting to some three thousand scudi per annum. In 1815, he was commissioned to superintend the restoration of the works of art to Italy.

Another, among the numerous gorgeous mausolea in the Frari church which will arrest the eye, is that of the unhappy Doge Francesco Foscari, immortalized by Byron in the tragedy bearing his name. His *dogat* of thirty-four years was one of the longest and most illustrious in the history of the Republic. Overwhelmed at length by the persecutions to which he and his family were subjected by his foes, and compelled, at the extreme age of eighty-four years, to abdicate an office he had reluctantly accepted, and had twice offered to resign, and had been finally forced to swear to retain for life—he fainted on descending the Giants' Staircase to leave his ducal abode. On hearing the great bell of St. Mark announce the election of his successor, Malipieri, five days later, he ruptured a blood vessel, and died, October 30th, 1457. It is a remarkable fact, that, never before, and never after, in all the long history of Venice, was there a Doge to mourn at the splendid obsequies of his predecessor. It was only after the death and burial of one Doge that another was ever chosen. In the garb of a simple Senator, Malipieri followed the remains of the great Foscari, decked with the insignia of the *dogat*, to the tomb.

In the biography of none of the noble families of Venice is the persecuting jealousy of that despotic Oligarchy so conspicuous, as in that of the Foscari. Many of these families, it is true, were victims of life-long martyrdom, because of their power and renown;* but there is none whose persecutions will compare with those of this celebrated house. Had the warning addressed by Foscari's predecessor, Moncenigo, to the Senate, against his elevation to the Ducal chair, been but addressed to himself, and been but better heeded than it was by those who received it, the old noble might have been spared the miseries of his protracted *dogat*, and, at length, have succumbed to a happier fate; while his mortal foe, Loredano, might never have inscribed on his ledger—*L'ha pagata*—"He has payed"—at the close of a long account of cruelties, because of imputed wrongs in a father and uncle slain. The studied and refined persecution of Foscari by the Venetian Senate, may be inferred from a single example. One day, while Doge, in his own gorgeous palace on the Grand Canal, surrounded by patricians, he was slightly wounded by a man clearly insane, pertaining to a noble family. Despite the manifest insanity, however, the man was arrested, tried and tortured by the Ten; and, although the Doge entreated his pardon, was actually executed. The tragedy took place in a boat moored opposite to the palace where the blow had been struck; and Foscari was forced to witness the pitiable spectacle from his own windows! And, a few years later, the old Doge was forced to witness a spectacle yet more pitiable—the torture of his own, and only, and innocent son! A fine painting of the last parting of the two Foscari, by Gregoletti, was executed, some years since, by order

* The family Da Moula, for example, whose splendid palace casts its shadow on the Grand Canal, was persecuted for years, because a member of that family, an Envoy of Venice to Rome, accepted the red hat of a Cardinal, without her permission. The old Republic, however, more than once, filled the Pontifical chair; and sons of St. Mark became successors of St. Peter. Antonio Ottobini, who became Alexander VIII., in 1689, and Carlo Rezzonico, who became Clement XIII., in 1758, may be named as examples.

of the Emperor Ferdinand; as was, also, one of the last parting of old Faliero with his wife. Engravings of both are common at Venice.

One other monument in the church of the Frari will attract attention for its unique, its grotesque design, if for nothing besides. It is that of the Doge Pesaro, who died in 1660, from the effects of a fall down one of the secret staircases of the Ducal Palace. He reigned but three years, and his pompous tomb presents one of the numerous instances at Venice, wherein the monument of the prince seems imposing and splendid, in exact ratio to the brevity and insignificance of his administration. The ponderous mausoleum presses with crushing weight on the shoulders of two unhappy negroes, black as the blackest marble can make them; their sable knees bursting through their white drawers, in their desperate efforts to sustain their burthen. In the centre of the monument, above all, complaisantly sits the marble Doge; and, on each side of him, is a bronze skeleton bearing a scroll, and a dragon bearing an urn! Another figure is, at the same time, offering the Doge a crown, which he is very modestly declining!

This church has half a dozen altars richly decorated; some fine paintings by Titian, Palma, Bellini, Salviati, and others; a choir celebrated for its exquisitely carved wood and *marqueterie*, and a large number of statues, urns, bronzes, sculptures, &c. The convent adjoining is a depository of the archives of the government, ancient and modern; and embraces, among other treasures, "The Golden Book," and numerous autograph letters of Charles V., Francis I., Henry IV., and of Napoleon.

The church of the *Frari*, or Monks, owes its name to the fact, that the site was once possessed by a convent of Minorities of St. Francis. The first stone was laid in 1250, by Cardinal Ottaniano,

Legate of the Pope. There is nothing in its architecture to demand notice. Its façade is enriched by three fine statues.

The church of *San Giovanni e Paolo*—"Saints John and Paul"—is to Venice, in connection with the church of the *Frari*, what St. Denis is to Paris, what Westminster is to London, what Santa Croce is to Florence, what the Escurial is to Madrid: it is the Pantheon, the Windsor, of the illustrious dust of the ancient Republic; it is the mausoleum of power to rank, "where pomp magnificently mourns departed pride." Externally, the edifice has not the slightest pretension. Its façade is not *finished*, although the structure was commenced in the thirteenth century, completed in the fourteenth, and consecrated in the fifteenth, more than four centuries since. Here are seen the monuments of about a dozen Doges, among which that of Andrea Vendramini, whose magnificent palace on the Grand Canal now belongs to the Duchess of Berri, is the most imposing. It is, indeed, deemed by many the most splendid tomb in Venice. This Doge was one of the first of the New Nobility created after the War of the Chioggia, in acknowledgment of extraordinary pecuniary sacrifices of patriotic citizens during that darkest epoch in the history of the Republic. Here, also, is the urn of the heroic Marc' Antonio Bragadino, the champion and the martyr of Cyprus, containing only his *skin*—ransomed by his family, at enormous cost, from the Moslem. Like Marsyas and St. Bartholomew, he was flayed alive! Here, also, among the numberless tombs of senators, generals, and illustrious men, that of Vittorio Cappello, brother of the frail but beautiful Bianca, to whose liberality he was indebted for the Trevisan palace, on the *Calle di Canonica*, near the Cathedral, one of the richest in Venice, will arrest attention; as, also, that of Edward Windsor, a military adventurer—a *Condottiore* in the service of the Republic, an Englishman, interred nearly three centuries ago. An inscription on the tomb of Alvise Michiele records the fact, that he fell dead, in 1589, in the Senate chamber, while urging the recognition of Henry IV., king of France, by the Republic;* and, in a corner is seen the new tomb of the Marquis de Chasteller, General of Artillery and Governor of Venice, who died in 1825. The celebrated Doge, Marino Faliero, who was beheaded for treason on the landing of the Giants' Staircase of the Ducal Palace as asserted by Byron and Delavigne—is declared in notes to their respective Tragedies founded on the subject, to be buried in an obscure corner of this church; but by others it is denied. Several of the monuments are surmounted by equestrian statues, and by marble effigies of armed men, who look out from their helmets as fiercely as executioners. A vast window of beautifully colored glass, executed at Murano in the fifteenth century, presents one of the few specimens of that art in the churches of Venice; although the staining of glass in a certain manner has been for ages, and is yet, a secret jealously guarded at that ancient manufactory. Over the grand altar, which is very rich, is a lesser window of similar character, a century later in origin. This church has some fine paintings, as well as some fine sculptures in marble; but the gem of the edifice is considered the celebrated *San Pietro Martire* by Titian. This painting is, by some artists, esteemed the second, in regard of merit, in the world—"The Transfiguration," by Raphael, in the Vatican, being ranked the first. Others consider, "The Assumption of the Virgin," by Titian, in the Academy of Venice, or "The Communion of St. Jerome," by Paul Veronese, in St. Peter's at Rome, or "The Last Judgment," at Paris—either one, or all, supe-

* Death, under like circumstances, has not been uncommon. Chatham and Adams are instances. The former fell in a convulsive fit, April 8th, 1788, when rising to speak in the House of Lords, and died a month later at his residence in London. Adams, as every one knows, expired in the ante-chamber of the U. S. Senate.

rior.* "The greatest masters have agreed," however, as we are informed by Algarotti, "that it is impossible to find a fault in this painting!" Whatever its merits, it has certainly received the highest honors which can be accorded a work of art. Having once been sold by the fraternity, for whose church it was painted, for the sum of 18,000 crowns, the Council of Ten annulled the contract, and forbade the Dominicans ever again, on pain of death to all concerned, to part with it! By Napoleon it was sent to the Louvre, where it remained fifteen years; and was there, by the ingenious process of *rentoilage*, restored to primitive perfection. It has been engraved a dozen times, and copied and imitated times numberless. A few years since, it was copied for the Emperor of Russia; and, in the summer of 1851, a copy was taken by Bartolomei, a Roman artist of distinction, for the Academy of Arts in Baltimore. The subject of this famous painting is the murder of a monk known as Father Peter of Verona, who was assassinated in a forest near Barlassina, when returning from a secret conference with another monk. This man flourished in the thirteenth century, and repaired from Verona to Milan to denounce heresies, and punish heretics. Indeed, a pulpit is still shown on the outside of the church of San Eustachio, in the latter city, whence he was wont to hurl his pious anathemas. But the worthy disciple of St. Dominic finding himself quite unsuccessful in his spiritual denunciations, had recourse to corporeal tortures, which, through the Inquisition of his dark order, he plied so mercilessly, that, at length, in 1252, April 6th, long-suffering patience was exhausted, and fear and vengeance dictated his assassination. A dozen years afterwards Rome canonized him; and three centuries after that, Titian was commissioned by the Domin-

* Titian himself regarded as his master-piece, the "Supper," painted for Philip II., for the Escurial, on which he was engaged seven years.

icans to confer more lasting immortality yet on the Martyrdom and the Martyr. The design, drawing, drapery, and coloring of this picture, even the most unprofessional eye must perceive to be exquisite; but *all* unprofessional people, and even all professors and *connoisseurs* of art, do not concede it to be the most attractive of the great master's works. The robust figure of an angel or two hovering in most palpable—nay, ponderous proportions over the tree-tops, detracts materially from the appropriateness of the design to a practical and Protestant eye. But, if this be a fault obnoxious to good taste, it is a glaring one in all the great religious paintings of all the great masters. The Deity presides in person at the "Paradise" of Tintoretto, and receives the Madonna into Heaven in the "Assumption" of Titian; while, in "The Venetian Slave delivered by St. Mark" of the former artist, the muscular body of the saint descending from the skies makes one shudder, from its similitude to the form of some stalwart and unhappy tiler tumbling headlong from a roof! "The Last Judgment," of Michael Angelo, also, whether as a fresco in the Sistine chapel at Rome, or as a painting in the Borbonic Museum at Naples, strikes the uninitiated more as a curious collection of well-developed arms and legs, floating by some "devilish cantrip slight" in mid-air, than for anything else!

In the *campo*, in front of the church of Saints John and Paul, is to be seen the only public equestrian statue in Venice; and this one proves, that its artist was not very "knowing in horse-flesh." Westmacott says, "it is heavy in form, and its action is untrue to nature." It is said to be the second equestrian statue erected in Italy after the *renaissance*, and is a monument to Colleoni, a general of the Republic, who is said first to have employed field-pieces in warfare, and who died in 1475. Count Daru states, that Colleoni bequeathed the Republic 216,000 ducats, on condition that an equestrian statue to his memory should be erected on this spot. The legacy was accepted, and a famous artist of Florence, Andrea Verocchio, painter, sculptor, architect, inventor of modelling in plaster, and master of the celebrated Leonardo da Vinci, was employed to execute the work. Vasari tells us, that the sculptor had moulded the horse, when he was notified, that he must mould the figure of Vellano of Padua, a living general, as its rider. The indignant artist, in a rage, broke the head of his mould, and then fled home to Florence! The Senate sent word after him, that his own head should share the fate of his horse's, if he was caught! His reply was, that they could restore his own head far more easily than they could that of his horse! There was so much of truth in the rejoinder, as well as so much of humor, that a pardon was sent him at once, when he returned to Venice, and worked with such zeal on his original design, that he ruptured a blood-vessel and died; and the statue was cast by Leonardo, whose name appears on the horse's girth.

This anecdote illustrates the fact, that St. Mark was always a stern task-master, whether dealing with artists or admirals, sculptors or soldiers. It is related of the celebrated Titian, who succeeded Bellini as painter of the Republic,—(for which service he received three hundred crowns per annum, being obliged to paint every Doge at eight crowns per head, paid by the Doge himself!)—that, on one occasion, having been commissioned to execute a battle-piece for the State, at twelve ducats per diem while employed, and having been paid in advance, and having been idle fifteen days, he was mulcted two hundred ducats—"obtained on false pretences!" Another artist, Tintoretto, perhaps, or Giorgione—having been paid in advance for a picture for the Ducal Palace, and having suspended the work and gone over to Padua to paint an altar-piece, an agent of the Ten brought the truant speedily back to Venice, and bade him resume, at once, and complete "the job of the Senate!" Again, while the great Sansovino, architect of the State, was erecting the Library of St. Mark, one of the vaults sinking, he was arrested and imprisoned, deposed from office, and condemned to repair the damage at his own cost. Through the influence of his friends, Titian and Pietro Aretino, he was restored to liberty and office, but soon after died. On the famous bronze door of the Sacristy of St. Mark, which "occupied thirty years of the artist's life," appear the heads of his two friends with his own. Aretino was a poet, infamous for debauchery. Once more—when Sanmichieli had erected the noble castle of Sant' Andrea amid the sands and waves of the Port of the Lido, his foes pronounced it insecure; and, not until it had been tested by a discharge of all its batteries at the same moment, was the architect released from arrest.

Adjoining the church of Saints John and Paul stands the fine edifice of the *Scuola di San Marco*, one of the six religious and philanthropic private institutions, which, to her honor be it recorded, have for four centuries, existed at Venice. This is a Hospital for the Poor, and among its inmates are several hundred insane women. A walk through its spacious wards is more impressive than would be a thousand homilies. Madness in all its horrible—in all its revolting forms is here—from moping fatuity to raving lunacy. The old system still obtains, with all its fearful results. The Hospital for insane men is on the island of San Servolo, in the direction of the Lido. "Here," says an eloquent writer, "the reason of a few Priest-Hospitallars, Monks of St. John, struggles with the madness of three hundred maniacs;" while, from the grated casements, the unhappy inmates look out on the melancholy Lagune, and send forth over the mirrored surface, as it reflects the lurid sunset, or the pallid moonbeams, their wild and unavailing shouts after the passing gondola.

"Oh, God! take what thou wilt, but spare my reason!" was the ejaculation of the great Johnson; and who that had visited the Mad Houses of Venice would not join in that mournful prayer?

Close beside the isle of San Servolo, and, as a contrast to its sad destination, stands the isle of San Lazzaro, the site of the peaceful Convent of the Armenians. The island owes its name to the fact that, in 1182, a Hospital for lepers from the Orient was here established. But, the curse of leprosy ceasing in 1715 Mechitar, chief of the Armenian church, driven from the Morea, by the infidels, received of the Venetian Senate this spot as an asylum for his faith—which faith is Catholic, certain rites and ceremonies only excepted. The voluminous registers of San Lazzaro show the names of half the distinguished people of Europe, to say nothing of Asia and America. In the year 1801, Pope Pius VII., after his consecration at San Giorgio, visited this convent, and recorded his name. In 1842, King Louis of Bavaria, on a visit there, addressed some verses to the monks, which were *done* by them into three different languages.

Not far from the church of Sts. John and Paul is *La Chiesa de' Gesuiti*—"The Church of the Jesuits." Externally, it is a vast barn; and, on entering, the first impression is, that the walls, columns, altars, pulpit, and even the pavement itself, have been daubed with a ground-work of whitewash, and then *grained* with coarse stainings of green. What then is the amazement, when, upon examination, the white ground proves to be purest marble of Carrara, and the green stainings—*verd-antique!* The illusion produced by this process in the drapery of the pulpit, is so perfect, that nothing less than the evidence of the sense of touch can convince the visitor that it is marble and not tapestry. One would suppose that only cloth of some description, could present a sweep and pendency so graceful. The grand altar is superbly rich. The spiral columns which sustain the *dais* or *baldacchino*, are of solid *verd-antique* marble; the tabernacle is of *lapis-lazuli*, and the steps are of Carrarese marble, vermiculated and arabesqued with yellow. The church has several fine paintings; among which is Titian's "Martyrdom of San Laurentino," which was at the Louvre from 1797 to 1815. It has, also, several Palmas and Tintorettos, and boasts the monument of the celebrated Doge Pasquale Cicogna, who substituted for the old Rialto Bridge of wood the new Rialto Bridge of marble, as it now stands. It has, moreover, the dust and tomb of the last Doge of Venice, Luigi Manini, with its affecting inscription—"*Æternitati suæ Manini cineres.*" Cicogna, whose tomb is as humble as those of most of the really great men of Venice, was elected to the *dogat* in 1585, after a stormy contest between the old and the new Patriciat and after no less than fifty-two ballotings—the infirm old man, whose ancestor, an apothecary, had acquired nobility two centuries before by furnishing an armed galley in the War of the Chioggia, being selected in a spirit of compromise. This Doge, who was a saint as well as a prince—who worked miracles as well as built bridges—completed the celebrated fortress of Palma Nuova, in the Friul, and, as already mentioned, erected the Rialto—which had been originally constructed of wood, in 1264, but repeatedly consumed by fire—of marble, in 1591. Its architect was the famous Da Ponte, its cost 250,000 sequins, or more than half a million of dollars; and no less than 12,000 piles of elm, we are told, were employed in its foundation. Its single arch of ninety feet span is exceedingly graceful.* It is crossed, like all the other bridges of Venice, by means of ascending and descending steps; and two ranges of shops divide it into three parallel streets. Here goldsmiths drive their trade, and here those extremely fine and

* The Canalazzo varies from one to two hundred feet in width.

pure yet strong gold chains, called *jaseron*, for which Venice has long been famous, are sold by the yard.

In the autumn of 1838, when the Emperor Ferdinand assumed the iron crown of Lombardy at Milan, it was contemplated to give the event a monumental commemoration at Venice, by throwing a second bridge of marble, like that of the Rialto, across the Grand Canal, opposite the Academy of Arts. Had this design been accomplished, the loss in point of scenic effect to this beautiful *Corso* would have been great; and so, probably, would have been the gain to the city, in point of utility. Which would have preponderated, however, different tastes would differently have decided. But the enormous expense, as estimated, forbade the enterprise being undertaken. The canal is, at this point, wider than at the Rialto, or, perhaps, at any other point above the *Dogana di Mare*, or the Marine Custom House; and any bridge would demand a single arch. It was also contemplated by the Government, in honor of the Emperor's coronation, to purchase and restore the magnificent Foscari palace, and found there a Polytechnic School. Well—the palace *was* purchased; but it was degraded into a Barrack for Bohemian soldiers!

Returning, however, to the churches:—If the visitor is astonished at the richness of decoration in the church of the Jesuits, what will he say of the *Scalzi*, the interior of which is entirely constructed of Carrarese marble, and is one continuous *congeries* of sculpture, statuary, and gilding? Every where is beheld only marble; and every possible shape, and many seemingly impossible shapes for marble to assume, are presented. In the words of a Frenchman—marble spreads itself in plates upon the walls, it twists itself into spiral columns, it moulds itself into chapiters, it curves itself into vaults, it breaks itself into angles, it denticulates itself into cornices it diffuses itself into every imaginable form of flourish and ornament; it floods the pavement engraved with epitaphs and sculptured with armorial bearings; it is red, it is green, it is white, it is black, it is veined, vermiculated, variegated, spotted; it shapes itself into statues and caryatides, winds itself into candelabra, effloresces into fruits, blossoms, and leaves; and even flings itself abroad into starry rays, to form a halo for the resplendent brow of the Madonna herself, and for the mysterious effulgence of the Holy Ghost! This church is about two hundred years old, and owes its costly decorations chiefly to opulent families—to the Venetian "Josephs of Arimathea," who have constructed here their "new tombs." Some of the most gorgeous of the chapels, indeed, were presented by individual families. It has two or three fine paintings. The Venetians are vastly proud of this church—more so, if possible, than of old San Marco itself. Yet, with all its marble, and golden, and sculptural sumptuousness, it is, by no means, pure in style or refined in taste; and, worse than all, it has attached to it not the slightest historic interest. It is a monument of mammon—not of religion—not of ambition—not of patriotism—not even of art. The tenants of its tombs are the rich, and the rich only—not of the great—not of the good; and, what that theatrical chapel, *La Notre Dame de Lorette* may be to Paris, that, to Venice, is *La Chiesa degli Scalzi.* During the bombardment of '49, several balls dropped through its gilded vault. One almost shudders at the idea of the irreparable damage which a bomb, bursting in its chancel, or its nave, would have accomplished; and it lay fully within the range of these terrible projectiles. The name is derived from that of the mendicant order of *bare-footed* friars—*Scalzi*—whose convent once possessed the spot.

Some eight or ten of the most noted churches in Venice have

now been noticed. But this brief catalogue includes not all among her three-score of sacred structures worthy of mention, whether we regard origin or history, architecture or ornament—their monuments, or their paintings. By no means. There is the church of *San Zaccaria*, with its vast dimensions, its singularly beautiful architecture, its costly decorations, and noted for the historic fact of the assassination of the Doge Pietro Tradenigo, in the ninth century, at its very portal, on the occasion of the annual procession to the edifice in honor of the saint—in which bloody catastrophe originated a decree of the Senate, that, in future, dignitaries of State should visit churches and convents only in gilded gondolas, although the decree was subsequently rescinded, and all gondolas, for the sake of equality, and to check prodigality, were restricted in hue to black only, as at present. Then there is the church of *San Francesco della Vigna*, a beautiful monument of the taste and genius of Palladio and Sansovino, in the 16th century, occupying the site of an ancient vineyard—whence its name—and honored by the tomb of that sage, brave, and astute old Doge, Andrea Gritti. And there is the church of *San Giuseppe*, distinguished by the splendid double mausoleum of the Doge Marino Grimani and his beautiful *Dogaressa*, both sleeping in one tomb; which lady, upon her coronation, a rare event,* received of Pope Clement VIII. the "Golden Rose," which gave her the rank of Princess, and of which she was subsequently deprived by the jealousy of the Senate. And there is *San Martino*, with its gorgeous paintings by Palma; and *San Sebastiano*, filled with works of the great master, Paul Veronese, and appropriately and deservedly honored with his tomb; and *San Nicolo*, celebrated for the antiquity of its origin, and its costly columns from Carrara, and its splendid stalactites from Corfu; and *Santa Maria del Car-*

* The Venetian Doges seldom had wives.

mine, with its paintings of Palma and Tintoretto, its tomb and statue of Foscarini, and its towering campanile, which, for two whole centuries, has been threatening to crush the adjacent roofs—although it varies scarcely more from an irreproachable perpendicular than all the other bell-towers of Venice, every one of which, St. Mark's not excepted, has, as before stated, a decided *lean*. And then, the vast and ancient *San Stefano*, with its rare marbles and rich sculptures—its bas-reliefs and statues—immortalized by the tomb of D'Alviano, the victim-hero of the wars of the League of Cambray—as, also, that of Morosini, the hero of the Peloponessus, who died at Napoli di Romania—while a rich urn of marble, in the cloister, contains the ashes of the Doge Contarini, one of the heroes of the war of the Chioggia: and *Santa Maria Formosa*, with its tombs and busts of the proud house of Capello, and its ancient tradition of the Brides of Venice, who, as before mentioned, in connection with *San Pietro di Castello*, on the annual nuptial feast, decorated for the occasion with all the costly jewelry of St. Mark's, and bearing their rich dowries, were abducted by the corsairs of Trieste, although in a few hours, and before nightfall, by Venetian gallantry, regained: and *San Salvatore*, with its three grand paintings by Titian, its precious *Icon*, a picture composed of gems like the *Pala d'oro* of St. Mark's, exposed only on occasions of special solemnity—with its tombs of the three Cardinals Conaro, and the two Doges Priuli, and, above all, its splendid mausoleum of Catarina Conaro, daughter of St. Mark and Queen of Cyprus, who died in 1510, and who is represented by a bas-relief on the marble offering the crown of her island-kingdom to the Doge—albeit, in very sooth, an *offer* more compulsory on the part of the spirited sovereign than spontaneous: and the *S. S. Apostoli*, with its strange altar of black touch-stone, in a chapel honored as the tomb of the remains of the Queen of Cyprus, before their final deposite in *San Salvatore;* and the *Tolentini*, on the Canalazzo, opposite the sumptuous gardens of the opulent Greek banker, Papadopoli—distinguished for its painting of St. Mark descending from Heaven to break the bonds of a Venetian slave, a duplicate of which is found in the Academy, and distinguished likewise for its mausoleum of the Conaro family, where again is told in marble the false tale of the proffering to the Doge Barbarigo, in 1490, of the crown of the isle of Cyprus, by its Queen; and *La Madonna dell' Orto*, with its numerous Tintorettos—the most remarkable of which is the enormous and singular representation of the "Last Judgment," sixty feet by thirty in dimensions—and its graceful campanile shattered by a thunderbolt some twenty years ago; and *San Giorgio dei Greci*, erected, as a Greek inscription declares, in 1551, three hundred years since, almost to a year, by Greeks residing at, or visiting Venice, on business or pleasure, in order that they might worship God according to the dictates of conscience and the laws of their fathers—the form of worship, and the mode of chanting prayers, and the separating of men and women, being much that of the Jewish Synagogue—the church itself being a monument of the characteristic toleration, both of the ancient Republic and the Austrian government, in matters of religion; and *San Rocco*, erected after the cessation of the plague in 1490—that event being attributed to the intercession of St. Roch, the protector against pestilence, by whose relics one of its tombs is hallowed—the edifice being adorned, as well as the *Scuola di San Rocco* adjoining, with numberless paintings by that everlasting Tintoretto,* the chief of which is the immense "Crucifixion;"

* The churches of Venice, alone, claim not less than 268 grand paintings from the prolific brush of this celebrated master; while the Ducal Palace has the "Paradise" and other vast works. The idea that he was aided by his pupils is, doubtless, correct. He is exceeded in the number of his works only by Rubens, who painted 1810 pieces, em-

and *San Paolo*, erected by the Doge Tradenigo and his son, in the 9th century, now remarkable only for its campanile, on which is a singular bas-relief of two Lions of St. Mark, one in the folds of a huge serpent, which threatens to crush it, and the other holding up in its paws a human head—alluding, as tradition asserts, to the conspiracy against Venice of Filippo Visconti duke of Milan, the device of whose shield was a serpent, in connection with the unhappy Carmagnola who was decapitated between the columns of the Piazetta, in 1432; and *San Jacopo di Rialto*, the oldest church in Venice, first constructed in the 5th century, in fulfillment of a vow of one Condiotto, a boat-builder, which vow is asserted to have saved all his little property from conflagration, when imminently menaced, by means of a sudden and miraculous torrent of rain! In the 12th century, this old church—then more than seven hundred years old—was re-constructed in the original form and on the original spot; and, in 1514, when two thousand houses all around it were swept away by the flames, this aged edifice, by miracle, remained untouched! In 1531, it was again rebuilt "in precisely the same form as at first, and on precisely the same spot," as is recorded in an inscription on its portico. It has two paintings by the son of Titian, noticeable only for their origin; also a humble, but beautiful altar, adorned with bronzes and marbles; and also two colossal statues—one of them a statue of its patron saint. Its site is indicated by its name. It stands near the Rialto Bridge, and faces the old Rialto square.

There are still other churches in Venice worthy of mention; but, as this, already almost endless, catalogue must somewhere close, it

bracing 14,864 figures. But the Flemish artist executed no such vast undertakings as "The Paradise" of the Ducal Palace, or "The Crucifixion" of the *Confrerie* of St. Roch, or "The Last Judgment" of the Madonna dell' Orto.

may as well close here; though fain would the writer allude to the unique and venerable cathedral of the deserted Isle of Torcello, and the aged church of Santa Fosca hard by, hallowed by the relics of the martyr-virgin whose name it bears, stolen, as were many other Venetian relics, from a foreign town, by Venetian merchants; and the old church of Murano, with a tesselated pavement like that of St. Mark, named and hallowed, in like manner, by the relics of a saint, of San Donato, Bishop of Evorea in Epirus, stolen, in like manner, too, by the Doge Michieli, in the 12th century, from Cephalonia; and fain, likewise, would he, for a few moments, dwell on the little church of San Lazzaro, buried in its green gardens on its quiet island, with its peaceful monastery of learned Armenians, its extensive library, its curious laboratory, its polyglott printing-press, its peculiar worship, its mosque-like minaret, its pleasant chimes, its Register of guests; and last, though far from least, its memories of Byron. There is, too, a gray old edifice on the island of the Lido, the age and the site of which might well claim a recording word:—the Lido, where the great melancholy voice of the Adriatic roars forth an eternal requiem to the buried Hebrews of the neighboring cemetery:—the Lido, where the brave French seaman, Admiral Count Villaret-Joyeuse, sleeps his last sleep, within reach, at his own petition, of the solemn and ceaseless murmurs and even of the dashing spray, of that ocean he loved so well:—the Lido, along whose drifted sands poor Byron daily galloped, composing his mournful verses the while, and longing for a quiet rest beneath:—the Lido, from whose bleaching shores is beheld a scene, when the summer-sun goes down behind the towers and domes of Venice—behind the blue Friulian mountains—behind the romantic Tyrol—behind the mighty Alps—flooding sea, and land, and city, and mountain-top with a deluge of glory—which neither pen nor pencil, nor poet, even, however inspired, can ever hope to portray!

But this must cease. What strange fascination have these old churches of Venice for an imaginative mind! What melancholy, yet absorbing, interest is inspired by their time-stained walls, their mouldering monuments, their crumbling tombs, their glorious paintings, their gorgeous altars! How many generations have paced their pavements and sleep beneath them! What wondrous scenes have they not witnessed in their centuries of by-gone existence! what startling events beheld! what strange histories recorded! What a world of august and mighty memories, and dim traditions, and solemn legends, and hoary chronicles, haunt and hallow their consecrated aisles!

For himself, the writer may well say, that some of the calmest and most contemplative hours he has ever known, have been passed in the churches of Venice; while, to that magic and beautiful city, so long his abode, in no terms could he more truthfully say farewell, than in those of her adopted bard—

"And of the happiest moments which were wrought
Within the web of his existence, some
From thee, fair Venice! have their colors caught."

Part First.

VENICE IN '96—97.

Her Fall.

How art thou destroyed that was inhabited of sea-faring men, the renowned city, which wast strong in the sea!

EZEKIEL xxvi. 17.

VENICE IN '96-97.

CHAPTER I.

ALLIANCE.

THE Fall of Venice, at the close of the last century, was one of the most memorable events in the annals of modern times. Despite her odious despotism, her incredible corruption, her detestable duplicity, her deplorable decrepitude, History has no record of a fall so sudden and so irretrievable, after a career so extended and so extraordinary.

In 1788, Luigi Manini, a member of the lowest class of the Venetian nobility—a class, which, in his person, for the first time and the last, attained the Ducal dignity—succeeded Paolo Reniero as Doge; and, nearly at the same time, the outburst of the French Revolution shook every state in Europe to its centre. Venice alone remained unmoved, or, if moved at all, true to her aristocratic instincts and interests, she sympathized and sided with the absolute Powers; although, unlike them, she raised no bulwark against the coming storm. Thus, in 1791, when the Count of Artois, brother to the unhappy Louis XVI., and subsequently King of France as Charles X., passed through her states, she honored him with every distinction due a prince of the blood. She signed, also, at Mantua, with the courts of the North and the court of Naples, a secret treaty, which had for its object the restoration of the French Monarchy; and she afforded to the fugitive Count of Lille, afterwards Louis XVIII., an asylum at Verona. But when, a few months later, by the Convention of Pilnitz, the basis of this treaty was annulled, Venice again fell back on her neutrality and aristocracy. She refused to receive a manifesto from the French National Assembly, but she resisted with equal obstinacy all the solicitations of the Coalition. In 1793, on the declaration of a Republic, she withdrew her ambassador from Paris—though a Republic herself in name; but, after the fall of Robespierre, impressed by the ascendancy of the new power, she, like Prussia and Tuscany, renewed with it her diplomatic relations, sent an Envoy to felicitate the Convention on its triumphs, consented to receive a Minister in return, and, in compliance with remonstrances of the Directory, gave notice to the Count of Lille to quit Verona.

In 1794, Louis XVI. having perished on the scaffold, and the heir to the throne, Louis XVII., being a minor, as well as a prisoner in the Temple, the Count of Lille assumed the title of Regent of the Realm of France. On his route from Turin for Vienna, he stopped at Verona, and there lived in seclusion in order to avoid honors from the Republic of Venice, by which it might become compromised. In 1795, by the decease of his nephew,* he became

* The unfortunate son of Louis XVI. as every one knows, is asserted *not* to have "died of scrofula, in the Temple, at Paris, at the age of ten, June 8, 1795, under charge of Simon the cobbler," as was given out by the Directory. The earliest tale of his evasion recites that he fled to Vendée from Paris, and thence to Venice *via* Trieste; whence, finally, he repaired to Rome, where he remained under the charge of Pope Pius VII., until the latter's seizure by Napoleon. A few years before, a young drummer, in the regiment Belgiogoso had declared himself the Dauphin, in order to escape a flogging; and he was so received at Turin, for some weeks. But, failing to convince his judges, he confessed himself the son of a watchmaker of Versailles. Shortly afterwards, the peasants of Western France were sure they had the Dauphin in the person of a young laborer: and, in

Louis XVIII., King of France; and England recognized his right by sending him an ambassador at Verona. It was then that the French Directory formally desired of Querini, the Venetian Envoy at Paris, the exclusion of the prince from the Venetian states. The request was granted by the Senate by a vote of 144 ballots to 43, and the exile was at once desired to withdraw: and it was then that the fugitive monarch returned his celebrated reply:—" *Je partirai, mais j' exige qu' on me présente le livre d'or, pour que j' en efface le nom de ma famille, et je reclame l' armure, dont l' amitie de mon aïeul, Henri IV., avait don à la République.*" The royal exile then retired from the States of Venice and repaired to the camp of the emigrant army of the Prince of Condè on the Rhine. Shortly after his arrival an assassin's ball grazed his head! The Aulic council at Vienna, thinking his presence in the camp liable to aggravate difficulties between Austria and the French Republic, desired him to depart; and he declining, a detachment of troops was despatched to enforce the request! He then retired to Blankenburg, in Prussia, while his brother, the Count of Artois, for some time resided in Scotland. English writers have not failed to denounce the conduct of Venice towards "the Pretender." They seem not to recollect, that their own government, just sixty years before, under the guidance of the Duke of Newcastle, had

1799, Fouché arrested and imprisoned another pretender. The stories of the later aspirants to royal birth—Hervagault, Richemont, Naundorff, Breman, and, latest of all, Williams, are familiar to all. Venice seems to have always been a famous resort for broken-down dethroned, disguised, or pretended princes. The Count of Chambord lives at Venice. In the *dogat* of Grimani, in 1598, a pretender to the crown of Sebastian of Portugal, who was slain at the battle of Alcazer, appeared at Venice. But, though claimed by the priesthood of the Peninsula as the "true prince," he was, upon demand of the Spanish ambassador, imprisoned during two years, when, being released, he was seized in Tuscany, and yielded to his foes.

indignantly ordered the Venetian ambassador to quit London in twenty-four hours, because the Venetian Senate had accorded the unfortunate Charles Edward, another "Pretender," distinctions due his rank, when, as Count of Albany, in 1737, he visited the Lagune; and that, during a period of seven years, no apology nor mediation could obtain renewal of amity!*

On the 21st of March, 1795, the same year of the occurrence of these events, General Bonaparte was promoted by the French Directory from the command of the Army of the Interior to that of the Army of Italy, in place of General Scherer, removed for incapacity. In high spirits the young General-in-chief, then in his twenty-seventh year, at once started for the Head-quarters at Nice, saying,—"In three months I shall be at Milan,† or at Paris,"—indicative of his desperate purpose.

"You are young to assume the command of the army of Italy," said Barras, as Napoleon was setting out. "In one year," was the prompt reply, "I shall be old, or—dead!" To Josephine, to whom he had been married but two days, and to whom he owed his appointment, he said,—"I owe you much; but I will either lose my head, or the world shall one day see me greater than it now expects."

The French army at Nice—numbering but 30,000 men, while that of Austria on the Italian frontier, strengthened by her allies of Naples and Sardinia, numbered 80,000‡—Napoleon found in the most destitute and disorganized condition; but from the summit of Mount Zemolo, he pointed out lovely Italy at its feet; and, breathing into it his own intrepid and enterprising spirit, he entered at once on that series of remarkable victories, commencing April 10th,

* The Earl of Holdernesse was sent as Envoy Extraordinary, 1745.

† Napoleon entered Milan, May 15th, one month after his first battle, Montenotte.

‡ Austria had also 200,000 men on the Rhine—Moreau's army being far less.

1796, at Montenotte, and terminating January 14th, 1797, at Rivoli—victories which have astonished, and still astonish the world. The results of these brilliant triumphs are condensed in his order of the day of March 9th, at Bassano, when about entering on his sixth campaign within a single year, by marching through the Tyrol and Carinthia over the snow-clad ridges of the Noric and Julian Alps, to dictate peace at the gates of Vienna:—"Soldiers! The fall of Mantua has terminated the war in Italy. You have been victorious in fourteen pitched battles and seventy combats. You have made 100,000 prisoners, taken 500 pieces of field-artillery, 2,000 cannon, and four sets of pontoons. The contributions you have levied on the vanquished countries have clothed, fed, and paid the army; and you have, besides, sent 30,000,000 francs to the public treasury. You have enriched the Museum of Paris with 300 *chefs-d'œuvre* of art, the produce of thirty centuries. You have conquered the finest countries in Europe. The Transpadane and Cispadane Republics owe to you their freedom. The French colors, for the first time, appear on the shores of the Adriatic, and within twenty-four hours' sail of the country of Alexander! Sardinia, Naples, Parma, the Pope, have ceased to be foes, and solicit friendship. You have chased the English from Leghorn, Genoa, Corsica. Of all the foes of the Republic the Emperor alone remains."

And thus, within a period of ten months, an army of 30,000 men, reinforced but once, and then by only 20,000 men, had defeated four Austrian armies, thrice reinforced, numbering 200,000!

It was early in the month of June, 1796, that the French army crossed the frontiers of Venice. On entering Brescia, Napoleon issued a proclamation, in which he declared, that, in passing through the Venetian territory, in pursuit of the Austrian army, to which passage had been granted both to come and to return,—he should respect the territory and the inhabitants of the Republic; that he should make his army observe the strictest discipline; that whatever it should take should be paid for; and, that he would not forget the old ties which united the two republics. "The French army," he said, "to follow the wreck of the Austrian army, must pass over the Republic of Venice; but, it will never forget, that ancient friendship unites the two republics. Religion, government, customs and property, will be respected. The General-in-chief engages the government to make known these sentiments to the people, in order that confidence may cement that friendship which has so long united the two nations."

His reception by the Venetian *Provveditore** at Brescia was cordial; and he continued his march until opposed by Beaulieu, before the Mincio, at the town of Peschiera, a place belonging to Venice, which the Austrian general had taken by stratagem and strongly garrisoned. Venice had not attempted to recover the place; it, therefore, ceased to be neutral, and cost Napoleon a battle to capture—an event of which he did not fail subsequently to remind her Senate.

In Venice, the rapid approach of the French army caused profoundest concern and agitation. By many of the citizens, Venetian despotism, it is true, was hated; but hatred of foreign domination was not less. Besides, there was a natural love of country, and a pride in a government, whose soil, for fourteen centuries, had been unpolluted by a foreign footstep. By the Senate, a question often agitated before, whether to take part with Austria, or France, or with neither, was now discussed anew. The old oligarchs advocated an alliance with Austria—a despotism herself and the natural ally of despotisms, whatever the name they bore. The young oligarchs

* Envoy, ambassador, minister proconsul.

proposed an armed neutrality of 50,000 men against both of the belligerents; while alliance with France was, by a third party—the Party of the People—deemed the only expedient course. In this dilemma, Battaglia, a sage old Senator, gave counsel to the Senate which the events of time have almost dignified into prophecy. Neutrality, whether armed or unarmed, he pronounced madness. Venice had no power to challenge respect; and, sooner or later, she would, inevitably, be crushed between the contending nations, and sacrificed by both in turn as a victim, when required. To decide for France, or for Austria, was, therefore, indispensable. Austria was driven from Italy. Alliance with her, at present, would draw down immediate vengeance from France. Besides, Austria had always coveted Upper Italy and Illyria; and, soon or late, would strive for them. The only protection against this ambition was France, a power which could never covet territory so distant from her own. The republican principles of France were, to be sure, repugnant to the nobility of Venice; but the old Nestor declared, that some sacrifices to the spirit of the age were indispensable, and that concessions to the nobles of the *terra firma*, and their admission to the Golden Book, could alone bind them to the Republic. A few modifications and reforms, and the old constitution of Venice might be rendered tolerable to all parties; and, then, in an event of aiding France by arms, Venice would, doubtless, receive a portion of the Austrian territory in fair Lombardy. At any rate, neutrality was the most perilous policy to be adopted.

But the pride and prejudice of the old Oligarchy, a lingering doubt of the permanence of French power, and a vivid dread of Austrian vengeance, unhappily forbade the adoption of this sage counsel, and drove the timid, but haughty, Senate into the unwise decision of unarmed neutrality—of all possible policies the very worst. To send *Provveditori* to the French general assuring him of the neutrality of Venice and presenting her claims to respect, and to issue general orders that the officers and soldiers of the army should be everywhere conciliated by the best possible treatment—this was the course resolved on.

As for Napoleon, prudence, just then, was hardly less essential to him than to Venice. Her power was still too considerable to be trifled with; while presence upon her soil for the French army, and provisions while there, were indispensable. Besides, neutrality had not forbidden her to supply the Austrians; and the fact that Beaulieu, by the possession of Peschiera, a Venetian town, though gained by stratagem, had cost him a battle, Bonaparte knew well how to use to advance his claims.

The *Provveditore* appointed, in accordance with the decision of the senate, to repair to Napoleon at Peschiera, was an old noble, a Venetian of the Venetians, an oligarch of the oligarchs, imbued with hate and horror of the French, whose name was Foscarinli. The conquest of Italy, the pillage of Pavia,* the furious passions of the conqueror, all had filled the old man with such terror, that, on setting out on his mission, which was to prevent the occupation of Verona, he is said to have written to the Senate—"May God be pleased to accept me as a victim!"

Verona, which had afforded an asylum to the Bourbon Prince, was in equal trepidation. Napoleon knew his advantages, and he did not fail to avail himself of them. He was, doubtless, often

* Pavia had been pillaged, and Binasco burned—but only to crush a dangerous insurrection, stirred up among the peasants by the priests, which menaced the massacre of the whole of the French army, then reduced to a fragment. It was Napoleon's only severity in Italy, and was, perhaps, unavoidable. Pavia was the only town he ever gave up to pillage; and he could endure the atrocities of his soldiers there [illegible] half the time he had promised.

unreasonably passionate; and, doubtless, he often assumed a passion when he felt it not, when it might tend to the accomplishment of his purposes. In the reception of the Venetian *Provveditore*, therefore, he assumed a passion, because the occupation of the fortress of Peschiera by the imperialists had cost him some troops; and bitterly did he denounce a neutrality which could not maintain itself. The blood of those troops cried aloud for vengeance, and should have it! On mention of Verona, and the prohibition of the Senate of its occupation by either of the belligerents, the young French general again affected a fury. "Venice," said he, "by daring to give an asylum to the Count de Lille, a pretender to the throne of France, has declared war against the Republic. I know not why I should not reduce Verona to ashes—a town which has had the insolence to esteem itself, for a moment even, the capital of the French empire! Massena has marched on that city. At this very instant, perhaps, he punishes it with flames." Finally, however, affecting to be somewhat appeased, he consented to delay entrance into the city for twenty-four hours, if Massena had not already taken it; but then, he should cannonade and bombard it, if not surrendered. The result was inevitable. The terrified Venetian ordered the French to be admitted at once to the military capital of the *Dogado;* and the wealthy Veronese, in great numbers, covered the roads to the Tyrol, bearing their valuables to escape French vengeance. But they soon found that their panic was vain, and returned unmolested to their homes.

At Verona, Napoleon received another commission from Venice, composed of the Senators Battaglia and Erizzo. Of these envoys he demanded supplies for his army, and requested the alliance of Venice with France. The *demand* was acceded to; and it was agreed that a Jew contractor should supply the army, and that

Venice should secretly pay him, and subsequently settle with France. The *request* of Napoleon, however, was declined, though strongly urged. "He had been sent," he said, "to drive Austria beyond the Alps, and, perhaps, to make Lombardy an independent state. This was direct service to Venice; and if, with her 50,000 Sclavonians and her brave mountaineers of the main land, she would assist him, her reward was sure." But it was all in vain. Venice clung to her ancient policy.

The presence of the French republicans in Italy had now begun to exert its natural influence. The despotism of Venice was deemed more intolerable than ever by the towns on the *terra firma.* Brescia was already prepared to revolt. A quadruple alliance between France, Spain, Venice, and the Porte, had been proposed, and was most pertinaciously urged by emissaries of France. Spain, however, was the only power that yielded to these solicitations. The Porte held back for Venice; and Venice, since she had witnessed the rapid propagation of democracy by the French, hated and dreaded them too much to become their ally. She even began secretly to arm against them. All her disposable troops and all her ships at the Ionian Isles were ordered to the Lagune; and her Sclavonian regiments were called from Illyria. Funds, also, were collected by taxes and donations, and the peasants of the Bergamesco were secretly armed and equipped by their *Provveditore*, Ottolini. All this Napoleon loudly denounced, though he was secretly not displeased, as it afforded him a pretext to demand continued supplies, and kept open a quarrel which might, eventually, facilitate his designs.

Affairs were in this position, when, late in July, old Wurmser debouched from the Tyrol at the head of 60,000 men; and, in a campaign of six days, the 30,000 French had routed twice their number, killing and wounding 25,000, and taking 15,000 prisoners, with a loss of only 7,000 men! All Venetia was horror-struck! In course of the campaign, when the French army left Verona, the citizens had openly expressed their joy, and had welcomed its foes; yet, when that same army again appeared before the city, and in triumph, the *Provveditore* modestly demanded a delay of two hours before opening the gates, in order to afford his friends, the Austrians, time to save their baggage in evacuating the place! The reply was a cannonade which soon put an end to all resistance. But, sparing the city and state any infliction of his wrath, Napoleon merely renewed his complaints to the Senate, because of its warlike preparations, and demanded supplies in future *at her own cost*, at the same time soliciting her alliance.

But it was in vain it was urged on Venice, that Russia coveted her colonies in Greece, and Austria her provinces in Illyria, while, alliance with the Porte and France would shield against both foes possessions of the Republic desirable to neither of her allies: that French valor insured her against the return and vengeance of the Austrians, which her own army and navy would render yet more impossible, if put on a war footing; while neutrality gained her not a single friend, but exposed her to the probability of being crushed by both belligerents, or of being made a medium of accommodation between them.* But Venice hated the French and their principles, and feared them, too, more than she feared or hated the ambition of Austria or of Russia. Under pretence, therefore, of maintaining her old policy of neutrality, she continued arming, and evidently against France; for she consulted the Austrian cabinet about a Gen-

* Lord Chesterfield, in the middle of the last century, predicted, that the security Venice owed to her neutrality would last no longer, than one of the great powers engrossed Italy—an event possible in his own century, probable in the next.

eral for her forces. Meantime, however, she supplied abundance of provisions to the French army. Meantime, also, came the victories of Roveredo, Bassano, and St. George; and, when the Veronese saw the French retreating one night by the Milan gate, and, three days afterwards returning by that of Venice, after the brilliant victory of Arcolo, they could no longer hope that the French could be driven out of Italy. The victories of Rivoli and La Favorita in January, and the surrender of Mantua on the opening of the following month, completed the conquest of Italy.* The equipment of armaments in the Lagune, and the arming of peasants in the mountains of Bergamesco, however, still continued; but the only step taken against this by Napoleon was the temporary occupation of the town of Bergamo, which, though it had a Venetian garrison, was declared unable to resist a surprise from the Austrians.

Prussia, at this time, proposed an alliance with Venice, offering to guarantee her integrity in case the belligerents should undertake to accommodate their differences at her expense. But the Queen of the Sea treated this proposal in the same manner as she had already treated those of the belligerents themselves. She would give her hand—she would yield her liberty, to none.

This was error—fatal error. In the iconoclastic strife, which, at that period, was raging throughout Europe, dashing sceptres into atoms and causing thrones to tremble and to crumble—breaking up the old order of things and fashioning all things anew—Venice should have foreseen, that her timid policy of neutrality was impossible to be sustained—that, of all other policies, it was the most perilous and impracticable—that of all other governments, hers was the most

* Mallet Dupan, of the French Directory, in his secret correspondence with Venice, writes from Paris after the battle of Rivoli, February, '97—"Half Europe is at the knees of this Divan, vying for the honor of becoming its tributary."

odious to the image-breaking reformers abroad, and most hateful to her own oppressed, but fiery subjects, at home; and that, by the one, or by the other, or by the combined assaults of both, she must finally fall—even as she did. More than once during the campaigns of 1796 was the balance of power in her own hands; and, had she, even as late as the month of August of that year, when the tide of war had reached her own border, and the invader with but 30,000 troops was about to encounter the veterans Wurmser and Melas with 60,000—had she even then let loose her 50,000 Dalmatians and her 20,000 peasants and mountaineers, the disastrous battles of Castiglione, Roveredo, Bassano, Arcolo, Rivoli, and La Favorita might have been attended with results far different, and her ancient nationality, for a time, at least, have been respected: or, had she accepted the proffered alliance of Prussia, that power might have been able to fulfill her promised guarantee, to protect her against the very evil by which she was finally overtaken, and which was then clearly foreseen by all but herself.

Napoleon was now more pressing than ever in his solicitations for alliance with Venice. He had determined on the grand enterprise of crossing the Julian Alps and advancing to the gates of Vienna; and the amity or enmity of Venice might become to him of the most vital moment. He sent, therefore, for the *Provveditore* Pesaro, and made the most frank and friendly overtures. He represented, that the Venetian towns on *terra firma* were imbued with the revolutionary idea, and that a word from the French would rouse them to insurrection; while, as the friends of Venice, the same French would not only abstain from instigating, but would strive to pacify public feeling, simply by suggesting a few modifications in the ancient constitution. At any rate, the French could and would guarantee their ally against, either the ambition, or the wrath of Austria. Had Venice yielded to these arguments, had she allied herself to France and modified her government, she might, for some years at least, have retained her nationality. But, true to her ancient policy, she once more declined all alliance.

CHAPTER II.

THE VERONESE EASTER.

True to her ancient policy, Venice declined all alliance. But Napoleon could not on this account defer his expedition to Vienna; and, finding further solicitation hopeless, he left behind him some 20,000 men to protect him against the treachery of the weak and perfidious Oligarchy that declined his proposals, but, as events proved, only awaited hoped-for reverses to crush him; and, on the eighteenth of March, commenced his perilous enterprise of crossing the Julian Alps, and dictating peace beneath the walls of the imperial capital. Hardly, however, had he sat out, when the revolutionary spirit in the towns of the *terra firma*, of which he had warned the *Provveditore* Pesaro, broke forth into downright insurrection. The discontent at the despotism of Venice, which had long existed, had been roused by intercourse with the French, and proximity to the Republics of the Po and Lombardy; and everywhere secret clubs and committees were formed, which, in correspondence with the republicans of Milan, openly avowed a wish to throw off the yoke of Venice. The towns of Bergamo and Brescia, which were nearest to Milan, were most agitated. The former secretly demanded of the Milanese whether, or not, they could rely on their support, and that of the Lombard battalion. This demand was revealed to Ottolini, *Podesta* of Bergamo, who had been so active in arming the mountaineers; and he at once sent a courier to inform the State Inquisitors at Venice. But the conspirators, apprised of the discovery, intercepted the courier, and published the names of those the *Podesta* had accused. Ottolini then ordered the arrest of all concerned, which, being attempted on the morning of the twelfth of March, became the signal for revolt.

Napoleon, in his confidential correspondence of the time with the French Directory, states that the revolt at Bergamo was instigated by Captain Landrieux, chief of the cavalry staff, and that he was paid for it; while, at the same time, he revealed the plot to the Venetian *Podesta*, and was paid a second time by him! But, while Landrieux was thus employed to stir up revolt, General Killmaine had received positive orders from Napoleon to take no part in political events; to give neither counsel nor aid to the disaffected, and, to the utmost of his power, to maintain tranquillity. When, therefore, aid was demanded by both parties of the Commandant of the French garrison, it was declined; and the precaution of doubling the posts, in order to maintain tranquillity in the place under his charge, was the only measure adopted. The insurgents then formed a provisional government, declared the town independent, expelled Ottolini and the Venetian troops, sent a request to Milan for aid, and, finally, an address to the Cispadine Republic, which concluded thus —"Let us live, let us fight, and, if necessary, let us die together: thus should all free people do."

From Bergamo a party of the patriots marched to Brescia, already prepared by Landrieux for revolt; and the *Podesta*, Battaglia, having fled, the city was on the 15th declared free. From Brescia, a party repaired to Salo, and thence to Crema, along the base of the mountains; and everywhere the Venetian authorities fled, everywhere the towns were declared free, and everywhere the French looked on as spectators. Roused by these events and by the priests, who came to preach in their hamlets, the mountaineers and peasants, long before armed by Ottolini, now mustered in vast numbers to pour down on the insurgent towns and reduce them, and perhaps, also, to massacre the hated French. Gen. Killmaine, made fully aware of this, sent the Lombard Legion to repress the rising; although had Venetian troops arrived to reclaim the revolted towns, neutrality would have forbidden his interference. Nevertheless, a general rising of the peasants and mountaineers might prove disastrous in the extreme, in the event of Napoleon's defeat in the Tyrol; and to the General-in-chief he, therefore, at once dispatched couriers with the exciting intelligence.

The Venetian Senate, terrified at these events, immediately sent a body of its Sclavonians against the insurgent towns, and, at the same time, demanded of Lallemant, the French minister at Venice, whether it could rely on the friendship of the Directory. The reply was, that, with modifications in its constitution, the Republic of France would support that of Venice. Upon this the lesser Council* assembled to deliberate. For centuries, no public proposition to amend the constitution had been made; and now, out of more than two hundred votes, it obtained but five. Fifty senators were for energetic measures, and 180 were in favor of gradual reform in more quiet times.

This decided, Venice again reverted to negotiation, and two deputies were sent to Napoleon, from the noble families of Cornaro

* *Il Consiglio dei Pregadi*, consisting at first of 601, then of 120, and, in the last days of the Republic, of 310 nobles. *Pregadi*—"selected"—from *pregare*, to pray.

and Pesaro. They reached the head-quarters of the French army at Gorizia, in Carniola, at the same time with the couriers of Killmaine, and just as Bonaparte was settling the capitulation of Trieste, having secured the line of the Alps. He expressed surprise at the intelligence communicated, and, perhaps, felt the annoyance of which he loudly proclaimed. The envoys then demanded that the French should aid Venice to quell the revolt, or restore to her the fortresses of Bergamo, Brescia, Peschiera, and Verona, that she might quell it herself. Napoleon declined to do either. To evacuate these strong places was to leave them open to the chances of the war; while, to arm against the friends of the French and their principles, in favor of those who hated both, was impossible. Besides, had not the French Republic emphatically declared, that it would sustain all nations desirous of liberty? and had it not issued explicit orders to its armies to succor all people oppressed, wherever found? Yet, if Venice would ally herself to France and modify her constitution, peace and order should be restored, by any means the French might possess, short of force. At this apparently wise counsel the envoys revolted, and the conference became warm. The subject of supplies was next treated of. Hitherto, Venice had furnished the French, even as, previously, she had the Austrians. But now, having left her territories, she objected to feeding an absent army: and, having failed to pay her contractors, they had failed to furnish supplies; and to levy "requisitions" on the people had, to the French, become indispensable. But Napoleon opposed such requisitions, either on the Venetians, or on the Austrians, because they vexed the inhabitants, and gave rise to abominable frauds: and he boldly and abruptly demanded a million of francs per month for supplies during the campaign. On being told that the treasury of Venice was bankrupt, the unscrupulous general bade them take money from the Bank-deposite of the Duke of Modena, who had fled thither with his treasures when the French first approached; or, levy it on property of the Russians, Austrians, English, or of any others of the foes of the French Republic, found in their city!

At a second interview Napoleon became furious.* "What would you have?" he exclaimed. "I offer you alliance; do you accept?" "No," was the reply: "Venice rejoices in the victories of France, and relies on her for existence; but, true to her ancient and wise policy, she would remain neutral. Besides, what could she effect as an ally? She is not now as when Louis XII. or Francis I. asked her aid." "But your armaments?" interrupted Napoleon. "Are indispensable," was the reply. "Brescia, Bergamo, Salo, Crema, Chiari, are in revolt. Verona is in danger. Venice itself is agitated." "Well," rejoined Bonaparte, "accept my alliance and these troubles cease: they are arguments for, not against it. But your fate hurries you on. Be then neutral, since you will! I consent. I march on Vienna; but I leave troops to control you. I know your designs. Beware! If, when on my distant campaign, you murder my sick, attack my depots, intercept my convoys, interrupt my communications, cut off my detachments, menace my retreat, you have sealed your own ruin! Your Republic is no more! Things pardonable while I was in Italy will be crimes when I am in Germany. If you take up arms, your Republic or my army must perish. Reflect; and hazard not the infirm Lion of St. Mark against the fortune of an army, in whose very hospitals could be found troops to cross your Lagune and crush you." With these words Napoleon sent home the terrified envoys, and at once ordered Killmaine to disarm all peasants and mountaineers, but, at the same time, to maintain the strictest neutrality.

* He was as fluent in Italian as in French.

There was necessity for this order. In the single month of March, from the 12th to the 28th, Bergamo, Brescia, Salo and Crema had thrown off the Venetian yoke. The Sclavonians were advancing to reduce them; and the Lombard Legion was marching to disarm the peasants. Skirmishes ensued, villages were burned, towns were sacked, the French, wherever met singly, were assassinated. Salo, a fortified place on the Lake of Garda, was seized; two hundred Poles of the Lombard Legion were taken and sent to the leads and pits of Venice, and the canal of Orfano was said to be choked with victims! The mountaineers of the Bergamesco, pouring down on 1200 Brescians who were advancing on Salo, had taken prisoners the two hundred Poles, as mentioned, and sent them to Venice. Immediately afterwards, 10,000 armed peasants appeared before Brescia; but they were driven back to their mountains by Killmaine, and Salo was retaken.

These events caused great excitement in Venice. The Senate resolved by a large majority to act vigorously against the insurgents, without openly declaring against the French,—deciding even by a vote of 192 out of 200, to give the million of francs a month demanded for supplies. Was ever duplicity more profound? It was worthy even of Venice! At the same time, the retreat of one division of the French from the Tyrol, an irruption of Croatians into Friuli, the re-capture of Fiume and Trieste, and the advance of the Austrian General, Laudohn, excited extravagant hopes of the speedy defeat of the French. Rumor proclaimed that Laudohn was descending from the Tyrol at the head of 60,000 men—that Napoleon had been defeated in the Alps, and that his ultimate ruin was inevitable—was absolutely certain!

Such was the rumor; but, far otherwise was the fact. It was true, that the French division under Serrurier had been driven out of the Tyrol by Laudohn with 12,000 Austrians and peasants, and forced to seek refuge in the fortress of Verona: and it was true that the Croats had expelled the French garrisons from Trieste and Fiume. But it was, also, true, that Napoleon by a succession of wonderful victories, had driven the Archduke Charles over the Julian Alps—had planted his outposts on the summit of the Sommering, whence they could look down on the towers of Vienna twenty-five leagues distant—had filled that splendid capital with such panic, that the crown and the imperial family—(among them Maria Louisa, the future empress of France, then six years old)—were embarked in boats on the Danube for Hungary—and, finally, had compelled the armistice and Preliminaries of Leoben; and all within the period of a single month! At the passage of the Tagliamento, on the icy summit of the *Col di Tarwis*, in the fearful gorge of Neumark, on every crag and in every pass of the dread Noric Alps, the impetuous charge of Napoleon had swept away the iron files of the Archduke Charles,* even as the howling blasts of winter had swept the sleet and the snow around him!

The bulletin of Napoleon, on commencing the campaign, had been dated the 9th of March, at Bassano, and the armistice bore date at the village of Leoben, on the 7th of April. Two days afterwards, Killmaine's couriers brought intelligence of the events at Salo, the irruption of the peasants, the seizure of the friends of France, the murder of the French, the imprisonment of the Poles. Furious at these accumulated outrages, Napoleon at once charged his first aide-de-camp, Junot, with "a thundering letter" to the Venetian Senate, in which, having recapitulated his alleged grievances, he demanded the disbanding of their forces, the disarming of the mountaineers, the delivery of the assassins, and the liberation of

* The Archduke, like Napoleon, was then about 27 years old.

the Poles and Patriots. "All the continent of the mighty Republic of Venice is in arms," he wrote: "on all sides the rallying cry of peasants armed by you is—'*Death to the French!*' Hundreds of soldiers of the army of Italy have fallen victims! In vain do you deny the organization of these assassins. Think you, because I am in the heart of Germany, I am unable to make the first nation in the universe respected? Think you the legions of Italy will suffer the massacres you incite? The blood of my brothers in arms shall be avenged! Not a battalion have I whose courage would not be redoubled by a charge of vengeance so noble. The Senate of Venice has responded with blackest perfidy to my generous treatment. I send you my first aide-de-camp bearer of this letter. War or Peace? If you take not immediate steps to disperse your brigands, if you do not arrest and deliver into my hands the authors of the assassinations you have perpetrated, war is declared!"

This menacing manifesto Junot was ordered to read to the Senate in person; and, if its demands were not satisfied, to bid Lallemant quit Venice at once, after having posted in the Piazza a declaration of war.

On the 15th, the rough soldier was introduced into the Senate, and read the "thundering letter" of his General in thundering tones, to the dismay of the intimidated nobles. They strove to palliate the offences with which they were charged, and, finally succeeded in pacifying Junot, by agreeing to write to the French General, and send to him two deputies to arrange the satisfaction demanded. The deputies selected were the senators Donato and Giustiniani.

But while, on the 15th of April, it was known at Venice that Napoleon had compelled the Austrians to ask an armistice, it was still believed at Verona that he had been utterly defeated. The retreat of Serrurier from the Tyrol before Laudohn and the peasants to Verona, and the retreat of the garrisons of Trieste and Fiume before the Croats, who had risen like the Tyrolese, to Palma Nuova —although events of but slight general importance, had served to confirm this belief, despite all the explanations of the French minister at Venice. Shut up in the mountains—with the Austrians in front, the Hungarians and Croatians on the right, the Tyrolese and Laudohn on the left—the infatuated Venetians supposed that they had only to rise in the rear to crush forever the last fragment of the French army in Italy. In the Veronese, therefore, the agitation had become intense and general; and the Venetian party, sanguine in their convictions of the overthrow of Bonaparte in the Alps, were resolved at once to expurgate their military capital of its abhorred invaders. This was to be effected in a manner truly Venetian—by a *conspiracy*, involving all the horrors of general massacre; and the day fixed for the event was April 17th, the very day when the Preliminaries of Leoben were finally signed—the very day that the Venetian envoys started from Venice to strive to appease the wrath of the French conqueror, infuriated by prior atrocities; it was Easter Monday, which, from the bloody events it was destined to witness, was henceforth to deserve a title as memorable in History as that of "The Sicilian Vespers"*—"*The Veronese Easter!*"

The citadel of Verona was held by the French troops of General Balland. The city was full of Sclavonian and Italian troops in the service of Venice; and, on the 16th, the number was augmented by

* The universal massacre of the French in Sicily was precipitated by a gross insult of a soldier to a young bride at Palermo, on her way to church, while the bells rang for vespers, March 30, 1282. The French were distinguished from Italians by the mispronunciation of the words *ceci* and *ciceri*, and 4000 were slain. The tyranny of Charles of Anjou and the Guelphs ceased with the Sicilian Vespers. An insulted husband brought the Gauls to Rome: an insulted bride drove the French from Sicily.

a reinforcement of 3,000, under Gen. Fioravente. On the same day, bands of peasants came pouring down from the Alpine valleys of the Tyrol and Friul, in advance of the column of Laudohn, roused by the fanatic harangues of their priests, and true to their nationality—which bands, added to those who had already descended, flooded the plains around Verona with 20,000 half-savage *contadini.* All communication between the French in the citadel with their compatriots in the neighboring towns was now cut off; and the indiscriminate slaughter of all detached parties who failed to reach the fortresses was at once commenced. Capuchins preached merciless massacre on Easter Sunday, which was the 16th, and a manifesto, invoking the people to sweep the French from the soil of Italy, was in every hand. This document bore the signature of Battaglia, *Podesta* of Verona, one of the wisest of the Venetian Senators, and one who had, from the first, counselled alliance with France. It was, of course, a forgery, and is said to have been written at Milan by a republican agent named Salvador, and distributed by the infamous Captain Landrieux, in order to involve Venice in strife with the French, and bring matters to a crisis. The manifesto more than fulfilled the purpose of its creation. It gave concentration to the movement, while it inflamed the people to fury. At length, all was completed, and on Easter Eve, a message was sent by the chiefs of the conspiracy at Verona, requesting Laudohn to advance the following day and receive the city. Bourienne passed through Verona, on his route from Paris to Napoleon, on the evening of the 16th; and, if the account of the scenes he witnessed was detailed by the secretary to his old comrade as vividly in person as in his "Memoirs" to the world, it is no wonder that the French General exclaimed in fury before he had half concluded—"*Sois tranquille; ces coquins lá me le paieront; leur Republique a vécu!*" After stopping two hours at Verona, the Secretary pursued his route, ignorant of the impending massacre. A league from the city, he was stopped by a band of 2,000 peasants who required him to cry—"*Viva San Marco!*" and then hurried on to Verona. "What would have become of me," naively asks Bourienne, "had I been at Verona on Monday, instead of Sunday?" On that terrible day the church-bells were rung while the French were butchered in the hospitals! Every one met in the streets was put to death. The priests headed the assassins; and—"*Death to all Frenchmen!*" was the rallying cry. The very day after Bourienne passed from Verona to Vicenza, *en route*, all Frenchmen on the road were massacred; and, hardly had he passed Padua, on his way to Venice, than he learned that he had escaped, as if by miracle, the assassin's dagger on the road from Vicenza! "Thus," says he, "assassination travelled as rapidly as the Post."

General Balland could not be blind to the menacing events of Saturday and Sunday; and, while he complained to the Venetian authorities of the insulting treatment of his troops, and in vain sought explanation of the military movements going on in the city, he ordered his men to be ready at any instant to retire to the citadel, and despatched couriers to Milan and Mantua for reinforcements. His apprehensions were not unfounded. On the morning of Easter Monday, bands of armed peasants poured into the city, shouting—"*Death to the Jacobins!*" At noon, shrill whistlings were heard all over Verona. It was the concerted signal for massacre, and the work of blood began. Every Frenchman, or "Jacobin," found in the streets was pitilessly slain; the guards at the gates were overpowered and butchered; four hundred French soldiers in the hospitals were slaughtered, and their corpses were beheld by the garrison crimsoning the waves of the Adige! The troops could no longer be restrained. A shower of red-hot balls was poured from the batteries of the fortress on the roofs of the city, and conflagration added its horrors to the scene. A flag of truce from the Venetian magistrates brought the menace of the indiscriminate massacre of a number of refugees, who had sought asylum in the Government Palace, if the cannonade did not at once cease. Balland responded with a demand for their immediate release, and, also, for the disarming of the populace, for the sending off the peasants and Dalmatians, and for the delivery of hostages in guarantee of submission : while the brave Beaupoil volunteered to beat his way through the raging billows which inundated the streets, to treat in the Government Palace on the surrender of the city. Hostages were refused ; guaranties against the wrath of Bonaparte were demanded ; the massacre continued all night, despite the truce ; the magistracy, powerless to restrain the masses, abdicated and fled ; the intrepid Beaupoil by miracle regained the fortress ; the cannonade and consequent conflagrations again commenced ; and, finally, another parley was demanded by prominent citizens who had now assumed command. But, even while this conference was going on, atrocities continued, and the garrison of Fort Chiusa on the Adige, which capitulated from famine, was butchered, in revenge for the cannonade of Verona ; and every Frenchman in every village around the capital was slaughtered by the ferocious peasantry !

Such were the massacres named by Napoleon—*Les Pâques Veronaises.* But retribution was at hand—close at hand. On Tuesday, the 18th, intelligence of the armistice at Leoben arrived, and Laudohn retired towards the Tyrol as rapidly as he had advanced. Thursday, General Chabron appeared with 1200 men, and, after a bloody fight with the Sclavonians under Fioravante, invested the town on every side. The Lombard Legion of 800 men, and General Baraguay d'Hilliers with his division followed. Sunday, the 23d, intelligence of the signature of the Preliminaries arrived. The die was now cast. The Venetian authorities of Verona repaired again to General Balland, demanding a parley, and guaranties against the wrath of Bonaparte. Both being refused, they once more abdicated, and on Friday, April 28th, after an insurrection of twelve days, the city was unconditionally surrendered by a "Provisional Municipality."

The populace were now as slavish in submission, as they had been atrocious in outrage. It was difficult to restrain the French troops, but the pillage and rapine were brief. The chiefs of the massacres were shot; the peasants were disarmed or cut in pieces upon resistance; a fine of 1,100,000 francs was imposed; a courier was despatched to Bonaparte; Generals Victor and Killmaine occupied Vicenza and Padua; and the Venetians, from the Campanile of St. Mark, beheld the flaunting tricolor and the victorious troops of France approaching their Lagune.

Meanwhile, a most unhappy event had occurred at Venice itself—an event not unlike those at Verona. On Sunday, the 23d of April, a lugger of four guns, belonging to the French flotilla in the Adriatic, and commanded by Captain Laugier, pursued by two Austrian frigates, sought refuge under the batteries of the Lido, with a salute of nine guns. An ancient ordinance of the Venetian Senate forbade the entrance of an armed vessel at the port of the Lido. Despite a storm that was coming up, and the presence of the hostile ships, the lugger was, therefore, at once ordered off; but, while obeying the command, the batteries of the fort opened upon her a tremendous cannonade. The captain ordered his men below, and went on deck with his trumpet to repeat that he was retiring; and while engaged in this brave act, was killed with two of his crew. Venetian galleys filled with Sclavonians then boarded the vessel. Several more of the crew were massacred, eleven were wounded, and the residue were carried to Venice captives. Next day the senate decreed a reward to the Commandant of the Lido "for having enforced respect for the laws of Venice!"

In view of this event, as also of those at Verona, the principle has been appositely cited, that pusillanimity and cruelty are closely allied with slavery; and that none are so humane as the brave and the free.

CHAPTER III.

VENGEANCE.

INTELLIGENCE of the massacre at Verona, of the suppression of the revolt, and of the signature of the Preliminaries of Peace at Leoben, reached Venice immediately upon the occurrence of the deplorable, and most unjustifiable outrage, at the Lido, and the Senate was in consternation. Fresh instructions were sent to the envoys despatched to Bonaparte; and, with fear and trembling, they obtained admission to his presence at Gratz, the capital of Lower Styria, on the 25th of April, on his return route to Italy. He had heard of the massacre at Verona of the 17th, from Bourienne and the couriers of Killmaine; and, in a dispatch to the Directory had said—"The only course left us is to destroy this ferocious and sanguinary government, and erase the name of Venice from the face of the earth." But he had not then heard of the affair of the Lido of the 23d.

Receiving with courtesy the trembling deputies, and dissembling his rage, he listened to them at great length. Then, without noticing their explanations, he exclaimed—"Are the prisoners released? Are the murderers punished? Are the peasants disarmed? I want no empty words. My soldiers have been massacred. I must have vengeance—vengeance!" The terrified envoys faltered forth something about the disorders incident to insurrection, and the difficulty of discovering murderers. "A government served by spies so well as yours should know the instigators and perpetrators of those murders," was the bitter reply. "But it is as despised as it is despicable. It cannot disarm those it has armed. I will disarm them for it. But my prisoners—are they free?" Donato began replying that the *French* were free. "I will have them all—all—all!" furiously interrupted Bonaparte—"all in prison because of political sentiments. I will go myself and demolish your dungeons—your leads—your Bridge of Sighs. I will be a second Attila to Venice. I will have no Inquisition—no Golden Book—institutions of a barbarous age; opinions shall be free. Your government is antiquated—it must be destroyed. At Gorizia I offered to Pesaro alliance. It was rejected. You awaited my return to cut me off. Well, here I am: but I treat no more. I dictate. I might have gone to Vienna, but I chose to accept peace. I have eighty thousand men and twenty gun-boats. Now, if all the prisoners are not at once set free, if the English Envoy is not dismissed, the people disarmed, the murderers surrendered, I declare instant war. If you have nothing new to reply, I can only add that you can go."

Upon reception of intelligence of the outrage at the Lido, the envoys, not daring to seek the presence of the infuriated general, addressed him a most submissive letter, offering every possible explanation and atonement. "No," replied Bonaparte; "I cannot receive you, covered all over with French blood. When you have delivered into my hands the three State Inquisitors, the Commandant of the Lido, and the Chiefs of the Venetian Police, I may hear your attempted palliation of unpardonable crimes." Atonement of another kind, which had often proven serviceable to Venice in her need—which formed, indeed, a part of her cardinal policy, was hinted at. "No—no—no!" replied the hero; "could you proffer me the treasures of Peru—could you pave your whole *Dogado* with gold—it could not pay me for the blood of the meanest of my Frenchmen, so treacherously slain!"

The envoys were dismissed. It was May 2d. War against Venice was next day declared. Assuming hostilities already commenced by Venice at Verona and the Lido, Bonaparte, whose powers did not authorize him to declare war, announced in his manifesto his purpose to repel the assaults of Venice to the utmost; and, to this end, he gave notice to Lallemant, the French Ambassador, to withdraw from that city, and ordered the Winged Lion of St. Mark to be overthrown wherever found, and the Tree of Liberty substituted in its place. He also ordered the towns of the main land to be municipalized, the old government to be declared defunct, and General Killmaine to proceed with the divisions of Victor and Baraguay d' Hilliers, to the border of the Lagune, there to await the troops coming down from the Julian Alps, to complete the besieging force.

Napoleon's manifesto declaring war, was published at Palma Nuova, on the 3d of May. It set forth, that Venice had availed herself of Holy Week to organize war against France; that vast bodies of peasantry were armed and disciplined by troops sent out of the capital; that a crusade against the French was preached in all the churches; that detached bodies were murdered and the sick in the hospitals massacred; that the crew of a French brig had been slaughtered under the eyes of the Senate, and the murderers publicly rewarded.

The manifesto concluded with the following directions:—"The General-in-chief requires the French minister in the Republic of Venice to leave that city, and the different agents of Venice in Lombardy and the Venetian states to quit the same, within twenty hours. The French Generals are ordered to regard the troops of Venice as foes, and to cast down the Winged Lion of St. Mark in every town where it is found displayed." In most of the Venetian towns were to be seen in the public Place, columns like those of the Piazetta at Venice—one bearing on its summit the Lion of St. Mark, and the other St. Theodore and the crocodile. These columns were emblematic of Venice—a portion of her arms, indeed, almost as much as the objects they bore.

To the manifesto of Napoleon the Senate replied that the massacres were not the work of the Government, but of individuals whom it could not control; that the people had been roused by the insolence of the French, and of the rebels whom they had seduced from their allegiance; that the first acts of aggression were committed by the French, in aiding the rebels against their lawful government; and, finally, that the only fault of which Venice had really been guilty was, her not having earlier foreseen the designs of France and united all her forces with Austria, when combating for a cause, which, sooner or later, must be that of every independent state.

The manifesto of Napoleon was the signal for revolt in all the Venetian towns of the main land. Prior to this, however, as early, indeed, as the 8th of April, and the very day after the signature of the armistice, he had issued a proclamation to the people of the Venetian towns, declaring that Venice could afford them no security of person or property, and by her indifference to their fate had roused the just indignation of France, and concluded thus:—"If

Venice rules you by the right of conquest, I will free you; if by usurpation, I will restore your rights." Each city declared its independence and appointed a Provisional Municipality, while the districts of Brescia, Bergamo, Bassano, Padua, Udine, and Vicenza shaped themselves into Republics on the model of that of France, abolishing feudality, suppressing convents, confiscating property, establishing national guards and hoisting the tricolor. The only recorded instance of opposition by the Venetian authorities took place at Treviso. Bonaparte, on entering the place, ordered its *Provveditore*, Angelo Giustiniani, to depart within two hours, on pain of being shot. The worthy descendant of Justinian replied, that his post had been assigned him by the Senate, and he should abandon it only with express orders from that source, adding much more of a very denunciatory character against the French. Bonaparte is said to have heard the old noble quietly to the end, and then to have dismissed him unharmed!

The French troops, returning from Carinthia, poured rapidly down the southern slope of those Alps, which, less than two months before, they had climbed; and, joining the forces already gathered, an army of 40,000 men gazed from the margin of the Lagune on the surpassing loveliness of the doomed city, while the French cannon again roared along those shores, which, for three centuries, had not echoed a hostile gun. The manifesto of Napoleon had been anticipated. The French troops under Baraguay d' Hilliers and Victor, joined by those of the new Italian Republics under La Hotze,* had already reached the Lagune; and, as early as the 30th of April, four days before the declaration of war, had begun planting their batteries at Fusina.

* La Hotze was a Swiss. He subsequently changed service and fell fighting under the Imperial banner. Scott pronounces him "a remarkable character."

The most delirious panic now took possession of the Venetian Senate, and, in some respects, the most causeless. Venice had known darker hours than this. Her position was far less desperate now, than when, centuries before, in the War of the Chioggia, her proud rival, Genoa, stood at her very threshold, and a blank sheet of paper was sent to Carrara, Lord of Padua, for the proposal of terms, and terms were refused. At the same time Prince Charles of Durazzo, nephew of the king of Hungary, was in the Trevisano, with 10,000 men, and offered peace only on condition of the payment of 500,000 ducats, expenses of the war—the treasures of St. Mark and the ducal *beretta* being the pledge, and, also, a tribute of 50,000 ducats per annum; also, that all future Doges should receive investiture and confirmation from the king of Hungary, and, as a mark of vassalage, that, on all festal days, the standard of Hungary should be displayed with that of Venice in the Place St Mark! No wonder the Great Council, at this crisis, debated the question of removal of the capital to the isle of Candia. Two centuries before, its removal to Constantinople had been proposed and negatived, although Venetian possessions in the Orient, at that era, exceeded far in value those on the Adriatic.

Nor was her position now so desperate as at the time of the League of Cambray, in the 16th century, when France, Spain, the Emperor, the Pope, the Duke of Ferrara, the Marquis of Mantua—all Christendom, indeed, preceded by the awful "Curse of Rome," united to crush, to dismember, to pillage Venice,—to wipe her out from the map of Europe and the world. This was not the first time her Lagune had resounded with the roar of French artillery—though all in vain—that it should now should so "frighten her from her propriety." Three hundred years before, when groaning beneath the incubus of all Europe in arms against her, the king of

France had established his camp at Mestre, planted a battery on the very spot where one was now erected, and had impotently discharged six hundred balls "in the *direction* of the capital, that posterity might be told he had cannonaded the impregnable city of Venice." The Viceroy of Naples, too, in course of the same disastrous conflict, had inflicted on Venice a similar insult; and, while from the summits of their bell-towers, the Venetians beheld the palaces and villas of the Brenta and Bacchiglione, and the towns of Mestre, Malghera and Fusina, on the borders of the Lagune, in flames, the balls of his heavy battery fell within the Monastery of San Secondo, on an island but a few hundred yards in advance of the city itself.

Nor was Venice now in such a condition of defenceless decrepitude as has been supposed. On the contrary, never had the Ocean Queen been better prepared to sustain her ancient pretensions. Her old fortresses were all garrisoned; new works had been constructed; she was amply supplied with stores and munitions for a siege; the sea was all her own, for her foe had no fleet; the Lagune was covered with her gun-boats, batteries, and large vessels heavily armed; her islands were filled with troops, and the masses in the Piazza still shouted the old battle-cry of her glory and her power—"*Viva San Marco!*" "*Fuori i barbari!*" * "Venice, the city of lofty remembrances, the Tyre of the Middle Ages, whose traders were princes, and her merchants the honorable of the earth, fallen though she was, from her former greatness, still," says Sir Walter Scott, "presented some appearance of vigor." She was

* "At no time," says the author of Childe Harold, "were the subjects of the Republic so unanimous in their resolution to rally around the standard of St. Mark, as when it was for the last time unfurled; and the cowardice and the treachery of the few patricians who recommended the fatal neutrality, were confined to the persons of the traitors themselves."

still Mistress of the Adriatic. " She could still," says the French historian, " present almost insuperable difficulties, even to the General who had just humbled Austria." For her defence, heavy batteries rose at every assailable point of the Lagune. Besides vessels of war, she had 37 galleys and 168 gun-boats, carrying some 800 guns, nearly 9,000 seamen and marine-gunners, nearly 4,000 regular Italian soldiers, 11,000 Sclavonians, provisions for eight months, water in her cisterns for two months (her only means of supply at any time), while the nearest islands of the capital were beyond the reach of the farthest cannon-shot from the batteries of *terra firma.* All historians—French and English, as well as Italian, concur in opinion that, Venice aided by England, though Austria was lost to her by the Preliminaries of Leoben, might have defied France.

" Venice, when she fell," says a Venetian writer, " certainly possessed great power and resources. She was mistress of more than three millions of subjects; of numerous fortified places; of armaments of the land and of the sea, and of an annual revenue of thirty millions of francs. The capital was defended by the surrounding Lagune from invasion by the French. It possessed two hundred vessels of war,* manned by 9,000 seamen and soldiers, and mounted by 800 guns. Munitions were abundant, and provisions plenty; and 140,000 citizens were eager for her defence, for which, also, she had over 20,000 regular soldiers. But the weakness of the government, the indolence of the aristocracy, the sluggishness of the people, concurring with other circumstances, caused that Venice came to be occupied by the French."

Despite all the boastings and blusterings of Napoleon, he had not a single gun-boat, with which to transport his troops across the

* Thirty-seven galleys and 168 gun-boats besides large vessels. Also, 300 merchant vessels and 8,000 sailors—say some!

Lagune; and, when the delay of construction had supplied him, he would have been forced to feel his way with the lead through the narrow and more intricate channels, exposed to a raking, point-blank, and murderous fire of numberless batteries. Whatever the ultimate result, delay of months seemed inevitable; and what might not months—even a few months, of such delay bring forth? Austria might again be in arms, and all southern and central Italy might be with her, instead of against her.

But Venice, however powerful without, was weak within. She was "a house divided against itself"; and she was doomed to its fate. With a good government, the stronger the pressure from without, the stronger is the resistance from within. With a bad government the result is the reverse. Her old and her new nobility were at feud. Her populace, ignorant, superstitious, half-savage, were their slaves and tools. Her *bourgeoisie*—her middle class—hated her hateful oligarchy; and from among this class was made up the party of "Jacobins," or Venetian Republicans. Then there was the Sclavonian soldiery, entirely indifferent which party prevailed, so long as an opportunity was presented them to pillage the opulent city, in the general anarchy. The old nobility dreaded the loss of their offices; the new nobility wished to retain their pensions; the middle class, composed of merchants, tradesmen, advocates, physicians, wished for equality and liberty, and welcomed the French, without daring to express it for fear of the lower class, composed of seamen, fishermen, gondoliers, artizans, who were ruled by the nobility through the priests, and whose rallying cry was *Viva San Marco!* This last class adhered steadfastly to the old order of things, to the government of their fathers, which, however hateful in its oppression of other classes, had never descended to oppress, but had always protected, them. All parties united in shrinking from a protracted siege, the chief horrors of which, however, would result from the internecine strife between conflicting factions within the Lagune, of which the mercenary soldiery would not fail to take advantage. United, Venice might perhaps, have resisted all Europe; divided, she could not control the factions by which her own bowels were torn. Venice, therefore, though beautiful in aspect, and, apparently, able to resist any assault, was liable to be dashed into pieces by the first rude shock. She was "a whited sepulchre—fair without, indeed, but within full of dead men's bones and all uncleanness." Besides, the *prestige* of that wonderful man—the "Man of destiny"—who, within a twelvemonth, had overrun all Italy, and compelled Austria to treat to save Vienna, appalled her. She trembled for her commerce and her mercantile marine. She dreaded the sequestration of her estates, and palaces, and villas, on the main land. She imagined that a few modifications of her old institutions would satisfy her foes within and without—would continue power to the old nobility, pensions to the new, commerce to the merchants, estates to the opulent: whilst it would obviate all the probabilities of civil war, the expenses of protracted siege and prevent the horrors of sack and pillage by the Dalmatians or the French—her *quasi* defenders or her real besiegers. She therefore, at first, resolved to attempt her ancient policy of corruption. We have seen the result with Napoleon at Gratz. He spurned the approach with scorn. Whatever the "price" at which *he* might be "bought," it could hardly be estimated in Venetian sequins.* With the Directory at Paris the attempt was more

* Venice strove to bribe Napoleon to spare her with the offer of a million and a half of dollars. The Emperor, after the peace, offered him a principality of 250,000 souls. He instantly rejected both. It is also stated, that, when Napoleon first entered the territory of Venice, in June 1796, her envoys offered him $1,200,000, desiring neutrality; and that, while granting the request, he declined the bribe. Some authorities, however, pronounce him less immaculate, and assert that he received a *douceur* of eight millions of francs

successful. Ten millions of francs in bills of exchange were transmitted for this purpose to Alvise Querini, the Envoy of Venice at Paris; and 600,000 francs in bills, as a private *douceur*, were placed in the hands of Barras, on condition of defending Venice in the Directory. The intrigue, with the names and sums, was discovered to Bonaparte subsequently, by the interception of certain dispatches at Milan, and the whole bribery was denounced. Venice was not saved, and the bills were not paid. The order of the Directory would, at any rate, have come too late to save the Bride of the Sea. She was already lost. Querini employed all possible means to gain favor for her, and availed himself of a crafty Dalmatian *intriguant*, intimate with Barras, to win him. And Barras was won.

On the 31st of April, the principal members of the Venetian government, forty-three in number, assembled on a summons of the Signory,* in extraordinary council, in the apartments of the Doge, to devise some escape for the doomed city, from the toils by which she was enveloped: but its deliberations were paralyzed by terror. The aged doge, Manini, tottered in, with his eyes full of tears, deploring the fact that "he was not sure of sleeping that night quietly in his bed!" Various modes of salvation were suggested. The timid proposed to treat; the rich and corrupt, who, as is ever the case, fancied that money was all-powerful and that "mammon could win its way where seraphs might despair"—insisted on augmenting the bribes; a few, and but a few of the heroic sons of heroic sires,—descendants of the Contarini, Pisani, Morosini, proposed to fight. But prudence, if not policy, prevailed. It was resolved to convoke the

from Austria, as the price for Venice by the treaty of Campo Formio, and returned to Paris with twenty-five millions in all!

* *La Quarantia*, the Council of Forty. *La Signoria*, the Doge's Council of Six.

Great Council, and to propose that modification of the constitution which the French general had himself suggested. This decision was quickened, as the day advanced, by the thunder of a distant cannonade, which announced that the Port-admiral, in obedience to orders reluctantly granted, had opened the batteries of his gun-boats on the rising works of the French, on the margin of the Lagune. Terrified at these terrible sounds, they were ordered to cease, and the Great Council, embracing the nobility, representing the republic, and numbering some twelve hundred members,* was convoked to meet the following day.

On the morning of the 1st of May, agreeably to this extraordinary convocation, 619 members of the Great Council assembled in their magnificent hall, one of the most spacious, and the most splendid in all the world. The question of the modification of the Venetian constitution had been, it will be remembered, already discussed in the month of March, when the Senate, terrified at the general revolt of the towns on the main land, had applied to Lallemant, the French minister, to know whether Venice could rely on the friendship of the Directory. The result was, then, that 180 voices out of about 200 were in favor of gradual modification in more quiet times. But, those times had not yet arrived, and there seemed no hope of their ever arriving. In silence—without a word of debate, the question was put; and, by a vote of 598 to 21, the Doge's proposition was adopted—that two commissioners should be sent by the senate to the French General, to lay before him the ancient constitution of Venice for modification, subject, for form's sake, to revision and ratification by the Council. With this resolution the *Provveditori* at once departed, and meeting Napoleon at the bridge of Malghera, on the margin of the Lagune, where he was making his dispositions

* Once twenty-five hundred.

for the siege, placed it in his hands. For an instant, he seemed astounded at the concession, but, immediately bursting forth in his usual boisterous manner, he exclaimed — "And the three State Inquisitors, and the Commandant of the Lido—are they in prison? I must have their heads. No treaty till French blood has been avenged. Your Lagune shall not deter me. I find it exactly what I expected. In a fortnight I shall be in Venice. Your nobles shall not escape death, except by going, like the French emigrants, and dragging their misery all over the world." The terrified deputies implored a delay of forty-eight hours, in order to obtain the consent of the Council to his demand. But, no. He would listen to no delay. French blood had been treacherously spilt. Nothing but the blood of the murderers could atone for it. "Venice *was!*" Her nobles should henceforth be wanderers forever from their hearths. He at length, however, granted twenty-four hours for the arrest of the Inquisitors and the Commandant; and promised to suspend his attack on the city six days, in order to afford the Council time to accede to his conditions, and forward them to him at Mantua or at Milan.

This was wise. Terror had now time to do its work. Indeed, it was Napoleon's only hope, despite all his bravado. "The Lagune *was* exactly what he had expected"—impassable without boats, and almost so with them; and he had not one! It is said that he had never been foolish enough to contemplate an actual assault upon the city. Had success been certain, still the Preliminaries of Leoben, as will be seen, and the unquestionable interference of Austria would have forbid. But his object was accomplished as surely as if his troops were already in Venice, and he set out at once for Mantua.

The *Provveditori*, immediately on their return, submitted their report to the Privy Council of the Doge, who, at once, resolved to convoke anew the Great Council, and submit to it a proposition to accede to all the French General's demands. On the 4th, accordingly, the Council met, and, on motion of the weak Doge, seconded by Pietro Antonio Bembo, by 704 balls to 10, it was resolved, that the Inquisitors and the Commandant should be arrested and tried—for doing exactly what they had been ordered to do, and applauded for doing!—and that commissioners should be authorized to treat on all conditions with Bonaparte. This was done, and the *Provveditori* departed for Milan.

Meantime, the internal affairs of Venice were every day becoming more desperate. The evils apprehended from a siege began to be experienced. The arrest of the three State Inquisitors—the terrible "Three"—had paralyzed the Police; the sailors of the fleet and the Sclavonians of the garrison were in a state of insubordination; the republicans, it was asserted, were conspiring to massacre the aristocracy, and the garrison was awaiting the event to pillage the city. It is very certain that the republican party was not idle. In the absence of Lallemant, the Minister, they made Villetard (the French Secretary of Legation, and actual *Chargè-d'affaires*,) the nucleus of their movements; and, while the more furious of the party paraded the streets, demanding with shouts the abdication of the Senate, abolition of the aristocracy, dissolution of the government, admission of the French, and a democratic rule, a revolutionary committee was in open correspondence with the besieging army and the revolted towns.

At one time terror had reached such a height, that the Senate authorized the military Commandant of the Lagune to capitulate to the Generals of the besieging force, in the absence of Napoleon, on the conditions of the reservation of nationality and religion, protection of persons and property, and safety of the Mint, Bank, Arsenal, and Archives. The response of the French generals was a prolongation of six days of the armistice, which expired on the 7th—the negotiations at Milan not having closed. Terror, they plainly saw, was performing their own task more perfectly than they could perform it themselves; and time only was requisite for its completion. The emissaries of France were busy in Venice. Two of these, Spada and Zorzi, chiefs of the democrats, suggested to the privy counsellors of the Doge, that they should address Villetard, the Secretary, desiring his advice at the existing crisis, for the salvation of Venice. Such suggestions would once have been answered with a sentence to the *piombi*, the *pozzi*, or the Canal Orfano, in those earlier days, when a mere approach to the dim and secret councils of a dread Oligarchy was sacrilege, and its penalty death.* But now, the crafty suggestion to conciliate their foes by anticipation of the contemplated reform, was gratefully entertained, and Battaglia and Donato were, on the 9th, commissioned to address the Secretary. He replied that he had no power to treat, but that his private opinion was, that, if the Sclavonians were disbanded and embarked—if a Civic Guard was established—if four thousand French were introduced into the city—if the ancient government was dissolved—if the aristocracy was abolished—if a municipal body of thirty-six members, chosen from all classes of citizens, with the Doge as Mayor, was instituted—if all political prisoners were released, and the Tree of Liberty was planted in the Square of St. Mark—why—that, then, he had little doubt the French General would—graciously pardon the three Inquisitors and the Commandant of the Lido!

* The extraordinary secrecy which characterized the Councils of Venice was instanced in the case of one of her admirals, who was on trial a whole month, and was finally condemned, but who knew nothing of the proceedings until arrested, although the whole nobility were, of coure, aware of the facts, and some of them were intimate friends of the accused, engaged warmly in his defence!

These modest proposals, as might be imagined, encountered furious opposition in the Privy Council, especially from Priuli, Pesaro, Calbo, and Erizzo. They prevailed, however, and were ordered to be laid before the Great Council, convoked to assemble on the 12th. The Sclavonians, also, were paid off at once, and embarked for Dalmatia, on the opposite shore of the Adriatic; but an adverse wind forbade their departure from the port, and the presence of these disbanded and semi-savage troops served to keep panic at its height.

CHAPTER IV.

"SPOLIATION."

On the morning of the 12th of May, 1797, the Great Council assembled. The vast and magnificent Hall of the Ducal Palace was thronged with citizens favorable to the abolition of the Oligarchy; and all its approaches swarmed with the populace in favor of the ancient order of things. The *Arsenalotti* were under arms: all the *guilds* of artisans were present in body: files of Sclavonians with artillery filled the Piazetta: guards patroled all the streets, and sentinels stood at the approaches to the Piazza, and in the courts, galleries, and lobbies of the palace.

The Council was opened by the aged Doge with an address, in which, with tears and lamentations, he deplored the desperate condition of his beloved Venice. Then presenting his abdication, the Council was proceeding to deliberate, when an irregular discharge of musketry in the Piazetta beneath the windows, filled the Hall with confusion and dismay. The members started to their feet. The Sclavonians are pillaging the city!—the French have crossed the Lagune!—the Jacobins have risen on the nobles!—the populace are murdering the republicans! Such were the ejaculations dictated by the various fears of the members of that august assemblage; and, without pausing to inquire the real cause of the disturbance, they united in a common cry—"To the vote!—To the vote!" and rushed to the urns as they were presented.

There could be but one result. The guilty city was doomed. Madness took possession of her councils. "As the fool dieth so died she." The only capital of Europe never yet soiled by hostile foot, yielded at last, without a struggle!—"Whom the gods would destroy they first make mad." Five hundred and twelve ballots, out of five hundred and twenty-nine cast, declared that the most ancient government in the world, and which had just completed its eleventh century of existence, was no more,* was at a conqueror's feet! The majority demanded by the statutes was six hundred, or one-half of the whole Council. The measures embodied in this vote were—surrender of the sovereign power by the Great Council to the Venetian nation—the institution of a Municipality—the establishment of a Provisional Government embracing deputies from all the Venetian States—consolidation of the public debt—pensions for the poor nobles, and admission of the French troops. The French tri-color displayed from the great window of the Council Hall, looking out on the *Molo* and the Port, was the signal to the Democrats without that the deed was done. The discharge of musketry, which had caused such panic in the Hall, and

* Venice existed as a *Republic* exactly 1100 years. The first Doge, Anafesto, was elected in 697; the last, and 122d Doge, Luigi Manini, abdicated in 1797. Fifty years from that date, 1848, Venice was again independent. There is a singular prophecy embodied in three lines of the Italian poet, Luigi Alamanni, respecting Venice—to this effect:—"If you change not, your liberties, already crumbling, will not survive the century beyond their thousandth year." From 697 to 1797 is just one century over a thousand years The prophecy was made two and a half centuries before the fulfillment, and was first pointed out by the historian Ginguene. Alamanni was born at Florence, 1495, was an exile at Paris, 1530, an Envoy of Francis I. to Charles V., in 1544, and died, 1551.

precipitated the sacrifice, had occurred in a casual rencontre between a band of those in favor of the measure and those opposed to it: and now, when the disgraceful consummation was received by one party with shouts of joy, it of course filled the other party with ungovernable rage. The narrow streets and public places were filled with armed bands, shouting—" *Viva San Marco!*"—"*Viva la Liberta!*" —the latter bearing as their symbol the tri-color of France, the former the image of St. Mark. A night of anarchy ensued. In the midst of the tumult, the insurrection, the horrible convulsion, threatening general pillage, rapine, and conflagration—the disbanded and semi-savage Sclavonians mingled with the populace, and terror and havoc were at their height. The houses of Spada, Zorzi, and others, charged with having urged on the downfall of Venice, were burst open and sacked: many of the most obnoxious of the "Jacobins" were assailed and maltreated; and one man, in whose pocket was found a tri-color cockade, being met by the mob, they nailed it to his forehead! To these atrocities, horrible and bloody reprisals were about commencing, when a brave band of the true sons of Venice, resolving to put an end to anarchy and restore *order*, at least, placed at their head an old Maltese, General Salembeni, long a victim of the State Inquisition, and boldly charged the insurgents. A conflict ensued on the Rialto Bridge, and order was at length restored. Next day a Provisional Government was declared, under the Advocate Dandolo as chief; and a Democratic Municipal rule succeeded that of the terrible Ten. The Sclavonians, after ravaging the Lido and Malamocco, were finally embarked for their native land across the Gulf.

On the morning of the 16th, Venice sent a flotilla to convey to the city a division of 4,000 French troops, under Gen. Baraguay d'Hilliers. And thus, having with her own hands torn down the venerable ensign of St. Mark, "with her own hands she ferried the invaders across the Lagune," which no enemy had ever passed before! The troops landed at the Piazetta. St. Mark's Place, the Arsenal, and other important points were, at once, taken possession off, amid the shouts of some and the execrations of others; and the tricolor of France was unfurled from those three celebrated masts before the Cathedral, which had so long supported the conquered standards of Candia, Cyprus, and Morea, and over which, for centuries, the Lion of St. Mark had, in triumph, expanded his wings.

The French were received with mingled shouts and sighs. The middle-classes and the lower nobility, which had long groaned under the hideous despotism of the State Inquisition, could but felicitate themselves on any change. The lower class, which had never felt the gallings of the chains, gazed on the strangers with frowning brows and flashing eyes; whilst those who saw in the fall of the institutions of their country, however hateful, the fall, also, of her ancient pride, independence, nationality, looked on in mournful gloom, and, in the words of Solkowski's report to Napoleon, "retired in silence to their homes, exclaiming with tears—"Venice is no more! St. Mark is fallen!'"*

Meantime, Bonaparte, at Milan, with the *Provvedatori*, was signing a treaty on the very day the French troops were entering Venice, embodying the same terms as those adopted by the Great Council, with the exception, that it enjoined the punishment of the

* "Venice, founded by Attila, fell by Napoleon." Figuratively, this is true. Honoria, a princess of Aquila, in custody for her amours, besought Attila to break her bonds, and accept her hand. He demanded half the kingdom as a dower, which being refused, he drove its people to the isles of the Adriatic, and—"founded Venice." A wanton princess gave Spain to the Moors for seven hundred years. Napoleon *accepted* Venice and gave her to Austria.

three Inquisitors and the Commandant of the Lido, and contained, also, several secret stipulations. The ratification of this treaty by the Venetian Government was, of course, impossible, even had it been necessary. There was no Venetian Government. It was ratified, however, at the instance of Bonaparte, by the Provisional Government of the city. The public debt was guaranteed by Napoleon, the pensions of the poor nobility were allowed, a general amnesty to all offenders—the unhappy Inquisitors and the Commandant alone excepted,* was declared, while the French troops, it was announced, would remain no longer in Venice than the tranquillity of the city required.

In accordance with the Treaty of Milan, Gen. Baraguay d'Hilliers entered Venice on the 4th of June with 16,000 additional troops, and the capitulation was complete. The Patriarch and his clergy administered the oath of fraternity, and the scriptural legend on the gospel held by the winged lion on the granite column of the Piazetta—*Pax tibi, Marce, Evangelista meus*, was erased, and the motto of the revolution—*Droits de l'homme et du citoyen*—was substituted—even the Lion of St. Mark, as was said by the gondoliers, being forced, for the first time, to "turn over a new leaf." The Tree of Liberty was reared in the centre of the Piazza, the only tree that ever cast its shadow over that tesselated pavement; and at its foot was burned (in effigy) the "Golden Book"—the long record of Venetian nobility, as, also, the ducal cap, the silver trumpets, the golden spurs, the cushions, the umbrella—nearly all of them presented as insigna of power by the Pope Alexander III. to the Doge Ziani, at the close of the twelfth century. The ducal cap — the *beretta* — the *corne dogale*, or "horned

* This prosecution soon dropped. Subsequently the Commandant applied to Austria for assistance, but died in poverty and neglect. In 1817, one of his sons was an artizan at Venice.

bonnet"—the republican diadem—with which the newly-elected Doge was crowned on being invested with power, claims an origin yet more ancient—as ancient, indeed, as the middle of the ninth century. Its shape was that of the *pilus*, or ancient Greek cap of liberty. It was of gold, gorgeously set with diamonds, rubies, and pearls. It was presented by Augustine Morosini, Abbess of the Convent of San Zaccaria, at Venice, to the Doge Pietro Tradenigo, on the occasion of a visit to worship some reliques donated her convent by Pope Benedict III., because of its hospitality and attention to him on a visit to the city. This was given by the Doge to the State, and, ever after, until the fall of the Republic, was it the diadem of Venice. When worn, its weight and pressure required a skull-cap on the Doge's head. On ordinary occasions an imitation of the *beretta* in cloth of gold, with the Phrygian shape of the *corno* was used.

The Golden Book, "that severe nomenclature of patrician rank in Venice," was instituted in 1315, and was thenceforth the index and standard of nobility, by which all claims were decided. Upon its pages were inscribed all the births, bridals, and deaths of the nobles. The names of a few foreign princes appear upon its leaves, and among them that of Henry IV., of France, placed there at his own request, on his marriage with the Italian princess, Marie de Medicis. This king and his posterity thus became nobles of Venice. Accompanying his request was a splendid suit of armor, yet to be seen at the Arsenal, and the sword worn by him at the Battle of Ivry, which disappeared in the spoliation of 1797. In 1795, when Louis XVIII., on demand of the French Directory, was exiled from his asylum at Verona by the Venetian Senate, it will be remembered, that he demanded the erasure of his great ancestor's name from the Golden Book and the return of his armor. This celebrated book consists of a series of manuscript volumes, bound in crimson velvet, preserved in the convent attached to the Church of the Frari, the depository of governmental archives, ancient and modern, and which can now be entered only on special permission from Vienna.

The secret stipulations of the Treaty of Milan were five in number. The first provided for certain exchanges of Venetian territory, made by the Preliminaries of Leoben; the second, the payment of three millions of francs; the third, as many millions in stores; the fourth, the delivery, armed and equipped, of three ships of the line and two frigates; while the fifth required twenty pictures and five hundred manuscripts. These articles being secret, were ratified, at the time of the ratification of the patent articles of the treaty, by the Provisional Government, by the signature of three of the members. We shall now see how they were executed.

Napoleon's objects in requiring the signature of the Treaty of Milan, after the voluntary adoption of most of its measures by the Great Council of Venice four days previous, were several, and are fully developed in a secret dispatch to the Directory three days afterwards, quoted by Alison: they were—to enter Venice and extract what he chose on pretence of executing the secret articles—to be able to avail himself of all the resources of the city, provided a treaty with Austria should not be ratified—to avoid odium in violating the Preliminaries relative to the Venetian territory, or to gain pretexts to facilitate their execution—to quiet Europe with reference to the occupation of Venice, since it would thus appear but temporary, and at her own request. A few days later he wrote—"Venice must fall to those to whom we give the Italian continent; but, meanwhile, we will take its vessels, strip its Arsenal, destroy its Bank, and keep Corfu and Ancona." On the 13th of

June he wrote to Gen. Baraguay d'Hilliers to present himself to the Provisional Government of Venice, and to represent, that her union with France, and the protection due to her from that Republic, rendered it indispensable, that her maritime force should be put on a respectable footing; on which pretext he was to take possession of everything, taking care to keep on good terms with the Venetians, enlisting all the Venetian seamen, and doing all things in the Venetian name. "In short," concludes this singular letter, "you must manage so as to transport all the naval stores and vessels in the port of Venice to Toulon. By secret articles of the treaty, the Venetians are bound to furnish to the French Republic five vessels and three millions worth of stores; but my intention is to take possession of all the Venetian vessels, and all the naval stores for the marine of Toulon."*

In obedience to these orders, everything found in the celebrated Arsenal, consisting chiefly of hemp, iron, and naval stores, was seized. All the vessels were, also, seized, either on account of the secret article, or on the pretext of occupying the Ionian Isles in the name of "Democratic Venice." A few of the vessels on the stocks were completed, and others were repaired, so that the Venetian fleet finally mustered six ships of the line, six frigates, and about a dozen galleys. Thirteen ships of war and seven frigates are said to have been found in the Arsenal, dating their commencement at different periods, from 1732—two having been begun in that year—two in '43, and two in '52—the oldest having attained the age of seventy-five years! But, had not these vessels been too dilapidated for completion, there was no material at hand for that purpose.

* The Directory subsequently wrote to Berthier, who succeeded Napoleon in the command of the Army of Italy in October of '97, that all the artillery and all the munitions, whether of war or of peace, should be transported to Corfu, Ancona, and Ferrara, so that Venice should not be left a single cannon!

Napoleon's object in this speedy seizure is said to have been to preclude the possibility of the repetition of such an event as occurred when the Dutch, dissatisfied with the revolution, delivered up their ships and islands to the English. He was, also, excessively solicitous to secure the Isles of Greece, belonging to Venice—Corfu, Zante, Cephalonia, Santa Maura, and Cerigo. He desired the Directory at once to dispatch Admiral Brueys with six ships to take the Venetian Navy and repair to the Archipelago; and, that there might be no pretext for delay for lack of funds, he sent, himself, two millions of francs to Toulon. He desired, also, that a body of seamen might be immediately sent him, across the Peninsula, by land, engaging to pay and equip them at Venice. Meanwhile, however, he united the French flotilla in the Adriatic with the Venetian vessels; and, intermixing the crews and embarking upon them two thousand troops, dispatched the combined fleet to take possession of the Grecian islands at once, for fear of the arrival of the French squadron too late. The Admiral reached Venice about the middle of July, where his fleet was paid, provisioned, and equipped, at the expense of the fallen Republic. It was then dispatched, with the remaining Venetian vessels, to the Archipelago, the Admiral being supplied with funds to enlist seamen on the coasts of Albania and Greece. Thus, not only were the important posts of the Ionian Isles secured to France, but a formidable French navy was created, as if by magic, in the Adriatic and Levant; while Corfu was selected as the principal naval station.

Immediately on entering Venice, the French had seized the public treasury; but they found in it only about two millions of francs, belonging to the Duke of Modena, which they, of course, appropriated as the property of an avowed foe. But, supposing this sum passed to the credit of Venice, there would still be due from her to

France, in fulfillment of the second of the secret articles, more than one million of francs. On pretence of making up this sum, various most unwarrantable modes seem to have been devised and resorted to. The Provisional Government was compelled to make forced loans; and even the celebrated *Bucentauro*, with which had so long been solemnized the symbolic nuptials of the Doge of Venice with the Adriatic, was broken up for the sake of its gilding, which is said to have yielded the sum of 18,000 sequins—about 220,000 francs. It was the third constructed since 1520, and was nearly seventy-five years old. At the same time the small museum of the Ducal Palace was conveyed to the Arsenal, and some of its most curious and valuable articles disappeared; among which was the sword of Ivry of the Chevalier-King, Henry Fourth, before-named, which is said now to be seen in the Cabinet of Medals of the Royal Library at Paris.

This museum of the ducal palace, which contained antique arms and curiosities of art, adjoined a small armory amply supplied with weapons and munitions, always kept ready for instant use by a special custodian, and sufficient to equip five hundred men. Thus, although no weapon could be taken into the council chambers, the patricians could, in five minutes, arm themselves to the teeth without leaving the palace, on the slightest cause. The chief of the decemvirs kept the key of this armory officially, and the significant letters C. D. X.—Council of Ten—is yet to be detected among the architectural ornaments of the walls.

The famous bronze steeds which so inappropriately stand over the grand portal of the cathedral, and that symbol of Venice, the Winged Lion of St. Mark, were also carried off. These horses, four in number, weighing each of them about two tons, are composed of pure copper, once covered with gold, and are remarkable, rather for extreme antiquity, than as works of art. They are supposed to have been the workmanship of Lysippus, a Greek of the Isle of Chio, and to have been conveyed to Rome, in the sixty-fifth year of the Christian era, by Augustus. Originally designed for a triumphal car, they are said to have been attached successively to those which surmounted the arches of Augustus, Nero, Domitian, Trajan, and Constantine. Early in the 5th century, they were transported to Constantinople by the Emperor Theodosius, and placed in the centre of the Hippodrome, a site far more appropriate, it will be admitted, than over the vestibule of a Christian church. In the year 1205, after the conquest of Constantinople by the Venetians and French, they were sent to Venice by the Podesta, Marino Zeno, as a portion of the immense spoil.* In 1797, they were sent by Napoleon over the Alps to Paris, and placed on the arch of the Carrousel, constructed for the purpose by Fontaine. By the treaties of 1815, they were restored, in common with all other works of art, to those from whom they had been seized, but not until exact models had been taken, which have replaced them, with the addition of an appropriate triumphal car, on the Parisian arch. Alison says, "The seizure of these horses was an act of pure robbery." Robbery?—Robbery from whom, and by whom? The Greeks were robbed of them by the Romans, and the Romans were robbed of them by the Byzantians, and the Byzantians by the Venetians, and the Venetians by the French, and the French by the Austrians! It would be exceedingly difficult

* The spoil of Constantinople has been estimated at the enormous value of 200,000,000 francs! Venice secured not only the bronze steeds and a vast quantity of marbles, statues and sculptures which enrich St. Mark's, but also, divers reliques deemed yet more inestimable—to wit—an arm of St. George, and one of St. James; the head of John the Baptist,—(the body having fallen to the lot of the French,)—the bodies of St. Luke and the prophet Simeon, and a phial of Christ's blood, and a morsel of his cross! The phial of blood was claimed by two soldiers, and one shed the other's blood to secure the precious booty!

to determine who have been the true robbers, though the Greeks of Chio were, doubtless, the true proprietors. Why Venice, in 1797, should complain of exactly her own act of 1205—or, complain that France, who aided her in that earlier spoliation, should begin to enjoy a period of possession after a lapse of six hundred years, is strange enough! It is also a little strange how the Allied Powers could have had the assurance to denounce this spoliation, and return the spoil to a city whose independence they had themselves just seized. The same treaties which provided for the restoration of works of art, provided, also, for the restoration of territorial and political rights to those equally despoiled. It was neither more nor less than a foul insult to Venice, to admit her right to her ancient independence, by sending back the treasures of which she had been despoiled, at the same time despoiling her of that independence itself, and more hopelessly than ever!

As for the Venetians themselves, they had been for some fourteen hundred years the veriest robbers in the world, as perfect Uscoques, indeed, as the Istriote corsairs whom they subdued and plundered! Saint Mark's Cathedral, in its absurd profusion of inappropriate, yet costly decorations, gathered from all the Eastern world, resembles more the den of the "Forty Thieves"—the hiding-place of their ill-got gains, than a Christian church; and the stolen bronze steeds over the portal are an appropriate sign for the place and its contents. The whole city of Venice, indeed, has been well said by Alphonse Royer to remind one of "the house of a pirate retired from business."

Not content to confine their robberies to profane objects, the Venetians extended their enterprise to sacred ones; and, not to name the sacred spoil of Constantinople, the bodies of San Marco, San Donato, San Nicolo, San Onofolo, Santa Fosca, and San Taraise, were the avails of some few of these "pious frauds;" while it was only because all their tricks did not prove successful, that the "crown of thorns" and the "robe without seam" and divers other reliques, equally rare and sacred, were not added to their collection!

To hear lamentations, therefore, or denunciations from, or for, such a people, and such a city, because of *spoliation*, recalls the musty adage of the devil rebuking sin. In 1797, at the very worst, the chalice often in her long career of conquest mingled by Venice for others, was only commended to her own reluctant lips. The "evil instruction" only came back to plague the instructor. After all, there is such a thing as retributive justice, on nations as well as on men.

The case of the Winged Lion of St. Mark, so far as France is concerned, is very different from that of the Bronze Horses. On the southern extremity of the Piazetta, looking down on the canal of St. Mark, stand two columns of granite, one red and one gray, and each about sixty feet high. They were brought, as before mentioned, from the Greek isle of Naxos, early in the twelfth century, by the doge Dominico Michieli; and here, for seven hundred years have they stood. On the summit of one, for more than five hundred years, has stood the statue of San Teodoro, the primitive patron of Venice, supported on the back of a crocodile; and on the summit of the other has stood the Winged Lion of St. Mark, which saint has been the patron of Venice ever since his remains, stolen by superstitious Venetian sailors, were brought to the city, early in the year 835. Both effigies are of bronze, and the work of the same artist, Pietro Guilombardo, in 1329; and neither of them have the slightest merit as works of art. The lion, indeed—if it be not a libel on the king of beasts to call this hideous monster by that name —is, in this regard, entirely beneath contempt, though for its antiquity, and as the national symbol of a world-renowned people for one thousand years, it is one of the most interesting objects in all Europe. Why Napoleon should have ordered this venerable emblem of a nationality to be borne away, only to be lost in the esplanade of the *Invalides*, at Paris, passeth comprehension; unless indeed, as has been suspected, he desired and designed, in a manner the most cruel possible, to mortify a people whom he despised, and to crush a city that he hated.

The lion returned to Venice and resumed his ancient position at the same time with the bronze horses, and by virtue of the same treaties of 1815. The horses are said to have been packed by the English, and sustained no injury in the journey; but the lion, less accustomed to travelling, perhaps, bore his journeyings less happily. It has even been asserted, that he sustained such damage at Paris, that another lion was substituted in fulfillment of the treaty. But this is improbable. Two such beasts as the Lion of St. Mark could never have existed! The damages of "the old original" repaired, the gospel under his right paw, abstracted at Paris, restored, he now rolls his hideous eyeballs as fiercely over the blue waves of the Adriatic, as he did five hundred years ago.

It has been remarked of the "Leonine City," that her emblem—her symbol—her device—her blazon—is anything but a lion; and the effigies of the king of beasts at the Arsenal and in the Cathedral Court, are hardly more fortunate in *vraisemblance*, than upon the column of the Piazetta. It may not be amiss to suggest, in this connection, that the idea of a lion with wings, owes its origin, probably, to the Vision of the Prophet Daniel—such a beast being one of the "four great beasts which came up from the sea," as described in the fourth verse of his seventh chapter—the first beast being "like a lion and had eagles' wings." His sitting posture indicates peace and wisdom, we are told; and his wings promptitude in execution. The legend on his book—*Pax tibi, Marce, Evangelista meus*—is said to have constituted the welcome of an angel to St. Mark, when, during his earthly pilgrimage, the saint landed on the islet where now stands the Church of St. Francis! The heraldic colors are said to be *azure* for the lion's body, *or* for his wings, and *argent* for his book—for which latter in time of war, to be substituted a naked sword. "A lion with two wings!" once remarked an Austrian, derisively—"from what clime does he come?" "From the same as an eagle with two heads," was the prompt reply of a son of St. Mark.*

As touching the return of the Bronze Steeds, it is mentioned as a somewhat noticeable coincidence, that the name of the ship-master who brought them back to Venice, was Dandolo, and that he was a lineal descendant of that same "old blind Dandolo" who, by conquest, brought them from Constantinople, six centuries before! † It is also said—"the name of the rebel apothecary, who received the Doge's sword on the final annihilation of the ancient Government, was named Dandolo." Another Dandolo—perhaps the same—a lawyer, and one of the only two men of merit whom, as Napoleon declared, he had met in Italy, was, as has already been mentioned, placed at the head of the Provisional Government; while, as late as the Greek Revolution of 1820, a Vice Admiral, Count Dandolo, commanded the Austrian fleet in the Levant. The name dates its origin as far back as the year 421—to the founding

* Smedley.

† After the conquest of Constantinople, Dandolo was chosen Monarch of the West, in the Church of Sta. Sophia, by a college of six Venetians and six Frenchmen: but, declining, Baudouin, Count of Flanders, was then elected. Dandolo died at Constantinople, in 1205, nearly a hundred years old, and was interred beneath the domes of the great Mosque. His was the first head stamped on the coin of Venice. Andrea Dandolo, a descendant, was the first historian of Venice, and the last of her Doges interred (1354,) in the Basilica.

of Venice. The oldest family names, indeed, in all christendom, are to be found in the island-city.

From the fifth century to the eleventh, Venice preserved family names according to the custom of Rome—a custom then abandoned by all Europe. Her Dukes and Counts had islands in the sea, but no castles on the land, and no vassals, with which to dispute the supremacy of the State. Titles, therefore, were powerless for good or for evil, and might well be allowed by the most jealous Government. What Dumas says of the nobility of Naples, is far more true of that of Venice:—"They may, perhaps, have an end, but it is very certain that they had no beginning! According to them, the most flourishing epoch of their houses was under the Roman Emperors; and they calmly name the Fabii, the Marcelli, and the Scipios amongst their ancestors. Those who are able to trace their genealogy back to the twelfth century only, are regarded as upstart nobility—mere young fry of aristocracy."

"As early as 1297," says Mariotti, "Venice boasted no less than four hundred and eighty patrician families; while to name not only the titled, but the historically noble houses, whose descendants still linger amid the desolation of that tottering beaver-city, would prove as arduous a task, as to compile the peerage of any of the great European monarchies. Among the houses that go back farthest into the past, a few are to be found in Rome or Florence, but a greater number at Venice." The destitution to which they are now reduced, he adds, is melancholy, though some have purchased a precarious subsistence by ignominious subservience to Austria: "but who that could die a Venetian patrician would live an Austrian noble?" The names of Tiepolo and Erizzo, go back directly to Rome; whilst the Giustiniani trace an unbroken pedigree to the Emperor Justinian, two thousand years ago! What is descent from William the Conquerer and his robber-band to this? What descent from the oldest houses of Germany and France? Well has it been said, that, "placed beside the aristocracy of Italy, the nobility of every other country in Europe sinks into comparative insignificance." The family of the Giustiniani, it may be remarked, has been preserved to the present day in a manner somewhat noticeable. In 1170, every male of the name had been cut off in the wars of the East—a pious monk of the monastery of St. Michael, named Nicolò, only excepted. To obviate the public calamity of the utter extinction of this great family, Venice obtained old Nicolò's release from his vows by special embassy to the Pope, and gave him a young and noble bride. For six years the devoted pair served most faithfully and successfully their dear Venice; and then retiring to the cloister, lived in the odor of sanctity, and, finally, thus died and were canonized! A century later, the Giustiniani had fifty branches, and two hundred Senators sitting in the Grand Council at one time! Forty branches were extinct at the time of the invasion of '97. It was one of this great house, Angelo Giustiniani, *Provveditore* of Treviso, who, it will be remembered, nobly refused to abandon his post, at the conqueror's mandate, until bidden by his true sovereign, the Signory.

The fifth of the secret articles of the Treaty of Milan exacted from subjugated Venice, was the delivery of twenty pictures and five hundred manuscripts. Very early in his Italian campaign we see Napoleon transmitting to Paris works of art. Indeed, not three months had elapsed after he took the field, and hardly was the Milanese in his hands, before we find him soliciting the Directory to appoint a committee of artists to make selections from among the master-pieces which his conquests placed at his disposal (in like manner as Canova was appointed in 1815 to superintend their return); while, in his bulletin at Bassano, less than one year after entering Italy, he enumerates among the spoils his army had taken, "three hundred *chefs d'œuvre* of art, the produce of thirty centuries." During the same period, Northern Italy had been forced to contribute 120,000,000 of francs; and during the whole two years of the war, an aggregate of 400,000,000 francs, a sum estimated by Alison to have been equal to £40,000,000 at that time in Great Britain! This is enormous—$200,000,000!—and seems incredible. But whatever may be said of the amount of spoliation to which other portions of the conquered country was subjected, or of the ethics of the system itself—it is very certain, that unhappy Venice did not escape the contribution of an ample quota. Some of the most splendid paintings transmitted to Paris were from the churches, and palaces, and public galleries of Venice. Among these was "*Saint Mark surrounded by Saints*," by Paul Veronese, which still fills a place in the *plafond* of the Louvre, and leaves one vacant in that of a chamber of the Ducal Palace. Another from the *plafond* of the chamber of the Council of Ten, representing a *Jupiter*, by the same artist, also remains at Paris; while a third, from the same place, by the same master, is at Brussels. Another, representing the "*Doge Grimani before the Virgin*," by Contarini, was returned among the rest; as, also, a superb cameo of "*Jupiter Protector of the Ægean*," which had been found at Ephesus in 1793, and which is now preserved in the library of St. Mark. Among the other works of art which have visited Paris, may be named the "*Martyrdom of St. Agnes*," of Tintoretto, at the church of *La Madonna dell' Orto;* the "*San Pietro Martire*," of Titian, at the church of Sts. John and Paul, which, while at the Louvre, was successfully restored; the "*Martyrdom of St. Laurent*," at the Jesuits, by the same master; the "*Virgin and*

Child and four Saints," by Bellini, at the church of San Zaccaria, of which picture there are three other copies by the same artist in the churches of Venice; and the "*Martyrdom of St. Bartholomew*," by Ribera (Espagnoletto), the only picture of the Spanish school in the Academy. It has already been mentioned, that the only picture of the French school at the Academy—"*The Magdalen at the feet of Christ*," by Lebrun, was sent from Paris in 1815, as a substitute for several Venetian pictures too old to bear removal. "*The Supper at Levi's house*," by Veronese, also crossed the mountains, as a pendant to his "*Marriage at Cana*," still at the Louvre. At one time more than a score of *chefs d'œuvre* of this artist were at Paris; but she lost half of them at the time of the general restoration. The celebrated "*Christ*," of Bellini, presented by that master to Louis XI. on his visit to Venice, at the close of the fifteenth century, is, however, still retained. It is said that Napoleon offered 20,000 francs in vain for the "*Ariosto*" of Titian, in the Manfrini Gallery. The picture of a *Berger*, in the same gallery, the only painting of Murillo at Venice, also arrested his attention, as well as a portrait of a lady, by Veronese, which was thought to bear a wonderful resemblance to Madame Elizabeth, sister of the unfortunate Louis XVI. The "*Rape of Europa*," by Paul Veronese, at the Ducal Palace, and the "*Virgin Enthroned*," at the Academy, by the same master, were also taken to Paris, as well as the "*Faith*" of Titian, in the Ducal Palace, and "*The Descent from the Cross*," by the same master, which is yet at the Louvre—Venice retaining two copies of the same picture—one at the Manfrini Palace, and one at that of Valmarana.

But Venice did not suffer alone. An armistice was granted to the Duke of Parma only upon payment of half a million of dollars, large supplies for the army, and twenty pictures. To retain the

"*Communion of St. Jerome*," the Duke offered the conqueror $200,000, but it was refused. To the Duke of Modena an armistice was granted only upon contribution of two millions of dollars, twenty pictures, and large supplies of provisions and horses. Milan contributed four millions of dollars and twenty pictures from the Ambrosian Gallery; while from the Pope was demanded, as the price of an armistice, four millions of dollars, one hundred objects of art, six hundred manuscripts, and a costly cabinet of medals: but the envoy of France had been assassinated at Rome without atonement. The treasures and reliques of the church of *Notre-Dame de Loretto* were also taken; as well as most of the best paintings of the churches of Bologna, and the jewels which adorned the shrines; and Paris yet possesses the celebrated bas reliefs by Riccio of Padua, taken from a church at Verona—a city which contributed nearly seven millions of dollars. At Leghorn, English goods, valued at nearly three millions of dollars, were seized in reprisal for the spoliation of French commerce by England on the high seas. But this latter spoliation was deemed only "the fortune of war;" and the money and merchandise, horses and provisions, legitimate prizes. The ravishment of the works of art seems alone inexplicable—albeit, they were but the luxuries of an opulent aristocracy, while the former were the necessaries of an impoverished people! *

The secret stipulation with Venice exacting [illegible] Manuscripts, was fulfilled from the depot of Government Archives in the convent adjoining the church of the Frari; and this article has been instrumental of more benefit to the world than all the others put together. Whatever the value attached to these archives, they embrace, per-

* English writers have been particularly severe on Napoleon's spoliation of Italy. Yet it would compare favorably, perhaps, with Lord Elgin's spoliation of the Parthenon, so bitterly satirized by Byron's "Curse of Minerva." The British Parliament voted £35,000 for these Athenian marbles in 1816, thus making the deed its own.

haps, the largest mass of written paper and parchment of an historical character in the world. There are not less than 8,664,709 manuscript volumes, arranged in 380 alcoves and cabinets. About 350 years ago, a portion of the Archives of the Council of Ten was consumed by fire. There remained, however, copies of all the decrees of this remarkable tribunal; and although the Ten were less given to writing than to acting, still, in a period of nearly five hundred years, a heavy mass of records would be apt to accumulate. There remained, also, that atrocious code—"the only code a legislative body has ever dared to erect on the avowed basis of perfidy and assassination,"* written by the Inquisitors themselves, and preserved in a casket, of which each one, by turns, kept the key. But for the conquest of Venice by the French, this extraordinary document would, in all probability, never have been laid before the world. The archives transported to Paris, in accordance with the fifth of the secret articles, furnished Count Daru, a Member of the *Académie Française*, with materials for his History of Venice,† which affords the only account of this ancient and mysterious government and city at all reliable or complete; while even this is disfigured by prejudice. The invasion of Venice was like the breaking open of the massive walls of a dungeon, and permitting the sunlight, for ages excluded, to pour in. Had she never been entered by a foe—a *foe*, however friendly the guise—her secret history would ever have remained as secret as it had, during her mysterious isolation of fourteen hundred years; it would never have been dragged out to the light and to the execration of mankind; but, like her *pozzi* and her *piombi*—her *pits* and her *leads*—have veiled its

* In a secret correspondence of a Venetian ambassador, published by Alfred de Musset, at Paris, is found recorded this:—"Pay to Signor A. the sum of fifty scudi, for having killed the Signor S., who spake ill of the Republic of Venice."

† Histoire de Venise, 8 tomes, 1821—recently published.

horrors in Cimmerian shades. Many of the darker evidences of the despotism of the Decemviri are said to have disappeared on the approach of the French. Hobhouse, in his notes to the fourth Canto of Childe Harold, says that the Venetians hastily blocked up the deeper of the dungeons of the Ducal Palace, and adds—"if you are in want of consolation for the extinction of patrician power, perhaps you may find it there." These dungeons are, indeed, dreadful; but the idea of them usually entertained, derived from these notes, as well as that of the *piombi* or *leads*, derived from "Cooper's Bravo," is, as before stated,* far from correct. One inmate only of these dungeons is said to have been found there by the French. He had been confined for sixteen years; and, on coming suddenly into the broad sunlight of the Piazza, was struck blind, and shortly died.

Among the few arrests made by the French on entering Venice, was that of the Count d'Entraigues, an emissary and agent of the Count of Lille, and of the emigrants, who had sought there an asylum. Napoleon might have sent him to Paris to be shot; but he did wiser: he gave the impoverished and terrified fugitive assistance in money, assigned him Milan as his prison-bounds, extracted from him all the secrets of the "Pretender" and the emigration worth knowing, as well as the whole history of Pichègru's treason, before undiscovered. Important disclosures, moreover, were made by the papers found in the Count's *portfeuille*. Subsequently, he broke his *parole*, and fled to Switzerland, where he published a shameful libel against the man who had spared his life.

* Introduction.

CHAPTER V.

CAMPO FORMIO.

INTELLIGENCE of the triumphs of Bonaparte was received at Paris by the friends of the revolution with unbounded joy, and by its foes with ill-concealed vexation—a vexation which was shortly manifested, by a motion of inquiry, on the 23d of June, by Dumolard, in the Council of Five Hundred, respecting events at Venice. "Rumor," said he, "diffuses everywhere our conquests over the Venetians, and the astonishing revolution which has crowned them. Our troops are in their Capital; their navy is delivered up to us; the most ancient government in Europe is annihilated; in the twinkling of an eye it again appears under democratic forms; and our soldiers, braving the billows of the Adriatic, are on their way to Corfu, to complete the new revolution! Admit these events as certain, and it follows, that the Directory has made war and peace, and in certain respects, a treaty of alliance, with Venice, and all without your concurrence."

This, certainly, was plausible—perhaps true. The historian of France* has well said—"The conduct of Bonaparte in regard to Venice was bold;" but, he adds—"it had, nevertheless, not ex-

* Thiers, on whom, as authority, collated with Alison, Botta, and Scott, the author has relied in all this narrative of the fall of Venice.

ceeded the limits of law." His manifesto of May 3d, was based on the necessity of "repelling hostilities already begun;" then followed surrender before war had actually commenced, succeeded at once by a treaty. Thus, Venice had been erased from the list of European powers, without a single consultation between the French General, the Directory, and the Council. The treaty forwarded by Junot to Paris, with the Austrian trophies, for ratification, was, therefore, almost the bulletin announcing the events.

But the motion of Dumolard failed of its object. It was one of the earliest and boldest of the movements of the Clichyans, in that conspiracy to overthrow the French Republic and restore the Bourbons, which was crushed by the prompt measures of the Directory, on the memorable 18th Fructidor, September 6th, 1797.

The interest felt by Napoleon in this event, and in those immediately preceding, was, of course, great. To leave Italy, in order personally to participate, however, was, of course, impossible. He, therefore, sent Augereau; and, subsequently, Bernadotte and his aide-de-camp Lavellette. The hero of Lodi and Rivoli, had been, indeed, severely assailed by the Society of Clichy. In journals, and in pamphlets, in the Council and in public meetings, they proclaimed, that Venice was the victim of his perfidy and private malice, and that the assassinations, so loudly complained of and so signally avenged, had been foreseen and contrived at his own Head-Quarters! Bonaparte replied in furious letters to the Directory:— "We have been assassinated by traitors," he wrote: "more than four hundred men have perished, pierced by innumerable blows with such daggers as the one I now send for inspection, yet the chief magistrates of the Republic would make it a crime to have it for a moment believed! I repeat, citizen Directors, the request I have made for my dismissal. I wish to live in peace, if the daggers of Clichy will permit me."*

But neither Napoleon's wrath nor his repeated request for a dismissal—of which, in all probability, he never even dreamed—diminished his wonderful activity. It was now, that, for the first time in his life, he visited Venice; and, like every one else, he was wonder-struck at its strange magnificence. He was shortly joined by Josephine, who had accompanied Junot on his return from Paris. "Come," he wrote to her—"come and enjoy the enthusiasm of which I am the object. Come and partake of the good fortune of a Frenchman, who is the first, since Pepin, to raise his flag on the monuments of the first of Republics." The young conqueror was too modest by half! Little Pepin never raised *his* flag on the "monuments" of Venice; and, in very sooth, she could have had but few monuments, if any at all, in the year of grace 804, for him to raise it on! But Napoleon was more versed in tactics than in chronicles. Josephine tells us, however, in her "Secret Memoirs," that she hastened to obey the summons, and "from Padua came to Venice by the canal of the Brenta, which communicates with the lagoons, a kind of ponds, or lakes, separated from each other by sand-banks, forming pretty islands." Josephine's topographical knowledge and graphical skill seem quite on a par with her husband's knowledge of history. "The beauty, the variety, the picturesque views, the delicious gardens along the banks of the Brenta," she continues, "enchanted me. In this country, nature everywhere presents a perpetual spring. The most magnificent

* Napoleon also refuted the calumnies of the Clichy faction in an anonymous circular, distributed throughout the army. In an address which he sent by Augereau to Paris, in the name of the Army of Italy, occur these significant words:—"Tremble, O, conspirators! From the Adige and the Rhine to the Seine is but a step! Tremble!"

palaces attest the wealth and luxury of their owners; the feathered inhabitants of this promised land, with their harmonious concerts, welcome the stranger, who comes to breathe the rich perfumes, exhaled from vast fields, almost without cultivation; for, along the road leading from Padua to Venice, the air is really embalmed. During all my travels in Italy, I found no region more delightful." Of Venice she says:—"Here stands that unique city, the strongest unfortified town known, impenetrable without any defence, and which has given the law to so many of the vanquished, without having ever yet fallen into the hands of a victor. My husband was now its conqueror, and I hastened to present him with the laurel, the symbol of his new glory. My presence seemed quite pleasing to the people of Venice. Those grave, illustrious Senators, whose fathers, if we are to believe an ancient tradition, descended in the direct line from the Adriatic Sea, (!) daily came and gave brilliancy to my court. Here, as at Milan, fête succeeded fête, and the thunders of Mars did not prevent the opening of the temples of Momus. All the authorities of the Cispadane and Transpadane Republics hastened to Venice to obtain a look at the French Washington. (!) I spoke Italian passably—enough, at least, to be able to reply to the compliments made me, and sometimes to the very wearisome speeches with which they honored the first *Citoyenne* of the French Republic—for thus they called me. I was in the midst of every kind of diversion, and for some time, the Carnival* furnished new varieties for our Venetian belles. I did my best to prolong the illusion."

The presence of Josephine, had, no doubt, a marked influence on Venetian society. The ladies fashioned their dresses upon hers, and abandoned the *zendale* for the cashmere. They also adopted

* This "Carnival" must have been at a subsequent visit; for it was now summer.

the French *etiquette* in visiting and entertaining. "Prior to the invasion," says a writer of the time, "a dinner-party furnished gossip for the whole town. In the largest palaces there were hardly a pair of chimneys: in private dwellings rarely but one, and that only for the kitchen, and seldom heated by a fire. But the Venetians are adopting French habits and employ cooks. They do everything, however, contrariwise from other nations. They enter their gondolas backwards; men wear their hats in the best company; the place of honor is on the left hand; few of the houses are open to visitors; they see each other only at places of refreshment—for a bench costs less than a supper."

Nearly sixty years have elapsed since these comments were made; yet they are hardly less true of Venice in 1853, than of Venice in 1797.

Napoleon's efforts to organize more permanent Governments for the City and States of Venice, were attended with no little difficulty, for the want of men whom he deemed suitable for the service. He seems to have felt the same contempt for the Venetians as that subsequently expressed in such bitter terms by Byron—"Good God!" he exclaimed:—"How scarce are men! There are in Italy eighteen millions, and with difficulty do I find two—Dandolo and Melzi!" Dandolo was a lawyer of Venice, and Melzi a lawyer of Milan.* Each was placed at the head of affairs in his respective city. This task completed, the young conqueror retired with Josephine to the beautiful palace of Montebello; and for a few months enjoyed some relaxation from his arduous and incessant toils.

The villa of Montebello, or, more properly, of Mombello, one of the most lovely in Italy, is situated about a dozen miles from Milan,

* Melzi d'Eril was a noble Milanese of Spanish extraction, uncle to Palafox, the defender Saragossa. He was framer of the Constitution of the Cisalpine Republic.

on the route to the Lake of Como. Its site is an eminence about a mile from the high road on the left, commanding an extensive view of the green plains of Lombardy. It formerly belonged to the Crivelli family, and was celebrated for its gardens and its exotics: but it is more celebrated now as the scene of those important negotiations, which, amid gayety and pleasure, preceded the treaty of Leoben, and for the most splendid Court which Northern Italy has ever known. Here were assembled Ambassadors from the Emperor, from the Pope, from Parma, Genoa, Venice, Piedmont, Naples, and Switzerland ; here the graceful Josephine—still a bride though more than a twelvemonth wed—received the homage due to the glory of her youthful husband ; and—far more dear to her—the adoring homage of that husband himself. Here Pauline exhibited those matchless fascinations, which later, were to irradiate her brother's imperial Court; and here was gathered all the rank, affluence, influence and loveliness of Italy, to swell the cortege of admirers of the most illustrious hero of the age, surrounded by a staff of officers worthy his renown. Balls, hunting parties, excursions to the Borromean Isles, to Lago di Como, to Lago Maggiore, and to the neighboring villages and towns, all of which vied in their homage with each other, hailing him as "the Saviour of Lombardy," formed a recreation to the severer tasks of diplomacy. "This," says Sir Walter Scott, "was, probably, the happiest period of Napoleon's life. Honor beyond that of a crowned head was his own, and the full relish of novelty, to a mind, which, but two or three years before, was pining in obscurity. Power was his, and he had not yet experienced its cares and risks : high hopes were formed of him by all around, and he had not yet disappointed them. He was in the flower of his youth, and married to the woman of his heart. Above all, he had the glow of Hope, which was marshaling him on even to more exalted dominion; and he had not yet become aware that possession brings satiety; and that all earthly desires and wishes terminate, when fully attained, in 'vanity and vexation of spirit.'"

As for Josephine, she was wont to call these days the happiest of her career. Not two years before, she had been a prisoner at Paris, awaiting the guillotine; and Napoleon had been a soldier out of employment—out of money—out of credit—with hardly a friend in the world! What a bewildering change for both! And both seemed now to enjoy their triumph to the full. Josephine, in her "Secret Memoirs," already quoted, can hardly find language to express her exaltation of feeling; "while Bonaparte," she says, "was utterly *intoxicated.*" "I am resolved," he said to her, "to be the great regulator of the destinies of Europe, or the first citizen on the globe. I feel myself capable of overturning all, even to the New World; and then, the universe will receive the law from my hands!"

The destinies of Genoa, Piedmont, Naples, the Grisons, the Cisalpine Republic, but, above all, those of Venice, which hung upon the treaty now being negotiated with Austria, engrossed the attention of Napoleon in the intervals of gayety, at the splendid Court of Montebello. The Preliminaries of Leoben, it will be remembered, were signed at that village on the 18th of April. By the articles of this convention, Flanders, Lombardy, and the frontier of the Rhine, were ceded to France—the whole of the continental states of Venice, including Illyria, Istria, Friuli, and Upper Italy, were secured to Austria—Romagna, Ferrara, and Bologna, taken from the Pope, were, with her Ionian Isles, secured to independent Venice; while Mantua, Peschiera, Porto Legnano, Palma Nuova, and Verona were, on the conclusion of a general peace, to be restored to the Emperor. Two Congresses were to be opened—one at Berne—the other at Rastadt; and peace was to be concluded within three months, on pain of nullity of the Preliminaries. Austria was, of course, anxious to withdraw Venice as speedily as possible from French influence. The occupation of Venice and the Ionian Isles by Bonaparte was certainly in derogation of the Convention of Leoben; but Austria herself occupied the Venetian provinces of Istria and Dalmatia in anticipation of a final settlement, and the offset was considered fair.

On the 24th of May the exchange of ratifications took place at Montebello, when the powers of the plenipotentiaries were verified, and the work of negotiation began. The conferences were, at first, excessively tedious. Count Cobentzel, aware of the re-action going on at Paris, protracted the negotiations on pretences the most frivolous; until all hope of the restoration of the Bourbons being crushed by the events of the 18th Fructidor, they began to proceed more rapidly, though still too tardily to satisfy the fiery spirit of Napoleon. The Count, with three colleagues, repaired to Udine, a town at the foot of the mountains, some sixty or seventy miles north-east of Venice; and Napoleon, with two colleagues, repaired from Montebello to the lovely villa of Passeriano, a few miles distant, the conferences taking place alternately at the two places.

One after the other the articles of a treaty were settled; but, on the subject of Mantua, it was found impossible to agree. Austria demanded it as the bulwark of Germany, while Napoleon insisted on retaining a place which had cost him so much, as the frontier of the Cisalpine Republic. In this emergency was it, that he seems, for the first time, to have resolved to sacrifice Venice, in order to secure a peace which the lapse of every day rendered more important. His *ultimatum* was this:—Venice to Austria—Mantua and the Adige to the Cisalpine Republic—the Rhine, Mayence, and the Ionian Isles to France; and this *ultimatum* he communicated both to Count Cobentzel and to the Directory. As for the latter, it had in June acceded to any disposition of Venice deemed expedient; but now, nothing less than the emancipation of all Italy would answer! Venice was, possibly, again busy with her bribes; and Barras, under date of September 8th, wrote to Bonaparte: "Let Mantua fall to the Cisalpine Republic, but Venice *not* go to the Emperor." Napoleon, on the 18th, replied—"If it is your *ultimatum* not to cede Venice, I much fear peace will be impracticable. Yet Venice is the city of Italy most worthy of freedom." The Directory replied with its *ultimatum*,—"Austria has long desired to swallow up Italy, and to acquire maritime power. It is the interest of France to prevent both these designs. It is evident, that if the Emperor acquires Venice, with its territorial possessions, he will secure an entrance into the whole of Lombardy. We should be treating as if we had been conquered, independent of the disgrace of abandoning Venice, which you describe as 'worthy to be free.' What would posterity say of us, if we surrendered that great city, with its naval arsenals, to the Emperor? Better, a hundred times, restore to him Lombardy than pay such a price for it. The whole question comes to this: Shall we give up Italy to the Austrians? The French Government neither can nor will do so: it would, in preference, encounter all the hazards of war." The same dispatch which bore these unwelcome instructions, informed Bonaparte that, on the resumption of hostilities, commissioners would be sent to relieve him of his diplomatic cares, thus affording him all his time to attend exclusively to his military duties. Enraged at these restrictions, the fiery Corsican at once replied—September 25th—"I beseech you, citizen, to appoint a successor to me, and accept my resignation. No power on earth shall make me continue to serve a government which has given me such a scandalous proof of its ingratitude." The prompt reply of the Directory, under date of the 29th, was utter inhibition of the cession of Venice! What was to be done now? Any man but Napoleon would have been at a loss—would have hesitated—might have despaired.

It will be remembered, that, by the Preliminaries of Leoben, three months only had been accorded for negotiations for peace. This period had expired, but the truce had been renewed. Still, Bonaparte was anxious for a speedy conclusion, and had resolved that such should be had by the opening of October at farthest. Then, in event of renewal of hostilities, he would at once cross the Alps, before the snow had blocked the passes, and thunder at the gates of Vienna: while, if the rupture were delayed until after the winter had set in, the Austrians, who could *descend* at all seasons, would meet him in Italy, and he might be in danger. His own reinforcements amounted to only 15,000 men, while Austria had thirty regiments and two hundred pieces of artillery on the Isonzo. She had, also, ordered a *levèe en masse* in Hungary; and 18,000 Hungarian horse had, for three months, it is said, "been in training on the banks of the Danube." Her preparations of all kinds had been immense. True, Napoleon had not been idle, but his position may be gathered from a dispatch of that date to the Directory, in which he says, that his foe had on the frontiers of Carinthia 90,000 infantry and 10,000 horse, besides 18,000 Hungarian volunteers; while *he* had only 48,000 infantry and 4,000 cavalry; and that, if Austria should assume the offensive, everything would become doubtful. There were, in reality, in Italy 80,000 French troops; but, of these, Bonaparte estimates not more than fifty or sixty thousand in the field. Besides, he urged that the war, once national, when the foe was on the French frontier, was now foreign —a war of governments, and that, in the end, defeat was inevitable. He urged, also, that it was indispensable for France to destroy the British monarchy. The "present moment," he writes to the Directory, October 18th, "offers to our hands a noble enterprise. Let us concentrate all our activity on the marine, and destroy England; that done, Europe is at our feet." Napoleon's desire to acquire the port and naval resources of Venice, is attributed to his anxiety to assail Great Britain in the East. Even then he contemplated the expedition to Egypt; and in a dispatch of a month previous, September 13th, he dwells upon this idea, and asks, also, "Why do we not lay hold of Malta?" Again, in his proclamation of September 16th, to the seamen of Admiral Brueys' squadron, then at Venice, he says,—"Without you, we could not carry the glory of the French name beyond a small corner of Europe; with you, we will traverse the seas and bear the standard of the Republic into the most remote countries."

At St. Helena, Napoleon revealed the value he attached to Venice in connection with that favorite scheme, the conquest of Egypt. He also highly appreciated the capacities of the city of Venice as the site for an emporium—whatever his appreciation of its people. "Venice," he says, "is better situated for commerce than any other port of Italy. The merchandise of Constantinople and the Levant arrives there by the shortest route, crossing the Adriatic; and thence it spreads itself over Upper Italy, as high as Turin, by the Po; over Germany, as high as Bolanzo, by the Adige; and thence by the passes of the Alps to Ulm, to Augsburg, to Munich, to Nuremburg. Venice is the sea-port of the Upper

Danube, of the Po, of the Adige; and nature destined her to be the storehouse of the Levant, of Italy, of Southern Germany."

Such were some of the reasons which urged Napoleon to present an *ultimatum* which he hoped would be accepted, though there were many other reasons of a private character hardly less powerful. He was weary of war—he had, like Macbeth, "won golden opinions from all sorts of people," and he wished to wear them awhile "in their newest gloss." He longed for peace and the society of his adored Josephine. He had been married more than two years, it is true; but he was still a lover, and, judging from his letters, a lover of the most ardent description. A new campaign could add but little to the glory of the past, and might detract much. It was too late to reach Vienna before Augereau with the army of the Rhine; while all the toils and all the perils of the campaign would fall on the army of Italy. Besides, he was anxious to be at Paris at this critical period—"Paris, the centre whence sprang all honors and all power," and where, already a warrior, he could appear with the double wreath of hero and diplomat upon his brow.

Regardless, therefore, of the express and reiterated injunctions of the Directory to "spare Venice," his mind was made up. Above all other considerations, he knew that the terms of this treaty were "glorious" for France. A slight event served to accelerate his resolution—as it were, to precipitate his purpose. On the morning of the 13th of October, on rising, he looked from his window away toward the Alps. Their peaks were white with snow! Winter was, indeed, at hand! He shut himself up in his cabinet, and marshalled his forces, and passed them in review. He had on paper 80,000 men—of these 60,000 in the field—of these 20,000 disabled, and no hope of reinforcements from the Rhine before it would be too late to cross the Alps; 40,000 French against 100,000 Austrians! "It is all over, Bourienne," he said to his secretary. "I shall sign the treaty. Venice shall pay the costs of the war, and guarantee the boundary of the Rhine. The Directory and the lawyers may say what they please."

The next conference was held on the 16th, at Udine. Napoleon resolved it should be the last. Both sides declared readiness to dissolve the Congress. Count Cobentzel recapitulated all his former arguments: Russia was the ally of Austria—the keys of Mantua were indispensable to the Emperor in exchange for the keys of Mayence, &c. Bonaparte sat indignant, but silent.

Rising as the Count concluded, he said, "This, then, is your last resolve? You would have war? Well, you shall have it!" Then, seizing from the sideboard a porcelain vase of great value, presented the Count by the great Catharine, he added, dashing it into a thousand fragments at his feet—"Thus—thus, within three months, will I dash your monarchy!"

Before the Austrian negotiators could recover from their astonishment, Bonaparte had left the room, and was entering his carriage. The Marquis de Gallo followed, and strove to detain him—"bowing most profoundly and in so piteous an attitude," says the Emperor at St. Helena, "that, despite my apparent anger, I could hardly restrain a laugh." An officer was at once sent to notify the Archduke Charles, that hostilities would re-commence in twenty-four hours. The Count alarmed, immediately sent the *ultimatum* signed to Passeriano; and, on the following day, the treaty was executed at that villa. It bore date, however, at Campo Formio, a small hamlet midway between the two armies, which could offer no accommodations for an interview to "the high contracting parties;" but it gave a name to a famous treaty, and received in return a name from that treaty itself, which it could have gained from nothing beside.

It has been said by one whose opinion is authority,* that never, during her whole existence as a nation, had France made so glorious a peace as that concluded by the first treaty between the Emperor and the Republic. By it she acquired—first, her natural boundary, the Rhine; second, the city of Mayence, the bulwark of the Empire; third, the city of Mantua, the bulwark of Germany on the south; fourth, the line of the Adige; and fifth, the Ionian Isles. In return she guaranteed to Austria, Venice and all her continental possessions on both sides of the Adriatic, including the towns of Verona, Peschiera and Porto Legnano; while Lombardy, with several of the Duchies and several of the Papal Legations, constituted the Cisalpine Republic. For Austria, also, a defeated power, the bargain was not bad. She resigned distant Lombardy and Flanders, with three and a half millions of people, and received Venice with all her continental possessions, embracing two seaports, with an equal number of people, equally rich and extensive, and above all, immediately adjoining her hereditary States.†

Among the numerous secret articles of this treaty, was one insisted on by Napoleon and reluctantly granted by Cobentzel, by which the illustrious Lafayette, with his colleagues, Latour-Maubourg, and Bureau-de-Pusy, patriots of the second, or Republican emigration, who, for five years, had been perfidiously incarcerated in the horrid dungeons of Olmutz—were set at liberty. A congress at Rastadt, for definitive settlement of the conditions of the treaty, was, also, stipulated: also, that Austrian troops should not enter Palma Nuova, until French troops had entered Mayence.

Anxious respecting the ratification by the Directory of a treaty

* Thiers. † Alison.

concluded in express contravention of its instructions, Napoleon sent Berthier and Monge to carry it to the capital. It was received by all Paris with unbounded joy, and was, of course, ratified. On the samé day, the hero of Italy was appointed "Commander-in-Chief of the Army of England!"

Napoleon now prepared to leave Italy—the scene of his glory for two years. He left an army of occupation of thirty thousand men, under Berthier, in Lombardy, and made his last appointments to office in the Cisalpine Republic. He ordered the withdrawal of his troops from Venice and her delivery to Austria. He provided an asylum in Lombardy for the Republicans of the fallen power. He ordered a funeral service for Hoche, just dead, and hastened the completion of the monument to Virgil at Mantua. Then taking a touching farewell of his army, and issuing an appropriate proclamation to the Italians, he proceeded rapidly through Lombardy, Piedmont and Switzerland to Rastadt, to exchange ratifications of the treaty and attend the Congress. This journey was one continuous triumph—a royal progress, though the young conqueror, moody and abstracted, seemed hardly conscious of his glory.* From

* Before leaving Milan, that capital presented Napoleon a medal struck in his honor, and decreed him the title of *Italicus*. But this, according to Josephine, seemed to elate him no more than all the rest. "Public favor, public favor," he repeated continually—"thou art as light as a zephyr—as inconstant as the seasons: thou wilt pass away like them; and, when the north wind blows, thou wilt cease to be seen. My deeds, history will transmit; but for myself, I may reap only oblivion." This said, he sank into the most gloomy and melancholy reflections. Wherever he went, rejoicings attended his footsteps: but Bonaparte was himself a stranger to the joy he inspired.—*Secret Memoirs of the Empress Josephine.*

This recalls Napoleon's reply to O'Meara, when it was remarked at St. Helena, that the triumphs of his first Italian campaign must have afforded him exquisite happiness:—"No—no—not one moment of peace. Life was only incessant strife and solicitude: and the inevitable battle of the morrow might annihilate all memory of the victory of to-day."

Rastadt, after arranging the delivery of Mayence, leaving the endless discussions of the Congress to his colleagues, he hastened *incognito* to Paris, which he reached on the night of December 5th, and repaired at once to a private house he had caused previously to be purchased. But, from this studied seclusion he was soon to be withdrawn, to receive an ovation such as French General had never received before.

CHAPTER VI.

"PERFIDY."

"No words," says Alison, "can paint the horror and consternation, which the promulgation of the Treaty of Campo Formio excited in Venice." A noble lady poisoned herself. The old Doge Manini fell senseless as he was about to take the oath of allegiance to Austria—even as did Francisco Foscari, three centuries and a half before, when he heard the great bell of St. Mark announce the election of his successor; and, like his deposed predecessor, Manini shortly died. The patriotic patrician Pesaro, who, as a *Provveditore*, and as an envoy to Napoleon, and in the Grand and Privy Councils, we have seen presenting, from the first, all the opposition in his power to foreign aggression, could not endure the sight of any standard on the masts of St. Mark, save that of the Lion. He became, therefore, a voluntary exile, and resided at London until his death—a period of eighteen years. In the church of the Frari stands the gorgeous mausoleum of his ancient family; on the banks of the Brenta its lovely villa; on the Grand Canal its immense, its massive, its magnificent palace—one of the architectural wonders of Venice—of Italy—of Europe—of the world. But he abandoned all—he abandoned his country, degraded and fallen, yet dearer than all—and died an exile in a distant land, rather than behold her in the stranger's grasp. Ah, had Venice had but more Pesaros! *

When, on the 16th of May, 1797, Venice admitted French troops within her sea-girt limits, it was with the distinct understanding of an independent and democratic existence thereafter. What then was the horror and indignation of those who had been favorable to that most questionable surrender, to find themselves yielded up to the darkest despotism in Europe? But, neither they nor the democrats of the continental towns, were alone in their profound emotion. Even the nobles and the populace, who had preferred Austria to France, revolted against the predominance of either over their ancient country. But it was now too late. Through their own insane and petty factions—through their own timid policy and almost judicial blindness—through their own degrading pusillan-

* The Palazzo Pesaro was constructed by Longhena, architect of the *Salute* Church. After the self-exile of its hereditary proprietor, it became the property of the noble Gradenigo family. In 1851, it again changed hands, and was in course of repair. Some ten or twelve years since, the Armenian monks of San Lazzaro had here one of their schools for the instruction of youths sent from the East for missionaries. It was called "The Raphael Armenian School," from the name of its founder, Alexander Raphael, of London—by birth an American, son of a rich merchant. He resided long at Venice, and became so attached to the Armenian monks of San Lazzaro, that, in 1845, he gave the Convent £100,000. He was a bachelor, a miser, a fox-hunter, very eccentric in dress and manner, and, at his death, in 1850, was member of Parliament for St. Albans. He left £300,000 in stocks, and £150,000 in estates. Leaving no will, his brother and sister, as heirs at law, received his property. He had taken offence at the Armenians on account of the manner of conducting his school, or he would, probably, have given them more. The school ceased some years since. A similar missionary school, or *Propaganda*, exists at the convent on the Isle of San Lazzaro, in the Lagune of Venice, and one, also, at Padua The entry of the Austrians exiled, also, the celebrated Ugo Foscolo—the dark, fierce, fanatic, hairy, bearded, poet, soldier, patriot. Driven subsequently from Lombardy by the French, he fled to London, and poured out his bitterness on the invader of his country in letters and lectures. An article on Venice from his pen appeared in the Edinburgh Review, June, 1827.

imity—their country had been lost—their ancient and beautiful capital enslaved. Their reward was appropriate—the contempt of foes, the hate of friends, the robbery of trophies, the dismemberment of territory, the extinction of liberties, the annihilation of nationality.*

On the 18th day of January, 1798, the French troops, by which for eight months Venice had been occupied, evacuated the place, and the troops of the Emperor entered. There was no resistance, no commotion, no disturbance—all was quiet; and, the only incident commemorative of the final extinction of the most ancient government of the world was the one already mentioned—its last chief magistrate, whose tomb is yet shown in the splendid church of the Jesuits, dropped lifeless when about to take the oath of allegiance to the stranger. "Thus," says Botta, "perished Venice. In these days, when Venice shall be spoken of, the name will signify Venice enslaved; but a time will come, and, perhaps, is not distant, when the name of Venice will mean ruins and sea-weed, covering the spot where once rose a magnificent city, the marvel of the world." And the British poet thus echoes the Italian historian:—"It may be safely foretold, that this unprofitable aversion (of the Venetians to the Austrians) will not have been corrected, before Venice shall have sunk into the slime of her own choked canals."

View these prophecies as we may, how fallible do they not prove the predictions of human wisdom. Venice died *not* when entered by France, nor yet when entered by Austria: and still she lives; and she still will live!

To Villetard, the Secretary of the French Legation at Venice, who remonstrated on her surrender to Austria, and who, an ardent

* Alison.

Jacobin, seems to have entered into engagements with her in behalf of France—Napoleon wrote in terms most contemptuous and harsh. "I have received your letter and cannot comprehend it," he said. "The Republic of France is not bound to sacrifice its interests to Venice. France does not make war for the benefit of others. It costs nothing to a handful of declaimers—madmen—to rave about republics everywhere. I wish these gentlemen would make a winter campaign. Venice exists no more. Effeminate, corrupt, treacherous—cowardly as hypocritical—divided into interests as numerous as there are cities—Italy, and especially Venice—is utterly unfit for freedom.* Yet, if she has the spirit to appreciate, or the courage to assert it, let her stand up for it—the time is not unfavorable." To Talleyrand he wrote—"You know not the Italians. They are not worth the sacrifice of 40,000 Frenchmen. You are under delusion. You think liberty can do much for a base, cowardly, and superstitious people. You wish me to perform miracles—I cannot. Italy has afforded me little support to liberty and equality. In my army I have only 1,500 Italians—rascals swept from the streets, and good only for pillage." "And thus, by denouncing Venice," says Alison, "would Napoleon fain strive to palliate his own unparalleled perfidy." "The history of the world," he continues, "contains no blacker page. To find a parallel we must search the annals of Italian treachery. It is difficult to say, whether most indignation is to be felt at the perfidy of France, the cupidity of Austria, or the insanity of Venice."

Is this just? Is it true? Is it reasonable? Let us examine.

* "Many politicians of our time," says Macauley, "are in the habit of laying it down as a self-evident proposition, that no people ought to be free till they are fit to use their freedom. The maxim is worthy of the fool in the story, who resolved not to go into the water till he had learnt to swim! If men are to wait for liberty till they become wise and good in slavery, they may indeed wait forever."

On the breaking out of the French revolution, Venice, as we have seen, sided with the absolute powers of Europe—signed with them the treaty of Mantua — afforded an asylum to the exiled Bourbons —withdrew her ambassador from Paris, and refused all communication with the Republic of France. Subsequently, however, impressed by the power of that republic, she exchanged ambassadors, and expelled the Bourbons. In June of 1796, Bonaparte, in pursuit of the Austrians, entered the Venetian States, and demanded as a right, from a neutral power, the same privileges which had been accorded his foes. The town of Mantua cost him a siege of three months and Peschiera a battle; and to prevent the occupation of Verona, Brescia, Porto Legnano, Bergamo, and other places in a similar manner, at his similar probable expense, he strengthened the Venetian garrisons with his own troops. The result was natural. The inhabitants had hated the despotism of Venice, and now hated it none the less by intimacy with the French republicans; though all political propagandism and proselytism had been expressly forbidden by Napoleon, as well as all interference with the existing government. To obviate the evils apprehended, Napoleon repeatedly urged on Venice French alliance, and also the quadruple alliance, promising a guarantee of the integrity of her ancient government and security against Austrian vengeance—all of which was as repeatedly rejected. He was accordingly forced to start on his expedition over the Alps to Vienna, leaving in his rear a covert and insidious foe ready to crush him, in case of reverse—leaving also menaces of terrible retribution, should his apprehensions be realized, and the pretended neutrality be infringed. It is probably true, moreover, that, in order to create a diversion in his favor, and to leave friends instead of foes in his rear, he now directly encouraged the propagation of free sentiments in the Venetian towns. Meantime Venice had begun mustering her forces, and arming and exciting the peasants and mountaineers against the French, and had consulted Austria about a Commander-in-chief for her army. It is plain, she had then no idea that the old saying, "Italy is the grave of the French"—was now, for the first time, to be falsified; and she as confidently expected, as she strongly hoped, soon to see back again, her friends, the Austrians, and in triumph; for her despotic spirit sympathized with despotism everywhere, even as much as it abhorred true freedom.

Well, hardly had Bonaparte started on his expedition over the Noric Alps, than an insurrection broke out in the Venetian provinces, and Brescia, Bergamo, Crema, and Salo declared their independence. To recover these places, Venice sent her Sclavonians; and the armed peasants were let loose to butcher the French and Jacobins, wherever found. The intervention of French troops now, of course, became indispensable; for, were the French defeated in the Alps, they would be cut to pieces in their retreat by this organized and ferocious force. Upon this, Venice at once despatched envoys to Napoleon, who overtook him at Gorizia, and demanded the restoration of the fortresses of Brescia, Bergamo, Verona, Peschiera, &c., which he had been forced to occupy, to keep out the Austrians; and, also, to aid the Sclavonians and peasants in putting down the *patriots!* Both demands were clearly absurd. Napoleon, so far from inciting, must have regretted this insurrection; for it was, at any rate, perilously premature for his purposes, and afforded Venice a pretext for unmasking a force which, in the event of his reverse, she might use to annihilate him. To give up the fortresses, his only retreat, were madness; while, to ask him to assist the avowed foes of the French against their avowed friends, and against the organic order of the Directory, was asking *rather* too much. "The French Republic," he said, "did not pretend to interfere in the internal dissensions of Venice; but the safety of her army required that he should not overlook enterprises hostile to its interests." And, once more he urged alliance with France, declaring that all should then be well. This alliance was again declined. It was never offered again!

But the surrender of the fortresses, and the putting down of the Jacobins being refused by Napoleon, the envoys of Venice declared that the Republic would no longer furnish the French army with supplies, especially as it was now no longer within her territory.—To this Bonaparte briefly and sternly rejoined, that Venice had fed his foe, and she should now feed him. If she called this *neutrality*, he would have the benefit of it. The result was sure and speedy. The envoys promised abundant supplies at the rate of a million of francs per month, for six months, charged to France, and were then dismissed with the distinct declaration, on the part of Bonaparte, that, should she, in his absence, prove hostile, he would return and crush her.

Well, she *did* prove hostile in his absence. The French and Jacobins were slaughtered everywhere, singly and in masses. Two hundred Poles, sent prisoners to Venice, were confined in the *piombi* and *pozzi* of St. Mark; and many friends of France were strangled, or were drowned in the Canal Orfano. Informed of this, Bonaparte sent Junot to the Senate demanding the release of the prisoners, and the disarming of the peasants, on pain of immediate declaration of war. But, on the very day before, April 9th, Napoleon had signed the armistice of Leoben, which he had forced the Archduke Charles, by a series of triumphs to demand, and by which, for Belgium and Lombardy, he had given Austria the continental possessions of Venice—compensating that Republic with Romagna, Bologna, and Ferrara. This compensation was adequate; if any one was to complain, it was the Pope, from whom, as a foe, a Legation had been taken: the transfer had been often before spoken of, and was strongly desired by Austria; and finally, if *she* had no scruples at the dismemberment of a friend, by which dismemberment she was to profit — of a friend who had incurred her present terrible troubles because of that friendship—how was France to be expected to have scruples at consenting to the dismemberment —with no hope of gain to herself—of an inveterate and irreconcilable foe? That such scruples would have been folly — or, at any rate, that, if there were "perfidy" in the transaction, on Austria alone should fall denunciation—events at that very time occurring in the Venetian states satisfactorily demonstrate.

But Alison says that the page of history has nothing more iniquitous to present; that it was darker in atrocity than the partition of Poland; and has only excited less indignation, because attended with no heroism or dignity in the vanquished. But Poland was partitioned by the very powers that had been her allies, and had promised her support! She was, moreover, an old and independent nation even as Venice, though with distinct natural boundaries, a reasonable government, and a brave race of people. But the natural limits of Venice were the Lagune and the Dogado. Nature never gave her provinces on the main land, nor beyond the Adriatic, nor in the Grecian Archipelagó. It was conquest—conquest only—unscrupulous conquest—the insatiate and grasping conquest of a thousand years. As for her government, it was abhorrent and abhorred, even by her subjects; while her perfidy and her cowardice were a by-word among the nations. Besides, Poland was *demolished*, while Venice by this arrangement of the Preliminaries, would be made stronger. The French historian is right then, when he says, that there was nothing in the partition of

Venice like that of Poland—except, indeed, *the perfidy of Austria.* It was she—Austria—who rendered both dismemberments indispensable.* The provinces of Venice were the only recompense she would accept for the line of the Rhine, which line France was bound in honor to demand, and the cession of Lombardy, which province, after its friendship and republicanism, it would have been base in France to desert.

But, to conclude all, Venice was the deadly foe of Republican France, had rejected repeated offers of alliance and protection, and lay in wait, like a lion—a "Winged Lion"—in his lair, to leap on her at her first reverse. True, she had, also, declined alliance with absolute Austria; but she was none the less her warm and close friend. Indeed, at the very time of the partition, she was aiding Austria—was asking a General for her army of Austria, and was assailing France!

Early in April, the retreat of the French before Laudohn from the Tyrol to Verona, and before the Croats from Trieste to Palma Nuova, confirmed prior rumors of Napoleon's utter defeat in the Noric Alps, and the advance of 60,000 Austrians on Italy. Venice now threw off her characteristic mask. Twenty thousand peasants poured down, at her command, from the mountains of Bergamo, and were joined by three thousand Sclavonians, sent by her to Verona. Then commenced the horrors of the Veronese Easter, continuing a whole week, wrapping the whole country in flames, and drenching it with French blood—the very hospitals of the sick supplying the butchers with more than four hundred victims! At the same time French blood was basely spilled on the deck of a French vessel, by the Commandant of a Venetian fort, and that Commandant was applauded by the Senate for the deed! There could be but one

* By the villany of Russia, and the perfidy of Austria and Prussia, heroic Poland fell.

possible result. *War*—agreeably to the customs of all nations, savage or civilized, ancient or modern—was inevitable. It was declared, and Venice, who could yet, after all, proudly have defied her adversary, yielded without a blow. Anticipating the Treaty of Milan, with a baseness and a cowardice unparalleled in history, and matched only by her own previously unmatched perfidy, she lay at the feet of one whom she regarded as her conqueror — though he was not so, and could not so have become— her ancient government, rights, powers—every thing most dear —and with her own hands, in her own barges, conveyed troops over her Lagune into her Piazza, which could never have otherwise been reached—conveyed troops to a spot, to save her from anarchy, which, for fourteen centuries, had been unpolluted by hostile step, and on which a transalpine soldier had not trod since the French crusaders knelt to implore the aid of Dandolo, eight hundred years before! True, Venice understood, that, by this submission she secured her old and independent nationality, with a democratic constitution; and such was, probably, the understanding and the design of her conqueror—a design which subsequent events, and the avarice of Austria alone, rendered it impossible for him to carry out.

As for "the spoliation of her arsenals, galleries, fleet, and treasury," so pathetically deplored by British historians, they seem not to consider that such spoliation is the prize—the penalty—the fortune of war: that, *Vae victis!* is the expression of an idea older even than the Roman phrase which conveys it: that the "spoliation" took place in direct accordance with treaty: that the conduct of their own nation—England—in seizing the Dutch fleet, led the same to be apprehended with reference to the fleet of Venice;* and that

* Copenhagen and the Parthenon, not to name India and China, one might imagine

the junction of that fleet with the squadron of Admiral Brueys was indispensable to secure the Ionian Islands, and to provide a sufficient French force in the Adriatic. That Napoleon at that time had the purpose of plundering Venice, and then handing her over to Austria, "like a squeezed lemon," as has been charged, seems improbable, if not absurd. It is plain, he had already begun to think of "fighting England in the East,"—the favorite scheme of his whole career—and deemed Venice inestimable as a port from which to fit out his "Expedition to Egypt." Why then despoil her, and give her to a foe?

The causes which led to the cession of Venice by France, or rather, her seizure by Austria, at Campo Formio, seem to have been abundantly developed during the negotiation. At first, such transfer was not mentioned; and it was only when Cobentzel utterly refused to forego his demand for Mantua, which had cost Napoleon a three months' siege, and was the bulwark of the Cisalpine Republic, as well as of the Tyrol—that Venice was named. Peace, we have seen, was indispensable to Napoleon; and Austria had long coveted another sea-port, besides Trieste, on the Adriatic. Venice had manifested as much love to Austria, as she had hate to France; yet, the cession of Venice was the sole condition on which Austria would cede indispensable Mayence and Mantua, and conclude an indispensable peace! There can be no doubt, therefore, that she was then as eager for the glittering prize, as she was, twenty years later, at

would render England silent, at least, if no more, respecting Napoleon and Venice. The capital of a neutral Power bombarded and nearly burned, and her fleet of thirty-five vessels seized and carried off! "Henceforth, treaties with that perfidious Power shall be written in blood and fire!" exclaimed the French Emperor, when told of the outrage of the Baltic. "Treaties are made to be referred to—not acted on," said the Marquis of Lansdowne, quoting the Great Frederick, in the British House of Lords, in 1791; "and the moment they are perceived to be against a country's interests, cease to bind!"

the Congress of Vienna in 1814–15, when it was demanded by her, and secured to her, in utter scorn of the great principles of the treaties of the time—the restoration of all Europe to its *status quo ante bellum* — its condition before the earthquake of the French Revolution—confirming thus her prior perfidy.

As for the people of Venice, the only portion of them really to be pitied, because of the transfer to Austria, were the flaming Republicans — the "Jacobins," as they had been stigmatized — who had overthrown their ancient government to receive the democracy, of which they were now deprived. To throw this red-hot and inflammable mass, which had endured so much for its French principles, and which, with such religious hatred, had hated all approach to despotism, into the freezing embrace of the most absolute despotism in Christendom — a despotism only less hideous than that they had just escaped — was, indeed, as has been well said, "cruel;" and must have caused in them sensations not unlike those attending a plunge into the ice-water of the Neva, after being steeped in the scalding steam of a Russian bath! No wonder that they denounced, loudly and deeply, both of the "high contracting parties;" pronounced "a plague on both the houses;" refused to be comforted; and failed utterly to appreciate, or to avail themselves of, the retreat provided them by Bonaparte, in the Cisalpine Republic.

As for the nobles, with their dependents and clients, the populace —the government, to whose tender mercies they were now committed, must have proven infinitely more consonant to their aristocratic feelings and their absolute principles, than the hated democracy which they owed to the hated French — a government infinitely nearer to their own old and cherished oligarchy. Indeed, it is asserted that this party, constituting the largest proportion of the

Venetian people — "celebrated with transports of joy the victory over the democratic faction, though obtained at the expense of the very existence of their country." This Napoleon had foreseen. "He disliked the Venetians; he saw that the change of government had produced no change of opinion; that the nobility and the populace were enemies of the French, and of the revolution, and well-wishers of the Austrians, and that a very small number of wealthy citizens approved the new order of things; that the democratic municipality manifested the worst disposition towards the French; and that almost every person in Venice desired a turn of fortune which would permit Austria to restore the old government."*

When and where, in his whole wonderful career, it may be asked, did the Man of Destiny endure from any government so much and so long, as from the government of Venice? Yet, without attempting any undue apology, or seeking any undeserved palliation for his

* The poet Moore in his "Rhymes on the Road," thus speaks of Venice:—

"Mourn not for Venice—let her rest
In ruin 'mong those states unbless'd,
Beneath whose gilded hoofs of pride,
Where'er they trampled, Freedom died.
Mourn not for Venice—though her fall
Be awful, as if Ocean's wave
Swept o'er her—she deserves it all,
And Justice triumphs o'er her grave.
Thus perish every king and state,
That treads the steps which Venice trod,
Strong but in fear, and only great
By outrage against man and God!"

The poet Shelly, in the "Lines Written among the Euganean Hills," represents the distant towers of Venice, under Austrian rule, as—

"Sepulchres, where human forms,
Like pollution-nourished worms,
To the corpse of greatness cling,
Murdered, and now mouldering."

conduct in its surrender, the sweeping declaration of his foes is by no means endorsed, that "no possible apology can be found." And, so far from just is viewed that other sweeping declaration, that "the whole infamy of the treaty, so fatal to Venice, rests on the head of Napoleon," that it may be unhesitatingly declared, that to AUSTRIA, and to Austria alone, is due "the deep damnation of her taking off." The Senate of Venice, in its proclamation of April 12th, 1798, after the occupation by Austria, sustains this view. "Venice, from the breaking out of the French revolution," says this paper, "though at times vacillating, had, on the whole, acted with the Emperor and against France; she had given safe-conduct, support, aid and comfort to the imperial armies; she had refused all alliance with his foes; and, at length, in support of his cause, and because of favor to him, she had compromised herself in open war against those foes." Was it just—was it honorable, therefore, when her evil day at last came—was it not, indeed, unutterably base, instead of defending an only too-faithful ally, to suggest her dismemberment, and greedily to grasp the spoil?—to seize on her capital and continue to hold it for half a century, and in perpetuity, indeed, despite all principles of justice, and of all international treaties and laws?—to blot out from the map of Europe that most ancient and illustrious of commonwealths, which, for fourteen hundred years, had maintained an independence of glory and of power? Well might her annihilation, like that of unhappy Poland—though less base—"cause a shudder throughout Christendom;" and well may the British historian, with all his prejudices, say of the perfidious instrument of her destruction, that "it was an act of rapacity which must for ever form a foul stain on Austrian annals."*

* Venice, undoubtedly, precipitated her own doom by her remarkable refusal of all alliance, and her obstinate adherence to neutrality. As early as 1791, Sardinia proposed

But not long was this perfidious power destined to retain her ill-gotten kingdom, as we shall see.

In 1798, Napoleon was in Egypt, and the following year was, to the combined armies of the Russians and Austrians, under Suwarrow, what 1796 had been to the French, under Bonaparte. But, early the ensuing spring, another Hannibal swept like an avalanche down the Alps, and the battle of Marengo and the Peace of Luneville restored Upper Italy, after an interregnum of a few months only, to its condition under the Treaty of Campo Formio. In January, 1802, was established the Italian Republic, of which Melzi d'Eril, the Milanese statesman, was nominated by the First Consul the

alliance; in '92, Sardinia with Naples did the same; in '97, Bonaparte urged it four different times, Austria twice, and Prussia once; but all the offers were alike rejected. The Ten, it is said, retained the proposals from the *Savii*, or Sages (there being five for the State, five for the Marine, five for the *Terra Firma*, &c.) and the *Savii* retained them from the *Pregadi*, or Senate; for they seem never to have been even acted on by the latter. So, when the Senate accepted 10,000 volunteers of Bergamesco, the *Savii* rejected them. Yet, as early as '91, Venice recalled her naval marine and refused it to Tuscany to defend Leghorn, because "needed for her own defence;" while, as early as '96, as we have seen, at Pesaro's instance, she began secretly to arm, after the stormy scene at Villagio, of Napoleon with Foscarini, the Proveditor of *terra firma*, and the occupation of Verona. Her people, also, voluntarily aided her with a million ducats of contribution. The secret of Prussia's zeal for Venice was fear of her ultimate possession, with the Adriatic, by Austria; and the fear did not deceive. Intrigue and corruption were the order of the day. A forged circular precipitated the Veronese Easter: two forged letters to the old Doge, May 11th and 12th, menacing conspiracy and promising democracy, precipitated the fall of Venice: Querini's bribe to the Director Barras of 700,000 livres *tournois*, in bills, at thirty days, was approved by Venice; but Querini was sent from Paris—Venice was not spared—Querini ignored the bills when presented—was arrested by the Directory, December 3d, '97, and sent to Milan—was thence sent off for Paris in March, and, on the 30th, *en route*, was suffered to escape! Among other charges of Vandalism against Napoleon is—that he suffered his soldiers to sell valuable archives of Venice for waste paper, while whole cart-loads that went over the Alps to France and Germany never returned. The latter clause of this charge is, certainly, more probable than the former, though both, probably, are alike untrue.

Vice-President.* On the 18th of May, 1804, the French Senate declared Napoleon Emperor, "through the grace of God and the principles of the Republic;" and the new Pope, Pius VII., crossed the Alps in mid-winter to officiate at the coronation at Notre Dame: but Napoleon took from him the crown he had consecrated, and placed it on his own head, and then placed her diadem on the head of Josephine. One year later—the Italian Republic had become "The Kingdom of Italy," at its own request, and the Emperor, after a triumphant progress through Piedmont, on the 26th of May, 1805, in the venerable Minster of Milan, in like manner violated the sanctions of antique usage, and himself placed on his head the Iron Crown of Lombardy, consecrated by Cardinal Caprara, repeating aloud its haughty motto—"*Dieu me l'a donnèe: Gare à qui la touche.*"†

An invasion of the new kingdom by the Archduke Charles soon followed; but it ended in his defeat by Massena on the banks of the Adige; and the great battle of Austerlitz, December 2d, 1805, forced the Emperor Francis to the Peace of Presburg. By this treaty, signed at the capital of Hungary, while Napoleon was at Schöenbrunn, on the 26th of December, and which concluded a campaign of only six months, signalized by only one great battle, Austria lost 20,000 square miles of territory, two and a half millions of subjects, and ten millions of florins (five millions of dollars), of annual revenue. She lost Venice and her States—consenting, at the same time, to their union with that new kingdom by an attack on which she had commenced the war. In exchange for Venice, Austria received the Electorate of Salzburg. Napoleon's ostensible

* Subsequently Melzi became Duke of Lodi; but he was suspected, and was excluded from active office.

† "God hath given it to me; woe to him that toucheth it."

purpose in this was to remove that warlike power from the eastern frontier of his empire.

For ill-fated Venice this change of masters could only be for the better. Under the Austrian rule of eight years, she is said to have been ill-governed and oppressed, and on Lombardy the leaden hand of despotism had begun to lie with ponderous weight. During this period, Venice witnessed but one event of political interest worthy of mention. In the month of March, 1800, the Papacy having become vacant by the decease of that feeble and persecuted old man, Pius VI.,* a conclave of cardinals, convened at Venice, elected the Cardinal Chiaramonti, Bishop of Imola, equally feeble, and destined to even more persecution, to the chair of St. Peter. He was crowned with imposing pomp, as Pius VII. in the spacious church of *San Giorgio Maggiore*, where his benevolent face is yet to be seen on canvass over one of the interior portals; and, a few weeks later, he departed for Rome, where he arrived early in July to assume the administration of the Tiberine Republic.

In September of the ensuing year he concluded a *Concordat* with the French Republic, by which, under the auspices of the First Consul, the Roman Catholic religion was made that of France. But strife arose; and, on the night of the 5th of July, French soldiers broke into the Quirinal, and carried off its inmate; and, for five years, he was the prisoner of Napoleon, against whom he launched the thunders of Rome. "Does he think his excommunications will make the weapons fall from the hands of my soldiers?" scornfully asked the Emperor of the Viceroy of Italy, in 1807. But himself, the Man of Destiny, recalled those words, and so did his

* Berthier proclaimed the Roman Republic February 15th, 1798. Pius died a captive in France, August 29th, 1799.

soldiers, during the unspeakable terrors of Moscow and a Russian winter. Cardinal Pacca with holy horror refers to the verification of the impious taunt.*

"If I mistake not," said the Emperor to his captive, at Fontainbleau, "the Conclave at Venice, by which you were elected, took its inspiration from my Italian campaign, and from words I had dropped respecting you." In 1813 a *Concordat* was concluded, but subsequently revoked.

In January, 1806, Austria evacuated Venice, and French troops under General Miollis entered. Its annexation to the kingdom of Italy by formal decree took place the following March. Dalmatia and Istria, three years later, were detached frrom it and incorporated with France.†

It was in 1807, that Napoleon, having visited Milan, prolonged his triumphal progress to Venice, in compliance with the invitation of her Patriarch Gamboni, who had conveyed it to St. Cloud, "laying the heart of the Sea-City at his feet." Napoleon had replied "that he would willingly visit Venice, well knowing the love she bore him." According to Botta, the whole city was illuminated to receive her Sovereign—the *Canale Grande* burning as light as day, and the Place St. Mark more brilliant still. "There were regattas, balls,

"On the 10th of June, 1809," says Pacca, "Napoleon published in Rome his decree for the deposition of the Pontiff. This the Pontiff met by a bull of excommunication, which was posted by his agents against the walls, in the most public places, in open day, and at the three Basilicas of St. Peter, St. John Lateran, and Sta. Maria Maggiore, at the hours when the people were gathering for Vespers. The agents were seen, yet none were betrayed; it was found impossible for the French to discover them by most searching inquiry. The whole population, also, resolved to obey the bull, and on the following day, Monday, every Roman in the employ of the French, down even to Custom-house porters and street scavengers, resigned their places." How diminished was Papal influence in 1849!

† Marshal Marmont, when Governor of Dalmatia, under the Empire of Napoleon, published a work descriptive of that singular country and people.

and operas," continues the unfriendly Italian ; "and what was even worse, there were plaudits of voices and hands. Every thing wore a cheerful and serene aspect; notwithstanding which Napoleon himself dreaded assassination: and Duroc, the Grand Master of the palace, was more than usually diligent, visiting cellars and cisterns. Some Venetians fluttered around their lord with joyful faces—for the age preferred a base but splendid servitude to honorable obscurity."

Eugene Beauharnais, son of Josephine, was appointed Viceroy of the new kingdom; and though but twenty-five years old, he governed wisely and well, and became, as some assert, as great a favorite of the Italians as he was of his imperial step-father. Others assert that he was as odious as he was pompous. Napoleon himself was but a year older when conqueror of Italy. Prince Eugene abode some time at Venice, and it was by his order the *Procuratie Nuove* was transformed into a *Palazzo Reale* for the residence of himself and court.*

Availing himself of the new kingdom, Napoleon established a new nobility, appropriating a portion of the revenue and the lands of the provinces for its support. In Parma and Piacenza were erected three of these fiefs or dukedoms; in Naples six; in Venice twelve, among which were Bassano, Dalmatia, Rovigo, Treviso, Vicenza; in the Papal States two, Pontecorvo and Benevento; and all were rendered noted by the celebrity of such names as Ney, Caulincourt, Bernadotte, Talleyrand, Mortier, Soult, and Savary.

* Eugene was made Prince of Venice and his infant girl Princess of Bologna. His wife's father, the King of Bavaria, with his queen, was present; also, Joseph Bonaparte, King of Naples, Eliza, Princess of Lucca, Murat, Grand Duke of Berg, Berthier, Grand Duke of Neufchatel; while Lucien from Rome, hitherto estranged, met his brother at Mantua, and was urged, in vain, to accept a crown.

CHAPTER VII.

LOMBARDO-VENETO.

The eight years of French rule at Venice, from 1806 to 1814, has left very different traces on that beautiful city, from those left by the eight years of Austrian rule, from 1798 to 1806, which immediately preceded. Everywhere in Venice, even now, may be seen the "mark" of Napoleon. It was by his order that the old structures at the eastern extremity of the city were demolished, among them being a church, and the beautiful Public Garden created —the only spot of the kind in all Venice, if we except the smaller garden on the Grand Canal, in the rear of the Royal Palace, or new Palace of the Procurators. Originally, this latter spot was the site of a dock-yard: subsequently it became that of a menagerie of wild beasts; and, in 1809, Napoleon transformed the fish-market, which then possessed it, into the lovely garden now existing. He also constructed the elegant and classical Greek Pavilion at its extremity, surrounded by water, whither he was wont to repair during his residence in the adjacent palace, while at Venice, to imbibe the exhilarating Mocha, of which he was so fond, and which, if "a poison," he considered a "very slow" and very delicious one. It was in this garden, as some assert, that Napoleon's statue was erected.

More probably, however, its site was the Piazetta, and opposite the great window of the Ducal Palace. It was inaugurated with much ceremony and solemnity, on the 15th of August, 1811. It was of marble, of colossal size, erect and naked, bearing in one hand the globe of Charlemagne, and in the other the sword of the Cæsars; and was sculptured by Dominico Bauti, an artist of Venice. A model may be seen, it is said, in the Brera Gallery at Milan, where is, also, to be seen a bronze statue of the Emperor designed for the Triumphal Arch of that city, representing Achilles, like that of Wellington over the entrance to Hyde Park. The marble statue at Venice disappeared in 1814; and its whereabouts seems not now to be known. It is said, that when the statue was about to be removed, a gondolier of the *Molo* cruelly exclaimed, "Let it stand, only turn the hands down." Such a change would have made the figure of an emperor the figure of a mendicant—the globe and the sword having been taken away.

Another memorial of Bonaparte—a bust which looked down from amid the old Roman heads which decorate the pediment of the *Fabbrica-Nuova*, now a portion of the Royal Palace, occupying the western extremity of the quadrangle of the Place St. Mark, opposite the Basilica, and uniting the old range of palaces on the north with the new range on the west—has, also, disappeared. Here stood, in 1809, the celebrated old church of *San Gimianino*, often before removed, containing the remains of the great Sansovino, removed oftener yet. In 1810, the church was demolished, the remains of the architect being transferred provisionally to the church of *San Maurizio*, and thence to that of the *Salute;* and the New Palace of Napoleon rose to complete the most splendid square in Europe. Napoleon strengthened, also, the defences of Venice, repairing the old fortifications and constructing new—the strong fortress of Malghera being the most considerable. He, also, improved the Arsenal, expending upon it a portion of the annual subsidy of thirty millions of francs which, after the annexation of Venice, was required of the Italian kingdom, on the pretext of supporting the French army of 30,000 men constantly quartered there. This entire sum was expended in Italy, besides other sums from France; and the effect was decidedly beneficial on the prosperity of the kingdom, though bitterly mortifying to national pride. This forced contribution and the military conscription were the chief subjects of complaint during Napoleon's rule. The annual levies, from 1806 to 1814, amounted, in aggregate, to 98,000 men, though but a portion were ever called into active service,—6,000 men being demanded during each of the first two years, and 15,000 during each of the last four. More than 30,000 Italian conscripts were sent to Spain, of which number less than 9,000 ever returned home! The loss in Russia is said to have been yet more severe, because it fell chiefly on members of the first families, who, as "Royal Velites," or Guards of Honor, were forced to accompany the Emperor on that disastrous expedition; and, unaccustomed to hardships and the inclemency of the climate, perished by the hundred.* In the winter of 1812, there is said to have been hardly a household of consideration in Lombardy not in mourning. Among the *Velites*, or volunteers of the Emperor's Italian Guard who died at the close of the Russian campaign in 1813, is enumerated by Count Litta of Milan, in his "*Famiglie Celebri d'Italia*," Francesco, "the last glory of the house of Foscari." Another Foscari, a lieutenant in the fourth regiment of foot, is mentioned by the same writer, as having refused to enter the Austrian service on the downfall of Napoleon, and as being, a few years since, a comedian at the Fenice Theatre. Domi-

* Spalding.

nico Foscari was, also, a player; while Marianna was the wife of a coachman of Pordenone, and Luigia wife of a tradesman of Dunkirk! Oh, what reverse! As for the great Conaro family—the last of the kindred of the Queen of Cyprus served Napoleon, and received the cross of the Legion of Honor. He was *aide* to the Viceroy of Italy, Eugene Beauharnais, and died some ten or twelve years ago.

Napoleon's policy of suppressing monastic institutions and religious establishments, found ample exercise in Italy, and especially in Venice. In 1805, the monastic orders were reduced, and in 1810 abolished. Napoleon found more than a hundred churches at Venice, and left little more than half as many. As for convents and monasteries, he suppressed all—that of the Armenians only excepted. Gamboni, the Cardinal Patriarch of Venice at this period, was highly esteemed by the Emperor for his charity, liberality, and learning. Early in life, Gamboni is said to have been one of the gayest of the clerical courtiers of Pius VI.

Napoleon seems to have done all in his power to restore Venice to her pristine commercial importance; and, if he failed to succeed, to the almost constant blockade of the port, and the restrictions thrown around trade by his "continental system," may the failure, in a great degree, be attributed. As early as 1806, he adopted, with slight modifications, the *projet* of a system of works to protect the port of Malamocco—the principal approach to the city—from the accumulating sands—which *projet* was presented by Col. Salvini, a distinguished Venetian engineer. The work was commenced, but was interrupted by the war, and the downfall of the Emperor. In 1825 it was resumed under the Austrian government, and the interior works, which were most imperatively demanded, were completed. Since then the two enormous dikes projecting into the sea, have, also, been completed. Napoleon, likewise, conceded the privilege of a free port to the island of San Giorgio Maggiore: and, in view of all his efforts for the advancement of the ancient emporium, it is not strange, perhaps, that he should have declared in 1810, "I have now recompensed Venice for all the ill I did her at Campo Formio and at Luneville;" and, possibly, he was more than half right. Yet, Venice was by no means peculiar in the reception of his favors. Which one of all his conquests bears not the mark of his mighty mind? His enterprise is not less plainly read in the docks of Antwerp and the dikes of Ancona, than in the Piazza of Venice and the *Duomo* of Milan.

For a period of nine years, from 1805 to 1814, the amount of revenue of the Italian Kingdom is estimated at one thousand millions of francs. Out of this, seventy-five millions of francs were expended on highways. The Simplon road over the Alps cost six millions of francs, of which Italy contributed five millions and France one. There were similar expenditures on bridges, canals, and embankments of rivers, and the civil list amounted to an aggregate of forty-five million francs—or six million francs each year; while the population was nearly seven millions. Money was also consumed in the drainage of marshes—in improvements of agriculture—for premiums, models, and other encouragements to the useful arts—in establishments for education—pensions to nuns and priests impoverished by the suppression of their institutions; and, finally, in the construction of splendid palaces, squares, public promenades, and gardens. The value of the monastic estates was estimated at four hundred million francs. They were sold as fast as possible, and the proceeds applied to extinguishment of the public debt. Two millions from this fund were appropriated to aid in the completion of the splendid Cathedral of Milan.

But nothing which Napoleon did for Italy, it has been said, conferred half so distinguished a benefit, as the imposing upon her the *Code Napoléon;* and, in view of his principal acts, there seems much truth in the remark, that, "whatever the Italians may have felt at the time, they now look back to the glory and activity of 'The Kingdom' with regret;" as, also, truth in this remark, for her consolation even at the worst—that, "if Napoleon chastised Italy with whips, he chastised France with scorpions." At Venice, the French rule seems now recalled, not only with regret, but even with attachment. Efforts, not unsuccessful, were made to reconcile the Venetians to subjugation, by means of public amusements.* An anecdote *apropos* of this is related. In May, 1812, the Admiral Count Villaret-Joyeuse, who then commanded Venice as Governor-General for France,† wishing to add a novelty to the splendid fête which he gave the city in honor of the anniversary of the coronation of Napoleon, ordered two of the celebrated masts which stand in front of the Cathedral of St. Mark, and which are each about seventy feet high, to be covered with grease, and the summits to be hung with rich prizes for those who could reach them by climbing. On the central mast rolled out the folds of the tricolor flag of France. A crowd of candidates presented themselves for the contest; but the first who attempted the task were the last. A sailor of the Arsenal had grasped the prize at the summit of one

* "The dull and death-like yoke of the Austrians," says Mariotti, "made a sad contrast to the activity and liveliness of the French dominion."

† The Admiral and Count Villaret-Joyeuse, whose name has been previously mentioned, was Captain-General of the Islands of Martinique and Saint-Lucie, when, in 1811, he was named by Napoleon Commandant of the Fourth Military Division of the Empire, and in 1812, Governor-General of Venice. He died the same year, and at his own desire was interred at the Lido, as near as possible to the sea, where his humble and moss-grown tomb is yet to be distinguished. Byron's wish to be buried at the Lido need not be recalled.

mast, when it broke from its base and he fell—himself being killed and several of the multitude beneath being severely wounded by the casualty. A gondolier on the other mast, also, at the moment of success, lost his strength, or his equilibrium, and his brains were dashed out on the pavement below. The Admiral gave pensions to the bereaved families of the victims; but the old Venetians said, that the punishment inflicted by Providence for the desecration of the masts which had borne the ancient standard of St. Mark for a thousand years, was perfectly just.

But Napoleon's downfall was at hand. His grand army of half a million perished amid the horrors of a northern winter. All Europe was aroused *en masse* to crush him with a promise of freedom never to be fulfilled. Italy, with chivalric constancy—sullen Venice only excepted—rallied to sustain him, when abandoned by all his other conquests, though with her young Viceroy Eugene, she proved no match for the veteran armies of Austria, led by veteran chiefs, which poured down the passes of the Alps in the summer of 1813. The dreadful battle of Leipsic took place the ensuing autumn, when, for two days, 500,000 men with 3,000 cannon, slaughtered each other, until 100,000 dead and wounded strewed the field, and every stream ran blood; and, on the 11th of April, 1814, Napoleon signed his act of abdication at the Palace of Fontainbleau. One month later, the dethroned Emperor, was an exile at Elba.

The battle of Austerlitz deprived Austria of Venice: that of Leipsic restored it. On the 7th of April, the Austrian General, Bellegarde, signed a convention with Murat, King of Naples, by which, on condition of the guarantee of his throne, he was to aid the Emperor Francis in expelling the French from Italy. On the 13th, Prince Eugene was repulsed with severe loss, and the passage of the Stura was effected by Bellegarde. On the 17th arrived intelligence of the abdication of Napoleon. A convention was immediately concluded, in virtue of which, Palma Nuova, Osopo, and Porto Legnano were at once surrendered, followed by Mantua on the 28th, with 6,000 troops, and by all other portions of Lombardy shortly after. As for Venice, she was subsequently besieged by an Austrian army; but the French seem not to have offered any very desperate resistance. They attempted but one sortie—a sortie against the post of Cavanella on the Adige, and in that were unsuccessful.

By the Treaty of Paris, of May 30th, France lost fifty fortresses of note, 12,000 pieces of cannon, a population of fifteen millions of souls, 100,000 men in garrisons, and was restricted to her old frontiers of 1792, all her subsequent conquests being restored to their former possessors. By the Treaty of Vienna of March 23d, 1815, these articles were confirmed, and details were settled. Then came, in rapid succession, the return of Napoleon from Elba in March, the scenes of the Hundred Days, the annihilation at Waterloo in June, and the successive acts of the Congress of Vienna during the ensuing November. By these acts the restoration of the conquests of Napoleon, begun in 1814, was completed. Austria received her ancient territories of the Milanese and Mantua; she also received, in violation of the very principle on which she had taken up arms against Napoleon, Venice, with all its continental possessions, and a portion of the Grisons. As for the Netherlands, which Austria, in '97, by the Treaty of Campo Formio, had, for Venice, ceded to France, they were seized by the Congress, and, with the United Provinces, were constituted one political body, under William, Prince of Orange, having the title, King of the Netherlands. And thus, Belgium not having been restored to Austria, she claimed to retain Venice. The claim was recognized, and the desperate effort to make of two wrongs a right has been ever since attempted in vain.*

On the 7th of April, 1815, the Emperor of Austria proclaimed the erection of his Italian territories into the "Lombardo-Veneto Kingdom," lying between the Isonzo and the Po, and the Ticinio and the Adriatic. Of this kingdom, Lombardy comprises seven districts, including the Duchies of Milan and Mantua. In Venice are six districts: the Dogado, or Duchy of Venice—embracing the city with the Lagune and isles, and a narrow zone around its margin, comprising no towns larger than Mestre or Fusina: the territory of Padua: the Polesina: the Veronese March:† the territories of Vicenza, Brescia and Bergamo: the province of Treviso, with the districts of Feltre, Belluno, and Cadore; and the ancient ducal province of Friuli.

On the 24th of April, 1815, the Emperor Francis gave his Italian Kingdom a charter, without, at the same time, however, conferring much liberty.‡ He, also, substituted the code of law which obtains in Austria for the *Code Napoleon*, to the great dissatisfaction of the Italians. Garrisons were then placed in every town, and most of the officers, civil and military, were entrusted to Germans. Melzi d'Eril, Duke of Lodi, however, retained both his title and his pension. Monastic institutions were not revived, though such restoration was urged by Venice; and there are said to be at

* "Of all that Napoleon had done for Italy," says Mariotti, "only the work of destruction was sanctioned, Austria, Sardinia, and the Bourbons: the Pope and the Jesuits returned: but Genoa, Venice, and Lucca had ceased to exist."

† A German word for *border*.

‡ Austria, in 1809, promised Italy a constitution, through the Archduke John: Naples was promised independence in 1813, through Gen. Nugent; and England guaranteed her the same, through Lord Bentinck, in 1814. But these promises were all forgotten at Vienna, in 1815; and "the insurrections of 1820-21, '31 and '48 followed, as a natural result."

this day hardly a thousand monks and nuns in the whole kingdom. But, discontent soon began to manifest itself, although it was said then, as it is now, to be the best governed state in Italy; and then, as now, the *secret* causes of dissatisfaction were almost as powerful as were those palpable to every eye. The everlasting interference of the government with private interests—the terrible retribution for political offences—the offensive pomp of foreign rulers—the ceaseless and senseless parade of foreign troops—the mystery and pedantry of German officials—that singular sullenness and haughtiness which makes even favors seem insults; but, above all, the eternal hate of race between the Italian and the Teuton—such are a few of the less obvious sources of irritation, always tending, more or less, to revolt, even from the very commencement of Austrian rule, forty years ago.*

* Byron, in 1820, writing at Venice, says, "Few individuals can conceive, and none could describe the actual state into which the more than infernal tyranny of Austria has plunged this unhappy city."

CHAPTER VIII.

INTERVENTION.

For a period of five years, from 1815 to 1820, Italy seemed perfectly quiescent under its "legitimate rulers." This, however, was far from being the fact. The masses were discontented—the higher classes disappointed with the restoration, and this discontent and disappointment first reached a crisis—a culminating point—at Naples. It is singular that the movement of 1820, like that of 1848, should have commenced under the coldest, darkest, and most odious despotism of Europe.* But there had long existed in the

* From 1759 to 1828, a period of 69 years, Ferdinand IV. was King of Naples. In 1797, Gen. Championet took Naples and declared the Parthenopian Republic, the king having been conveyed to Palermo by Lord Nelson. But Cardinal Ruffo drove out the French under Macdonald, and a capitulation was signed by the representatives of England, Russia, the Porte, and Naples, and the lives and property of the republicans were assured upon surrender of the forts. This capitulation was repudiated by the king; and, supported by Lord Nelson under the baleful influence of Lady Hamilton, 25,000 lives were sacrificed, and Admiral Carracciolo was hanged from the yard-arm of his own frigate, the Minerva! But the tyrant's triumph was brief. The French returned—he again fled to Palermo, where, during the successive reigns of Joseph Bonaparte and Joachim Murat, he remained, until June, 1815. On the night of January 3rd 1828, Ferdinand died of apoplexy, as was *said:* he was found dead in his bed at 10 o'clock the next morning. He was 76 years old and had reigned 65; and, despite three revolutions and three restorations, is said to have been "the most popular monarch that Naples ever had," in like man-

Abruzzi and Calabria—for a period, indeed, of ten or twelve years—a secret society, with signs, symbols, forms of initiation, and modes of recognition, called *Carbonari*, or Charcoal-burners—(the chief vocation of the peasantry of that region being to manufacture charcoal)—while, carrying out the idea, a meeting was called a *Vendita*, and a lodge a *Baracca*.* The members of a counter-society were known as *Calderari*, or Braziers.

Originally Republicans, the Carbonari declared themselves, after the restoration, in favor of a constitutional monarchy under the Bourbon dynasty, though always distrusted by the Constitutionalists, whom they, in their turn, charged with lukewarmness. They had lodges in Piedmont, Lombardy, and the Popedom, and a general and simultaneous rising in each government is said to have been at one time designed; this rising having been encouraged by the declaration of the principle of non-intervention by the Allied Powers, in the late successful revolution of the 8th of May in Spain.

A history of the Secret Societies of Italy, during the half century last past, would fill volumes. First in chronological order here, as everywhere else, indeed, stands the order of Ancient Free Masonry, the order of *Liberii* or *Franch*, *Muratori*, or *Francs Maçons*. It is a remarkable fact, that a lodge of this fraternity existed for some time under the jealous and argus-eyed Oligarchy of Venice; and was not discovered until 1785, when it was suppressed, and all its furniture and archives committed to the flames, by order of the "Supreme Court of the Ducal Palace." In the secret records of the old Republic appears a catalogue of the singular articles found in

ner, probably, as Naples herself is called "the faithful city of Naples," despite her twenty-six insurrections! But old King *Nasone*—Big Nose—was always the idol of his Lazzaroni.

* *Vendita*—a Sale: *Baracca*—a Hut.

the Lodge Room, as, also, a detailed account of *a* form of initiation, and a list of members' names. The whole number was fifty-four, and the list embraced names of some of the most distinguished men of Venice. Among these were Querini, subsequently Ambassador to France, Battaglia, Envoy to Napoleon in '96 and one of the Grand Sages of the Senate, Albrizzi, Inquisitor of State, Pindemonte, the distinguished poet, Fontana, the celebrated engineer ; likewise several ecclesiastics of high rank, as well as members of the noble families of the Pisani, Morosini, Giustiniani, Gasparoni, and persons bearing the well-known names of Memo, Soranzo, Paleocapa, and Camerata.

Under French rule, Masonry seems to have been *tolerated* in Italy, although by an official act of December 9th, 1806, the order is declared "perilous to government and subversive of religion and society." Another protest, under date of March 6th, 1813, also appears, although the order seems not to have been suppressed. But, if France tolerated Masonry in Italy, not so, certainly, did Austria. Her first official anathema against it bears date 1820, followed up by one yet more severe in 1824, and another in 1826.

As early as April 28th, 1738, Masonry was denounced by the Papal See. A second denunciation appeared May 18th, 1751, a third, September 13th, 1821, and a fourth March 12th, 1825, since when, it seems not to have been denounced by its distinctive appellation, but to have been included in the wholesale anathemas of the Italian despots against "Secret Societies." Of these societies, not less than thirty-four have been formally denounced by the Austrian Police, by respective names, as appears by official records. According to Italian writers, the first of these secret societies—"the first sect of Italian Independents"—arose among the Venetian and Lombard patriots with the first oppressive acts of French rule. It was known by the name of the "*Ligue Noire*" to the French, who dreaded, and hated, and left nothing unattempted to exterminate it; but, thriving and increasing during the whole French occupation, it aided materially in the expulsion. It enlisted malcontents of all parties, and its sole object was to drive out the barbarians.* With this league, under the general name of *Carbonari*, originated towards the end of 1814, a project for the liberation of Italy—a project crushed before any overt act had transpired, and punished by years of captivity of its chiefs in the dungeons of Milan and Mantua. But the fraternity was not crushed, and with that fraternity originated, subsequently, the Revolution of 1820.

The rising at Naples commenced on the 2nd of July, with a mutiny in the army, because of dislike to General Nugent, an Irishman, who was Commander-in-chief. The result was entire desertion of the royal cause by the army, led by its officers, who were mostly Carbonari,† immediate adhesion on part of the people, and a demand for a liberal constitution. The old King Ferdinand acceded to the demand, and gave power to Francis, the Crown-prince, to carry it, out. The Carbonari then proposed the Spanish constitution of 1812 recently revived—which was, also, the constitution of Sicily in 1812, —the most democratic charter ever framed for a monarchy, and deemed by conservatives as utterly unfit for Naples as for Madrid. It was, however, accepted and sworn to by both king and prince. Gen. Pepé at the head of the army and the people then entered Naples, and a provisional commission entered on the administration of government. But difficulties innumerable, at once arose, and among them was a revolt at Palermo, in the island of Sicily, the people demanding restoration of their independent government, and

* Mariotti.

† The Carbonari, from 1808 to 1821, had their head-quarters at Naples.

12*

their constitution of 1812, granted by Ferdinand and guaranteed by England—yet annulled at Vienna in 1815 which revolt was only quelled by bloodshed, and by an armed force despatched from Naples.

On the 1st of October, the king opened the parliament in the church of Spirito Santo, and, during the same month, the Holy Alliance, embracing Russia, Austria, and Prussia, met at Troppau and resolved, in violation of their own declared principle of non-intervention, to crush the constitution of Naples by force of arms. France approved, but gave no aid; England remained neutral, and Spain, Sweden, Switzerland, and the Netherlands, recognized the new government. The King of Naples was invited to the Conference, and was suffered by the Parliament to go, with a protest on one side, and a promise on the other, against any change in the constitution.* But, once at Laybach, where the Congress now sat, the old despot was easily and speedily convinced that his promise was null, having been "extorted by violence;" and an army of 43,000 Austrians, which for six months had been on the Po, crossed that river and was on the frontiers of Naples and entering the passes of the Abruzzi, led by Gen. Frimont, with a proclamation from the king calling on his people to receive the invaders as friends—almost before the danger was suspected.

It was at this time, or a few months previous, that Lord Byron, then at Ravenna, who had warmly sympathized in the whole movement, addressed the Neapolitan government, presenting to "the good cause" a thousand *louis*. His address concludes thus:—"Distance from the frontier, and the feeling of personal incapacity to contribute efficaciously in the service of the nation, prevents the

* Naples sent Prince Cimitilò to Laybach to deprecate the intervention of the absolute powers.

writer from proposing himself as worthy of the lowest commission for which experience and talent might be requisite: but if, as a mere volunteer, his presence were not a burden to whomsoever he might serve under, he would repair to whatever place the Neapolitan government might point out, there to obey the orders and participate in the dangers of his commanding officer, without any other motive than that of sharing the destiny of a brave nation defending itself against the self-called Holy Alliance, which but combines the vice of hypocrisy with despotism."

Fortunately, the services of the noble Lord were not accepted, although his contribution was.

On the 7th of March, 1821, the army of the Constitutionalists of 25,000 men under Gen. Pepé, joined battle with the foe at Rieti; and, on the ensuing morning, that army numbered but hundreds in place of thousands! The Neapolitans had fled! On the 10th, the Austrians were in the fortress of Aquila and resistance was at an end. It was on learning the entry of the Austrians into Naples without even a shadow of resistance, that the poet Moore, as every one knows, penned his spirited verses commencing—

"Ay, down to the dust with them, slaves as they are,
From this hour may the blood in their dastardly veins,
Which shrank from the first touch of liberty's war,
Be sucked out by tyrants, or stagnate in chains."

In palliation of the apparent poltroonry of the Neapolitans, it has been urged with much force, that "the leaders had before them Austrian bayonets, and saw behind them the piles and scaffolds of '99. They knew that they were betrayed at Naples, whilst they had come to die on the frontier." Treachery has been attributed, also, to some of the leaders themselves; and the malign influence of Jesuitism, it is said, was also busy.

On the 15th of May, Ferdinand was again in his capital. But his promise of general amnesty was forgotten. A hundred heads fell; many persons were sent to the galleys, to dungeons, to convict islands. Pepé and Carrascosa escaped to England, and Colletta and two other generals were exiled to remote provinces of Austria. On the 26th, a decree was issued by the king in the nature of a charter, by which Sicily was rendered, in a manner, once more independent of Naples.

It was at the Congress of Troppau, which was in session from October to December 1820, caused by the recent revolutions in Spain, Portugal and Naples,—convoked by Prince Metternich, and held by Russia, Prussia and Austria, that the principle of *Armed Intervention*, as understood in modern times, may, perhaps, be viewed as having been first formally and definitively announced:* for, at Troppau, it seems to have been distinctly agreed, that Austria should fight, and Russia and Prussia hold at bay the rest of Europe; while the doctrine put forth was this,—"The Powers have an undoubted right to take hostile attitude in regard to those States, in which the overthrow of government may operate as an example."

At the Congress of Laybach, held by the same powers, under the name of "The Holy Alliance," from January to May, 1821,—the

* A well-informed writer in the "Democratic Review," January, 1852, dates the birth of Intervention with the adoption of the 17th article of the Treaty of Westphalia, signed by France and Sweden, in 1648—exactly two centuries before it was so fatally exercised in 1848. The effect of the principle was to wipe out Germany by the intervention of France and Russia, and to establish Austria, Prussia, and thirty-eight lesser sovereign states. Philip II. of Spain intervened, also, in France, and William II, of Prussia, in Holland. Then followed the interventions of Russia in Poland and the infamous partitions, the intervention of the Allies in the affairs of France for twenty-five years—the intervention of Napoleon in the affairs of Europe for fifteen years—the intervention of the Allies by the Treaties of Paris and Vienna, of 1814-15—followed by the subsequent interventions, more particularly noticed in the text—and the yet more recent intervention, that of England in Central America.

Emperors of Russia and Austria being present in person, and England, France, Prussia, Naples, Modena, Popedom and Tuscany, by envoys—the same principle became a portion of the international code of the continental powers; and in pursuance thereof, Naples, Sicily and Piedmont were occupied by Austrian troops, and the Spanish constitution they had adopted was abolished. The doctrine of this Congress, as put forth in the Laybach circular of May 12th, 1821—a circular distinct from that signed by Russia, Austria and Prussia, and signed by Metternich alone in behalf of Austria,—was this:—"That useful and necessary changes in legislation ought only to emanate from the free will and intelligent conviction of those whom God has rendered responsible for power; and all that deviates from this line, necessarily leads to disorder, commotions, and evils far more insufferable than those which they pretend to remedy:" or, in the language of Daniel Webster, in reply to Chevalier Hülsemann in 1849,—"That all popular or constitutional rights are holden no otherwise than as grants and indulgences from crowned heads." Against this monstrous principle, even Lord Castlereagh, in behalf of England, entered his solemn protest.

At the Congress of the five great powers at Verona, held from October to December, 1822, the same principle was avowed by the Emperors of Russia and Austria; and, in accordance therewith, France was suffered, in 1823, to restore the Bourbons to the throne of Spain, and suppress the Cortes and Constitution, and was promised aid if required. At the same time the Greek resistance, which had always been encouraged by one of the powers, Russia, was pronounced "rash and culpable"—"a firebrand of rebellion in the Ottoman Empire!" To all this, and especially to the intervention of France in Spain, England again protested, September 27th, 1822, through her then Premier, the great Canning. But, four years later, England herself intervened in Portugal, in favor of Donna Maria against Don Miguel; and, in 1833, intervened in Belgium, with the other great powers, to place Leopold on that throne, instead of the Russian Leuchtenberg, or the French Nemours, inhibiting all idea of a Republic! So much for England in the past—an index and a prophecy of the future.

In 1836, the Emperors of Russia and Austria, the king of Prussia, and all the other European Sovereigns, those of England and France only excepted, met in Congress at the Baths of Tôplitz, in Bohemia. The cause of this meeting was the Quadruple Alliance of England, France, Spain and Portugal, for the expulsion of Don Carlos and Don Miguel from the Peninsula. Armed intervention was then urged by the Emperor of Russia, in order to prevent the evil influences of the Revolution of 1830, in France, the defeat of Don Miguel in Portugal, and the failure of Don Carlos in Spain. This was opposed by the King of Prussia and Prince Metternich; and, on the 4th of March, the Congress broke up—no intervention being resolved on, save that of a pecuniary character proffered by the Czar—the principle of *non*-intervention, being, in fact, virtually re-declared!

All Europe, however, and especially the Peninsula of Italy, as we shall see, continued to be oppressed by this incubus of armed intervention, by which not less than a score of insurrections were crushed within as many years; and it was this same despotic principle which crushed the liberal cause in Europe in 1849. Rome and Hungary threw off a yoke which could never have been replaced, but by the armed intervention of France and Russia. Had England, France and Prussia forbidden, as they might have done, the invasion of Hungary by Russia, Europe had now, perchance, been comparatively free. "With Hungary triumphant and independent," says an able writer, "Austria could not have bullied Prussia, could not have trampled on the constitution of Hesse, could not have conquered Venice, could not have retained, though she had recovered Lombardy, and could not have given France even the paltry and miserable pretext for that attack on Rome, which has covered both her arms and her diplomacy with indelible infamy."

On the very day that the Austrian troops occupied the city and castle of Aquila, near Naples—(on the 10th of March, 1821)—a mutiny broke out in the army of Piedmont. Several officers and nobles, members of the Society of the Carbonari, were at the head of the movement, and it was secretly countenanced by Charles Albert, Prince of Savoy-Carignano. The citadel of Turin was seized on the 12th, and next day the king, Victor Emmanuel, abdicated in favor of his absent brother, Charles Felix, appointing Charles Albert, Regent, who, on the 14th, swore support to the same Spanish Constitution adopted by Naples. A ministry was then formed and a Junta constituted. On the 23d, Genoa declared her independence of Piedmont—as Sicily had declared hers of Naples a year before—and proclaimed the same Constitution.* But already the cause was lost. The Austrian troops in Lombardy were on the Ticinio; Charles Felix had disowned and denounced the acts of the Regent; and Charles Albert himself, on the night of the 21st, had fled to the Austrian camp. On the 8th of April, the royal troops, united with the Austrians, routed the insurgents at Novara—a spot fatal to Piedmont:—on the 9th the Junta dissolved; and, on the 10th, Charles Felix† was at Turin, and the whole affair was over.

* Genoa and Sicily did each precisely the same thing in 1848–49, under precisely the same circumstances.

† This king, whose Italian name was *Carlo Felice*, earned by his tyranny another cognomen more appropriate than *Felice*—happy—before his decease: it was *Feroce*—savage!

An insurrection in the Papal States seems to have been designed, simultaneous with that at Naples. As early as February, Lord Byron, then at Ravenna, writes to Mr. Bankes—" Be assured there are troublous times brewing for Italy." Again, in April, he writes to Murray—" there is that brewing in Italy which will speedily cut off all security of communication, and set all your Anglo-travellers flying in every direction. The Spanish and French affairs have set the Italians in a ferment; and no wonder: they have been too long trampled on. I shall think it by far the most interesting spectacle and moment in existence to see the Italians send the barbarians of all nations back to their own dens. I have lived long enough among them to feel more for them as a nation than for any other people in the world. But they want union, and they want principle; * and I doubt their success. However, they will try, probably; and, if they do, it will be a good cause. No Italian can hate an Austrian more than I do." On the 23d of the same month, he writes that the walls of Ravenna were that morning found covered with placards—" Up with the Republic!" " Down with the Pope!" " Down with Priests!" " Down with the Nobles!" and adds—" I dislike the Austrians, and think the Italians infamously oppressed." In the month of August he writes, that " the Huns" were on the Po, and that if they crossed it there would be fighting. A month later he writes that all were looking on each other like wolves, only waiting for the first falling on to do unutterable things, and that the government had begun to look on himself with a suspicious eye: also, that the Austrians were masters of the Papal Police: " but some day or other they will pay for all; it may not be very soon,

* " The Italians are mere children," writes Mazzini, Oct. 4, '47, " but with good instincts. They have not a shadow of intellect or political experience. I speak of the multitude, and not of the few leaders, whose sin is want of resolution."

for these unhappy Italians have no consistency among themselves." On the evening of the 9th of December, the Commandant of the troops, who was very obnoxious to the people, was shot down at his door in the street at Ravenna. Byron had him taken to his house where he died. Subsequently, an Austrian spy was stabbed. In the month of July, 1821, he writes—" The tyranny of the Government here is breaking out. They have exiled about a thousand people of the best families all over the Roman States." And again —" you have no idea what a state of oppression this country is in— they have arrested above a thousand of high and low throughout Romagna—banished some and confined others, without trial, process, or even accusation! Every body says they would have done the same by me if they dared proceed openly.* Every one of my acquaintance, to the number of hundreds, has been exiled. It has been a miserable sight to see the general desolation in families." During this period Byron received an anonymous letter styling him " Chief of the Americans"—*Capo di 'Mericani*—the Carbonari of the Romagna being honored with that name: and threatening him with assassination. Byron, soon after, left for Pisa.

A large portion of a Journal kept by Byron at Ravenna, during the eventful months of January and February, 1821, is devoted to the political movement by which all Italy was at that time engrossed. No doubt is left by this Diary that the poet, together with his friends, the elder and younger Counts Gamba, father and

* Byron seems to have been an object of special *surveillance* to the Italian Police. As early as October 2, 1819, a notice was issued by the Police of Bologna to that of Venice, warning them of the poet as a member of the Secret Society of *Roma-Antica*, and minutely detailing his habits and principles. This curious document is to be found on the 205th page of vol. 1st of the " *Carte Segrete e Atti Ufficiali della Polizia Austriaca in Italia, dal* 4 *Giungo*, 1814, *al* 22 *Marzo*, 1848;" and thus opens—" On the 12th of last month, the noble English Lord Byron left this city for Venice."

brother of the Guiccioli, were active Carbonari, and participated in the frequent assemblages in the Forest of Ravenna—the Forest of Boccaccio's and Dryden's "Huntsman's Ghost." His Lordship's house became a depot of arms and ammunition, and he declares himself in constant readiness to lead an outbreak. He also contributed liberally in money. He seems to have had many doubts as to the issue, however; and respecting his coadjutors, too, despite his enthusiastic hopes. The revolution in the Papal States was, at first, fixed for October, 1820. The time was postponed, however, to the 7th or 8th of March, 1821. But the chapter of accidents had then closed. It was too late. The night of the 7th of January was, also, fixed for a rising at Ravenna. It was a tempestuous night, and Byron watched till the dawn in expectation; but in vain. The counsel urged by the poet—"to attack in detail, and in different parties, in different places,"—was wise, and indicates zeal. But a few extracts from the Diary will better indicate the spirit of the writer:—

Jan. 8th.—"I wonder what figure these Italians will make in a regular row? I sometimes think, &c. And yet there are materials in this people and a noble energy, if well directed. But who is to direct them?

9th.—"The Austrian barbarians are again on war-pay, and will march. Let them—'they come like sacrifices in their trim'—the hounds of hell! Let it still be a hope to see their bones piled like those of the human dogs at Morat, in Switzerland. Onward! It is now the time to act. It is not one man, nor a million, but the spirit of liberty, which must be spread. The waves which dash upon the shore are, one by one broken, but the *ocean* conquers, nevertherless.

12th.—"The Austrians I abhor, loathe, and—I can not find

words for my hate of them, and should be sorry to find deeds correspondent of my hate.

13*th.*—"The Powers mean to war with the Peoples. The king-times are fast finishing. There will be blood shed like water, and tears like mist; but the peoples will conquer in the end. I shall not live to see it, but I foresee it.

28*th.*—"The Austrian brutes have seized my three or four pounds of English powder at Venice. The scoundrels! I hope to pay them in *ball!*

29*th.*—"Met a company of *Americani* in the Forest, all armed, and singing with all their might in Romagnuole—'We are all soldiers for Liberty.' They cheered me as I passed. I returned their salute, and rode on. This may show the spirit of Italy at present."

It seems, that every thing was arranged for a rising on the 10th and 11th of February, with the idea that the Austrians would cross the Po on the 15th. But this passage was effected on the 7th, and Romagna could only stand on the alert, and await the advance of the Neapolitans.

Feb. 14*th.*—"Another assassination at Cesenna—in all about *forty* in Romagna, within the last three months.

18*th.*—"To-day I have had no communication with my Carbonari cronies; but, in the mean time my lower apartments are full of their bayonets, fusils, cartridges, and what not. I suppose that they consider me as a depot, to be sacrificed in case of accidents! It is no great matter, supposing that Italy could be liberated, who or what is sacrificed. It is a grand object—the very *poetry* of politics. Only think!—a free Italy! Why, there has been nothing like it since the days of Augustus.

20*th.*—"The *Americani* give a dinner in the Forest in a few days, and have invited me as one of the Carbonari. I will get as tipsy and patriotic as possible.

24th.—" The secret intelligence this morning is as bad as possible. The plan has missed—the chiefs are betrayed, &c. Thus the world goes; and thus the Italians are lost for lack of union among themselves. I always had an idea that it would be bungled. Whatever I can do by money, means, or person, I will venture freely for their freedom. I have five hundred pounds in the house, with which I have offered to begin."

In his "Detached Thoughts" Byron says, " The Neapolitans have betrayed themselves and all the world; and those who would have given their blood for Italy, can now only give her their tears. Atrocious treachery has replunged Italy into barbarism. However, the *real* Italians are not to blame; merely the scoundrels at the *heel* of *the boot* which the Hun now wears, and will trample them to ashes for their servility."

With such terror did the movements of the Carbonari at Naples, Turin, and in Central Italy strike the imagination of the old Emperor Francis of Austria, that it seems to have haunted his mind like a monomania for years afterwards. Not the slightest movement had as yet become apparent in the Lombardo-Veneto; nevertheless, Count Strassoldo, Governor of Milan, received orders from Schönbrunn to leave no stone unturned to develop the designs, and discover the members of the Carbonari in that kingdom. To this end, a special commission was instituted at Venice; and soon, on pretence of having detected perilous plots against the government, the society of learned men, " *Scienziati Italiani*," at Milan was dissolved—its periodical, " *Il Conciliatore*," was suppressed, and several of its members, among whom were Count Confalonieri, and Silvio Pellico, were arrested. At the same time, October, 1820, Maroncelli, Pallavicini, Moretti, Munari, Foresti, Oroboni, Ressi, Solera, Villa, and Andryane were also seized and imprisoned.* Tried at Venice, or at Milan, by extraordinary tribunals, in the Fall of 1822, the accused were all condemned, and several were doomed to die. Their sentences were commuted, however, to various terms of imprisonment at Spielberg, *in carcere duro*—from imprisonment for life, to imprisonment for eight, twelve, or fifteen years. Among those tried at Venice and doomed to die, were Foresti, Solera, and Munari. Of these Foresti, a native of Ferrara, was, at the time of his arrest, Judge of a Tribunal in the Polesina; and, for two years, from October 1820 to November '22, was he confined beneath the *leads* of the Ducal Palace at Venice, awaiting trial, with his associate, Pellico, and the rest. He found the "terrible *Piombi*," however, the most agreeable of all his various prisons! Light, airy, with large windows commanding a magnificent view of the port, the shipping, the bustle of the *Molo* beneath, the isles of the Lagune, and the daily arrival of the steamer from Trieste, the only disagreeable characteristic of these chambers was a rather uncomfortable warmth of an August noon. But his reminiscences of the *Pozzi*, in which he was confined during forty days after his sentence to death—from St. Martin's day to Christmas—are by no means so delightful. Foresti and his associates, were, probably, the first who, for years, had been incarcerated in these horrible dungeons; for, under French rule, their use was, by express decree, forbidden. And here, in these deep, damp, and mouldy dens, lighted dimly only by artificial means, looking daily for the fulfil-

* These were not the first political seizures under Austrian rule in Italy. As early as 1814-15, five years before, numerous arrests, civil and military, of all classes, had been made at Milan, and elsewhere. Some of the accused were sentenced to imprisonment for years, or for life, and some were sent to fortresses in Hungary.

ment of a dreadful doom, no wonder that reason tottered, and relief was sought in the hoped-for oblivion of suicide; and then, worst of all, in each narrow cell, every moment of every night and every day, watched two barbarian sentinels over each manacled captive. But the death on the gallows was commuted to living death *in carcere duro.* On Christmas Eve, in the Piazetta of St. Mark, opposite the *Porta della Carta,* rose a scaffold. The immense quadrangle, together with that adjoining, bristled with Austrian bayonets; a vessel-of-war, with guns loaded and matches lighted, lay moored opposite the fatal Columns: the windows and arcades, and roofs of the surrounding palaces swarmed with a sympathizing people. And then were proclaimed the warrants of death—for Austria never sentences in vain: and all the terrible forms of public execution were observed—the last only excepted: and then the prisoners were remanded to their dungeons for life. They were now conveyed to the Convent of St. Michael, where many had been previously confined, and whence some had well-nigh effected escape, and where now Venetian sympathy was expressed by nightly serenades:* and at midnight, on the 12th of January, in silence and in gloom, they were all embarked for Mestre, and thence by carriages conveyed over the Tyrol to Moravia, for life-long incarceration. To some of them, it was, indeed, life-long, and yet brief: but some outlived their turnkey, and were once more free; and some had been previously released by imperial policy, as well as some by more merciful death. On the 10th of February, 1836, Francis of Austria died: Francis of Austria confronted his victims at the bar of God! Ferdinand, his successor, for once remembered a promise, and released all the residue of the prisoners, after confinement of sixteen years—

* The advancement of the Italians, not only in appreciation of their rights but in boldness of expression, is well illustrated by the sympathy of Venice and Milan for the condemned of 1822.

among whom were Foresti, who, from the age of twenty-four to forty, was a captive, and the Count Confalonieri, on condition of exile to the Western World. One after the other was subsequently called home—Foresti excepted, who is now a resident of the city of New York—an occasional sufferer from maladies contracted in his Moravian dungeon, to which so many succumbed, though, generally, stout and strong in body as in mind, and who, had he but condescended to accept amnesty from Pius, in 1846, as a citizen of Ferrara, might now be a dweller on his native soil.

As for the Count Confalonieri, doomed also to die, he is said to have owed life to the heroic devotedness of an heroic wife, although, like Foresti and his associates in the Square of St. Mark, he mounted a public scaffold surrounded by bayonets and a sympathizing people in the market-place of Milan, and was then remanded to perpetual incarceration, like the rest. And the meek and gentle poet, Silvio Pellico—the whole world has been made familiar with his ten years' incarceration beneath the *leads* of Venice and in the dungeons of Spielberg, by his touching narrative—"*Le Mie Prigioni.*"

And all this for what? Who shall tell? Yet, had these men been the vilest of political offenders, the atrocity of their several punishments would have disgraced Austria—even as it has done—for ever—for ever! For, well has it been said, that the imprisonments of Venice and Spielberg, described with such terrible faithfulness by Andryane and Silvio Pellico, have made the Austrian name a name of horror!—the very synonym of despotism. By the former especially, "the prison doors have been thrown open; the graves of Ressi, Villa, Moretti and Oroboni, the madness of Pallavicini, the mutilated frame of Maroncelli and the walking skeletons issuing from that living tomb, all are brought before our view."

Pellico, since his ten years of *carcere duro*, has taken no part in politics. Was he bound to quiescence by an oath and the terms of his release? Some years since, he was assailed by Gioberti's *Primato*, because of sympathy with the Jesuits, and was defended by his more radical brother, Francesco, who, nevertheless, could but unite in the lamentation of the poet's former associates—"Better had he died at Spielberg!"

Tuckermann, who met Pellico at Turin, where he resides, some twelve or fifteen years ago, describes him as a man of small stature, about thirty-eight years old, wearing glasses—his complexion deadly pale, "as if blanched by the blighting shadow of a dungeon"—his brow broad and high—his expression serious and thoughtful—his manner courteous and affable—all his time devoted to the care of a father rapidly declining with age, of whom he spoke with deep emotion. He was then librarian of a wealthy Marchesa. His pen was chiefly employed on Catholic hymns and religious odes. He was a devotee, and leaned towards the Jesuits. For his beautiful and touching work descriptive of his Prisons, though translated and sold by thousands in every language in Europe, he had received but two thousand francs, and that from its original publisher at Turin. Its popularity in England, Germany, and the United States is said to be far greater than it could ever have been in Italy. "Pellico is even now living at Turin," bitterly remarks Mariotti, "pensioned by a charitable Piedmontese lady, walking arm in arm with a Jesuit, praying, praying!"*

* Pellico was born in 1789, and is now, therefore, about sixty-four years old. He is the author of numerous celebrated works—dramas and poems—besides the Prisons. He was arrested Oct. 18, 1820. and liberated Aug. 1, 1830. He disclaims all knowledge of the Carbonari. His devotedness to his home and family is remarkable. He went to Rome for the Papal benediction in 1851. He is very poor, though his works have made fortunes for piratical publishers. And so, Botta was a mendicant exile at Paris, while his great History was rendering Geneva printers opulent; and Manzoni could get but a gratuitous pittance for his beautiful "*Promessi Sposi*," which has made its thousands for publishers. Now, however, there is said to be a common copyright for all Italy, Naples excepted.

CHAPTER IX.

"YOUNG ITALY"

Resuming our rapid sketch of movements in Italy since the Restoration:—In 1822, a conspiracy was detected in Sicily, and, in 1828, an insurrection at Salerno, a fortified town of Naples, on a bay of the Mediterranean bearing the same name. Both, however, were promptly suppressed in the usual manner—by arrests—executions—fines—imprisonments. In 1830, Ferdinand II. at the age of twenty-one, succeeded on the throne of Naples, his father Francis I., who had succeeded his father, Ferdinand I., in 1825, and had reigned feebly enough for a period of five years. From 1830 to 1848, the government and governor of the kingdom of the Two Sicilies were infamous; and, as a natural consequence, political eruptions were numerous—more numerous, indeed, than those of the national volcano, and more devastating—numbering in all, half a dozen at the least. In 1835, a movement was planned at Messina, which, it is thought, might have proved successful, but for the cholera, which carried off 9,000 people in a few weeks. There were movements, also, in Syracuse and Catania; but they were speedily suppressed by the exile and executions of martial law. Sicily then became the plotting ground of all Italy, and the influence of its secret league was felt from Turin to Trapani—from the Alps to the Straits—with hardly a suspicion on the part of government: but, local and partial risings excepted, the kingdom of Naples was, for ten or twelve years, comparatively quiet.

It was within this period transpired the melancholy tragedy of the Venetian Brothers, Bandiera, whose affecting story is known throughout Christendom, and whose name is a watchword of liberty to the oppressed of all Europe. These young men were two in number, natives of the sea-girt city, and sons of the Baron Bandiera, a Rear-Admiral in the Austrian service, who had disgraced himself by arresting at sea, in 1831, despite the capitulation of Ancona, the patriots *en voyage* for France. To wipe out this blot on their family escutcheon was, apart from all other influences, natural and laudable in his sons. They were both officers in the Austrian service. The elder, Attilio, a senior lieutenant, about thirty-four years old, and married, had distinguished himself in the Syrian war, and been eulogized by Napier in his dispatches. The younger, Emilio, was about twenty-four, unmarried, and adjutant and secretary to Paoluzzi, Port-Admiral at Venice. Irritated by the disgrace of their father, and groaning beneath the despotism which oppressed their country, they conceived that their rank and influence would enable them to command the service of the Austrian Marine, and thus achieve their country's emancipation. To this effect, on the 14th of August, 1842, the elder brother addressed Mazzini, the chief of "Young Italy," then at London, and implored acceptance of his scheme. The illustrious exile responded with commendation and encouragement, but with counsels of prudence and delay. Suspicion, however, fastened on the young patriots, and, to avoid arrest—the warrant being already in the hands of their father, the Admiral—they deserted the Austrian fleet, in the port of Trieste, and fled to

Corfu, in the month of April, 1844. Here had gathered a large number of Italian exiles; and, encouraged by the excitement in Calabria to hope once more to see their native land, they addressed Mazzini at London imploring aid from the "Association," and counsel from himself, for their contemplated expedition. Their chief, however, not only refused the aid desired, but strongly denounced the enterprise as premature, and as calculated to injure, and not to advance, their common cause; and, for a few months, the mad scheme was abandoned.

Meantime, the young and beautiful wife of the elder Bandiera, at Venice, sank under solicitude and suffering. "She was fair, good, and brave," writes Mazzini in his tribute to the victims' memory. "And, if I had not long firmly believed, that the woman and the man, who, loving each other, die of suffering, must one day be reunited, as angels, in some holy mystery of eternal love—the sole thought of this woman, dying of a broken heart, without unjust irritation, and without complaint, for the man, who, himself, some months after, was to die in his turn, bearing witness for his faith, and doubtless, thinking of *her*, this sole thought would be sufficient to give me such belief."

Subsequently, the younger son, Emilio, resisted all his mother's tears and adjurations to accept the offer of the Viceroy, Archduke Ranieri, of full restoration to rank, nobility, and honor, if he would return to Venice. "To me," says Mazzini, "he appears yet greater at this moment, than when he fell cool and calm at Cosenza."

After this, the brothers were summoned to an Austrian Court-Martial; and published their refusal to obey in a Maltese paper. Craft was then resorted to. Excited by false intelligence communicated by emissaries of the despots, they led an expedition to Calabria, composed only of eighteen men! On the evening of the 12th of June, having eluded the vigilance of the English police, they were conveyed to a *trabacolo*, some five miles distant from Corfu; and, two hours after sunset, on the 16th, landed at the town of Cotrone, in Calabria, exclaiming—*Ecco la patria nostra! Tu ci hai data la vita, e noi la spenderemo per te!*—"Land of our nativity, hail! Thou hast given us life, and we will give it for thee!" But the spy commissioned to guide, betrayed and denounced them; and, after wandering in the mountains for three days, they were surrounded by troops and taken. Captured on the 19th and incarcerated at Cosenza, on the 23rd of the ensuing month they were condemned by a court-martial, and, at five o'clock on the morning of the 25th of July, 1844, with seven of their companions, were shot! *Viva l'Italia!* were the last words on their lips; and never was death more calmly and heroically met, or under circumstances of more peculiar and appalling horror. A Catholic priest who presented himself, was, we are told, mildly repulsed. "We have sought," said they, "to practice the law of the gospel, and to make it triumph, at the price even of our blood. We hope that our works will recommend us to God better than your words. Go and preach to our oppressed brothers."

Among the seven associates of the brave Bandiera who perished by the same fate, at the same time, was a young Venetian, by name Dominico Moro, about twenty years of age, a lieutenant in the Austrian service on board the *Adria* corvette, until his desertion and flight to Corfu with the Bandiera in April. He is said to have been distinguished for gallantry on the Syrian coast during the late war; and, like his comrades, was descended from the proudest nobility of Venice. As for the others—Berti was about fifty-five, an old officer under Napoleon, and served at Waterloo; Nardi was forty-three, a solicitor, a native of Modena, a Secretary of Government during the insurrection of 1831 ; Lupatelli was a brave man and a violent politician, and for several years was a prisoner at Rome on account of his opinions; Ricciotti was a Roman, forty-five years old, married, of small stature, a soldier, a prisoner—his whole life a romance. He had been sent by Mazzini from London with strong dissuasions against the enterprise, which, nevertheless, immediately on his arrival at Corfu, he conducted as a leader! The two last of the victims were Rocca and Venerucci, mechanics of Romagna, of intelligence and probity.

Thus fell, in all, nine brave and patriotic, though misguided men, victims to Austrian and Neapolitan vengeance—victims to treachery —victims to a rash and ill-advised enterprise; but, above all, victims to the shameful detection, and still more shameful betrayal, of that enterprise, by the official spies of a Government called "liberal!" Yes—it was through the perfidy and fraud of the Right Honorable Sir James Graham, Chief of the British Post-office, that the whole correspondence of the exiles of Corfu with Mazzini, was laid bare to the cabinets of Vienna and Naples; and it was at the instance of the *Piedmontese* ambassador at London, it is said, that the deed was done! Mazzini was first led to suspect some tampering with his letters by an editorial article in the *Times* newspaper, which alluded to an Association in London for the emancipation of Italy, referring to facts which could have been legitimately known to only a few members of that Association. Prior to this, however, frequent delays of twenty-four hours had been observed in the delivery of his letters; and now he noticed that they all bore two post-stamps, one designed to efface the other. Thus, letters posted early in the day, which should bear the mark of 10 o'clock, would bear that of 12, the cypher being effaced by the figure 2. Again, letters posted to other persons at the same residence with himself, invariably reached their destination two hours before his own—all tending to show, that letters bearing his address were opened at the Office. To prove this, letters directed to Mazzini were posted containing grains of sand, poppy-seeds, hairs, &c., so placed as not to fall out, unless the letters were opened. Invariably the sand, seeds, and hairs were gone. Wafers peculiarly shaped always underwent a change in going through the Post-office; and, when wax and seals were used, the private marks on the seals were never retained in the counterfeits, and a purposely imperfect impression was always perfected! The result of the whole investigation was a chain of irrefragable evidence, that the London Post-office, under Sir James Graham, was guilty of all the infamous frauds of those of Paris and Vienna, without their palliations, and to accomplish an infamous design. To "*graham*" letters long remained, at London, an appropriate and retributive term of ignominy for similar violations in the British Post-office. The Right *Honorable* Sir James condescended, it seems, to attempt no defence of himself, until the matter was referred to in Parliament, when he declared that *his* department of the administration was not the one guilty of the charge!—in other words, that he had been but the tool of the Earl of Aberdeen, then, as now, Premier, at the instigation of the absolute Powers, to perpetrate an act, which has covered all concerned with deserved and undying infamy! And yet, the Duke of Wellington asserted at the time in the House of Lords—and thus upon legal investigation it was fully proven—that, for more than a century and a half, the Premier of England had claimed and exercised the same prerogative!*

The career of that celebrated man, Giuseppe Mazzini, seems almost as remarkable as his character. Born at Genoa in 1805, he

* Mariotti.

commenced the study of Law, but soon devoted himself entirely to politics. In 1830, suspected of being a Carbonaro, because of certain contributions to the "*Antologia*," a literary journal of Florence, he was imprisoned for five months in the castle of Savona, and then banished. It was from France, in the month of June, he wrote his celebrated address, "*A Carlo Alberto di Savoia, un Italiano*." Subsequently he established a journal at Marseilles, called "*La Giovine Italia*"—to which the venerable Sismondi of Geneva, author of the "History of the Italian Republics," contributed—in which he boldly depicted the despotism of Rome, Naples and Austria, and which he distributed broad-cast from one end of the Peninsula to the other—albeit, the penalty for the possession of a single copy was the galleys for three years. Movements in Savoy, Sardinia, and Lombardy, followed; and twelve executions by Charles Albert—three at Genoa, three at Turin, and three at Chamberry, and the crowded dungeons of Spielberg, Venice, and Olmutz, betrayed its influence. Then came the ill-advised and most disastrous attempt of 1834 on Savoy, entrusted to General Ramorino, a Pole, with a few hundred followers, at Geneva, whom he was the first to leave to their fate. Exiled from Italy, France, and Switzerland, Mazzini fled to London, where he commenced another journal—"*Apostolato Popolare*"—and founded a school for the poor Italian boys of that capital. In '48 he was at Milan, during its brief period of independence; and, after its fall, shared in the perils and privations of the Lombard soldiery. In March '49, he was elected to the National Assembly at Rome, by a majority of a thousand votes more than either of the seven others elected on the same ticket. A month later he was, with Armellini and Saffi, appointed a Triumvir with dictatorial power. His brave and blameless career in this position, even the French Envoy, Lesseps, has warmly certified. His whole salary he gave to the hospitals. With the fall of the Republic, and entry of the French, he repaired to his native Genoa. Driven thence by the Government of Turin, he sought refuge at Geneva, where he narrowly escaped assassination at the hands of Visetta, a tool of tyranny, in January, 1850. Thence departing, he closed his pilgrimage once more at London, where, with his pen he eloquently defended Italy and assailed her foes. Carlyle has pronounced him "a man of genius and virtue—a man of sterling humanity and nobleness of mind." It need hardly be added, that he is "the life, the soul, the perfect embodiment" of "Young Italy."*

The fate of the brave Bandiera seems to have paralyzed liberalism in Naples for some years; but, at length, on the 27th of January, 1848, to the amazement of all Europe, burst out at this point a Revolution which proved the precursor—the forerunner—the Avatar of the wonderful events of that and the ensuing years.

If we now glance at the Papal States, since the movement of 1820, we read the same dark tale of the frantic struggles of thirty years for freedom, stifled, one after the other, in blood.

In 1823, the Cardinal Della Genga was Pope as Leo XII. successor to Pius VII. The Carbonari were active, and political assassinations were frequent. In August, 1825, Cardinal Rivarola was Legate at Ravenna, and passed sentence on more than five hundred persons accused of political offences, without trial and without defence—some to imprisonment for years, in *carcere duro*, some to

* The League of "Young Italy" superseded that of the Carbonari. It was secret—it had an oath and a sign of recognition—its symbol was cypress, "in memory of its martyrs"—its motto—*Ora e Sempre*—"Now and Ever"—its standard—the Italian tricolor—white, red, green—bearing "Liberty, Equality, Humanity, on one side—"Unity, Independence, God, and Humanity," on the other. "*Young Italy* closed her martyr-mission with the appalling tragedy of the Bandiera." Mazzini was its President, and Guerrazzi, of Florence, Secretary.

imprisonment for life, some to exile, some to death, amounting in all to one hundred and more. The residue were sentenced to *discipline*, civil and ecclesiastical—that is, they were forbidden to leave their native places, or to be absent from their houses after a certain hour of the night; and were forced to report themselves to the Inspector of Police once a month, &c. &c. &c., on pain of three years of public labor for each disobedience! Rivarola's life was attempted: and then the prisons ran over with convicts, and the overplus was received by old convents, and seven Carbonari were hanged in the Piazza of Ravenna, and their bodies were left hanging a whole day on the gibbets!

In July, 1830, Charles X. of France was dethroned, and a liberal monarchy, under the Orleans branch of the Bourbon dynasty, was instituted. On the 30th of November of the same year, Pope Pius VIII., who, in 1829, had succeeded Della Genga, died; and, during the conclave, a conspiracy excited by late events at Paris, burst out at Rome. Charles and Louis Bonaparte, sons of the late king of Holland, the latter present Emperor of France, headed an attempt to seize the castle of St. Angelo, but failed as signally as did the same Prince Louis, subsequently, at Strasbourg and at Boulogne.

On the 2nd of February, 1831, the Cardinal Mauro Cappellari, General of the Carmelite order, was Pope Gregory XVI. Revolution then broke out; and, on the 4th, Bologna had expelled the Papal Legate, had formed a Provisional Government, and had organized a National Guard. On the 26th, deputies from the revolted Legations, denounced the temporal power of the Pope, and proclaimed a Republic.

But Austria came with her bayonets; the insurrection was crushed before the end of March; the general amnesty guaranteed by

Cardinal Benvenuti designed to disarm resistance was repudiated; the dungeons were again crowded, and the revolted provinces were again garrisoned by foreign troops.

Under the same influence of the French Revolution of 1830, Modena and Parma rose. The insurrection in the former Duchy was precipitated by the arrest, on the night of February 3d, 1831, of the heads of the conspiracy, in the house of Ciro Monetti. The Duke Francis, one of the basest tyrants as well as one of the vilest cowards in Italy, fled, as had his father, in '97, and as did his son in '48—fled to Mantua. The Ex-Empress, Maria Louisa, the wanton, widow of Napoleon—the paramour of Neipperg—fled, also, from her Duchy of Parma—as did her successor Lodovico of Lucca, twenty years later. In a month, the Duke Francis entered his capital at the head of Austrian troops: Monetti and Borelli, chiefs of the revolt were publicly hanged, and a hundred others were sentenced to imprisonment for life. As for the Duchess of Parma, to her credit be it recorded, she inflicted no penalties and redressed some grievances, on her restoration by the same means.

In July 1831, the Pope by a *Proprio Motu*, at the instance of the great powers professed to make concessions; but they proved a mere mockery. May 10th, 1831, the five great powers, in a "Memorandum," recommended Pope Gregory XVI. to give the higher civil offices in his states to laymen, and to suffer the indirect election by the people of a legislative body to vote taxes and control expenditures. This advice Gregory almost utterly disregarded. England alone protested. Her envoy, Sir George Seymour, in 1832, retired from the conferences, and the other powers receded from the "Memorandum," and, in January of 1832, the eastern legations were again in insurrection. The slaughter of forty inhabitants of Forli, however, and the presence of Austrian bayonets, again, within a month, suppressed every movement.

But the influence of the double-headed eagle in Italy had now become too palpable; and, on the 22nd of February, 1832, a French fleet anchored off Ancona and occupied the town,—to the excessive scandal of immaculate Austria! Anarchy at Ancona ensued, and the Pope launched against it his impotent interdict. Its occupation by France he consented to, however, so long as Austria continued to occupy Bologna and Ferrara; and in the autumn of 1838, the Papal states were evacuated by both of the intervening powers.

In 1845, an insurrection roused by the oppression of Cardinal Massimo, Legate of Ravenna, broke out at Rimini, but was at once crushed by the atrocities of a military commission.

On the morning of June 1st, 1846, the last of the Gregories died, at the age of eighty-one—and to the great joy of his people. On the 17th, the Cardinal Johannes Maria Mastäi-Ferretti, Bishop of Imola, to the amazement of everybody, though elected with unexampled despatch, was proclaimed Pope Pius IX.;* and, within a month, as his first official act, and as the first of that series of reforms—voluntary or compulsory—which precipitated the events in Europe of 1848–49, declared a political amnesty. This accustomed clemency on the accession of a new pontiff affected not less than three thousand of his imprisoned and banished subjects, proscribed during a despotism of fifteen years! Only seventy persons, who had added breach of trust to political offences, were, it is said, excluded from the benefits of this popular concession; while the returning exiles were exalted to place and power.†

* Pius, at his installation, was the youngest Pope since Innocent III., in 1196, who assumed the tiara at thirty-seven. Pius was but fifty-four.

† Six thousand state prisoners in a state of two millions, were a formidable item for a

The influence of the position assumed by Pius, was electric throughout Italy. At Florence, at Lucca, at Turin, all over the Peninsula, "*Viva Pio Nono!*" was an incantation to dash down despotism. A free press—a Civic Guard—these were the only demands, and they were granted. Leopold of Tuscany imitated Pius, and Lodovico of Lucca imitated Leopold; while the Customs Union, which, for months, had been canvassed, linked Rome, Florence, Lucca and Turin by the strongest of ties—their interests. There was some opposition at first, of course, on part of the despots, especially on part of the silly young Duke of Lucca, who terribly stormed, and then as meekly succumbed; but they all gave in a sullen and hypocritical adhesion in the end. Their faith in the unthinking bayonets of Austria, at last seemed diminished or dead. Ever since 1815, that despotic power, by her possession of the Lombardo-Veneto, and by her military, diplomatic, or family influence in Tuscany, Parma, Modena, Naples, and Rome, had been virtually mistress of Italy; and, as occasion offered, had extinguished from time to time, as we have seen in this hasty sketch, beneath her armed heel, or by means of her dungeons at Venice and Spielberg, and on her scaffolds at Modena, every spark of freedom as it rose. But that misused power was about to cease, or, at any rate, for a time to intermit. In July, 1847, alarmed at the movements of Pius, Austria plotted and protested, and, finally, by an ill-advised occupation of Ferrara, on a frivolous pretext, roused the nationality of the whole Peninsula. Rome thundered at the aggression, while even the Bourbon of Naples and the Hapsburg of Florence, were forced to swell that cry, which had now become the slogan of all Italy, from the Alps to the Straits—that cry first raised by Julius

bankrupt political budget. Every new ruler in Italy clears the prisons of the late monarch's victims to make room for his own.—*Mariotti.*

II., who yet died of impotent rage while it remained unfulfilled—"Away with the Barbarian!" Venice and Milan excepted, Austria was virtually excluded from Italy. Her "occupation"—that of "restoring *order*"—for doing which in Parma, Modena, and Rome, in 1831, she was apotheosied by conservative Christendom—was now, in 1847, clearly "gone"—at least for a season. A nation *in carcere duro!*—that was hardly to be thought of. "A nation cannot be sent to Spielberg." "Ah, had but Ferrara in 1847 imitated Moscow in 1812!" sighs the chivalric Mariotti,—another Palfox yearning for another Saragossa to quicken every patriotic pulse to frenzy to accomplish freedom!

If we now glance at Piedmont, we shall find that the extreme north of the Peninsula had been hardly more quiet than the extreme south, during the twelve or twenty years last past.

At Turin, in 1830, Charles Felix, King of Piedmont, died, and Charles Albert of Savoy-Carignano, the Prince-Carbonaro, ascended the vacant throne, with the most sanguine anticipations of every liberal in Italy. Mazzini, in his celebrated address to the new monarch, already alluded to as having been sent from his exile at Marseilles, gives utterance to these sentences among others:—"God created in six days the physical universe; France in three days has created the moral universe, and like God reposes; yet the French Revolution, Sire, has but begun. Rise, then, and, like God, bring forth a world from this chaos. Unite the scattered members and say—It is mine, and it is happy; and thou wilt be great, like God, the Creator; and twenty millions of men will cry aloud, "God is in heaven, and Charles Albert on earth!"*

* This remarkable letter bore the motto—*Se no—no!*—"If not, not!"—and concluded thus—"Posterity will proclaim you first among men, or the last of Italy's tyrants! choose!" This address, says Mariotti, possession of, or acquaintance with which, cost many

But Charles Albert was then hardly ready to become "The Sword of Italy"—*La Spada d'Italia*—to drive out the barbarians, and, like the flaming sword at the gates of Eden, to keep them out: and so Mazzini continued an exile more hopelessly than ever.

In 1833, a conspiracy involving numerous advocates, and numerous officers in the Sardinian army, was discovered at Genoa, Alessandria, and elsewhere, and Charles Albert, whilom "Prince of Carbonari," but now "King of Piedmont," was deemed to have entitled himself to yet another title less honorable than any yet conferred on him—*Il Traditore**—by dooming several of the conspirators, even associates of his own in an earlier conspiracy, to the scaffold. The following year, the equally mad attempt, already mentioned, by a few Polish and Italian refugees, to occupy Savoy, as the first state of "Free Italy," proved equally abortive. In 1843, the Abatte Vicenzo Gioberti, an exiled court-chaplain of Turin, and who, like Mazzini, had cherished the doctrine of expelling all "barbarians" from Italy—published his *Primato*, followed, in 1845, by his *Prolegomeni*,† advocating the immediate expulsion of the Jesuits as the worst of "barbarians"—for the expression of which sentiments, a dozen years before, in 1833, he had been banished the capital and the realm. But, in February, 1848, the Piedmontese rose in their power, and Charles Albert conceded the French Charter of 1830, and Vincenzo Gioberti, the exile, was in 1849, Premier of Sardinia.‡

a young enthusiast his head in Piedmont and Genoa in 1831, was for sale in every book-stall of Rome and Florence in 1847!

* The Traitor.

† *Del Primato Civile e Morale degl' Italiani*—"The Pre-eminence Civil and Moral of the Italians." *Prolegomeni del Primato.*

‡ The Marquis Massimo D'Azeglio, the champion of the 'Moral Force'—the 'Passive Resistance'—Party, which, for a score of years, ruled the Peninsula—was the associate of Gioberti; and, upon the Ministerial crisis of May, 1852, was called to form a cabinet. As for Gioberti, after the fall of Charles Albert, he was sent Minister to Paris, where he

At the same time, Pellegrino Rossi, "the exile of Bologna of 1815," who, from an humble Professor at Geneva, had become at Paris a peer, and had, in 1843, been sent by Thiers, Premier of France, as Envoy to the Pope, to negotiate the suppression of the same Order of Loyola, was Premier of Rome, and subsequently the victim of the very movement he had apparently inspired.*

As for Lombardy, her abortive attempt of 1820–21, had filled her cities with spies, and her castles with "barbarians;" and, under a despotism less leaden, perhaps, than that by which other portions of unhappy Italy were oppressed, but with 30,000 Austrian bayonets at her heart, she remained quite quiescent for nearly thirty years, amid convulsions almost ceaseless on every side. And yet, if the earnest protest of an able Italian writer is to be taken as true—that all the movements in Italy from 1820 to 1848 were, absolutely, only preparatory, preliminary, provisional, transitional steps to Revolution, and not Revolution itself—mere trial-tilts for the grand tournament of the expulsion of the barbarians, and not the tournament itself—not even excepting the three days of '31, when ten millions of Italians became free only to become more surely enslaved—why, then, we are rather to commend the forecast and policy of the Lombards and Venetians for failure to participate in premature attempts, than to condemn their apparent supineness!

In the autumn of 1838, Ferdinand I., who, in 1835, on the decease of the Emperor Francis, had ascended the throne of Hapsburg-Lorraine, and who had succeeded to his father's Premier,

died of apoplexy, October 30th, 1852, at the age of forty-five. His obsequies were celebrated at Turin with exceeding pomp, in the Church of Corpus Christi, on the 22nd of November ensuing.

* "Count Rossi will only return to Paris from his important mission to Rome, to be trusted with some of the most responsible offices in the government.' This prediction of an able writer in 1848, met but a mournful fulfillment in '49.

Metternich, as well as to his father's crown, visited the Lombardo-Veneto with imposing pomp; and, on the 6th of September, was crowned with the iron crown of Lombardy in the Cathedral-church of Milan. This ancient diadem was taken from its recess, in the centre of the large cross over the altar in the Cathedral of Monza, and was conveyed to the capital in a royal carriage by itself, resting on a cushion, preceded and followed by a guard of cavalry, and attended by other carriages containing the great officers of state. Subsequently, it was re-conveyed to Monza with similar ceremony.* At Venice, the Imperial visit was characterized by a pomp and pageant, which the old city had not witnessed for more than half a century, and which was more like the ancient splendors of the Ascension and the Nuptials of the Adriatic, than to any Festa, even in Italy, of modern times. This visit was signalized by an amnesty for political offences, and opened the dungeon-doors of Spielberg to the condemned of '31, after an imprisonment of nearly eight years. All state trials, also, then pending, were quashed, and all exiles, absentees, and refugees, were permitted to return, upon application within twelve months—a dozen persons—and among them Foresti—only excepted. The Institute, also, which had been suppressed at Milan and Venice in 1820, was suffered to resume its sessions.

As for the Ocean-Queen, she seems to have slumbered quietly on in her vassalage for a period of fifty years, amid all the vicissitudes attending her own government, and amid all the commotions in the governments around—without a single thought of independence—without a single throb for liberty; without one dream of her glorious past—without one hope for her gloomy future. And thus, as if

* Murray. † July 1853, Foresti was appointed U. S. Consul to Genoa.

dead and dust—as if whelmed in the waves of her own Adriatic—as if—

> "Sunk, like a sea-weed, into whence she rose"—

slumbered she on in her dreadful slumber—a slumber more terrible than death—until roused with the whole Peninsula—the whole Continent—the whole of Europe—by the tornado of 1848!

Part Second.

VENICE IN '48—49.

Her Rise.

Down in a Southern clime, amid the silent waves of a tideless sea, there lies a weary land, whose life is only in the Past and the Future.—Mariotti.

VENICE IN '48—'49.

CHAPTER I.

RETROSPECTION.

From the Treaty of Vienna, in 1815, to the Revolution-Spring of 1848, Venice remained under the unquestioned rule of the House of Hapsburg-Lorraine. The form of government bestowed on the Lombardo-Veneto kingdom—comprising nine Lombard and eight Venetian provinces, with a population exceeding five millions, may be inferred from the *Patent* of the Emperor Francis, April 7th and 24th, 1815. By this proclamation a *Municipality* was granted each town; and a Representative Assembly, College, or Congregation, was granted to each province, making seventeen colleges in all, the deputies being elected by the people, one half being nobles and the other half commoners. A similar assembly was granted to each of the two capitals, Milan and Venice, which were ruled by an Imperial Viceroy, and by resident Governors who acted as Presidents of these central assemblies, or congregations. The members of these councils consisted of two deputies from each province, one a noble and one a commoner, selected by the provincial assemblies from lists presented by the qualified voters, and also one deputy from each royal town. The qualifications for the Central Council were possession of taxable property worth four thousand crowns, citizenship, and thirty years of age. The term of office was six years; the salary two thousand florins—$1,000. The conditions of eligibility to the Provincial Assemblies were the same as to the Central Assembly, except that a capital of only two thousand crowns was required, instead of real property to the value of four thousand, while the position conferred rank but not salary. As to the powers of these Congregations, they seem to have been limited to deliberation only upon matters of municipal policy, upon questions of assessment of taxes, upon the superintendence of roads, canals, rivers, schools, charitable institutions, &c. They could make no laws, levy no taxes—in fine, they were expressly inhibited by the imperial proclamation the exercise of any power legislative, administrative, or judicial. They could only *deliberate* and lay the result of their deliberations before the Vice-regal government for ratification; and if this ratification were refused, the Central Congregation could then lay the matter before the Imperial government at Vienna. Indeed, the whole duty and power of these representative assemblies seems embodied in the following provision of the Imperial edict creating them:—

"We permit the Central Congregation to communicate the necessities, wishes, and petitions of the nation, and reserve to ourselves to ask them for advice, when it shall seem good to us."

But, if this representative government did amount to little more than "A Board of Commissioners to superintend roads and schools," it seems to have performed its limited duties by no means ill. In 1814, before the French expulsion and Austrian return, the roads are described as mere goat-paths; but, in 1834, not less than eleven millions of dollars had been expended during a period of fifteen years, on roads, bridges, canals, and other internal improvements; and Lombardy had become the garden-spot of Southern Europe. Since the period of these primary improvements, the annual expenditure for repairs is estimated to have reached nearly half a million of dollars each year.

Popular education, of a certain character, for which the Austrian Empire is somewhat remarkable, seems, also, to have been fostered. A national school system was put in operation in Lombardy some thirty years ago, and it now embraces more than two thousand schools for boys, and twelve hundred for girls, divided into two classes, upper and lower. One of these schools every boy and girl in every parish, from the age of six to twelve years, is obliged to attend. The teachers are regularly educated for their vocation, and receive salaries of from fifty to one hundred dollars a year. Books are supplied gratis as well as tuition, and the whole establishment is supported by a parish-tax, augmented, if requisite, by aid from the public treasury. The course of study seems, in some respects, quite complete: corporeal punishment is not permitted, and the moral and sanitary regulations seem worthy of imitation. In the Venetian provinces the same system has been introduced. It now embraces, probably, about two thousand schools and more than sixty thousand scholars. It embraces, also, eighty-six *gymnasia*, or colleges, with three hundred professors and seven thousand pupils, and thirty-four colleges for girls: also, twelve Lyceums for philosophical studies, and the two Universities of Padua and Pavia,—the whole system both in Lombardy and Venice being superintended by general boards at the two capitals.

These statements, it should be remarked, are based on data

furnished some years ago, since when great advances are said to have been made. "Every town and village," says Mariotti, "has its university, college, gymnasium, lyceum, or seminary, almost free of expense"; and, were it not that the jealousy of government, in its system of elementary education, utterly excludes all inquiry, or study, on principles of politics, public law, political economy, and even mental and moral philosophy, while it strictly prescribes the course of instruction to be pursued, the books to be used, the teachers to be employed, and even the subjects to which each hour of the day shall be appropriated, down to veriest details most contemptibly and punctiliously minute, — the Austrian system of intellectual culture might, possibly, merit the encomiums passed on it, of being "the best in the world."

The condition of Lombardy and Venice, in an industrial point of view, under the Austrian government, is not easy to estimate, on account of the absence of reliable data. It is stated, however, on good authority, that, in thirty years, the production of silk, for which Italy now ranks above all other nations, has grown from a small value to 300,000,000 Austrian *Lire*, about fifty millions of dollars. Of this sum about one-third belongs to the Lombardo-Veneto kingdom; while, in 1800, the whole annual produce did not exceed two million pounds of silk. In twenty years, the silk produce of this kingdom has trebled; and, besides supplying its own extensive manufactures, its exports, amounting to an annual value of from fifteen to twenty millions of dollars, now rule the market, for this staple, of the world.

Besides silk and silk goods, Venice exports, also, wheat and other grains, glass and glass wares, paper, jewelry, books, "Venetian treacle," and, likewise, many of her imports; which latter are chiefly sugar, coffee, olive-oil, salted-fish, cotton and wool with their fabrics, hardware, and dye-stuffs. Smuggling constitutes a very active and very lucrative branch of industry, two-thirds of all the coffee and sugar which enter Venice being contraband! As for manufactures, they are principally glass, treacle, soap, earthenware and candles. Book printing and ship-building are, also, carried on to some extent. The steam-engine, as a manufacturing agent, first appeared in a sugar refinery at Venice so lately as 1836. The shipping aggregate has been estimated at 30,000 tons, exclusive of fishing smacks.

If now, in this cursory and general view of the Lombardo-Veneto, we glance at the two capitals of the Imperial Kingdom, we shall observe facts equally deserving notice. Milan, that "most luckless of cities," as the Italians call it—having been beseiged forty times, taken twenty times and razed to the ground four times, is, at this day, one of the most opulent and magnificent capitals of Southern Europe. As for Venice, when, in 1797, she basely yielded to Bonaparte, she was, no doubt, in a most deplorable condition. Once "Mistress of the Adriatic," her power was now a mere shadow. She was an object at once of infinite contempt, infinite wonder, and infinite pity. Her commerce, which once whitened every sea, had, in the comparison, hardly an existence; her navy which had numbered hundreds of armed vessels was reduced to a few scores; her revenues were insufficient to sustain her inquisitorial government; her manufacturies, once so numerous and so noisy, were silent and few; while the dissoluteness and debauchery of her citizens were beyond all conception and all belief. Mothers sold the honor of daughters and law recorded the covenant. There were twenty thousand licensed courtezans; and a thousand applications for divorce crowded the docket of the patriarchal tribunal! Such was Venice, when, after an independence of nearly fourteen centuries, her soil was first polluted by the invader's foot. During the twenty years which immediately ensued, the condition of Venice became, materially no better; and, if possible, it became worse: and, when, in 1814, the Austrians again took possession of the city, they found her, as they say, stripped of her ornaments and treasure, her commerce ruined, her harbor filled with sand, her Arsenal deserted, her manufactures annihilated, her palaces crumbling piece-meal into her canals and filling them with the *debris*, her ships rotting on the stocks and at the quays, her pauper list numbering fifty-four thousand persons, and her charitable institutions, on which she had always prided herself, utterly bankrupt.

True, Napoleon during the eight years he held rule in Venice, was not, as has been already stated, idle. He left there the print of his mighty tread, as he did wherever he went; and the Public Gardens, the Royal Gardens, and that splendid pile of architecture on the western side of the Place St. Mark uniting the old and new Procuratorial Palaces, will ever remain among other monuments to his memory in the City of the Sea. He vastly augmented her military importance, also, by enlarging and completing her lines of fortification,—among the works designed by his genius being that massive structure, Fort Malghera, which defends the approach to Venice by land on the north. He suppressed many of the innumerable convents and churches with which the city was filled; and, while he annulled all remnants of aristocratic institutions, put a limit to the pernicious influence of the clergy. He, also, roused a warlike spirit in the young Venetians by enrolling them in his armies, and strove to foster commerce by conceding a Free Port to the Island of St. George. But the endless blockade maintained by a British fleet rendered utterly ineffective every effort, however energetic or well-directed, to revive trade and industry; and the once-proud Queen of the Sea seemed, no doubt, as is said, to sink every day into deeper and deeper depression.

That she owed all this ruin to invasion is not true; and, perhaps, had she now been restored to independence—as of right she should have been restored—as, by the Congress of Vienna, all other powers with few exceptions were,* to the *statu quo ante bellum*,—she might never have been able to sustain it. Her old Oligarchy was out of the question, even had it been desirable, or endurable. Her only hope, it is urged by absolutists, was union with Tuscany, Genoa or the Papal States; while, united with either, she could have proved but little better than a cypher. To Austria, and to Austria only, they say, could she be of value. Trieste, at the foot of the Adriatic, had hitherto been her only port, and Venice afforded a valuable depot of trade between Germany and the Italian Provinces. The value attached by Austria to her new possession may be inferred from the fact, that, during the first twenty years of her rule, she expended more than ten millions of dollars in reparations. The popular idea, therefore, that that Empire strove to prostrate Venice by advancing Trieste, is hardly reasonable. As business revived, convents and churches were converted into magazines; and a ruinous custom, already alluded to, was pursued by the impoverished proprietors of princely mansions of selling them to Jews, who demolished them for their costly materials. Many of these antique marbles and rich sculptures were conveyed to other capitals of Europe, and a splendid palace, which once cast its shadow on the waters of the Grand Canal, is said now to stand in almost equal splendor in Belgrave square, London! The Imperial Government, however, very soon put an end to this barbarous desecration, and even purchased, itself,

* Netherlands, Genoa, Parma, Venice, Saxony, Parma, Lucca, Ragusa, &c.

the palaces of those most clamorous to sell.* The rise in the value of property which has since taken place is astonishing. Palaces are pointed out on the Grand Canal which only ten years ago could have been bought for $20,000, which could not now be obtained for thrice that sum. The Savorgnani palace is said to have been bought in 1817, by the Baron Galvagna, Imperial Counsellor, for $3,000: in 1846, $50,000 was repeatedly offered and rejected for the same palace! The Grassi palace was bought for about $20,000, by a company of merchants in 1840: in 1847, the sum of $80,000 was offered for it in vain! In 1840, the Angarini, or Manzoni palace was sold for $4,000: now, four times that sum, it is said, could not buy it! In 1840, also, a portion of the Palazzo Labia was purchased by the Prince Loboskowitz with a view to its restoration; but although death arrested his purpose, the property has vastly increased in value since. The Vendramini palace, erected at enormous expense in 1483, by the Doge Loredano, and sold to the Duke of Brunswick in 1681, two centuries later, for about $120,000, in 1817 would not bring one-fourth part of that sum, although since purchased at more than one half by the Duchess of Berri. The original cost may have exceeded half a million of dollars. It is in perfect preservation, despite its four centuries of age. Palaces have been purchased, also, and restored as residences by the Count of Chambord, son of the Duchess of Berri and "last of the elder Bourbons," by Gen. Gorzkowsky, Governor of the city, Admiral Wimpfen, Taglioni the *danseuse*, and numerous others. Rents, also, have doubled at Venice during the twenty years last past.

* In a note to Childe Harold, written in 1817, is found the following:—"Most of the patrician mansions are deserted, and would gradually disappear, had not the government, alarmed by the demolition of seventy-two, during the last two years, expressly forbidden this sad resource of poverty."

These facts certainly indicate prosperity, and this comparative prosperity may be attributed to several causes. Venice, with the return of the Austrians became a capital of a kingdom, the seat of a Vice-regal court, a port of the imperial fleet, the residence, or summer watering-place, of numerous dethroned or reigning princes, banished nobles or prominent persons of either sex bankrupt in position or health, the rendezvous of a numerous garrison, and the resort of travellers from all Europe and all the world. It was not, however, until 1830, that the Imperial Government manifested any marked solicitude for the commercial prosperity of Venice. Prior to that period, the popular idea seemed somewhat justified, that it was disposed rather to foster Trieste, even at the expense of Venice. Having manifested an effective zeal for the return from Paris of the three Bronze Steeds, the Winged Lion, and the other works of art and antiquity carried off by Napoleon, and in the preservation and repair of the old palaces and monuments, it there seemed to rest. About the year 1830, livelier interest was exhibited. The Arsenal, so long deserted, began to assume its old activity; vast sums were expended in deepening the approaches to the port blocked up with sand, and immense sea-walls and dykes were constructed to meet and repel the storms of the Adriatic. The magnificent Railway-bridge was, also, constructed, being the first link in the iron road connecting Venice with Verona and Milan and even Genoa—connecting, indeed, the Adriatic with the Mediterranean. The privilege of a Free Port was, also, extended from the Island of St. George to the entire city, and every effort was made to encourage commerce. At the same time, as if to leave nothing untried—prominent Venetians began to be invited to participate in the civil administration of government; and their sons were called to office in the imperial army and navy. Indeed, to such extent had this system of appointment, say the conservatives, been practised, that, upon the breaking out of the Revolution of '48, most of the naval officers were found to be Venetians!

But, despite all the efforts of the invaders—often mistaken and always selfish—to reconcile a conquered people to their rule; despite all their exertions to induce prosperity, and even, despite their extraordinary success, still that conquered people, though degraded and subdued, could but remember, that, for fourteen hundred years, their fathers had possessed national independence, if not much freedom—that, prior to the present century, the armed tread of a foreign foot had never once polluted their soil—that they were, to all intents and purposes, the debased and despised slaves—not even of conquest, but of base bargain and sale—that they had been and were the victims of treachery, perfidy, and ambition—that their tyrant had, and could have, no possible shadow of right to rule them; and that, by the Congress of Vienna, they should, agreeably to its own edict, have been restored, like all the other minor powers of Europe, to their condition prior to the French Revolution. Nor could they forget that native, ineradicable, undying hate, which the Italian has ever borne the Teutonic race—that utter and reciprocal antipathy to his language, to his person, to his habits, to his manners, to his dress. The idea, so often urged, that Venice was governed better now than by her ancient Inquisition, and better, possibly, than she could govern herself, never once entered their heads, or, if it did, it only roused intenser bitterness and more inveterate hate against the haughty and despotic foreigners who at once ruled and despised them. Among the more substantial sources of complaint was the fact, that the Lombardo-Veneto Kingdom, though embracing but one-seventh of the inhabitants of the Austrian Empire, yet furnished one-fourth of all the taxes. But this extraordinary fact proved—urged the tyrants—only the extraordinary productiveness of the country, as appeared by statistics of the income-tax; while it also appeared, that this people paid one-third less per head than those of some other provinces of the empire.* It was, however, admitted that Venice had a right to complain that her Railroad to Verona was controlled by Jews and bankers at Trieste and Vienna, and that the Austrian Lloyd Steam Company enjoyed a virtual monopoly of the trade of the Adriatic; that Milan, not without reason, complained of being denied a Bank; Pavia of being deprived of her Arsenal; Brescia of being forced to stop her Armories, and Bergamo of being forced, in like manner, to quench her Foundries; the interests of all these cities being, thus, in a measure, crushed for the sake of rearing stupendous and iniquitous imperial monopolies. In addition to these branches of industry, the manufacture of tobacco at Venice, and all over the kingdom, was, also, a monopoly: and there were others still. The people complained, moreover, that the civil officers placed over them were nearly all Germans; that the members of the Central Colleges failed to convey their wishes to the imperial ear; that the press and the tongue were fettered, and that the land was swarming with troops and spies.

The apologists for Austrian domination in Lombardy maintain it

* Thus, Lombardy and Venice paid about $4 per head; Austria above and below the Enns, $6; Bohemia and the Tyrol, $2; Hungary less than $1. The only direct tax was the *Prediale:* the indirect was on salt, oil, sugar, tobacco, coffee, stamped paper—total amount 129,000,000 of Lire per annum, of which 80,000,000 was transmitted to Vienna, and 70,000,000 retained to pay the 36,000 Austrian *employeés* in the kingdom, and for other purposes. Under Napoleon, 29,000,000 of Lire, at one period, are asserted to have been annually transmitted to Paris. The condition of the peasants, they also insist to have been favorable, *Conscription* being the chief tyranny they endured. Foreign soldiers, they add, were seldom seen, except in the large towns, before the revolution; and the landed proprietors were generally well off, and, often, opulent.

to be "popular with the peasantry, and attacked only by intriguing nobles, priests, physicians, and lawyers."* But, granting this, what must be that government, as has been forcibly asked, which has for its implacable foe every educated man whom fate has subjected to its despotism? As for the peasantry, Mazzini was, probably, right, when in 1845, he declared the Austrian government to be the best in Italy; but to the high-born, the emulous, the educated, no tyranny which merely affects the body could be so intolerable as that which forbade as crime one aspiration for influence, one throb of generous ambition, one effort for the free expression of thought or sentiment. What wonder, then, that the young, the aspiring, the educated men of Lombardy hated her oppressor with hate the more undying and ineradicable because forced to be suppressed? What wonder, also, that impelled by this patriotic and pious hatred, the gallant young victims of Cosenza, worthy sons of St. Mark, rushed upon their fate, as already detailed;† and what wonder, that hate was roused to frenzy in their native town against its oppressors, for their cowardly share in that tragedy of blood?

But, blind to this inveterate and deadly hate, as if impelled by fatality, the besotted and despotic government which oppressed Venice, seems to have made not the slightest attempt to allay the constantly increasing spirit of discontent. It made no attempt, like the tyrant of imperial Rome, to divert the thoughts of the conquered from their real or fancied wrongs by brilliant fetes and public shows. With the single exception of the custom brought from Vienna of having music in the Place St. Mark every other night by one of the garrison bands,

* "The populace," says Byron in his Private Journal, January 24th, 1821, "are not interested in the revolt—only the higher and middle orders." It was very different in '48-49, and is more different yet in '53. All orders are now interested.

† Part First, chap. ix.

no effort was made, as under the more politic rule of Napoleon, to seduce the pleasure-loving Venetians from brooding over their degradation. Possibly, it was thought by the invaders, that the people of Venice lacked spirit ever to take the initiative in an Italian revolution, even if they had sufficient to follow the lead of others. In this idea they were more than half right; for, in all probability, but for the work of reform commenced by Cardinal Mastäi-Ferretti, on his exaltation to the Papal chair in the summer of '46, but for the insurrectionary spirit all over Italy in '47, but for the revolution in Paris in February '48, and the outbreak at Milan, Vienna and all over Europe immediately after, the revolution in Venice would never have taken place. Even Luigi Mariotti, who was hopeful even of Naples, and who predicted that "the day of awakening in Italy would have all the consequences of an earthquake," seemed utterly hopeless of Venice. In his first work he speaks of the poor Queen of the Sea, as if "dead to hope, or worth, or aspiration," and as if—"however soon the hour of Italian redemption might strike for others, it would always strike too late for her." And these lines, written on the very eve of her awakening, came before the world at the same moment with the startling intelligence, that she had, at last, risen from her slumbers, and with one mighty struggle had burst her fetters and flung them off!

CHAPTER II.

REVOLUTION!

In detailing the form of government imposed on the Lombardo-Veneto kingdom, it was said, that the whole power and privilege of its Representative Assemblies seemed embodied in the permission to "communicate the necessities, wishes, and petitions of the nation," to the Imperial Council at Vienna.

But this privilege, poor as it was, appears never to have been exercised,—this duty, so heavily incumbent, was never performed by these Assemblies—either because of a desire of conciliating, or because of a dread of displeasing their masters at Vienna. The first movement in opposition to this apathy was manifested by a resolution offered in the Central Congregation of Milan, on the 9th of December, 1847, by Nazari, deputy of the city of Bergamo, demanding that a commission should be appointed to lay before the Emperor a *projet* of reform for the Lombardo-Veneto kingdom, based on the universal discontent. This proposition was opposed by the governor of the city, Count Spaur, President of the Assembly, who declared, that the Viceroy, the Archduke Ranieri, was himself engaged in preparing such a *projet*. The resolution was adopted, however, by a unanimous vote, and approved by the Viceroy; and the people of Milan flocked to the residence of Nazari to do him honor. A committee of six, consisting of deputies from Milan, Mantua, Lodi, Como, Cremona, and Brescia, with the bold deputy from Bergamo at their head, was appointed, and at once prepared their plan of reform, which was laid before the Emperor, though audience to the deputation was declined; but the only reply from Vienna was augmentation of the garrison of Milan!

On the 21st of December, two weeks after the passage of the resolution of Nazari at Milan, a similar proposition was presented in the Central Congregation of Venice by Daniele Manin, a deputy for that city. In this communication it was set forth, that, during the thirty-two years of the existence of national representation in the Lombardo-Veneto kingdom, the constitutional duty of the Central Congregation, to present the wants and desires of the country at Vienna, had never once been performed, thereby deceiving the Imperial Government into the belief, that the country had no wants or desires to express, when such was far from being the fact. The Venetian Congregation was then conjured to imitate the Lombardian Congregation, and, by so doing, promote the national prosperity, and public tranquillity. The wishes of the nation were embodied in fifteen articles, the most important of which were,—the creation of a Council of State, reforms in criminal jurisprudence, the possession of all civil offices by Italians, and the employment of all Italian troops exclusively in Italy.

On the 28th, Morosini, a deputy in the Provincial Congregation, caused Manin's proposition to be endorsed by that body; and in an address to his constituents, urged, that a demand for reform should, for its honor, originate with the Provincial Representation. On the 29th, a deputation of prominent citizens solicited the Municipality of Venice to desire the Central Congregation to act in concert with that at Milan; and, on the 30th, a prayer to that effect was presented.

The unanimity of this movement induces the idea, that it may have owed its inception to the ninth Congress of the Association of *Scienziati Italiani*—the Athenæum of Venice—at that time in session; for, about a week after Manin's first motion, and on this same 30th of December—the last day but one of the year '47—an address was delivered before that body, assembled at the Fenice Theatre, by Nicolò Tommaseo, deploring the condition of letters in Upper Italy, attributing it to the fact, that the clause in the Patent of 1815 securing liberty of the press, was not observed; and urging a petition, respectfully praying for the practical enjoyment by the people of Venice of the privileges in this regard, by that instrument vouchsafed. He also urged the general signature by the people of other petitions against other abuses. This production was received with great applause, although an attempt at response was made by the Abbate Zantedeschi; and both discourse and petition were forwarded to the Imperial Minister, Kübek, at Vienna. On the 14th of January, the Advocate Avesani urged the Central Congregation to appoint a commission to collect and transmit complaints to Vienna, which was done.

The two boldest leaders in this movement, it is seen, were Manin and Tommaseo. Nicolò Tommaseo is one of the most distinguished authors of Modern Italy. His chief productions are a Dictionary of Italian Synonyms, Philosophic Studies, Dictionary of Æsthetics, Commentaries on Dante, Popular Modern Songs, and a political romance entitled "The Duke of Athens," which has been translated into several European languages. Another of his works is "*Rome et le Monde*," and, in 1838, while an exile at Paris, he extracted from the Royal Libraries, with permission of Louis Philippe, the *Relations des Ambassadeurs Venetiens sur les affaires de France au XVI me. Siecle*, which appeared in two volumes. He has, also, become known among scholars for the causticity of his critiques on foreign authors. By birth he is a Dalmatian, and was once expelled the Austrian empire because of liberalism in political sentiment. His father, the Advocate Tommaseo, is said to have been chief of the Carbonari at Ferrara, in 1818. In person, Tommaseo is diminutive, while he is almost blind from ophthalmia.

Daniele Manin, the coadjutor of Tommaseo in demanding the rights of Venice, is a native of that city, the only son of Pietro Manin, an advocate of Padua. Daniel was born on the 20th of June, 1804, and was, therefore, at the commencement of 1848, in his forty-third year. His father was a Hebrew; but, having become a proselyte to the Christian faith, he assumed, as was customary, the name of the noble who officiated as godfather at his baptism. In this instance that noble was Pietro Manini, brother to Luigi Manini, the last Doge of Venice. The mother of Daniel was Anna Bellotto, a beautiful girl of Padua, to whom his father was never married.* His education was received at the College of Santa Giustina at Padua, and, from his earliest boyhood, he was noted for his talent and industry. In addition to law and the exact sciences, he applied himself to the Hebrew, Greek, English, French and German languages. During his studies, he translated Justinian's Pandects, and published several minor works, which gained him considerable reputation. An affection of the eyes was caused by his intense studiousness; and the kindness of Teresa Perisinatti,

* One account states that the lady was married—though not to Manin. There seems no doubt, however, that her son, like some others whose names are prominent in history, was illegitimate. Several *brochures* in Italian relative to Manin appeared a few years since, the author of one of which was killed in a duel by a friend of Manin, because of injurious assertions.

the fair daughter of an Advocate of Venice, in reading to him, because of this affection, caused, also, an affection of the *heart*, which resulted in marriage. At the age of twenty-seven he received a diploma as a member of the Venetian Bar, and entered on the practice of law, with some success. The bar in Italy, however, presents but a narrow field for an Advocate. All the pleadings are conducted in writing; the accused has no counsel; the trial is secret, except at Naples and Parma; * there is no jury or audience; the Judge indicts, prosecutes, and sentences; and anything like the exhibition of eloquence seems utterly out of the question. Nevertheless, during the stormy sessions of the Congress of Stockholders deliberating on that great enterprise, the Venice and Milan Railway, Manin is said to have given indication of those wonderful powers as an orator, and "that vehement and passionate flow of language which takes a multitude, and especially a southern multitude by storm," which, in a few years, were to enable him to rouse and direct, or to soothe and quell, the passions of a Revolution.

In person, Manin is small, with an oval face, dark hair, eyes and whiskers, a pale and contemplative countenance, capacious brow, simple and unassuming manners; and, though wearing spectacles, younger, apparently, by some years than he is. In general aspect, he is not altogether unlike a distinguished American poet.

On the night of the 18th of January, 1848, Manin and Tommaseo were arrested in their own houses, by the Austrian Police—their papers were seized and their persons imprisoned—the former being engaged at the moment upon a circular to the Bishops. The

* At Naples and Parma, trials are public—except the *Corte-Statario*, or the *tribunale-straodinaria*, or courts-martial, which may at any time be held; and then "the stroke falls suddenly, invisibly, as the decree of Heaven." There are seven judges on the bench, and no check in free speech, pen, or press.

charge against them was the crime of high treason, because of their addresses and petitions of the 21st and 30th of December preceding! But this violent and tyrannical act, together with others of a like character, failed entirely of its object. Instead of intimidating the Italians, it roused their nationality and fanned into fury the fire which had long secretly flamed in their breasts. Placards and inscriptions the very next morning were reported by the Police as having been found on the walls all over the city—"*Viva Pio Nono! Viva l' Italia! Viva Manin e Tommaseo!*"—followed up in a few days by some of a still more significant character—"*Morte a Palffy!*"—"Death to Palffy!"—the Civil Governor—"*Morte ai Tedeschi!*"—"Death to the Germans!" A general explosion was kept down only by the severe measures of the *Giudizio Statario*, a police provision permitting the trial and punishment of accused persons within two hours after the offence charged, which went into operation at Venice on the 25th of February,—although demonstrations of unequivocal indignation were of daily occurrence. Indeed, hardly a week had elapsed after the arrest of the two patriots, when the national enthusiasm was roused to the highest pitch by appearance on the stage of the magnificent Fenice Theatre of the celebrated *danseuse* Fanny Cerito, decorated with ribbons of white, red and green, the tri-color of free Italy; and, when the Police entered and drove out the excited audience and closed the doors, only the overwhelming force which had been detailed for that service prevented an immediate outburst of revolt. Nevertheless, in the *Politico-Amministrativo* Monthly Bulletin for January, from the authorities at Venice to the Imperial Government at Vienna, the excitement arising from this arrest is declared to have subsided: —although Manin and Tommaseo still continued in close confinement, despite an eloquent memorial of Teresa Manin to the

Governor, in her husband's behalf—a memorial which gave rise to several replies and rejoinders, and which proved, that, though she had a weak woman-heart in her bosom, there was a man's brain in her head; and which, moreover, offered an early refutation of the calumny, that, "in Italy, woman's politics are limited to wearing tri-color ribbons, and refusing an Austrian in the waltz!"

It has been remarked, that the people of Venice would not, in all probability, have taken the *initiative* of revolution; for, up to 1848, "order" reigned at Venice more thoroughly undisturbed than in any other town of Italy.* But now, revolution was on every side. Every breeze brought to the ear the clash of arms and shouts of revolt. The declaration of a Republic at Paris, February 25th, precipitated by the revolt at Naples a month before, was the signal for revolution all over southwestern Germany; and, before the middle of the ensuing month, all the secondary powers—Bavaria, Wurtemburg, Baden, Saxony, Brunswick, Hanover, as well as the Dukedoms of Weimar, Gotha, Reuss and the Hesses, had yielded to the popular demands for trial by jury, freedom of the press, a general German Parliament, a burgher-guard, and other franchises, of less prominence. At length, on the morning of the 13th day of March, the storm of revolution, long brooding, burst on Vienna—Vienna, the only capital of Europe, which, for half a century had slumbered profoundly on amid all the popular uproar around! A company of students repair in procession to the *Landhaus*, with a petition to the Stände, for enlargement of political liberty—they are fired on at order of Archduke Albert, and many fall slain: the whole city is roused—the Burgher Guard fraternizes with the people—the dismissal of Prince Metternich, Premier of the empire, of Archduke Albert, Chief of the Army, and of the hated Count Sedlnitzky,

* Mariotti includes Milan also in this category.

Chief of the Secret Police, is peremptorily demanded and obtained: the students and the people then receive arms, and, on the evening of the 15th, appears an imperial proclamation, granting a National Guard, granting a free press, and promising an immediate convocation of representatives from all parts of the empire, elected by the people, to frame a Constitution. Never was more strikingly exhibited "the sympathy and solidarity of the peoples." Revolution bursts at Naples: within twenty-four days it bursts at Paris; and then, within twenty-four hours, it bursts at Vienna! The old aphorism of the absolutists—"*Tant que Louis Philippe sera à Paris, et Metternich à Vienne, l'Europe ne bougera pas*"—was now to them a prophecy of doom. Louis Philippe was no longer at Paris: Prince Metternich was no longer at Vienna, and all Europe was in commotion. The effect of intelligence like this on the inflammable minds of the Venetians may be imagined. At the same time, vague rumors of revolution in the cities of Lombardy began to be heard.

It was as early as the 5th and 8th of September, '47, that the first popular demonstrations transpired at Milan. Prior to this, some students of the Universities of Padua and Pavia had been maltreated or murdered by Austrian officers, for the expression of liberal views; but the matter had not attracted general notice. At Padua, on the 8th of February, some eight or ten students had been wounded at the celebrated Café Pedrocchi; and at Pavia, six or seven other students had, at another time, been killed, and thirty wounded, and the University temporarily closed; while, at Treviso, near the close of the year, December 16th, the name of Pio Nono having been rapturously applauded at the Theatre, during the performance of the Opera "*I Lombardi*," an order was issued forbidding henceforth all allusion by the people to the reigning Pontiff—

"*tutte allusione, prossima o rimota, diretta, od indiretta, alla persona del regnante pontifice!*"

The agitation, also, of the question of the right, under the treaties of 1815, of the occupation of Ferrara by Imperial troops, during the summer of the same year, and the arrangement of August, by the mediation of France, had also aroused deep feeling in every city of Italy, from Rome to Genoa, against the Emperor of Austria, and for the Pope.

Ah! had poor Italy had but then a Paul, or an Alexander, or an Urban, or a Julius, or a Hildebrand, to verify the subsequent words of Charles Albert—"*L'Italia fara da se*"*—that heroic motto which found an echo in every Italian heart!

On the 19th of July, the Austrian troops entered Ferrara with loaded guns and lighted linstocks, as if advancing on a foe; but, on the 23d of December, the protest of the Papal Nuncio at Vienna, backed by the denunciations of all Italy, had forced an evacuation. At the same time, however, the army in Lombardy was reinforced from 35,000 men to 70,000, so as to leave a disposable force of 40,000 men, after providing for the garrisons—the great powers being notified, that the only object of this increase of force was the better security of the Austrian possessions; while it was publicly announced by the directors of the Imperial foundry at Mariazelle, in Austria, that, for six months, no private orders could be executed, as, night and day, the entire works would be employed in casting cannon and projectiles. Most of the reinforcements sent were Croats, from the brave and hardy Ottochan and Ogulin border regiments, until the number in Upper Italy attained more than 30,000. These men are said to make the best infantry in the world. They are tall, bony, all muscle and sinew, with sharp faces, and long

* Literally—"Italy will do for herself."

moustaches—patient, enduring, frugal, disciplined, and, at eighty paces, dead shots. Their women are perfect Amazons, and fought well beside their lovers and husbands throughout the whole war. Over their shoulders they wear a Red Mantle, whence their popular name. No wonder that these barbarians should have been viewed with horror and hate by the Italians as they disembarked at Venice, or came pouring down the passes of the Tyrol; being then "consigned to their barracks, where horses where always saddled, and cannon was always in readiness." And no wonder that, by all these events, and others of like character, popular feeling had been deeply roused.

When, therefore, in the month of September, the people of Milan were brutally assailed, and slaughtered by the Austrian police, simply for singing the "Hymn of Pio Nono"—the *Marseillaise* of Italy in 1848—on the occasion of the investiture of the new Prelate of that See—Archbishop Romilli, an Italian, being successor to the deceased German, Gaisruck, with his Archiepiscopal robes—indignation knew no bounds, and insurrection assumed its date. Subsequently to this, a studied system of mutual annoyance and exasperation seems to have existed between the garrison and the people. The shape or color of a hat,* the fashion of a vest, the style of the beard, or the cut of the hair, seems to have been deemed sufficient cause for controversy. At length, to manifest opposition to the government, and to diminish its revenues, the liberalists of Milan resolved to abstain from the use of tobacco in every form—that manufacture being an imperial monopoly, bringing to the revenue nearly a million of dollars, or 4,000,000 of Lire; and the refusal of the Americans to use tea, and its destruc-

* After the revolt in Sicily the Calabriase hat, with feathers, and with the buckle in front, was viewed as revolutionary, and prohibited!

tion in Boston harbor was instanced, in a circular of the day, in support of their determination, and as an earnest of their ultimate success. Nor was this all. The Lottery was a most lucrative monopoly, and it was renounced; the Theatre paid tribute, and La Scala was deserted; the Corso was Imperial, and its promenades were abandoned. And thus, not only were the lottery and tobacco—the darling vices of Italy—renounced, but, also, the use of sugar and coffee, which were likewise taxed; while the velvet of Genoa was substituted for the broadcloth of Germany. As for the theatre—La Scala was so deserted, that "the insolent minion," Fanny Ellsler, a German, was forced to throw up her Carnival engagement; and Tadolini sang to empty boxes! One may naturally suppose Italians in earnest, when they sacrifice to any cause the theatre and the *tombola*, tobacco, and coffee!

But, exactly in proportion as the citizens deserted the theatre and the Corso, did the soldiery frequent them; and the less the Milanese smoked, the more smoked the Austrians. The soldiers were encouraged in these demonstrations by their officers, and especially by the counsel and example of the Count Von Neyperg; and in citizen garb they often paraded the streets smoking cigars with the most insulting *sang froid*. At length, one day—it was the 3d of January, 1848—a cigar having been stricken from the lips of an insolent soldier by an exasperated citizen, a rencontre ensued, in which eight of the Milanese were killed and fifty wounded. Among the slain was Magnanini, an old man of seventy, a Councillor of the Court of Appeals. Popular indignation was now roused to fury; and, although in a proclamation of the 9th, by the Viceroy, Archduke Ranieri,* redress was promised, it was by no means wholly appeased.

* This old man was the weakest of all the Archdukes of Austria, and the most un-

On the 14th, at Turin, obsequies for the martyrs of Milan and Pavia were celebrated with imposing pomp, and, subsequently, at Rome, notwithstanding the protest of the Austrian Ambassador. From Venice, despite the prohibition of the Police, eight thousand francs were, by the ladies, forwarded to the wounded at Milan, with a letter of sympathy. The Mayor of Vicenza forwarded two thousand francs contributed by the inhabitants; and, at Verona, sixteen hundred francs were contributed in eight hours, when the contribution was arrested by the Police.

On the 15th, at Milan, appeared an Order of the Day from Radetsky of characteristic sternness; and, on the 17th a letter from the Emperor to the Viceroy, which was published, caused a profound sensation. It was as follows:—"I have duly examined the events which occurred at Milan on the 2d and 3d instant. It is evident to me that a faction, desirous to destroy public order and tranquillity, exists in the Lombardo-Veneto kingdom. All that you deemed necessary to satisfy the wants and wishes of the different provinces I have already done. I am not disposed to grant further concessions. Your Highness will make known my sentiments to the public. The attitude of the majority of the population of the kingdom, however, induces a hope that similar distressing events shall not occur. At all events, I rely on the loyalty and courage of my troops."

This was one of the last of Metternich's manifestoes. A few weeks later, and he was a fugitive and an exile!

On the 22nd, the *Judicium Statuarium*, a provision permitting the trial and execution of accused persons within two hours after the offence charged, equivalent to martial law—already mentioned at

popular—and that is saying a good deal of him. The Archduke Charles was a soldier; the Archdukes John and Stephen were esteemed liberals; the Archduke Ranieri was only a despot and a fool.

Venice—which was signed November 24th, 1847, went into effect on demand of the Police. Arrests now became numerous. Some of the prominent citizens were seized. The prisons were crowded, and numbers were sent to the House of Correction at Porta Nuova. Of the lower class four hundred were arrested. One hundred and eighty of the ablest were sent as recruits to the squadron at Trieste; and the residue, without trial, were transported as galley-slaves to Moravia and Illyria. Terror now seized Milan! The massacre of Gallicia, which chilled all Europe with horror, was remembered and dreaded! The Gyulai Regiment was in Lombardy! On the 21st, three hundred of the most respectable citizens applied for their passports. On the three last days of January, the railroad from Treviglio to Milan was exclusively occupied in the transportation of troops. On the 6th of February, a fete in honor of the Constitution granted January 29th, by Ferdinand of Naples, was celebrated with rejoicings. A month later and the revolution at Paris, which, according to Carlyle, would never have "broken out so and then, but later and otherwise, had there been no insurrectionary Sicily and reforming Pope"—was celebrated with mingled dismay and exultation; and the crisis was at the very door.

Early on the morning of the 16th of March, the Viceroy had received intelligence of the revolution at Vienna of the 13th; and, long before dawn on the morning of the 17th, under a strong escort, with his family and all his effects, he was off for Verona—in obedience, to be sure, to an order from Vienna, dated a fortnight before. The Governor of the Province, Count Spaur, had, also, left Milan some days previous, and his duties had devolved on Count O'Donnel,* the Vice-Governor. At nine o'clock on the

* This same Gen. Count O'Donnel, it probably was, who saved the Emperor's life from an assassin in February, 1853, and in April received the order of St. Stanislaus from the despot of Russia, for the feat.

morning of the 17th, a telegraphic dispatch from Cilley, a town in Styria on the route from Trieste to Vienna, announced that "the Emperor had determined to abolish the censorship, and to publish without delay a law on the Press, as well as to convoke the States of the Kingdoms, both German and Sclavonic, and, also, the Central Congregations of the Lombardo-Veneto,—the meeting to be held on the 3d of next July, at latest."

Upon this intelligence, all Milan at once repaired to the Town-Hall, shouting—"Arms and Civic Guard!"—and then, bearing along the *Podesta*, or Mayor, Count Gabrio Casati, repaired to the Governor's Palace to present a petition for the annulment of sumptuary laws, the release of political prisoners, the election of deputies, the enrollment of a National Guard. The petition was rejected and the palace was stormed and taken! Two millions of francs were found in the military chest: and old Radetsky's flight for the Citadel was so precipitate, that he left his sword of "sixty-odd years' service," and his vest behind! O'Donnel, failing to effect his flight, was made prisoner, and in agonies of terror issued orders for a Civic Guard, and every thing else demanded.

Barricades now arose as if by magic in every street, of enormous dimensions, and to the incredible number of two thousand! The most costly furniture furnished by patrician hands, and the imperial coaches, were added to augment them. The Town-Hall was burst open by Radetsky's cannon, and three hundred insurgents were made captives. The fighting in the streets of Milan then commenced, and continued with unabated fury five days—until the evening of the 22d. The tocsin pealed incessantly from every campanile. All night of the 18th raged a terrific storm, but the storm of civil war was more terrific still. Next day was the Sabbath; but for Milan it was no day of rest. Musketry rattled from every window and roof; while women and children showered down paving stones on the foe. " The very foundations of the city were torn up," says Radetsky in his official report. " Not hundreds, but thousands, of barricades crossed the streets. Such circumspection and audacity were displayed, that it was evident military leaders were at the head of the people. The character of the Milanese had become quite changed. Fanaticism had seized every rank and age and both sexes." The proudest ladies ministered to the wants of the wounded in the hospitals. The "military leaders" alluded to are said to have been veterans of Napoleon's army in Italy, and adventurers from Algiers, the Levant, France, and South America; while a body of Italian Swiss riflemen, from the Canton of Ticino, did deadly service from the marble roof of the Cathedral and the windows of houses. Long before—nearly a year, indeed—had Radetsky foreseen all this, and even the advance of Sardinia to the rescue, and had demanded of Metternich an army of 150,000 men in Lombardy; but in vain. The old veteran states, in his report of April 8th, that he had even been informed that the insurrection would break out on the 18th.

The loss of life during these five days fighting in the streets of Milan, has been variously stated. It has been placed as low as 700 slain on part of the Austrians, and 250 on part of the people; and as high as 5,000 dead and captive of the former, and 329 of the latter. Radetsky's force has, also, been variously stated at from 8,000 to 20,000 troops, many of them Italian, with from fifty to seventy pieces of artillery. As for the Milanese, they had, at first, but a few hundred fowling-pieces, though shortly supplied from the barracks, the Custom House, the shops of armorers, and from the hands of Austrian soldiers taken prisoners. Most of the body of nine hundred armed Police, also, took sides with the people from the first. As for the Italian troops, though many remained and were forced to fight against their countrymen as mere machines, yet a regiment of grenadiers had been ordered from Milan only the week before. On the first alarm, Radetsky sent for the two frontier brigades of Strassoldo and Maurer, on the Ticino, but they came too late, and only joined him outside the walls of Milan on the 23d.

The Croats, during the bloody strife, are said to have been guilty of atrocities too abominable to pollute the printed page. Women were violated and bayoneted; unborn babes were torn from the maternal womb; children were nailed by the hands to the doors of their homes, or spiked against walls or trees; the white hand of a lady ornamented with rings was found in the pocket of a Croat; men were flayed—were covered with pitch and burned—were deprived of hands and feet—were buried alive! Eyes and tongues were torn out, and living bodies were cut into fragments!

Such atrocities would be incredible were they not incontestibly attested. The Milanese, on the contrary, seem to have been humane. Even the infamous Count Bolza, a spy of the Police, dragged from a hay-loft, was spared. The 541 sick and wounded Croats in the military hospital of San Ambrogio were studiously tended, though heartlessly left to perish by their comrades. Baron Landsfeld, chief of the Police, was, with his family, respected. Delicate ladies dressed wounds;—and they made them, too; for one lady slew three Croats with her own hand! Beardless boys wrung bayonets from veterans. Those who lost one arm still fought on with the other; while the last words of the dying ever were—*Viva l'Italia!* Radetzky's uniform, found in the castle, was hung on a pole and riddled with balls. The projectiles flung by the foe, were sent back by cannon of wood and leather, hooped with iron. One species of

Austrian projectile was a leaden head of Pio Nono! Ammunition was abundant, 48,000 pounds of powder having been discovered in the Barracks of the Incoronata.

Radetsky repeatedly menaced the city with bombardment from the castle, despite the protest of the foreign Consuls, and kept up a ceaseless cannonade from his sixty guns with red-hot shot, which set on fire many houses near the walls. An armistice of three days, which he proposed on the 22nd, was instantly rejected by the Provisional Government. The destruction of property was great. Provisions became scarce and dear. The people cut off entirely from the city gates, could only communicate with the country through bold contrabandists, or by means of small balloons, at which latter the ignorant Croats vainly discharged their muskets! Some of these aerial couriers fell in Sardinia, some in Switzerland, some in Piacenza, and bore this message among others, signed by the Committee of War:—"Brothers! Fortune smiles! Austria, vanquished, retains only the castle! Hasten on! Let us secure but one gate between two fires and we conquer!"

In a similar manner, news of insurrection in Pavia and Bergamo came over the walls; and soon, from the tower-tops, troops of hardy Lombards were beheld swarming across the rice-fields to the rescue.

On the evening of the fifth day, one of the gates, that of Tosa, defended by seven guns and 2,000 men, was gallantly carried by the brave Luciano Manara, by means of moveable barricades. News was now received that Padua, and Venice, and, indeed, that all Lombardy was in revolution—that thirty thousand peasants were pouring over the plains to relieve Milan—that ten thousand Swiss had crossed the frontier; and that Charles Albert himself, King of Piedmont, with fifty thousand men, was on the Ticino!

Evacuation of Milan seemed now to Radetsky inevitable, and on the evening of the 22nd of March, he issued the necessary order. Eight hours were required for its execution, and it was morning before the last Austrian soldier had left the ramparts. Three hundred German families left Milan with them. A terrible fire was kept up on the retreating troops, and their path was lighted by conflagration. The Italian regiments of the garrison, during the retreat, were under severest *surveillance.* At some doubtful points, the Austrian artillery was turned upon them, and the slightest hesitancy, or delay was met by the terrible menace—"Advance or die!" Nevertheless, Radetsky, in his report of April 8th, declares that no Italians deserted during the strife at Milan, and that all did their duty!

A constant cannonade was poured by the castle from sixty guns, shifted from point to point, while from the seventy bell-towers of Milan pealed out the unceasing tocsin of alarm. From every roof, window, tree, tower, wall, was showered a deadly *fusillade;* while even women and children poured down boiling pitch, and oil, and lead, on the hated foe.

It must have been a wild—a fearful scene, that evacuation of Milan on the night of Wednesday, March 22nd, 1848! The thunder of the castle-guns—the fitful rattle of musketry—the incessant peal of hundreds of alarm bells*—the screams of the wounded—the groans of the dying—the blasphemies of the retreating foe—the triumphant shouts of the heroic Milanese—the blood-red glare of burning houses and the blazing citadel which lighted up a midnight sky! "Never, while I live," writes an Austrian officer, "shall I for-

* The superstitious and semi-savage Croats are said to have been so panic-struck by the bells, as to have become utterly bewildered and powerless. Radetsky accordingly issued an order, at a subsequent period, declaring, that every town which rang the tocsin, should be razed to the ground—a threat which he fearfully fulfilled in the cases of Molignano and Castelnovo

get that Milan night!" Well has the scene been termed "The Lombard Vespers!"

On the following day, the Provisional Government of Milan—which was formed on the night of the 21st—issued a manifesto, in which they detailed their wrongs at length. This powerful document, which, for boldness and precision, recalls our own Declaration of Independence, may be viewed as embodying not only the leading grievances of the Lombardo-Veneto kingdom, but those, also, of most of the other despotisms of Italy. To the capitals of Milan and Venice, however, it applied with peculiar force. "Two thousand millions of Italian money," says Cattaneo, "were buried in the Imperial treasury; and, although the Italians formed but one-eighth of the population of the Austrian empire, they had to bear one-third of the public burdens!" The swarms of haughty and sullen officials were all of the abhorred Teuton-race—as ignorant generally as they were presumptuous always—"the very judges dispensing justice through interpreters!" And then the hated and hateful Police; and the despotic Conscription, which exiled the young Italian half his life to the frontiers of the Empire.*

But, for the moment, these atrocious wrongs were well-nigh forgotten, in the general jubilee, at the wonderful triumph that had just transpired. That an unorganized mass of unarmed citizens, without experience or discipline, should have driven out from among them some ten or fifteen thousand of the best troops in the world, commanded by the oldest and, perhaps, the ablest military chieftain of modern times, seemed incredible—were it not true; and presented the only instance of the kind on record in all history, if we except the expulsion of the Spaniards from Naples by Massaniello in 1647—of the French from Palermo, in 1282—of the Austrians

* In 1814, the term of service was three years, but in 1843 had been extended to eight and fifteen. So says Mariotti, to whom the writer is indebted for valuable facts.

from Bologna, in 1848, and of the insolent soldiery of Maria Theresa, from the walls of Genoa, by an infuriated populace, armed only with knives and stones, just one century previous, 1746. And yet, "The Italians dont fight," said Blackwood's Magazine only two months before! What thought Marshal Radetsky? And in what capitals of all Europe, save in Italy, have similar deeds of daring ever been witnessed?

As the Austrians poured out of Milan in their precipitous flight, the peasantry poured in no less precipitously from the surrounding country, until, it is estimated, not less than 30,000 of these rough patriots inundated the streets of the capital.* But their stay was short. Two Legions were formed—one to defend the city as a Civic Guard, and the other, under the name of "Legion of the Alps," to follow the foe. The latter under guidance of Manara, Cattaneo, Villani, and others, pursued the retreating Radetsky and harassed his flight, until joined by the serried battalia of the King Charles Albert. The hope of Austria—vile as it was vain—that, in event of strife, the Lombard peasant could always be incited against his master the noble, proved utterly futile; for patrician and plebeian found a foe alike in the abhorred Teuton.

Meantime, and almost simultaneously with the events detailed at Milan, panic or mutiny took possession of the entire Austrian force in the Lombardo-Veneto; and post after post, town after town, corps after corps, surrendered, almost without a show of resistance. "Out of twenty battalions at the outbreak of the insurrection," says the Prussian General Willisen, "seventeen passed over to the enemy." Among these was a battalion of the regiment Haugwitz, commanded by Prince Schwarzenberg, subsequently Premier of the

* "The peasantry of the Venetian provinces continued, it is true, in their stupid and pusillanimous apathy, but in Lombardy they rose *en masse*."—*Mariotti.*

empire. The impregnable strongholds of Osopo, Palma Nuova, Rocca d' Anfo, and Pizzighettone yielded almost without a summons, and opened to the insurgents their vast supplies of arms and munitions ; while Brescia, Padua, Vicenza, Monza, Bergamo, Treviso, Rovigo, Como, Udine, and all the lesser towns, posts, and villages followed their example, even to, and even beyond, the frontier of " the ever-loyal Tyrol." The Laggo di Garda, the boundary of Lombardy, was, also, taken possession of by means of its gun-boats and steamers, and 500 barrels of powder secured. " The Lombards were free !"

Verona and Mantua were saved only by the firmness of their Governors, Gorzkowsky and Gerhardi, and the folly or treachery of the insurgents. The fortress of Peschiera, on the Mincio, at Lake Garda, held by the stern old Baron de Rath, is impregnable, and was not approached. Neither was that of Legnano on the Adige. The cowardly Francis of Modena fled to Mantua, at the first outbreak at Milan ; and the still more cowardly Carlo Lodovico of Parma " was too cowardly even to attempt flight," and so became a prisoner in his own palace, his strong citadel of Piacenza being at once evacuated by its Austrian garrison. The Austrian garrison at Ferrara was unmolested, and that at Comacchio capitulated. As for Venice, she was evacuated by the Austrians on the same day as was her sister-capital, Milan, March 22d, and in " manner and form as hereinafter to be written."

Thus, out of Ferrara, Peschiera, Mantua, Verona and Legnano— Austria had not left her, before the close of March, 1848, a single inch of firm ground, in all Italy ! *

* Mariotti.

CHAPTER III.

BLOOD!

It was on Thursday, the 16th day of March, that those vague rumors, which so often and so mysteriously, yet, with such strange truthfulness, anticipate more certain intelligence of momentous events, were in full circulation, respecting the revolution of three days previous at Vienna,—under the arcades of St. Mark. Yet, vague and uncertain as these rumors were, they met a reception as undoubting as it was welcome from the ever-sanguine Venetians. Their exultation was all the more intense for being half-suppressed; and their joy and triumph was more vividly declared by the flashings of their dark eyes, and the enthusiasm of their expressive features, than it could have been even by their lips.

At about the hour of four that evening—the usual hour at that season for fashionable appearance on the Piazza of St. Mark—the feelings which now possessed the people were betrayed by the fact, that Marshal Marmont was hissed while promenading with the Countess Palffy, wife of the Civil Governor of Venice, and that, too, by persons not of the lowest class. Marmont was one of Napoleon's Marshals who betrayed his master, and for many years resided, with other fallen dignitaries, in fallen Venice.* Some hours afterwards, when the people repaired to the Fenice Theatre with the purpose of there celebrating the revolution at Vienna, they found the doors closed, and an overwhelming Police force stationed within the iron railings, by which, on the side of the Campo San Fantino, the edifice is surrounded. Contenting themselves, therefore, with applying to the guardians of the building those terms of ridicule which only a Venetian can conceive, they shouted—"Death to Metternich!" "Death to Palffy!" and dispersed for the night.

Next day, the 17th, about noon, the Austrian Lloyd Steamer, *Venezia*, from Trieste, brought the Vienna mail of the 14th, detailing the extraordinary events which had transpired in that city. Hardly had the anchor of the steamer found the bottom, at her usual mooring opposite the two granite pillars of the Piazetta, when her remarkable news was known throughout the city; and, hardly was it known, before an immense multitude began assembling in front of the Governor's Palace.

So indispensable to a correct apprehension of scenes and events is a distinct idea of the theatre on which they are enacted, especially in a city so unique as Venice, that, even at the hazard of repetition,

* Frederic Auguste Louis Viesse de Marmont, born 1774, died at Venice, March 2nd, 1852. He was the last survivor of Napoleon's celebrated Marshals, created May 19th, 1804, the day after the proclamation of the empire. At the age of eighteen he attracted Napoleon's attention at the siege of Toulon, and was, in '95, made by him one of his aids when General of the Army of the Interior, and taken by him to Italy in '96. Marmont took the first gun at Lodi, and subsequently bore the trophies, 82 flags, to Paris. He was with Napoleon during his whole career, and was made Duke of Ragusa, but was denounced as a traitor for the capitulation of Paris in 1814. He was in command of Paris in 1830; and, after his expulsion with Charles X., went into exile and obscurity. His name was stricken from the list of the Marshals of France and a black veil was hung over his portrait. For many years he resided at Venice, and received much attention from the vice-regal court. He died at seventy-eight, leaving most of his small property to his *maitre d' hotel.*

a second glance at some of her more prominent features—a rapid recapitulation, as it were, of the characteristics already presented, together with the supply of such additional suggestions as may occur, seems advisable; and the same course, as it may be required, will hereafter be pursued.

The Piazza of St. Mark is, probably, the most magnificent, if not the most capacious, square in Europe. Napoleon said of it—"*La Place Saint-Marc est un salon, auquel le ciel seul est digne de servir de voute!*" It embraces an area of 576 feet in length, by 269 in width at its widest point. At the eastern extremity rises the facade of the Cathedral of St. Mark—172 feet long by 72 in height, with five domes from 80 to 90 feet in altitude—gorgeous with mosaics and oriental with minarets—completed more than eight centuries ago—its famous bronze horses prancing above the chief portal; while, in front, rise three masts, from which in the proud day of the Republic's power floated the conquered *gonfalons* of Cyprus, Candia, and the Morea.* At the western extremity of the Piazza stands the palace erected by Napoleon in 1809. On the north, the old palace of the Procurators of St. Mark; and, on the south, the new palace of the Procurators, now occupied by the government—each structure being more than three centuries old.†

* These masts were originally erected to sustain the silken standards of Cyprus, Candia and Negropont; but, at a later period, the standard of Morea was substituted for that of the last; while, at the commencement of the 16th century, two Procurators of St. Mark, Barbo and Loredano, substituted the present splendid pedestals of bronze, decorated with syrens and tritons, the work of Leopardo, for the original frames of wood. The masts themselves are about seventy feet high, painted red and surmounted by the winged lion, gilded and crowned. The silver towers of Cyprus first floated from a mast of St. Mark, February 26th, 1489, upon the abdication of the Conaro Queen in favor of the Republic.

† The *Procuratie Vecchie* was erected in 1500, as a residence for the *Procuratori* of St. Mark, officers of high dignity, and, originally, the wardens of the Basilica, the trust being instituted about the middle of the 11th century, and the term of office being for

Thus, the northern, western, and southern sides of the Square of St. Mark are completely closed in by the walls of these splendid and lofty palaces, the only ingress or egress being through low arches. Around these three sides of the Piazza runs a continuous Arcade, beneath which are the Cafès of Florian, Suttil, Quadri, and others, and numerous offices, bookstores, and repositories of fancy goods of every description. The fourth side of the quadrangle is occupied by the Basilica. At right angles with the Piazza, at its eastern extremity, extends towards the south to the quay, the Piazetta, or "little square." In the angle of the Piazza and Piazetta rises the Campanile, or bell-tower, of St. Mark—more than three hundred feet high, and more than seven hundred years old. This tall tower is tenanted by watchmen night and day, whose office is to strike the hours on the huge bells in echo to those struck by the sledge-hammers of the two Moors on the platform of the opposite *Torre del' Orologio*, or "Tower of the Clock;" also, to peal the changes required by the innumerable solemnities of the Catholic church, even from dawn until dusk, and from dusk until dawn; also, to watch over the city, and, in event of conflagration, to raise the alarm and direct the *Pompieri*, by concerted signals, to the scene; and, lastly, to sweep the port and the Adriatic with glasses, and communicate the approach of vessels, and the various circumstances of interest which may present. These men—these watchmen of the bell-tower of St. Mark, are, indeed, the veritable and most vigilant guardians of Venice. They maintain regular watch and ward, and a small

life. As the trust increased in importance, the number of Procurators was augmented to some thirty; and, among other prerogatives bestowed on it, was that of an Orphan's Court. To it was often committed the execution of wills, not only in Venice, but in distant cities of Italy. In this manner the power of the body became vast, and it usually supplied a doge. In the decline of the Republic, the office was often sold—the price to the old nobility being $30,000, and to the new $100,000. The *Procuratie Nuove* were erected because the old palace was not sufficiently spacious.

THE PIAZETTA.

Page 317.

apartment in the belfry of the tower affords them a couch, and protection against the chill sea-breeze of the night, or the sultry sun of the day, as they alternately sleep.

The Piazetta is about one hundred feet in width by one hundred yards in length. On the east side, in a line with the Cathedral, extends the immense Palace of the Doges; and on the opposite side is the Library of St. Mark and the *Zecca*, or Mint—one continuous mass of structure, with an arcade continuous with that of the Piazza beneath. The Ducal Palace has, also, its arcade, which, more than six centuries ago, under the name of the *Broglio*, was the privileged promenade of the haughty patricians. At the southern extremity of the Piazetta, not far from the water-side, rise the famous pillars of red and gray granite, so constantly mentioned—each of a single block—one surmounted by the winged lion of St. Mark, which in 1807 visited the *Invalides* at Paris, but came home in 1815, and the other by a statue of St. Theodore, the earliest patron of Venice, standing, sword in the *left* hand and shield in the right, on the back of a crocodile.* From this spot stretches away towards the east, along the port, or Canal of St. Mark, the *Molo*, or quay, in front of the Ducal Palace, succeeded by the *Riva degli Schiavoni*, and a continuous line of quays extending to the extremity of the islands, nearly two miles distant, at the Public Gardens. This

* These columns, it is said, lay for half a century on the quay after their arrival at Venice, and one fell into the canal and was lost in attempting to land it. At length, Nicolo, a Lombard, raised the two which remained to their present position, and claimed from the Senate, as compensation, that games of chance, prohibited elsewhere, should here be permitted—in accordance with their promise to pay him "whatever he demanded." To obviate the evils, however, which soon became apparent, and at last intolerable, the same spot, four centuries later, was designated for public executions, and by the gamblers was deserted. Henceforth, to pass between the columns was deemed a sure omen of evil, and the saying "*Guardati d' all inter colonne*," became common. The unhappy Faliero landed "between the columns," owing to a dense fog, on his return to Venice, after having been chosen Doge, as already mentioned.

broad and continuous quay is cut by numerous canals, which are crossed by peculiar bridges, composed of steps ascending and descending. The Arsenal stands not far from the Gardens, and the corvette, or sloop-of-war which guards the harbor, a vessel of sixteen guns, lies at her moorings opposite the mouth of the canal leading to its gates. The Piazza, Piazetta, and Molo, are paved with variegated and ponderous flag-stones, though no animal larger than a dog is ever seen upon them,* and the clatter of hoofs, the crack of the whip, or the rattle of wheels is never heard.

The continuous pile of structure called the Mint, the Library, and the New Palace of the Procurators, forming the west side of the Piazetta and the south side of the Piazza, constitute the residence of the civil and military Governors of Venice, and accommodate most of the Governmental offices. At the southeastern extremity of this angular pile, in the front of the edifice called the Mint, the windows and balconies of which look out on the harbor—out on the Postal steamer from Trieste—out on the blue Adriatic—down on the quay, to the Gardens, the Arsenal, and the corvette—down on the Piazetta with its two granite pillars, and on the Ducal Palace directly opposite—while, near the water, in the rear, on the south, extend the Royal Gardens planted by Napoleon—at this southeastern extremity of this angular pile, on the 17th day of March, 1848, were the apartments of Count Palffy, Civil Governor of Venice. Forty years before they were the favorite abode of Napoleon while at Venice; and, in less than forty days after, they were the residence of Daniel Manin, Dictator of the Queen of the Sea!

One hour after noon, on this 17th day of March, the Piazetta

* The young Venetian knows nothing of horses: and, as for sheep, calves, and oxen—why, he believes that cutlets grow on trees, and steaks on vines—perhaps! At least, so it has been suggested by a droll Frenchman.

beneath the windows of these apartments seemed the rendezvous of all Venice. One large band of citizens, consisting of several hundreds, came pouring through the Piazza by the *Sotto Portico* of the Clock tower, while another band, with rude streamers and ruder shouts, came rushing up the *Riva;* and, "Liberty to Manin! Liberty to Tommaseo!" was the burthen of the cry of both. In the basement and arcade of the Ducal Palace, on the opposite side of the Piazzetta, is a *corps de garde*, with two field-pieces always standing in front. The drums now beat to arms, and the whole detachment seized their muskets and fell into line. The shouts increase. Count Palffy appears on the balcony, and essays to speak, but his voice is drowned by the uproar. A deputation from the people demands the immediate release of Manin and Tommaseo. With fear and trembling the demand is accorded, and again the old Count essays to address the excited populace, to palliate his indiscreet act.* But they listened not. They had rushed across the Piazetta, "between the columns," past the guard of soldiers with their artillery, past the Ducal Palace, over the *Ponte della Paglia*—from which you look up to the melancholy "Bridge of Sighs," connecting "the palace and the prison on each hand;" and, bursting open the doors of that same "prison," had released their persecuted and incarcerated favorites within a period less than that required by

* Palffy's order to Linder, Chief of the Police, for the release of Manin and Tommaseo runs thus:—"In view of the imperious circumstances, I have thought proper, on my responsibility, to order that Nicolo Tommaseo and Lodovico Manin, now in arrest, shall be at once set free from arrest, and set at liberty." The old Governor, in his trepidation, seems to have forgotten that Manin's Christian name was *Daniele*, and not *Lodovico!* "I do what I ought not," were the only words of the palliatory speech which accompanied the order which seems ever to have been heard—sufficiently significant and sufficiently true, no doubt, and sufficiently complete also, one would think, notwithstanding the conciseness. For, what could the old Count say more? These words embodied every thing for him!

this description of the event. At the same time, despite fierce and even sanguinary resistance on the part of the prison-guard, several other individuals, confined on political charges were set at liberty, among whom were two citizens of Padua, who were subsequently welcomed to their home by an enthusiastic ovation of their fellow-citizens.

Tommaseo, at once, at his own desire, was conveyed to his abode: but Manin, in prison garb, squalid and livid, with neglected hair and beard, was borne on the shoulders of the enthusiastic multitude beneath the windows of the governor, where, despite official menace and entreaty, by word and sign, he prolonged an eloquent discourse—the people swarming the arcades "to listen to the thunders of eloquence of the man, who, from that day, was to be to them, all that Kossuth was to the Hungarians,"—until, fainting from excitement and fatigue, he sank, and was borne on their shoulders to his home.

Venice was electrified! Cafès in the Piazza at once threw off their old appellations, and, re-christened, appeared as "Cafè Tommaseo"—"Cafè Manin." Universal jubilee and rejoicing seemed the order of the day; and, in the excitement of the moment, the remarkable spectacle of the conquered embracing the conqueror—the Venetian embracing the Austrian—was witnessed in the Place St. Mark.

But this could not last. Suddenly, to the amazement of all, at the summit of the central mast of the three which stand before the cathedral, where once waved the conquered standards of the Eastern Archipelago, and where, for more than fifty years, had waved the tricolor of France, or, the imperial *Schwartz-gelb** of Austria, on all days of festivity or solemnity, now rolled out to the

* Black and yellow.

setting sun, in the evening breeze, the bright folds of the glorious tricolor of independent Italy.* A detachment of the Kinsky regiment, on guard at the time, were, at once, despatched with an imperial standard to replace that of revolution; but it was wrested instantly from their hands, torn into fragments and trampled contemptuously into the dust! A few moments and six guns in rapid succession from the guard-ship, *La Clemenza*, spoke alarm to all the forts and barracks in and around Venice; and, at once, St. Mark's Place bristled with bayonets. A ladder was brought to remove the obnoxious tricolor from the mast; but, strange to tell, the attempt utterly failed! *How* it chanced to fail is not narrated, and can not well be conceived; but, so long as one ray of the fading light permitted that symbol of liberty to be distinguished, the eyes of the triumphant Venetians rested on it with joy and pride. And all that night it waved on, and it was still waving in triumph when the next morning's dawn broke over Venice.†

At a late hour in the evening the great bell of St. Mark began tolling; and the whole city, roused by its deep tones, which they regarded either as the tocsin of conflagration or of revolution, poured like a flood from every avenue into the Piazza. On the balcony of the Governor's palace appeared the Cardinal Patriarch Monico in his priestly robes; and, bestowing on the excited masses his benediction, besought them to repair in peace and order to their homes. A movement of the people towards the palace, the better to catch the Archbishop's words, was interpreted as a signal for attack, and the order was at once given to clear the square, which,

* Green over white, over red, longitudinal, or at right angles with the staff. The Hungarian tricolor is the same inverted—red, over white, over green. The French tricolor is blue, white, red, latitudinal, or parallel with the staff, the blue being attached to it and the white in the middle.

† This is affirmed by Venetians, though denied, of course, by their foes.

with much unnecessary roughness, was executed with fixed bayonets. The people were driven off: "a solitude was made and called peace:" but, strange to tell, the tricolor of free Italy still floated from the summit of the central mast of St. Mark! All that night, also, Count Palffy held a council with the Municipal authorities, and the Central Congregation, as to the best mode of quelling the tumult. Manin, a member of the College, suggested a Civic Guard; but a suggestion from *that* source was, of course, sternly disregarded.

Thus ended "the first day in Venice." The blunders of the Austrians were great and palpable. To release Manin and Tommaseo was a blunder: to permit the symbol of revolt to float for one moment over Venice was a blunder: to suffer, by carelessness, the alarm-bell of St. Mark to be tolled was a blunder: to charge with fixed bayonets on an unarmed multitude of men, women, and children was a great blunder: but, the greatest blunder of all was, not to have cleared the square, by fair means or foul, six hours before!

On the morning of the 18th, a powerful, though suppressed, sensation evidently pervaded the City of the Sea. On the ponderous pillars of the arcades of St. Mark, at the portico of the clock tower, in the Campo San Luca, upon the columns of the Ducal Palace, and all along the *Molo*, and *Riva*, and, indeed, at every public place, revolutionary placards of the most inflammatory character had been posted during the night; and they were, of course soon surrounded by excited groups, which every moment received fresh accessions to their numbers. In some quarters of the city, especially in the *sestieri*, or wards, of San Polo and Cannaregio, the masses became turbulent, and some arrests of ringleaders were made.

But the rendezvous of the boldest and most belligerent of the populace seemed to be the Piazetta, near the granite columns, beneath the windows of Palffy, and before the Guard-post of St. Mark, already alluded to. An assault on this station was soon commenced by means of those insulting jests, for which the gondoliers, fishermen, *flaneurs*, *facchini*, and lower classes of Venice have always been famous. But the Croatian sentinels could comprehend nothing of all the insolence addressed to them, except the significant Italian pantomime; and their proverbial patience was not soon exhausted, nor were their stolid comprehensions soon aroused. About noon, however, a detachment of the Kinsky regiment, numbering about three hundred, was marched up to the post and took position. Nearly at the same time the Postal steamer from Trieste anchored opposite, bringing rumors of the concessions of the Emperor at Vienna on the evening of the 15th, and his promise of a Constitution and Parliament. This intelligence was variously received. By the well-informed and conservative, it was welcomed with joy, as an augury of a brighter future, and a better government. By the radical, it was viewed with distrust, or, as a forced concession, indicative of feebleness; and, instead of satisfying, only roused hopes or fears, as touching entire, and, perhaps, immediate, emancipation from a hated foreign rule. As to the masses, they comprehended precious little of the whole matter; and the only meaning they attached to "constitution" was concession, or a "showing of the white feather" on part of the old Emperor. Of course, therefore, they were easily roused to insurrection, and to demand that all the rights, instead of a part only, should be restored to their ancient Republic. Rushing, therefore, into the Piazza, with tri-colored banners and cockades, they continued their insult and derision towards the soldiers on guard at the Post St. Mark; and, at length, began tearing up the huge flags which pave the place, and breaking them into fragments, to supply themselves with missiles. A platoon or two of soldiers with fixed bayonets soon put an end to this amusement; but, as they were regaining their post, a volley of rocky fragments came showering on their heads and shoulders. Instantly wheeling, the soldiers discharged their pieces in the air. This clemency was, of course, attributed by the thoughtless masses to cowardice, and the assaults and insults instead of being checked, were only encouraged.

The indifference of the populace to danger, however—the very boys dancing in the smoke of the musketry up to the very points of the serried bayonets, and even, in some instances, managing to unfix and carry off from the carbines those long and sword-like weapons—was certainly remarkable, and gave an earnest of the intrepid spirit, at a later period, to be by those same boys displayed in their country's cause.

But all things must have an end; and, at last, stung by rage and pain, "the long-suffering German patience" was exhausted; and like the troops of the British garrison at Boston, more than seventy years before, and, like the troops of the line at Paris, less than thirty days before, and with an ultimate result similar to that in each prior case, they delivered their fire on the unarmed masses. In an instant five Venetians lay dead on the *pavè*, and nine more, dangerously wounded, lay weltering in their gore.*

"To arms! To arms!" was the startling cry which now rang along the canals of Venice, and which was echoed and re-echoed from her lofty palaces! "The Germans have fired! Venetians are murdered!"

At once the drums of the Austrian garrison began beating

* Among those severely wounded was an old woman of sixty-two, named Maria Cordella.

the *generale*, and the Place of St. Mark, in a few minutes, was filled with bayonets. The order was then given, which should have been given hours before, to clear the square and the streets; and a charge with fixed bayonets swept the infuriated but unharmed multitudes into their houses. Audacious to the last, however, they ascended to the lofty roofs, and showered down all sorts of missiles on every unlucky *pompon* that was spied below. Long before this, all the shops and cafes on the Piazza had been closed, in apprehension of an *émute;* and the danger of a premature explosion being imminent, all the powers of the republican leaders were called into requisition, to restrain the ignorant and fiery masses, by means of promises of speedy and complete recompense, from attempting immediate vengeance for the slaughter of their comrades. The shout for "vengeance," therefore, was, through their influence, adroitly changed into the cry—"A Civic Guard!" Already, that day, early in the morning, had Manin represented to Count Palffy the intense odium existing between the garrison—composed of Hungarians, Germans, and Croats—and the Venetians, and the utter powerlessness of the former to maintain order, except by force and bloodshed; and had renewed his counsel of the previous night for a Civic Guard. This counsel had, a second time, been disregarded. At the present crisis, however, the persevering patriot again appeared before the Governor, accompanied by the Mayor, or Podesta, of the city, Count Correr, at the head of the municipal authorities and the most influential men of the city, when the weak old man relented, and the order for enrolment was issued. The number of citizens he at first consented to arm was 400; but the Municipality caused the number to be raised to 1,000; and, at the urgency of Manin, the order, at length, at 5 o'clock in the evening, was issued for 3,000!

It was near nightfall when placards all over the city announced this event, and served partially to arrest the infuriated masses, who, armed with every imaginable implement which might serve for attack or defence, were hurrying to some rendezvous to prepare for vengeance.

The order for the enrolment of a Civic Guard having been signed, municipal registers were at once opened in the Piazza, and the ranks were speedily filled to the number of two thousand strong, and Manin was chosen captain.

Arms from the Arsenal soon made their appearance; and, at six o'clock that evening, not a *gendarme*, a *sbire*, or a soldier of the old police, was visible; while the streets and piazza were patrolled by the citizen-militia. Meantime the people were addressed by persons of influence and popularity, many of them republican leaders, in all the public places, and exhorted to become tranquil. The new police, as yet without uniform, were temporarily distinguished by white scarfs; and entered on the discharge of their functions with promptitude and zeal, amid the acclamations of the people.

But, while order and tranquillity were thus restored in the heart of the city, it was far otherwise in the distant *Sestieri* of Castello, Cannaregio, Dorsoduro, and other quarters remote from the Place St. Mark. Here, fierce and fiery groups of the lower orders were assembled, and menace of terrible vengeance for those who had fallen in the morning was openly made. These dark threats may, perhaps, be viewed as the inception of a later sequel of horror and blood. A large number, also, of excited men, armed with clubs, pistols, and daggers, had previously assembled at the palace of Count Salvi, bent on mischief; but, upon his arrival with the order for a Civic Guard, he was received with cheers, and the crowd dispersed.

In the *Sestiere* of St. Mark, however, all was peace and order; and, as a proof of the fact, and to give this state of things encouragement, the vast Fenice theatre, which can seat nearly 3,000 people, was thronged with a brilliant audience. A few hours later, and this brilliant audience was poured into the Place St. Mark. A joyous event had transpired. A swift express steamer, dispatched from Trieste, had brought the welcome intelligence, that the principles of the promised Constitution had been propounded in that city, and that the official declaration had arrived. The magnificent square of St. Mark suddenly assumed the aspect of a gorgeous saloon flooded with illumination. From the centre poured forth the inspiring strains of the Austrian bands—the finest in Europe—while flags and hangings waved from the windows of the surrounding palaces. Into this splendid square all Venice seemed assembled in mass; and, when, on the balcony of the Governmental Palace appeared Count Palffy, with his wife and the Podesta Correr, and in person read the imperial proclamation,* the same populace, which only the night before had heaped curses on the Governor's head, now applauded him to "the very echo that applauds again!" Intoxicated with a senseless, yet sympathetic enthusiasm, they filled the air with *Vivas*:—"*Viva il Imperatore!*"—"*Viva l'Italia!*"—"*Viva la Costituzione!*" And thus passed the entire night of the 18th—in songs, and shouts, and embracings, and felicitations, and fraternizations, and illuminations—in mad and blind rejoicings—the entire night, even to the morning's dawn.

The next day was a holiday—it was the Sabbath. It was a bright and beautiful morning; and, as is usual on that day, the first rays of the sun fell on the "*Schwartz-gelb*"—the imperial gold and

* Probably the dispatch from Cilly posted at Milan by Count O'Donnel on the morning of the 17th.

black of Austria—the standard of Maria Theresa, of Hapsburg Lorraine—as its voluminous folds rolled out in the fresh breeze from each of the tall masts of St. Mark, from the tower of the Campanile, and even from the turrets of the Cathedral of St. Mark itself. A portrait of Pio Nono, crowned with laurel, was exposed in the Piazza: brilliant carpets, tapestry, hangings of every texture, description, and character flaunted from the palace windows, looking down on the square; and, conspicuous among the colors, were the white and red of Austria—the colors of her army and marine. Before the sun had gone down, however, a new combination had, here and there, unobservedly, crept in; and the red, white, and green proclaimed the tricolor of Italy. At night the spacious Fenice was filled with applauding multitudes, although the tricolor with which it had been decorated was removed by an armed force; while illumination and exultation possessed the Piazza. Thus the day passed peaceably off in rejoicings similar to those of the preceding night. All classes were glad they scarcely knew why; and shouted they scarcely knew what, or for what. It is very certain that but very few of that vast multitude were capable of appreciating the imperial concessions; and it is equally certain that those few were by no means the most clamorous. Fraternization, which had been commenced the night before, and which, indeed, had for some days been going on, was now more conspicuous than ever, between the Italian troops in the service of Austria and the citizens of Venice. Everywhere, in the cafes and restaurants, beneath the arcades and promenading the Square of St. Mark, might be seen the officers and men of the Italian grenadiers arm in arm with citizens, each decorated with the ominous white, red, and green; for, they supposed that a constitution implied nationality, and nationality implied a symbol and banner. Every one saw this: many applauded: none denounced.

And thus passed away Sunday and Monday, the 19th and 20th days of March, in feasting, rejoicing, fraternizing, and that, too, although rumors of convulsions in Milan, and all over Lombardy, had become rife in Venice. Order the most punctilious was, however, meantime maintained throughout the city by the newly-enrolled Civic Guard.

It requires no remarkable perspicacity to detect three great blunders, at least, in the Austrian policy at Venice, on the 18th, 19th, and 20th days of March. Indeed, so numerous were the Austrian blunders committed at this time, that never was the Roman maxim, that "madness precedes destruction," more strikingly illustrated. It was madness to permit the populace to assemble and continue their insults and assaults on the soldiery, and, at last, to fire on them, instead of dispersing them with the bayonet at first. It was madness to grant the demand for a Civic Guard, and to place arms in the hands of the excited population. This was fatally proven—yet most fortunately—fatally to despots, in almost every city in Europe, in 1848. The first demand was always a National, a Civic, a Burgher Guard, to "maintain order;" the second, "like unto it," was sure to follow—*Liberty*; and, thanks to the arms granted by the tyrants, there was power, generally, to enforce that demand. Finally, it was great error on the part of the Austrian officers and authorities, to suffer the fraternization of the Italian citizens and troops under an insurrectionary badge; and this they very soon discovered—but discovered it, as was usual, when it was too late.

CHAPTER IV.

MARINOVICH.

"An assassination seemed the necessary precursor of all reforms —the indispensable prelude of all the political changes of the year 1848. At Vienna, Prague, Pesth, Frankfort, Baden, Rome, this method was pursued, under various circumstances of treachery and cruelty."

Such are the words of a British Tory in the "London Quarterly Review;" and to the names of Count Auerswald, Count Latour, Count Lamberg, Count Rossi, the Princess Windischgraëtz, and Prince Lichnowsky, he would, probably, add that of Colonel Marinovich, the Commandant of the Arsenal of Venice. How he would have characterized the martyrdom of such men as Messenhauser, Bassi, Blum, Becher, Jellinek, and the murders of the thousands equally guiltless swept down by *fusillade*, or *mitraillade*, by musketry or artillery, in the streets of Paris, Berlin, Vienna, Prague, Pesth, Baden, Venice, Milan, Naples, Rome, Palermo—in the streets of almost every considerable city on the Continent of Europe, to say nothing of the martyrs of battle and siege, hardly need be asked.*

* Latour, War Minister, slain at Vienna, October 6th; Lamberg, Governor of Hungary, slain at Pesth, September 29th; Rossi, Premier of the Pope, slain at Rome, November 15th; Princess Windischgraëtz, wife of the Austrian Marshal, slain at Prague, May 12th, by a shot from an opposite window while in her own apartments. Auerswald and

The intoxication of the 19th and 20th of March, seems to have been succeeded by a sullen reaction on the 21st. The intelligence that Milan was in full revolt—that Radetzky with 10,000 men had taken refuge in the citadel from the fury of an unarmed mob, and that all Lombardy was in insurrection, had, of course, its effect, and was not neglected by the exceedingly shrewd and astute men by whom the republican party was led. Emboldened by events and by comparative freedom, these matters were not now, as formerly, alluded to with "bated breath," in a corner, but were freely and openly discussed in cafès and restaurants. It was plain that Venice was anxious to imitate Milan, and brooded in sullen silence over some plan to effect her purpose. That the Austrian authorities should not perceive this menacing attitude of affairs was impossible. Ever provident, and thoughtful, however, only of their own personal safety, they, to a great extent, confided the preservation of public order and the maintenance of municipal rule to Manin, Chief of the Civic Guard; while, for their own protection, the sentinels were trebled, and the courts and corridors of their palaces were invested by a large portion of the most reliable regiment of the garrison—the regiment Grentzer.*

Lichnowsky, slain at Frankfort, in September, were members of the German Parliament. Lichnowsky was aid-de-camp of Don Carlos of Spain, when residing at Brussels. Blum, "the lamplighter of Leipsic," also a member of the Frankfort Parliament, was shot by order of Windischgraëtz, October 9th. Messenhauser, Commandant of the Academic Legion, at Vienna, shared the same fate, at the same time and place, by the same sentence, for the same offence: as did also Drs. Becher and Jellinek, editors of the "Universal Gazette of Austria," a radical journal. Of the martyrs of Italy, "whose name is legion," poor Ugo Bassi, the monk, shot at Bologna, August 8th, 1849, must serve as the representative.

* The Austrian force at Venice in March, 1848, consisted of one brigade—comprising 4,000 Italian troops in four battalions, with 2,500 Austrians and Croats in three battalions—two of Germans and one of Borderers. The Italians, though not in a mutinous state, were not deemed reliable: neither was the Marine force of the guard-ship, or of the Arsenal. At Padua, however, an hour or two distant by railway, Baron d'Aspre had 33

In the course of Tuesday, the 21st, rumors were circulated throughout Venice, that the city was to be destroyed! "A diabolical scheme," it was said, "had been devisedby Marinovich, with the concurrence of Vice-admiral De Martini, First Commissioner of the Admiralty, and the civil and military Governors Palffy and Zichy, to bombard Venice from the surrounding forts, and to blow the city up by means of mines and other infernal devices, centering at the Arsenal, in event of the slightest insubordination being again evinced." To the excitable and credulous Venetians of the lower class nothing seemed more probable than this "infernal plot" —more infernal, even, than that supposed to have been subsequently detected at Rome. Indeed, the idea seems not to have been without some credence even on the part of those who should have known better; for the British Consul-General, Mr. Dawkins, in behalf of the Foreign Consular corps, demanded an explanation of the rumor from the Austrian authorities. The prompt rejoinder was, that no such purpose had ever been, or was then, contemplated.

The discovery of "the infernal plot" found, however, undoubting believers in the masses, especially among the workmen of the Arsenal—the *Arsenalotti*—upwards of a thousand in number, to whom the Commandant Marinovich, had become excessively odious, because of his severe discipline, his searching correction of abuses, and his reduction of their wages and perquisites, whilst those of his own office had been, by his superiors, increased in reward of that very severity. Indeed, he seems to have been appointed to this post expressly on account of his ferocity of character, for the purpose of reforming irregularities; and he is said to have performed the functions of his appointment with stern fidelity to his

battalions—eleven being Italian—16 squadrons, 56 cannon, and one battery of congreve war-rockets—in all some four or five thousand strong masters. That fidelity and foresight cost him his life; while to it Austria owed the fact, among many others, that most of her fleet, instead of being at Venice at the period of the revolution, was in the harbor of Pola, on the opposite side of the Gulf, and thus in safety. That Marinovich was hated, however, by the *Arsenalotti*, and, perhaps, deservedly so, cannot be doubted; and even now he is spoken of by intelligent foreigners, resident in Venice at the time, as "a fool-hardy brute, who rushed on his fate." *

On the evening of the 21st, the *Arsenalotti*, on leaving the Arsenal at the regular hour of four, lingered in groups in the adjoining *campo* and on the contiguous bridge, with the avowed purpose of slaying their hated Commandant—or, in the expressive phraseology and imagery of the country—"to watch the wild beast as it issued from its lair—to assail it with stones and brickbats—to knock it down and drown it!" † His life was saved this time, however, by the bravery and promptitude of Manin, who, having gained information of the plot, hurried to the spot with a detachment of his Civic Guard, and with infinite difficulty, with a promise of Marinovich's immediate resignation of his office, withdrew him from the hands of the enraged workmen, and conveyed him on board the guard-ship, *La Clemenza*, anchored off the Arsenal, to pass the night.

That same night Manin and Tommaseo with other patriots assembled at the house of the former to take counsel on the present

* This man's unpopularity is attributed to the fact also, that, years before, "he had broken the heart of the young Archduke Frederick, the hero of Syria, and idol of Italian sailors and marines," who, nominally Commander-in-chief of the Austrian navy, was placed under the *surveillance* of his stern lieutenant to cure him of an unfortunate passion. But jailors are rarely popular. Even Marshal Bugeaud, Louis Philippe's custodian of the Duchess of Berri, when her last child was born, was no exception.

† Official account.

attitude of affairs. We are told that various schemes and propositions were discussed. The first object of the republicans had been triumphantly accomplished. The people were armed. A numerous and well-appointed Civic Guard under command of Manin himself had been secured. The next step resolved on was to secure the Arsenal, which, from time immemorial, rightly or wrongly, had been viewed as the citadel of Venice. No spot in Venice, indeed, is more intimately associated with its ancient greatness, than its celebrated Arsenal. It was commenced in 1304 by Andrea Pisano, and completed in course of twenty years, although subsequently enlarged and improved. Its walls and towers, macchiolated and crenulated, embrace a circuit of nearly two miles. It has four basins; and the dock-yards, work-shops, foundries, &c., surrounding, are almost numberless. Its graceful arches, surmounted by antique shields and inscriptions, and its ponderous pillars with their chaste capitals, render its architecture almost as observable for decoration, as for its antiquity and strength. The Porta Leone, with its trophies of ancient Grecian art, the armory, with its strange weapons and instruments of torture, the Model-room, with its representation of the famous Bucentaur, and its extensive rope-walk, or the tower of the Tana, erected a century and a half since, are among the most striking objects it presents.

To rouse and concentrate the people who still retained a most enthusiastic, yet reverential, regard for the old Republic, despite all its traditional horrors, Manin proposed that the ancient battle-cry—*Viva San Marco!*—with which Venice had become "Mistress of the Seas and the glory of the whole earth," should again be raised. With the pristine splendor of Venice under the auspices of the Winged Lion of St. Mark, no gondolier even was so debased as not to be intimately familiar; albeit, he knew but little, and that but by dim tradition, of her tyranny, and nothing, of course, by experience. *Viva San Marco!* In these three words was embodied whole centuries of most brilliant and wonderful history—yet, history which the humblest son of Venice could read and comprehend. The word *constitution*, on the contrary, conveyed to his mind no distinct or tangible idea whatever, even were it comprehensible at all. *Viva San Marco!* became, therefore, at once the motto, and the Winged Lion became the device of "Young Venice."

On the morning of the 22nd, Marinovich, despite the counsel and entreaties of his friends, and especially of those of the Vice Admiral—General De Martini, repaired, at his usual hour, to the Arsenal, but not by his usual route, or to his usual entrance. He avoided the principal portal, beside which stand the old lions of Athens, brought by "Morosini the Peloponesiaque" two centuries ago from Mount Hymettus, and which for more than twenty centuries before, even from the date of the battle of Marathon, had stood in like manner the guardians of the capital of Greece and of its port, the famed Piræus. Not by this entrance did the doomed Marinovich, following the suggestion of friends, and, prompted by a vain and tardy prudence, seek admission to his post; and by this very act of "prudence" his fate was, perhaps, precipitated. A side-door at which he applied was found locked, and one of the conspirators who was despatched for a key apprised his comrades that their victim was in their power. Alarmed by the shouts of the approaching mob, the unhappy man, now too late, sought a hiding place in a tower near the Porta Nuova. But doors were burst open, the crowd rushed in, and, on the upper landing of the staircase, stood the Commandant with two pistols and a drawn sword in his hands. "Would you take me alive or dead?" was his desperate demand. "Alive!" was the stern reply: and instantly his weapons were wrested from his grasp, his body was impaled on a pike, and, dashed to the floor, was dragged by the feet down the staircase to the bottom. "A priest!" was the only prayer of the wretched man. "Next week!" was the bitter response—a response long since taught by his own lips to the importunate. Frightfully mangled—mutilated by a thousand wounds from a thousand weapons, long after life had fled the infuriated *Arsenalotti* continued to insult the senseless carcase of their abhorred despot.

"Thus died this bad man," says the official notice of his death, "by the hand of God for the horrid plot to destroy a country of which he was an unworthy son,"—for Marinovich was himself by birth a Venetian.

This was lamentable; yet, deeply as we may lament, we can hardly wonder at the result. In the eloquent words of another*— "We deplore the outrages which accompany revolutions. But, the more violent the outrages, the more assured we feel that *a revolution was necessary*. The violence of those outrages will always be proportioned to the ferocity and ignorance of the people: and the ferocity and ignorance of the people will be proportioned to the oppression and degradation under which they have been accustomed to live." But, though we may wonder not at the occurrence of this bloody catastrophe, what we *may* wonder at, and what, indeed, can be viewed only as incomprehensible, is the insane rashness of the unhappy man in returning to the scene of his doom. Equally incomprehensible, also, is his utter dereliction from duty—a dereliction which should have cashiered him had he survived, in not demanding of Count Zichy, the Military Governor, a guard for the post entrusted to his discretion and defence, if not for his personal protection; and even more incomprehensible and reprehensible is

* Macauley.

the neglect of the powers at St. Mark's Place to send from the ample garrison ample defence. But the old Counts Palffy and Zichy throughout the whole insurrection seem to have been stricken with judicial blindness, or to have been utterly incapacitated by the extremity of bodily terror for the most common exercise of the most common powers. No wonder, that the superstitious masses of Roman Catholic Venice should have viewed the fate of this bad man as "a real miracle of Providence." No wonder that, astonished at his insane return to his post, after an escape from destruction so narrow, it was declared in the official bulletin of his death, that, "by the special permission of Heaven, blinded by obstinacy, he rushed on a fate which saved Venice from destruction and insured her immediate liberation from the barbarian yoke." No wonder that, on every wall and every column of Venice, on the evening of the same day, appeared in flaming posters these startling words—"*Giudizio di Dio! Viva Maria Salvatrice di Venezia! Viva la Republica Veneta! Viva l' Italia! Viva Pio Nino!* The infamous traitor who for years tyrannized cruelly over all in his power—the vile Satrap of the Aulic iniquities of Vienna—the hated tool of crime, has, by God's hand, been stricken with that chastisement so long merited and defied! His hand—his soul sold to Austria,—thirsted only for blood! God's finger, like that of the angel of Israel in Egypt, marked the last hour of his perfidy. Blind to all he had seen, deaf to all he had heard, he rushed on his doom. He died—died in torments—a second Prina!" *

The slaughter of Marinovich was the breath which loosened the

* Prina—Chief of Police of Milan under the French rule—torn in pieces by the people in the streets. It is said that the man who struck Marinovich the fatal blow was subsequently appointed chief keeper of the Forest of the Montello above Treviso, and afterwards a master workman in the Arsenal, a position which he held until the final capitulation.

avalanche! One might suppose that the prior slaughter of five of their unoffending fellow-citizens would more effectually have roused the Venetians. And it had roused them. To that rash act, doubtless, is directly traceable this second—this retributive deed of blood. Deeply had vengeance been sworn, and with difficulty had its immediate gratification been postponed by the more wise republican chiefs. An attempt, which, on the 18th, could have met only certain defeat, on the 22nd might prove, and did prove, triumphantly successful. There was on the 18th no Civic Guard—the people had no arms—and the very act which roused popular insubordination demanded a popular police for the maintenance of order. The Civic Guard was secured—arms were secured, and the return of Marinovich to the Arsenal on the morning of the 22nd, and the scene of violence which ensued, affording a pretext for an immediate demand for the delivery of that important post to the protection of the Civic Guard, would almost seem to justify the popular belief in the special providence of God. No doubt the schemes of the republicans were wisely conceived and deeply laid; but they could hardly have embraced—yet might not very deeply deplore—the death of Marinovich, since his life had been saved only the evening previous with great difficulty, and only by the unlooked-for appearance of Manin with his Civic Guard at the Arsenal; while his ultimate doom was the direct result of a rashness so utterly fool-hardy, that it must have been utterly unforeseen. No doubt Manin was ready with his citizen soldiery to march to the Arsenal, or to any other important point, at an instant's warning, on that momentous 22nd day of March; and had Count Zichy been equally ready with his Croats, he would never have been forced to sign a disgraceful capitulation, and the Mistress of the Adriatic would not that day, at least, have changed masters.

The death of Marinovich was the torch to the Revolution of Venice, and, in a space of time incredibly brief, the entire city was in a blaze of conflagration! From Mestre to the Lido, from Burano to the Giudecca, went up the wild slogan—"*Fuori lo Straniero! Morte ai Tedeschi!*" Away with the foreigners! Death to the Germans! This was the signal for Manin to act. At the head of only two hundred men of the Civic Guard, led by Major Olivieri, he marched at once to the Arsenal by way of the Molo, and peremptorily demanded the keys. The demand was refused. The gates were then forced, the most important posts were occupied without effusion of blood, the armory was entered and its contents distributed, and the acting Commandant, Vice-Admiral De Martini, was made prisoner. Members of the Civic Guard to the number of more than five hundred had now reached the spot, and the Arsenal was declared to be in their possession. Major Bodai, at the head of a body of marine troops, made up principally of Venetians, having ordered them to fire on a company of the Guard encountered on the *Via dei Giardini*,* was not only disobeyed, but was impaled on his own sabre by one of his own lieutenants. The soldiers then grounded their arms, tore out the Austrian *pompon* from their caps and replaced it with the tricolor cockade. This example was followed by all the Italians of the garrison, by all the *Arsenalotti*, as well as by all the naval troops on the spot. The artillery battalion of Grentzers which had come up and opposed the guns of the Civic Guard, —(which guns subsequently proved not to have been charged)— with loaded cannon and lighted linstocks, laid down their arms on the first invitation. All the vessels, as well as all the arms and munitions of war contained in the Arsenal fell, of course, into the hands of Manin, and the free tri-color superseded the imperial red and

* A street leading to the Public Gardens.

white at the peak of the guard-port corvette. Immediately nominating Col. Graziani to the command, already twice vacated in a single day, the eloquent Advocate addressed the multitude in a few of those vigorous sentences which he so well knew how to make effective. Then unfolding the glorious old standard of St. Mark found in the Arsenal, and drawn forth, at length, after a lapse of fifty years, from some secret receptacle of the past, he led the people up the Molo, a distance of more than a mile, with shouts of "*Viva San Marco! Viva la Republica!*" to the great square of the capital.

"But where, during the enactment of these strange scenes, was the Austrian garrison of more than six thousand men which held possession of Venice?" The question may well be asked, and it is as easily answered. They were in their respective barracks! "And the civil and military Governors, Counts Palffy and Zichy, where were they?" They were in the vice-regal palace, almost beside themselves with terror, vainly seeking counsel from their equally terrified counsellors! The incompetence—the cowardly inaction of these men is incredible! Not one measure had they taken to arrest the insurrection now raging in Venice! They had not enforced respect to the flag they had sworn to maintain with their blood, but had suffered it to be torn down and replaced by a symbol of rebellion. They had not sought to secure the safety of the German troops, nor the loyalty of the Italian; while Venetians were permitted to retain undisturbed possession of the Arsenal and of the corvette which protected the port. Palffy was a Hungarian; but he had passed most of his life in Italy and was personally exceedingly popular. He was *ex-officio* President of the Central Congregation, Sabregandi, a Venetian, being his Vice-President. A son of his fell at Presburg in '49, fighting against the Hungarians. The house of Palffy-Shandor is said to be one of the oldest, noblest, and wealthiest in Hungary.

Zichy was also of Hungarian origin, and belonged to a noble, powerful, and somewhat extensive family. He had three brothers, and the name frequently occurs in the story of Austria and Hungary in '48–9. It was, possibly, a son of his who was hanged by Gorgey as a traitor. In his early life he had been a brave, high-toned soldier; but now, though but fifty years old, emasculated by dissipation and prematurely old, he had long felt his incapacity for the responsible station he filled, and had desired recall to Vienna. That desire should have been gratified. It was not. When, therefore, he did return, it was in deep disgrace, only to be rendered yet deeper by the sentence of a court-martial.*

* There is some romance attached to Count Zichy's career—if *rumor* is not even falser than usual. When quite a youth, he was attached to the Embassy of Prince Esterhazy at London. On his return, he became the lover of a beautiful gipsey-girl—educated her—was anxious to marry her, and finally went with her to Bohemia, where they had two children. Subsequently he gave her a castle in Hungary and married a noble lady, at Pesth. President of the Council at Pesth, Imperial Counsellor at Vienna, Commandant of Fiume—finally he was sent to Venice. Here he is said to have led a most licentious life, and the Princess of Belgiojoso attributes his remarkable infirmness of purpose to an intrigue with a Milanese girl of the humblest extraction, of whom he was foolishly fond.

CHAPTER V.

EVACUATION.

On the morning of the 22d of March, there appeared in the official Gazette a notice from the Central Congregation of the city of Venice, that, in view of existing emergencies, it had been thought proper to invite to a seat in its counsels some of the most extensively-known and highly esteemed of the citizens of the place, not members of that body. In accordance with this notice, there assembled, at the hour of ten of that morning, at the Palace of the Municipality, the Podesta Correr, with the six Assessors and their Secretary, together with the citizens Reali, Revedin, Avesani, Pincherle, Castelli, and Costi, who had been invited, as mentioned, to assist in the deliberations. Thus assembled, they were discussing the state of affairs and the measures proper to be taken, when intelligence arrived that the hated Colonel Marinovich, Commandant of the Arsenal, had been killed by the *Arsenalotti*, and that Olivieri, Chief of the Civic Guard of the *Sestiere di Castello*, in which the Arsenal is situated, had with his troop occupied the place, and had despatched another troop to take possession of the *Goletta Guardaporto*, or Guard-ship, *La Clemenza*, a corvette of sixteen guns, lying at anchor in the Canal of St. Mark. Almost immediately upon this startling announcement appeared the Advocate Angelo Mengaldo,* Commandant of the Civic Guard, who had been previously commissioned by the Municipal Council to wait on the civic and military Governors of Venice, Counts Palffy and Zichy, and demand the evacuation of the Arsenal by the Croats. He now reported, that he had been favored with an audience by these functionaries, in presence of the Vice Admiral Martini and the council of the government; that, in reply to his demand, it was remarked, that the requisitions of the Municipality were rapidly increasing, and that it was to be apprehended, that, were even the demand now advanced acceded to, like those which had already been granted, still other demands would be preferred, and order in the city would not yet be restored. It was desirable, therefore, frankly to be advised of the real intentions of the city. To this Mengaldo answered, that order would not be restored until all means of defence and offence were yielded to the citizens. "Why, that is neither more nor less than abdication!" cried Palffy. "It can not be granted. Nevertheless, you are desired to request the Municipal Council to present itself before the government, and explain the wishes of the people." But scarcely had this refusal to surrender the Arsenal to the people been uttered, before shouts in the Piazza beneath the windows of the Palace announced that surrender to be already complete!

* It is not improbable, that the father of the Advocate Mengaldo was the Chevalier of that name, with whom Lord Byron had a swimming match in 1819, at Venice, together with an Englishman named Scott. Mengaldo was then 30, Scott 26, Byron 30. Byron took the palm. He was in the water four hours and twenty minutes, and swam some four or five miles, and up the whole length of the grand canal, from the direction of the Lido towards Santa Chiara. On leaving Venice, Byron gave his friend Mengaldo, as a *souvenir*, a cross of the *Legion d'Honneur* found at Waterloo. The chevalier had been himself decorated by Napoleon.

The Assembly having heard the report of Mengaldo, at once despatched a deputation, consisting of the Podesta, with the delegates Michiel, Medin, Avesani, Pincherle, Fabris, and Mengaldo himself, to wait on the two Governors, and demand, that, for the tranquillity of the city, and to prevent the needless effusion of blood, the government should be reposed in the hands of the citizens.

It was nearly four o'clock when this deputation was introduced into the presence of the Civil Governor, whom they found surrounded by his council. It was received with bitter reproaches by Count Palffy, who declared that imputations against the government had been circulated among the people for the express purpose of causing agitation; and, proceeding to enumerate them, he pronounced them, with great vehemence, utterly false, and was pouring out indignant denunciations without stint, when he was unceremoniously interrupted by Avesani, with the remark—"Are we invited here, as formerly, to be reproached, or to negotiate?" At this cool interruption, the old Count became yet more furious, but observed that his words were directed not to Avesani, but to the Podesta and the others who had promised, that, upon the granting of the people's wishes respecting a Civic Guard, order should be restored; whereas, both the disorder and the demands were on the increase. He concluded by stating, that the Government Council was now assembled to hear these demands, and to decide whether they were such as could be discussed. To this harangue the Podesta replied, that the present deputation had been sent by the Municipality to communicate to his Excellency measures it was deemed indispensable to adopt, in order to prevent bloodshed, and that the Advocate Avesani would now, in its behalf, present them.

Avesani at once took the floor. He said that the Governor must be aware, that no ordinary demand was to be made, or of which the Council of Government could have cognizance; that all dissimulation was vain; that there was no time to be lost; that no reply would, therefore, be made to his Excellency's speech, nor would any discussion be admitted on the rights of the people, or the cause of their agitation, or the tardy concessions of the government. Events demanded instant decision, and that decision must be this—"The Austrian Government abdicates its power!"

"If that be your demand," indignantly rejoined Palffy, rising from his chair, "I at once renounce all power, and, in accordance with my instructions, repose it in the hands of the Military Governor. Henceforth the city will treat only with him."

Avesani replied, that he had but the moment before, by an accidental opening of the door, caught a glimpse in the passage of Count Zichy, Commandant of the city and fortifications, and desired that he might be at once summoned to hear the demand and return his response. The request was conceded, and the Civil Governor immediately announced to his military colleague that the deputation had preferred demands, which it was impossible should be entertained by himself and council, and that, therefore, he deposed all his powers into the hands of the Commandant of the City and Forts; desiring him at the same time to spare, as much as was consistent with the discharge of his stern duties, that monumental and beautiful capital, which they both loved so much. The Commandant expressed surprise at this request and pronounced it inadmissable. His long residence in Venice, he said, had inspired him with profound affection for her; but, much as he loved Venice, his duty was dearer than her welfare, and this duty, he added, would be rigorously discharged.

"Then our demand is refused?" said Avesani. "Be it so; but

upon your Excellency will rest all the bloodshed which this announcement will cause."

"Your demand requires modification," was the conciliatory response.

"Modification!" cried Avesani: "It is too late!" and he at once began reading terms of abdication already drawn up, which he held in his hand:—

"1st. The German troops, and all troops not Italian, will evacuate Venice. The Italian troops will remain."

"Impossible!" exclaimed the Count. "We will fight!"

"Be it so," quietly rejoined the Advocate, about to depart; "we will fight."

"But to consent to such a demand would cost me my head!" faltered the Governor.

"There are more heads in peril than your Excellency's just at present," dryly answered Avesani.

"But my orders from Vienna—"

"Your Excellency will receive no further orders from Vienna."

"A few hours for reflection—"

"Not a moment! Too much time has been already wasted! Each hour, each minute, the work of blood may begin! The demand is Spartan—it requires a Spartan answer."

"But a portion of the troops"—began the Count—"should they be unwilling to depart—"

"Every Teuton must go, or his blood be on his own head!" was the stern response. "There can be no half measures now—no temporizing."

"Then the demand must be accorded," said Zichy, sadly.

"The second demand," continued the Advocate is this—"The troops shall depart immediately for Trieste, and by sea."

" But I cannot prevent the troops from rejoining their respective corps, and they must depart under protection of the forts," urged the Count.

" The forts, also, must be evacuated," replied Avesani. " Besides, the Venetians have no wish to present to their brothers of the province a body of troops, of which they have themselves become tired and are happily free : in fact, we have no wish for a single Austrian soldier on our Lombardo-Veneto soil !"

The Count attempted to reply, but every objection was cut short by the declaration, that discussion was impossible, and that the demand must either be accorded, or responded to by force.

" Then it is accorded," said Zichy.

" The third demand," continued Avesani, " is this"—" The material of war of every kind remains at Venice."

There was the same refusal, the same persistency, the same final forced accord.

" 4th. The military chests remain at Venice."

" But the pay of the troops and their transportation"—

" Both shall be provided," interrupted the Advocate.

" And the extra pay for three months, which is always paid to the soldier on his discharge ?" inquired the Count.

This demand was, at first, opposed, but was finally granted. The fourth condition was then agreed to like its predecessors. The fifth and final demand was this—" The two Governors shall remain as hostages for the complete execution of the Convention."

To this Count Palffy most earnestly objected. Possibly the old man's perceptions of peril in longer continuance at Venice, and his desire to depart were quickened at the moment by the shout of the slaughterers of Marinovich beneath the windows—" One more !' He urged, that, having resigned his office before the Convention was opened, and having taken no part in it, the measure could have no propriety with reference to him. He appealed, also, to Avesani, whether he had not always deported himself in office as a man of honor, undeserving treatment like this?

"Yes," replied the Advocate, "you have always acted with honor and affection towards Venice until recently; but, during the three months last past, you have committed grave faults, and have been guilty of acts of oppression even surpassing your orders from Vienna—your orders from that man who boasts himself the Nestor of diplomacy—Metternich, yet, whose obstinate and blind opposition to the torrent of the time has conducted the Austrian monarchy to the very verge of the precipice."

Count Zichy, also, objected to being retained as a hostage. Necessarily, in the execution of the Convention, he should be the last to leave. Why, therefore, subject him to the mortification of a specific condition to the same effect? And he was so urgent in his entreaties, that some members of the deputation interposed in his behalf.

"Well," said Avesani, yielding, at length, to the general solicitation, and extending his hand to the Count—"give me your word of honor, General, that you will be the last to depart, and your wish shall be observed."

This *parole* was, of course, given, and a stipulation was embodied in the Convention, that a steamer should be placed at the disposition of his Excellency to transport himself and *suite*, with the last remaining soldiers from Venice. It was, also, stipulated, at the instance of the Count, that transportation should be provided for the families of all the civil and military officers, and for those of the soldiers. The convention was then executed in duplicate, one of the original documents being placed in the hands of his Excellency, the Lieutenant Field Marshal, late Commandant of the City and Forts of Venice, Count Zichy, and the other being committed to the deputation, to be solemnly deposited in the archives of the city.

It was now six o'clock, two hours having been consumed in these important transactions, and the deputation, departing from the Palace, proclaimed to the people, assembled in immense multitudes in the Place St. Mark, that the Austrian rule in Venice had ceased.

Such were the circumstances attending the capitulation of the Austrian Government in Venice, on the 22nd day of March, 1848. We are left in doubt upon no point in the entire transaction, inasmuch as a precise and detailed account of the whole interview, signed by the deputation, appeared in placard the same evening, posted at every corner, to which was subjoined the Convention itself and a Proclamation to the people.* The Convention was as follows:—

" His Excellency, the Signor Count Luigi Palffy, Governor of the Province of Venice, in order to avoid an effusion of blood, and, having been informed by his Excellency, the Count Giovanni Correr, the Podesta of Venice, and by the Municipal Assessors, and by other citizens delegated for the purpose, that this would be impossible, except upon the conditions underscribed—deposed his powers into the hands of His Excellency, the Signor Count Ferdinando Zichy, Commandant of the City and Forts, warmly recommending to the said Signor Commandant to exercise great consideration for this

* " *Capitolazione Del Governo Austriaco in Venezia, Addi* 22 *Marzo*, 1848. *Dal Librario Pietro Milesi al Ponte di S. Moise.* (*Tip. Merlo.*)" This singular document is now exceedingly rare—all copies found on the return of the Austrians having been destroyed, together with all other records of the revolution or republic of '48-9, whatsoever—the only copies spared being those in the archives of the foreign Consulates. Detection of a copy of this " *Capitolazione* " in the possession of a Venetian at the present time would be deemed warrant for instant arrest.

beautiful and monumental city, for which he (Count Palffy) had always professed the most vivid affection and the most loyal attachment, and which it afforded him pleasure anew to repeat. In consequence of this recommendation, the Signor Count Zichy, impressed with the urgency of circumstances, and with the same desire to avoid useless effusion of blood,* has agreed with the undersigned to establish the following Convention:—

1.—From this moment the civil and military government, both of land and sea, ceases, being remitted to the hands of a Provisional Government to be established, and now assumed by the citizens undersigned.

2.—The troops of the Regiment Kinsky, as well as of that of the Croats, the Artillery of land, the corps of Engineers, shall abandon the city and all the forts, and all the Italian troops and the Italian officers shall remain at Venice.

3.—The *matériel* of war, of every kind, shall remain at Venice.

4.—The transportation of the troops shall ensue immediately, by all possible means, by the way of Trieste, by sea.

5.—The families of the officers and soldiers shall depart, and shall be protected, and means of transportation provided for them, by the Government about to be instituted.

6.—All civil officers, Italian and not Italian, shall be protected in their persons, families and goods.

7.—His Excellency, the Signor Count Zichy, gives his *parola d' onore* to remain the last in Venice, to secure the execution of the above conditions. A steamer will be placed at the disposal of His

* If this were the motive for evacuation, it proved fallacious. The seventeen months' siege of Venice caused greater "effusion of blood"—greater destruction of life and property, than would any act, however severe, to quell the rebellion of March '48. Besides, why are garrisons supplied with carbines and bayonets, if there is to be such chariness in the "effusion of blood?"

Excellency for the transportation of his person, and the persons of his *suite*, and those of the last soldiers who shall remain.

8.—All the chests shall remain, sufficient money for the pay and transportation of the troops being taken out. The pay shall be given for three months.

Executed in double original. (Signed) Count Zichy, Field Marshal, Commandant of the City and Forts, Giovanni Correr, Luigi Michiel, Dataico Medin, Pietro Fabris, Gio. Francesco Avesani, Angelo Mengaldo, Commandant, Leone Pincherle: witnesses, Francesco Dott. Beltrame, Antonio Muzzani, Costantino Alberti."*

The following Proclamation completed the placard :—

"VIVA VENEZIA! VIVA L'ITALIA!

CITIZENS! the victory is ours without blood! The Austrian Government, civil and military, is fallen! Honor to the brave Civic Guard! The undersigned, your fellow-citizens, have stipulated a solemn Treaty. A Provisional Government will be instituted; meanwhile, compelled by the necessity of the moment, it has been assumed temporarily by the undersigned. The Treaty will be published this day in an appropriate supplement of our Gazette. *Viva Venezia! Viva l'Italia!*

VENICE, *March* 22, 1848."

This Proclamation, like the preceding documents, bore the signatures of Correr, Podesta, Michiel, and Medin, Municipal Assessors, Fabris, Central Deputy, Mengaldo, Commandant of the Civic Guard, Avesani, Advocate,† and Pincherle, Hebrew Banker.

* Literal translation. The military chests proved to contain 36,000,000 Austrian Lire—about $6,000,000: the "*matériel* of war" amounted to 30,000 muskets, with other arms; the Italian soldiers remaining were nearly 4,000 in number, and the Croats and Germans sent off nearly 3,000.

† "The Revolutions, not only of Italy, but of all Europe have been raised and directed

Thus fell the Austrian power in Venice, with not one effort to maintain it! Never was there exhibited a more extraordinary instance of the paralyzing effect of panic. A well-appointed garrison of nearly seven thousand troops, in full and unquestioned possession of a city like Venice, easily held, laid down their arms at the bidding of a mere mob—(so far as *power* was concerned)—without attempting a single blow! Well may this event be viewed as among the most wonderful of all the wonderful events of that remarkable epoch; and, if it astonished all to whose knowledge it came, hardly less did it astonish those by whose cool intrepidity and dogged persistency, it had been accomplished. In view of the pitiable and humiliating scene of the capitulation in the Governor's Palace, there must be admitted, for its comprehension, either a most imposing display of energy on one side, or the presence of the most abject and deplorable imbecility and cowardice on the other. Judging from the detailed report of this conference, of which translation has been given, and which it is not surprising the Austrian government should have subsequently manifested some zeal to suppress it, it is probable there was no lack of either. The Advocates Avesani and Mengaldo proved themselves brave, firm men; and the Counts Palffy and Zichy proved themselves very arrant cowards.*

by lawyers." So says the London Times. In Venice, Manin, Avesani, and Mengaldo; in Florence, Guerazzi; in Milan, Casati; in Hungary, Kossuth; and numerous less prominent names all over Europe, would seem to corroborate this. In the American Revolution, lawyers took so active a part, that Burke called the country "a nation of Lawyers.' Avesani was one of the most prominent advocates in Venice, son of the learned Baron Avesani.

* Of one of these worthies, it is related, that, terrified by the tragedy at the Arsenal, and in constant apprehension of sharing the fate of Marinovich, he retired to his bed, from which he emerged only when informed that he must sign articles of capitulation. This done, "Richard was himself again;" and, thanking God that he might now devour his dinner in peace, he at once seated himself at table, and commenced a valorous and vigorous assault on the contents of his trencher!

So rapidly had the events transpired which have been detailed, that the sun had been gone but an hour when the capitulation was proclaimed to the immense multitude which now swarmed the Place St. Mark. Among these were about two thousand of the Civic Guard, with their chief, Manin, at their head, who, in response to enthusiastic *Vivas*, addressed them in one of his brief but fiery harangues. He told them that their freedom was achieved—that a Provisional Government would be at once declared—that the independence of all Italy would follow, cemented by a Republican union to be ratified at Rome. Thus early in the struggle did Manin put forth the principle of Mazzini—the independence—not alone of Venice and Lombardy, but the independence, union, and republicanism of all Italy. And it was amid enthusiastic shouts of *Viva l'Italia! Viva Republica!* that this eloquent man thus concluded:—"Venetians! I know that you love me,* and, in the name of that love, I know you will permit me to enjoin upon you moderation and order. Be joyous!—be exultant!—it is your right!—it is your duty! But you will never forget to conduct yourselves with the dignity and propriety of men worthy to be free."

The articles of the Convention were carried out without delay; and the three thousand Croats and Germans were embarked for Trieste. This evacuation, however, was not unattended with some little excitement, which, in one instance, menaced results, which might have utterly changed the whole face of affairs. The third article of the Convention declared—"The material of war of all kinds shall remain at Venice." Under this article the soldiers were required to leave behind them their arms. This the German Kinsky regiment refused to do. Indignant at what was deemed

* "*Veneziani! So che mi amate.*"

designed disgrace, General Culoz ordered the men back to their *caserma*, which was on the *Riva degli Schiavoni*, looking upon the Port, and barricaded the portals. Gun-boats, brought up from the Arsenal, were moored opposite, to batter them down; but the brave fellows absolutely and stubbornly persisted in ignoring the disgraceful condition of Zichy's convention for hours—some say for days. Manin, on the other hand, as obstinately insisted on literal compliance with the terms of the capitulation; but he was overruled by his colleagues, and unwisely the regiment was suffered to depart with the honors of war.

That same evening, the 22nd of March, at nine o'clock, the fortress of Malghera, which defends the approach to Venice on the west, was occupied by the Civic Guard of Mestre; and on the succeeding night, the fort of San Felice, which guards the entrance to the port of Chioggia, some twenty miles distant from Venice, was taken possession of by the citizens of the former place, and all the other forts and batteries which circle the Lagune shortly shared the same fate.

The possession of these fortresses, and especially, of that of Malghera, was of the utmost importance. Had they not been surrendered, they could not have been taken, and the resistance of Venice would have been materially shortened.

Immediately upon the execution of the Convention, the deputation of seven by which it had been signed, and by which temporary rule in Venice had been assumed, appointed one of their number, Angelo Mengaldo, to act as Chief of the Civic Guard, in place of Manin, who had previously resigned; and, investing the former with their powers, gave him in charge to form a Provisional Government.

Meantime, the Counts Zichy and Palffy remained prisoners on

parole in their palaces. Two days afterwards, they were both embarked with their *suites* on a steamer for Trieste. The light in which their conduct was viewed by the Imperial Government at Vienna may be inferred from the fact, that Zichy was subsequently condemned by a court-martial at Olmutz,* and that the humiliating apology of Palffy met with cool indifference. In this apology, or "explanation," the Count expresses "an afflicting feeling of sorrow," which, no doubt, he felt—for the loss of Venice; but he solemnly protests, that he not only took no part in the capitulation of the garrison, but was absolutely in ignorance of the event until it had transpired! He states, that, immediately upon the commencement of the Revolution, he perceived the necessity of placing unlimited power into the hands of the Military Governor, which he accordingly did, agreeably to existing laws, at two o'clock, P.M., on the 22d of March! Subsequently, he asserts, he was placed under guard in his own apartment, and was conducted to the steamer for embarkation, without being suffered to communicate with any one but his escort. On the 26th of March, he made a full and detailed report of the whole affair to the ministry. His concluding words are these:—"All then must be convinced, that I neglected no duty either before or after the unfortunate catastrophe, as a servant of the state and as a man of honor." But poor Count Palffy's hopes deceived him. "All" were *not* "convinced." Indeed, very few were convinced of anything—save his own deplorable weakness and incapacity.

On the morning of Thursday, the 23rd of March, the Piazza of St. Mark contained all Venice. Two battalions of the Civic Guard

* From Trieste, Zichy is said to have repaired to Jellachich at Agram, whence he despatched an apology for his conduct, to Vienna. Ordered to a fortress in Silesia, he was there put under arrest. Condemned at Olmutz, he was sent to Klagenfürth, but was set at liberty the ensuing October.

were drawn out by their Commandant, Mengaldo, and amid enthusiastic shouts, which echoed throughout that magnificent square—shouts, which, for more than half a century, had been hushed—*Viva Venezia! Viva San Marco! Viva Republica! Viva l'Italia! Viva Manin!*—the Republic was proclaimed, a Provisional Government was nominated, and upon the tri-color of liberty was solemnly invoked a benediction by Monico, the venerable Patriarch of Venice.* The members of the Provisional Government were nine in number—Daniele Manin, President, and Minister of Foreign Affairs; Nicolo Tommaseo, Minister of Worship and Instruction; Antonio Paoluzzi, Minister of Marine; Jacopo Castelli, of Justice; Francesco Solera, of War; Pietro Paleocapa, of Public Works; Francesco Camerata, of Finance; Leone Pincherle, a Jew, of Commerce; and Angelo Toffoli, *Artiere*,† who had been efficient with the people, who was connected with the Cabinet as Minister of Arts, though without portfolio, or specific trust.

Among the earliest decrees of the Provisional Government was that establishing a standard, which, as the symbol of the Republic of Venice of the nineteenth century, was thenceforth to float from the masts of St. Mark, so long as that republic continued to stand. The standard of the Old Republic, which for fourteen centuries had led the Ocean-Queen to glory, had been of royal purple or of snowy

* A good poet, an elegant writer, and an excellent man, though rather Austrian in sentiment and predilection. His installation to the Patriarchal office in March, 1817, thirty-one years before almost to a day—is said to have presented one of the most pompous ecclesiastical pageants that even Venice ever beheld, a portion of which was a procession of 650 priests marching around the Piazza with bell and book, cross and candle. The Aulic Council at Vienna, in its programme of the ceremony, prescribed "a coach and four horses,"—a prescription wonderfully "*German* to the matter," says Byron, who mentions the event in a letter to Murray. "A coach and four horses" in St. Mark's Square! A barge and twelve rowers in Hyde Park!

† Artisan. Toffoli was a tailor. In like manner, "Albert *Ouvrier*," in Paris.

white,* charged with the device of the Winged Lion of St. Mark in gold. The standard of the New Republic was of three colors—green nearest the staff, white in the middle, red at the end, while above, on a white field bordered by the three colors, was the golden lion;—the flag thus uniting the symbols and associations of the Venice of the past with those of the Italy of the present. The decree by which this standard was instituted, bears date March 27, and thus concludes:—"The tricolor is the common banner of all Italy, implying Italian unity. The lion is the special symbol of one of the Italian family."

But no celebration in Venice is complete which is not consecrated by the solemnities of her religion. Upon all great occasions, an ancient painting of the Madonna, said to have been executed by St. Luke, which is preserved among the most precious treasures of the cathedral, is exposed to the gaze and adoration of the people. A similar painting is seen at Florence. This picture is said to have worked many miracles. In the autumn of '51, it was exposed for the worship of all Venice, and was even carried in procession around the Square of St. Mark, with a view to the cessation of a protracted season of rain, which it was apprehended would blast the vintage—albeit, no effect on the heavens was observable. But now, it was not to implore, but to celebrate a miracle, that the old painting was exhibited to the people; and no wonder that the Venetians, superstitious beyond all belief, in view of the extraordinary occurrences of the twenty-four hours last past, should cry out, as they did, with one voice, when the Madonna was elevated before their eyes—"The downfall of Marinovich, the Virgin's first miracle!"

* Both colors are cited by chroniclers: but purple has the preference. At the imperial coronation at Milan in 1838, Venice was represented by a standard of purple with a blazon of azure and emerald—the sky and the sea.

In this general and enthusiastic inauguration of the Republic of Venice, only two members of the numerous corps of foreign consuls officially participated. These were the Consul-General of France, and the Consul of the United States—the late William A. Sparks of South Carolina;* and, of these two, the latter was by far the most prominent. In person, he assisted at the celebration; and the bright stripes and stars of our own glorious republic waved fraternally beside the tri-color of young Italy, amid exultant shouts—"*Viva gli Stati Uniti! Viva la grande Republica! Viva il Console Americano!*" It was a strange spectacle this recognition of an ancient republic, so long dead, once more revived, by a sister republic six thousand miles distant, which had been struggling into birth when the other was ceasing to exist! The prompt recognition of the Venetian republic by the American Consul met a hearty response from President Manin; and, in an autographic note, bearing date the 24th, warm gratification is expressed; and the hour of one of that day is designated by the Provisional Government for special audience.

The first official act of the Provisional Government was most commendable; it was to assure security to all strangers in Venice of whatsoever nation, or political creed. The second was equally so: it was to adopt as "Sons of the Republic" the sons of Eugenio Zen, who fell in the massacre of the 18th of March, in the Piazza of St. Mark—a decree as profoundly politic as it was just. On the same day a Provisional government was proclaimed by the towns of Rovigo, Treviso, and Udine, which towns, together with all other

* Mr. Sparks died of cholera at Venice during the bombardment by the Austrians, August, '49. His remains were disinterred, by order of the U. S. Government, in July '51, and sent on board the Razee Independence, at Triesto, for transportation to the United States. See Vol II.

provinces of the old Venetian republic on *terra firma*, very shortly sent in their adhesions. Each of these provinces, it was decreed, should depute to Venice three counsellors, which counsellors uniting with three others elected by the Capital herself, should on the 10th of the ensuing month, assemble in the Ducal Palace, appoint a president, adopt rules for their own government, and maintain a direct and constant recommendatory correspondence with the Administrative Government.

It may as well be here remarked, that the promptitude with which Venice declared herself a republic, was viewed, at first, by no means favorably at Milan, and even at Genoa. By the patriots of those cities, it was deemed the duty of Venice to have awaited the expulsion of every " barbarian " from Northern Italy, before determining a form of government. But Milan and Genoa were situated far differently from Venice. The former cities might be assailed and reduced by Austrian, or even by Sardinian arms, almost any day,—as events proved,—despite all declarations and inaugurations of a republic. But the Ocean-Queen, once evacuated of foreign foes, might boldly lift up her " tiara of proud towers," circled by the protecting waves and a double zone of batteries ; and, for months, nay, for years, even—as events also proved—defy all the power which Austria could array against her. Well, then, might she proclaim herself an independent republic,—albeit she did so but provisionally —even before the last Croat had ceased to pollute her soil,—" well" might she do this, though, perchance, in so doing, she did "not wisely."

The exciting events of the memorable 23rd of March closed with a splendid illumination of the Fenice Theatre, the entertainments of which were enlivened by a song written for the occasion in honor of the brave Civic Guard.

CHAPTER VI.

"THE HOLY WAR."

THREE days have usually been deemed indispensable for the accomplishment of a Revolution on the Continent of Europe. But the revolution of 1848 in Venice was commenced and completed within a space much briefer—within the space, indeed, of about one-half of a single day, and that day the 22nd day of March, exactly one month subsequent to the commencement of the revolution in Paris. Before that month had expired, every Austrian soldier had evacuated Venice; every port, battery and barrack was in the hands of the Republicans; nearly every provincial town of the ancient *Dogado* had sent in its adhesion; while a Provisional Government, with Daniel Manin, the Advocate, as its chief, was in steady and successful action.

Measures were immediately adopted for the defence and welfare of the city, and for the confirmation of the new order of affairs. The enrolment of ten battalions of volunteers as a Civic Guard, embracing all citizens between the years of 18 and 55, whose term of service should be one year, was decreed, as was, also, that of an artillery force, a cavalry force of two hundred men for service on *terra firma*, and a volunteer marine force. A Committee of

Safety was also instituted ; the salt tax was abated and the personal tax abolished : importation of arms was encouraged ; the chiefs of ports and fortifications were instructed to sink all foreign vessels attempting to approach the city without examination and permission ; the tariff of duties in various forms was modified ; the reception of bank-notes at the public offices was forbidden ; the department of Imperial Engineers was suspended ; duties on Sardinian wines and stamp duties on newspapers were abolished ; a free press was decreed—every publication bearing its author's name ; all forms of religion were declared equally privileged, and all citizens, whatever their faith, were declared equally eligible to all offices in the state. A Commission for the revision of all civil and criminal laws and forms of action was appointed ; protection of the rights of minors was assumed ; all prisoners on political charges were released ; the deliberation of a tribunal on all accusations was declared indispensable ; also, that all accused persons should be provided with an advocate ; the people were enjoined to express their wishes and sentiments by means of memorials and the press, and, under no circumstances, to resort to tumultuous assemblages ; a Commission of revision superseded the Senate or supreme tribunal ; loans were negotiated, contributions solicited, money was coined at the *Zecca*, or Mint, bearing the winged lion, the device of the republic of former days ; the *Palazzo Reale* became the *Palazzo Nazionale ;* a body of *Gendarmerie*, or civic police, was created ; the terms of payment of bills of exchange were extended ; a garrison force to occupy the fortifications was instituted ; the enrolment of a battalion of Swiss was ordered, and Major Olivieri and Major Canetti of the Civic Guard departed for the Canton of Zurich for that purpose. The entry of the steamers of the Austrian Lloyds into the port of Venice was prohibited ; and the functions of the Central Congregation were declared to be superseded by the Council of State convened April 10th. A national cockade was adopted; the Arsenal was entrusted to a guard composed of tradesmen of standing, and the mercantile marine was encouraged to transfer its service to the "marine of war." The little brothers of Lieutenant Moro, executed at Cosenza, in 1844, were declared sons of the republic, and a pension was settled on his widowed mother. The government monopoly of cotton was abolished, as, also, the penalty of imprisonment for certain financial offences, all persons who were then in prison convicted on such charges being liberated.

Numerous other measures were adopted and provisions decreed in course of the first month of the republic; but those cited will indicate the general tenor of all. Meantime, those civic and religious fetes, which are ever so rife in pleasure-loving Venice, were not neglected; while obsequies for the illustrious dead, the consecration of banners, and the inauguration of civic and military corps were of almost daily occurrence. On the 25th of March, the fete which commemorates the founding of Venice was celebrated with most imposing solemnities in the cathedral of St. Mark and throughout the city. The coincidence was viewed as significant and propitious, that the anniversary of the founding of Venice should be almost identical with the date of her freedom from bondage and the founding anew of a republic. The Feast of the Annunciation fell, also, on the same day. On the 2nd of April, at Campo-Sampiero, a benediction of the banner of the Civic Guard was solemnized with great splendor, in the presence of an immense assemblage of citizens; on the 4th, obsequies for the sons of Lombardy and Venice, fallen in the cause of Italian liberty, were celebrated at the church of *S. S. Apostoli*, as well as on the 13th at the cathedral of St. Mark; while, on the 19th of the same month, the Hebrews celebrated similar obsequies with great pomp in their principal synagogue. Venice, as already remarked, has ever been distinguished for most commendable liberality in matters of religious faith and worship; and, although the religion of the state has always been that of Rome, the Jews, Greeks, Turks, Protestants, &c., &c., residing within her jurisdiction, have always enjoyed entire freedom to worship agreeably to the dictates of their own consciences. On the 25th of April, a benediction of all the banners, and the administration of an oath of allegiance in the Place St. Mark, formed a portion of the celebration of the *Festa di San Marco;* and, on the 30th, was inaugurated the banner of the *School of St. Mark*, a discourse on the occasion being delivered by Father Tornielli.

The first duty which devolved on the chiefs of the revolution was to secure their conquest, and to this end, a military force was indispensable. Here was a task by no means easy. The Venetians, though overflowing with enthusiasm, patriotism, and courage, were yet utterly ignorant of the use of arms, which, indeed, most of them, had never seen except in the hands of their oppressors; and were equally ignorant of discipline, tactics, or the art of war. As for the four battalions of Italian grenadiers, with the 800 dragoons who had manned the fortifications, as a portion of the Austrian garrison, they are said to have become almost useless when freed from their Teutonic taskmasters and the terrors of the rod—albeit, with Jellachich in Hungary, and even with Radetzky in Italy fighting against their own countrymen, at that very time, they won the warmest encomiums for bravery and discipline! But, of all the eighteen or twenty battalions that deserted the Austrian standards, hardly as many hundreds ever became reliable soldiers in their country's cause. After rioting a few days at Venice, Milan, Brescia, Cremona, or elsewhere—offering for sale their arms and equipments, they became clamorous for home, and home they were gladly sent —to be a curse to themselves and everybody else to the very end of the chapter.*

In looking abroad for aid, the Swiss, whose services at Rome, Naples, and Milan, had distinguished them in Italy, at once attracted attention at Venice; and, in April, as already stated, Canetti and Olivieri, of the Civic Guard, were dispatched for Zurich, where they negotiated the enrolment of a company of one hundred men, under command of Captain Jean Debrunner, "to serve the Republic of Venice faithfully and loyally two years." The principle of neutrality had been recently proclaimed by the Swiss Diet; but Debrunner managed to get his company out of the Cantons; and, after various adventures, reached Venice on the 11th of June.†

On the 24th of March, the day after the evacuation of Venice, intelligence arrived of the evacuation of Milan, which event caused great rejoicing and an illumination of the Fenice Theatre, renewed from the night before. The same day Padua was evacuated by the Austrian troops, and the fortress of Palma Nuova was surrendered to the National Guard, under Gen. Zucchi, who, a state prisoner, was released from the fortress to take command. Deputations, also, arrived from many provincial towns, recognizing the Republic,

* Belgiojoso. This, perhaps, is too sweeping. Col. Forbes says that a battalion composed of deserters, commanded by Major Gallateo, did good service.

† As a corps of chasseurs this body of Swiss served faithfully throughout all the residue of the siege, and the narrative of its adventures detailed by its captain is piquant and graphic. Its service was chiefly demanded in the fortifications of Lido, Malghera, Burano, Murano, Chioggia, &c., &c., and it suffered so severely from disease and the casualties of war, that not one half of the company returned to their native mountains. Recruits, however, were constantly arriving to fill the vacant places.

and giving in their adhesion in the name and behalf of the citizens of those towns which they represented. To strengthen these places against the Austrians, by whom they would, of course, be speedily menaced, numerous corps of volunteers, called "*Crociati*," or Crusaders, from the tri-colored cross which they wore on their breasts, were enrolled and sent off. The first of these bands, commanded by Giorgio Gritti, and called "*La Legione Trivigiana*," departed on the 30th for Treviso. One band of these Crusaders, it is said, was composed almost entirely of women! But these Amazons seem never to have rivalled in bravery or discipline that ancient sisterhood which furnished them an example and a name; while the bands of their male compatriots, made up of gondoliers, *facchini*, *flaneurs*, and vagabonds, and officered by young students and artists, became, it was complained, rather a terror than a succor to the country they professed to protect. One of these bands was commanded by Col. Davido Amigo, commissioned by the Provisional Government, and another by Ernesto Grondoni, both of which marched to the relief of Palma Nuova besieged by the Imperial troops, early in April. In a sortie, shortly afterwards, twenty-three of these Crusaders were taken captive by the Austrians, but, from some cause or other, were at once set at liberty. The first bands of these *Guerilla* troops departed with the benediction of the Patriarch of Venice and the eloquence of Manin to nerve their arms and fire their breasts; while they were, by official decree, elevated to the grade of regular troops, being promised the same pay; and, if they fell, support was guaranteed to their families. Still more to inflame the fever for arms, Ugo Bassi, a Barnabite monk, assisted by Allessandro Gavazzi, Frate Tornielli and others, traversed all Lombardy and Venetia, preaching a "crusade." The effect of these inflammatory appeals was at once apparent; and bands of armed men sprang up as if from the dragon's teeth of Cadmus, all over the north of Italy, every town, hamlet, and village sending forth its quota.

On the 26th of March, the Viceroy, Archduke Ranieri, departed from Verona for the Tyrol. On the first of the ensuing month, Field-Marshal Radetzky arrived at that city in full retreat from Milan, and immediately held a council of war, composed of generals and colonels. The result was witnessed in a proclamation two days afterwards, declaring Verona in a state of siege, imposing on the citizens a forced loan of three millions of Lire (half a million of dollars), and enjoining the surrender of all arms within twenty-four hours—those of the Civic Guard alone being excepted.

Radetzky having accomplished his perilous retreat from Milan on the terrible night of March 22nd, had directed his march towards Lodi. But his progress had been slow, owing to the destruction by the peasants of roads and bridges, and the rearing of barricades. "The weather, also, was terrific during all that terrific contest." At Molignano, the tocsin was rung—his interpreter was seized, and his troops were even summoned to surrender! But he soon taught the little town by bombardment and conflagration the folly of its audacity, and thus all other little towns inclined to imitate its example. On the night of the 23d he reached Lodi, which was held by the Archduke Ernest.

On that same 23d of March, Charles Albert, "by the grace of God King of Sardinia, Cyprus,* and Jerusalem," had issued a proclamation to the people of Lombardy and Venice, declaring that the destinies of Italy were maturing—that a happier fate awaited

* Venice disputed the pretensions of the Duke of Savoy to Cyprus a century ago. "It is surprising," says an old writer, "with what heats these two powers have contested their title to a kingdom that is in the hands of the Turk."

the defenders of down-trodden rights—that affinity of race and community of feeling had caused his people to be the first to manifest the admiration felt by all Italy—that his armies, already concentrated on the frontier in anticipation of the liberation of Milan, were now coming to offer that aid in future trials which brother expects from brother, friend from friend—confiding in that God visibly present—that God who had given Italy a Pius—that God, who, by such miraculous influence, had enabled Italy to act alone. The Proclamation thus concludes :—" And, that the sentiment of Italian unity may be further manifested, we command our troops, on entering the territory of Lombardy and Venice, to bear the escutcheon of Savoy on the tri-colored flag of Italy."

Upon the appearance of this proclamation at Turin, the Envoys of Austria, Russia, and Prussia at once demanded their passports. A diplomatic note from the Premier Pareto suggested to Austria, that the Sardinian government was forced to the measure it had adopted, in order to protect its throne, as well as all Italy from the baleful effects of a republic in Lombardy and Venice ! The same plea had formerly been rendered to account for the extraordinary concentration of forces on the frontier. At variance with Austria for three years, in January, '48, when Austria resolved on a garrison of 15,000 men on the Ticino, Sardinia placed her army on a war-footing, enlisted volunteers, established depots at Chivasso and Vercelli, and, on the first alarm from Milan, mustered a force of 60,000 men on the frontier, with reserves at Genoa, and Turin, and elsewhere, of, perhaps, as many more, ready at a trumpet-call for motion ; while 300 cannons, 60,000 muskets, and two millions of cartridges were stored in the fortress of Allessandria !

Nor was Piedmont alone in this concentration of military force. In the spring of 1848, Austria had 70,000 men in Northern Italy in two divisions, one at Milan, the other at Padua, subdivided into fifty-seven battalions and thirty-two squadrons. There were parks of artillery at Magenta, Padua, and Varese, numbering more than one hundred cannon, and two siege batteries of the heaviest metal and largest calibre. Munitions of war were, also, pouring constantly into Italy, and the forges of Mariazelle were ever active; while not even a pound of nitre, or a single sword-blade was suffered to cross the frontier, the exact destination of which was not surely known. All Lombardy had bristled with bayonets, and the palaces of Venice had become the barracks of Croats. Princes Schwartzenberg and Lichtenstein had been dispatched to Italy with large commands; and Austria, by her railroads and steamers could pour fifty thousand men from Vienna on Milan in less than a week—provided always she had them to pour.

Charles Albert, only one month before his proclamation, in announcing to Austria his purpose of giving his four millions of people a constitution like that of France in 1830, had assured her of his continued friendship, and of his design to maintain all treaties as faithfully as ever. To the remonstrances of the Austrian minister against the violent tone of the press towards his Government, and its direct appeals to the Lombards and Venetians to revolt, as, also, to his demands for explanation of the unusual concentration of troops on the frontier, repeated assurances of friendliness were alone obtained, and the utter absence of hostile intent towards Austria declared. When, too, the Austrian envoy, Count Buol Schauenstein (subsequently minister to England, and more recently premier by the death of Prince Schwartzenberg), protested against the enrollment of a corps of volunteers at Turin, manifestly for the invasion of Lombardy, which had been decreed, and into which foreigners might enlist, inquiring at the same time whether subjects of

Austria would be received, he was assured by the Marquis of Pareto, Sardinian Minister of Foreign Affairs, that "he would do all that depended on him to insure amity between the two states." Yet, at that very time, Charles Albert had promised Milan, upon a direct demand of its people, a military subsidy, and the next day issued his proclamation! Comment is unnecessary. There can be but one opinion of the conduct of Charles Albert—diplomatically speaking—in this violation of the Treaty of Vienna—a treaty to which Sardinia was a party; and which, while it secured Genoa to her, by the same right or the same wrong secured to Austria the Lombardo-Veneto. But Charles was possibly "whirled along" by his new Ministers, Pareto and Balbo, even as was Pius by his. This seems his sole apology.

On the 26th, 5,000 Piedmontese troops entered Milan;* another division of 8,000 was at Crema on the 28th, while the King at Lodi on the 31st with 40,000 men, or as some say only 25,000 men, issued a proclamation, stating that his army had advanced 110 miles in seventy-two hours, and rejoicing at the call of Lombardy and Venice for aid.

Nor did this gratification seem unreciprocated. At Milan, on the 26th, a proclamation had declared Charles Albert the faithful ally of Lombardy; and that it was agreed, that, during the coming contest, the army furnished by him should be provisioned by that city. The king had now under his command some 53,000 men, while 17,000 Romans, 3,000 Modenese and Parmesans, 5,000 Tuscans, and 17,000 Neapolitans were on the march to join him.

The revolutionary movements at Paris, Vienna, Milan, Venice—in all the cities of Central Europe, had forced the liberal pontiff,

* One of Charles' first acts effect the enlargement of the Duke of Parma, who had been virtually a prisoner in his own palace, in his own capital!

Pius, who had himself, unwittingly struck the first blow two years before, on his accession to the Papal See—as well as the despot Ferdinand, the Duke of Parma, and the grand Duke of Tuscany, to yield to the voice of their people and send auxiliaries to aid in driving the barbarian from the soil of Italy.

As early as the 23rd of March, Gen. Ferrari led 10,000 militia and volunteers from Rome; while Gen. Durando, an exile from Piedmont, a soldier in Spain, recalled to Italy by the amnesties of '46, followed immediately with 7,000 Swiss infantry and Roman dragoons. On the 17th of April the divisions met at Ferrara; but it was not until the 21st, that Durando ventured over the Po, because forbidden to cross without orders, and placed himself under the direction of Charles Albert. Subsequently, after some further delay, his command, joined by some 6,000 Lombard and Venetian volunteers and Ferrari with his 10,000 Crociati, who had preceded him, making an aggregate of about 23,000 men, hastened to Treviso in order to prevent the advance of Nugent.

As for Tuscany, her Grand Duke early sent 5,000 volunteers under Gen. De Laugier, and a Legion of Students led by their Professors, to the frontier, on the plea, at first, of "maintaining order;" but, finally, April 9th, he bade them "fly to the rescue of their Lombard brothers," and, with "extreme regret," gave his passport to the Austrian Envoy! These troops, therefore, with the 3,000 men of Parma and Modena who reached the camp April 24th, and the Students' Legions from Genoa and Turin, formed from the very opening of hostilities a portion of the Sardinian army.

As for Naples, her first band of volunteers, 184 in number, embarked for Genoa on the steamer *Virgilio*, on the evening of the 29th of March, amid enthusiastic shouts, led by the Princess Christina Trivulzio di Belgiojoso, who bravely bore the tri-color throughout the war and published the story of her adventures at its close. Two days later, three other legions followed, numbering some 600 volunteers; and, in a week, the 10th regiment of the line was on its voyage to Leghorn—at all of which movements, be it noted, Lord Napier, the British Envoy, expressed unqualified dissatisfaction. Just a month subsequent set out the "Neapolitan Army of Expedition for Northern Italy," under the veteran Pepé.

This old man's name fills a large space in the events of '48–49. Exiled in 1799, at seventeen, for liberalism, from his native Naples—a hero of the Italian Legion under Napoleon at Marengo—an ornament to Murat's staff in Sicily, 1810—at the head of 50,000, at the acmé of military rank, the liberator of his country, in his thirty-eighth year, in 1820—an exile then for twenty-seven years in England and France—in the March of 1848, at the age of sixty-two, a Neapolitan war-steamer was ordered by Ferdinand to convey Gen. Pepé from Marseilles to Naples, under the amnesty of the New Constitution.

And this New Constitution? On the 2nd of September, 1847, a demand, suggested by the reforms of Pius, was made for "independence and liberty," at Reggio and Messina, but was at once stifled, as usual, by bombardment and blood. Nothing daunted, however, the people of Palermo publicly proclaimed a purpose of rebellion,—an act of daring of which all history has no other record—were not a constitution granted them prior to January 12, 1848, the birthday of the king. None was granted, and they were as good as their word, and sustained the revolt against nine war-steamers and some 14,000 troops.* Salerno next rose with 10,000 men,

* On the 18th of April, the Sicilian Parliament met—adopted their constitution of 1812—declared Ferdinand of Bourbon no longer their king, and on the 11th of July, proceeded to elect the Duke of Genoa, younger son of Charles Albert, to that office. Ferdinand at

followed, on the morning of January 27th, by Naples herself, with 20,000. The result was resignation of the Ministry, expulsion of the infamous Del Carretto, Chief of Police, and the outline of a constitution, the French charter of 1830, modified by Bozzelli, proclaimed on the 29th for both of the Sicilies.

At Genoa, Pepé learned of revolutions at Berlin, at Vienna, at Milan, at Venice; volunteers were flocking to Milan and Charles Albert's camp, and the old chief himself, reviewed the Civic Guard of 5,000 men. Arrived at Naples—closeted with the king—desired to form a Ministry—offered an army of 40,000 men to cross the Po—overruled in a demand for seven steamers to convey as many battalions to succor Venice and capture Trieste—delayed unhappily by illness—at last, on the 4th of May, a brigade of 17,000 men of all arms was *en route* for Lombardy, to be followed by 24,000 more, and the veteran was himself *en voyage* for Ancona to join them, in the steam-corvette *Il Stromboli*—having received at the moment of embarking, instructions to confine himself to the right bank of the Po until subsequent orders—instructions which the old hero was resolved to regard as "never received." On the 10th of May, arrived at Ancona, was issued the first of those Orders of the Day which became subsequently so celebrated—rousing the nationality of the troops and abolishing the lash. In the port was the Vice-Admiral De Cosa with seven Neapolitan war-steamers, two frigates, and a brig, with 4,500 troops of Pepé's force on board. On the 16th, this squadron joined the Sardinian, under Admiral Albini, at Venice, and on the 22nd, the united fleet was off Trieste.

At Bologna Pepe received a despatch from President Manin, ap-

once recalled his Minister from Turin. Sicilian independence was, however, short-lived; and the Bourbon tyrant got back again, thanks to bombardment and massacre and the acquiescence of England and France.

prising him that the whole of Friuli swarmed with Austrians, who were advancing to blockade Venice by land, whilst a blockade by sea was already declared; and fervently invoking his immediate advance and aid. Here, also, the old general received a communication from the king of Sardinia, and at once despatched Captain Ulloa to place the Neapolitan troops under the king's command. But that very day—May 22nd—came a despatch from the Ministry at Naples, recounting disturbances of the 15th and recalling all the troops, except the volunteers, and adding, that, if Gen. Pepé did not think proper to conduct the retreat, that duty should be assumed by Gen. Statella, whom he had himself selected as Lieutenant-General on leaving Naples. Accepting the alternative, Pepé at first resigned the command, but, immediately, moved by the remonstrances of the brave Bolognese, re-assumed it and despatched Gen. Scala to Naples with a definitive declaration, that he would neither send back the troops, nor conduct them back, and that the duty of a citizen, superseding all others, was to consult the welfare and glory of his country. Admiral De Cosa was more obedient with the squadron, though not until positive and reiterated orders a month later; while Statella who had resigned at once, narrowly escaped being burned—thus sharing the fate of his carriage, in Tuscany, in his retrograde flight.

The insurrection at Naples which afforded a plea for this recall, originated in a difference between the king and the liberal deputies, on Saturday, the 13th of May, as touching the form of oath to be taken on the opening of the Assembly, on Monday the 15th. Sunday night the Swiss were under arms—the National Guard were ordered out—barricades rose—the Ministry resigned—the King conceded everything as to the oath; but the removal of the barricades was refused, except upon further concessions. At noon, on the

15th, the streets were crowded; the Swiss and the National Guard were in presence, and a chance shot was the signal for the commencement of a scene of massacre for fifteen hours which beggars all description. The National Guard was annihilated; the Lazzaroni declared for the king and perpetrated unutterable atrocities; nearly every house on the Strada Toledo was riddled by artillery or sacked; the white flag of the Bourbons superceded the tri-color, and from every house hung a white sheet or handkerchief as a protection. The victims were hundreds.* Many sought refuge on the English and French ships in port. Levraud, the French *Chargé*, went on board the flag-ship *Friedland*, to solicit interference from Admiral Baudain, who, to that end, despatched a memorial to the king. An indemnity of 50,000 francs was subsequently awarded the French in Naples for losses. The king was asserted to have had 20,000 troops in the city. Del Caretto and Campo Basso, the old executors of Ferdinand's cruelties, recently returned from their brief and forced exile, are said to have presided at this *fête* of blood, at sight of which the infamous Cardinal Ruffo himself, might have shivered in his shroud!

On the 18th, a new ministry as its first act, recalled the troops and the fleet from the North; and truly has it been declared, that, if the King of Naples wished to earn the everlasting gratitude of Austria, he chose wisely his time; for it was, perhaps, the exact moment when these troops were recalled, that even the sword of Naples might have turned the scale. The Neapolitan troops under Pepé, united with the Roman and Lombard troops under Durando and Ferrari, would have numbered nearly 40,000 men—strengthened by which, Charles Albert could, doubtless, have driven Radetzky over the Isonzo. But the Neapolitans turned their backs on

* More than five hundred. The white badge recalls the horrors of St. Bartholomew.

the Po—the whole of the first Division quartered at Ferrara being first led off by a Sicilian regiment—the 12th—of "galley-slaves and pardoned highwaymen." These were followed, on the 10th of June, despite the positive Order of the Day of that date of Gen. Pepé at Rovigo to cross the Po—by all the residue of the Neapolitan force, as well as the 10th regiment that had fought well and bravely at Curtatone—a single battalion of Rifles, a single company of Sappers, a body of Volunteers and a train of field-artillery only excepted. With this force, together with a second battalion of Neapolitan Rifles, and several field-officers who had managed to escape from their retreating troops,* numbering in all some 2,000 men, the old veteran directed his steps towards the City of the Sea, in compliance with the repeated and earnest entreaty of Manin; and, on the 13th of June, entered the Lagune just in season to save her from capture and to prepare her for a siege of fifteen months.

Nor was the defection of Naples the only one which the "Holy War" was at this time called to suffer. Bitterly was Italy taught, in '48–49—"Put not your trust in Princes!" On the 18th of April, Ferdinand called home his troops, and on the 29th Pius IX. did the same by his! Yes, Pius IX., who had not only—voluntarily or compulsorily—authorized his subjects to aid the cause of Italian independence, in which he had himself assumed the initiative, but who had, in a manner, given their banners his apostolic benediction, as they defiled before St. Peter's, on leaving the gates of Rome! Scarcely had they departed, however, when, suddenly, early in April, his confessor, whose influence had been for liberalism and had been very great—died—it was said, by poison; and, on the

* Gen. Lahalle, dragged along by his troops, took his own life in despair; and Col. Testa was struck with apoplexy.

29th of the same month, appeared the Pope's famous *Allocution*, in the Consistory of Cardinals, taking decided stand against the Italian cause, by declaring the war himself had originated against the Germans to be " wholly abhorrent from his counsels !"

If now we look for mundane causes for this spiritual horror, we shall find, that, on the 25th of April, the Ministry of Pius urged war on Austria: that the German cardinals, at once, in a body, apprised him, that such a step would cause their immediate renunciation of all allegiance to the Holy See; whereas, by a counter course, the Papacy *might* receive all the advantages promised by Joseph II.; and, finally, that, April 29th, appeared the Allocution of Pius, without consultation with his Ministry, or even with Cardinal Antonelli, his most intimate counsellor! The people of Rome were indignant, and no wonder. To withdraw the Papal Crociati, already in Lombardy, Pius then sent " the sainted legate" Corboli Bussi—a saint in fact, it is said, as well as in face—and, whose words by the superstitious Charles Albert were deemed little less than " the will of God," although announcing a most dishonorable defection. And this was the same Pio Nono whose reforms of 1846–7 were the cause—the origin—the inception of the events of 1848–9 in Italy—in Europe; and who, upon the occupation of Ferrara by these same " Germans," had been the first to protest, and had led the cry which went up from one extremity of the Peninsula to the other—from Sardinia to Sicily—from Venice to Leghorn—*Fuori i barbari!* Away with the barbarians! It was the same Pio Nono whose acts had directly originated disturbances in Naples and Sicily, which, as we have seen, extorted from Ferdinand of Bourbon the constitution of January 29th; disturbances in Piedmont, which gave her a constitution, February 8th, commemorated by splendid rejoicings on the 27th; disturbances in Tuscany, a few days later, with like result; disturbances in Paris, which made France a republic, February 25th; disturbances, within the space of the following week, in the Dukedoms of Baden, Bavaria and Nassau, the Kingdom of Wirtemberg and the Electorates of Hesse Darmstadt and Hesse Cassel, which resulted in concessions and reforms; disturbances at Munich, on the 6th of March, which resulted in abdication of the King; disturbances, on the 14th and 16th, in Hanover and Saxony, extorting reforms; disturbances at Berlin, which resulted, on the 21st, in the promise of a German Empire with a constitutional government; disturbances at Vienna, which exiled Metternich and proclaimed, on the 15th, the basis of a constitution; disturbances at Milan, which evacuated that city of Austrian troops, on the 22nd, and disturbances at Venice, which made her a republic on the same day; to say nothing of like disturbances in every capital and every large town on the continent, with like results. Rome received her *Statuto* on the 14th of March.* On the 26th of that month, Charles Albert was in Lombardy at the head of a Piedmontese army; and volunteers and troops of the line from all Italy were flocking to his auspicious standard. In the language of the celebrated historian of France, Mignet—" *Toute l' Italie s' élançait sous les étendards du noble Charles Albert!*" And, at that moment was it, of all others, that Pope Pius thought proper to ignore the work of his own hands—to repudiate the putative offspring of his own head and heart! He would neither nourish the flame he had kindled nor quench it. By his famous Allocution he declined to declare war;

* At Rome the Imperial arms over the Austrian Embassy were torn down by the people March 21st, at Florence and Leghorn the 24th, at Naples the 26th. Count Lützow the Austrian Envoy at Rome, recalled April 10th, left, May 5th, on a British steamer, protected from the mob by the British Consul. Prince Schwartzenberg, the Austrian Envoy at Naples, escaped by means of a British man-of-war boat on the night of March 28th.

and yet, had he not blessed the banners of his crociati, who, though ostensibly sent "to defend his frontier" against Austrians already flying over their own, had yet crossed the Po with his apparent assent? Nor was this all. At the same time, he addressed a letter to the Emperor of Austria, calling him the "Prince of Peace," and advising him most paternally to resign his Italian Provinces, at the very moment his own troops under Durando and Ferrari were doing their best by force of arms to take those provinces from him! At the same time, moreover—or rather two months later—on the 27th of June,—he addressed in autograph to Venice, through Castellani, her Envoy at Rome, the following words:—"God give his blessing to Venice, and deliver her from the calamities she apprehends, in such manner as in the infinite resources of His Providence shall please Him for the purpose." Could inconsistency, vacillation, or duplicity well go farther? And is it wonderful, that even at this early period Pius began to meditate flight, and asked for a refuge at Naples, that Medina of Papal Hegiras, from the terrible storm his incantations had conjured up? In view of this deplorable defection, how like a mockery and a lie seem his early benedictions of the Italian cause—his early and enthusiastic words—"*Benedite, O Dio, l' Italia!*"—so often quoted.

The army of Charles Albert at the close of April, according to General Pepé, numbered 60,000 Piedmontese, 5,000 Tuscans, 3,000 Modenese and Parmesans, 17,000 Romans, and 5,000 Lombards—in all 90,000 men—though not more than 70,000 were under his immediate orders. The field-artillery, consisting of one hundred and twenty twelve-pounders to oppose the Austrian eight-pounders, is said to have been "faultlessly equipped and well trained;" and was under the command of the Duke of Genoa, the King's younger son; while the six regiments of lancers, almost equally unexceptionable, were under command of the Duke of Savoy. The *Commissariat*, however, is said to have been in a sad state of confusion; while the general staff "seemed to have lost the very rudiments of strategy."

To oppose this gallant array, "Father Radetzky" had an army of 135,000 men *on paper*, though less than 80,000 *in fact*, and only 50,000 in the field, of which some 10,000 were tried Italians: and he was hoping for a reinforcement of 25,000 troops from Vienna, for which he had applied, together with vast munitions.

We left the old Marshal at Lodi on the night of the 23d, resting his exhausted troops, after their protracted strife of five days at Milan, and their perilous evacuation of the previous night, and their harassed retreat of the previous day. But that repose was brief. The whole country he soon found was in arms—3,000 Italian troops deserted him, and went to their homes, and Charles Albert, with 40,000 men, was in hot pursuit. Any attempt *then* to re-take Milan, as he says he had at first purposed, would have been madness. On the 25th, therefore, he continued his retreat eastward to Crema, where, in a proclamation, he announced, that "peaceful inhabitants had from his soldiery nothing to dread; but that all persons taken with arms in their hands should be judged by a military commission; and, on conviction, should be immediately shot." From Crema, the Marshal continued his retreat—imposing a heavy contribution of supplies on the defenceless village of Montechiari, the Austrian muster-field for spring reviews—until he reached Verona, which, with Mantua, Peschiera, and Legnano, constituted the only places in all Lombardy and Venice now in the hands of the Austrians! Within the period of a single week, the yoke had been thrown off from all the residue of what had been the "*Regno Aus-*

triaco Lombardo-Veneto;" and the troops by which it had been garrisoned had either capitulated, been imprisoned, or suffered to retreat.

Thus, "within five days, a host of 70,000 combatants was routed and scattered with a panic and confusion, such as the world never witnessed since the days when angels smote the host of the Assyrian. On the 16th of March, Austria seemed invincible: on the 22d, it was thought she had ceased to exist."

On the 23d of March, the people of Como declared a Provisional Government, seized the barracks of 12,000 troops, and, securing their arms, hurried off to aid Milan. At Varese, two hundred Croats were compelled to surrender. The cattle of Pizzighettone was given up with all its ordnance, and that of Piacenza was evacuated. The people of Pavia, Lodi, Dezensano, and Cremona, drove out the "barbarians" with considerable effusion of blood; while the garrisons of Udine and Treviso were permitted to capitulate. The citizens of Brescia expelled the Austrian troops from their walls, having first arrested their commandant General Shoubals, with some fifty of his officers. The garrison at Bergamo, consisting of eight hundred men, retreated to their barracks on the breaking out of the insurrection, when, their arms being demanded on condition of an undisturbed evacuation, they seized the deputation of citizens who made the demand! To release this deputation they were permitted to depart with their arms in their hands, in the same unwise manner as at Venice, Parma, and, indeed, all over Italy.

At Verona, Mantua, Legnano, and Peschiera, by order of the weak old Viceroy at Milan, arms had been placed in the hands of the citizens at their request, on the plea of "maintaining order" as a National Guard. The result was as inevitable as, under like circumstances, it was elsewhere and everywhere, invariable. The Imperial garrisons in these towns, as in all others, were at once assailed, and owed their safety only to precipitate retreat to the massive fortresses—none of which, however, were prepared or provisioned for a siege. At Verona, when the castle was summoned by the people to surrender, the prompt reply of its Commandant, General Gerhardi, in the spirit of General Taylor, at Buena Vista—" Come and take it"—seems to have quieted effectually the aspirations of the most enthusiastic. The garrison of Mantua was commanded by General Gorzkowsky, a Pole by birth, and, since the capitulation of Venice in '49, Military Governor of that city. His entire force consisted of three hundred artillery men and a few hussars. With this handful of men he retreated from the menacing aspect of the National Guard, which, by order of the Viceroy, he had been compelled to arm; and, having dispatched urgent request for reinforcements, shut himself up in the citadel, to await the sequel. Hardly was this accomplished, when a deputation of citizens, led by the Bishop of Mantua, appeared at the gates, and formally demanded the keys of the fortress, and its immediate evacuation by the Austrian troops. The plea urged in justification of this peremptory demand was, the prevention of needless effusion of blood—the fate of the garrison being declared inevitable, should the citizens, now fully armed and sanguine of success, pour themselves *en masse* on the castle. The city is situated on an island formed by lakes and the Mincio, and approached only by five long and narrow causeways, raked by batteries. In the midst, the citadel rears its massive pile, which, for nearly five hundred years, was alike the palace and the fortilace of the Gonzagas, the " Captains" of Mantua. It is now a prison and a castle, flanked by proud towers heavily macchiolated, but enfeebled by antiquity, decay, and the storms of war, which have for ages beaten against its rugged battlements. Nor was it now prepared to sustain a siege, nor could its garrison be relied on. Upon the first visit of the deputation of citizens, it is related that Gorzkowsky, having listened courteously to its mission, replied—" Gentlemen, you say that you urge capitulation to prevent effusion of blood. But I shall not attack you, and if you attack me, your blood and mine be on your own heads. As regards this fortress, the Emperor, my master and yours, has committed it to my trust. If in person he demands its keys, they are his: but to you, be assured, it will be yielded only as a ruin!"

On the second visit of the deputation, the Governor took the Bishop into the magazine, and then, pointing to a flint and steel in his hand, he pronounced these emphatic words—" When I can defend this fortress no longer, with this flint and steel I will blow it into the air, and, with it and myself, half of Mantua!" The old Bishop dropped trembling on his knees, and implored the abandonment of so desperate a resolve. " So help me God, I will keep my word!" was the brief, stern answer; and the terrified ecclesiastic, with his single companion, was dismissed to spread the panic. Despite this frighful menace, however, the fortress would, doubtless have been assailed by the infuriated citizens of Mantua on the ensuing morning; but the morning brought relief, in a reinforcement from Radetzky, then at Verona, and Mantua was preserved.* For this intrepid behaviour, which so strongly contrasts with the pusillanimous conduct of Count Zichy, Governor of Venice, under circumstances far less desperate, the rough old Pole merited well the distinction to which he was advanced on the fall of Venice—the military command of that beautiful city, from which Zichy had been degraded.

* London Quarterly Review.

One other instance—and few enough there were—of firmness and courage among the panic-stricken Austrians of the time is recorded in the person of General D'Aspre. This distinguished officer was in command of the garrison of Padua, when orders came from Milan to establish and arm a National Guard. D'Aspre hesitated obedience. Deputations of citizens remonstrated. Intelligence of revolution poured in hourly from every side. Austria in Italy was crushed! On Mantua and Verona depended the fate of her army, and at all hazards they must be retained. To arm the citizens of Padua would endanger this, as well as his own retreat. The arms demanded were refused! "But we are already partially armed," was the response. "Refuse our request and your own safety is compromised." "Be it so. Come on. My troops ask no protection but from their own weapons. My artillery frowns from your ramparts and at the heads of your streets. I am about to retreat. If I am attacked I will lay your town in ruins. I quit you as a friend: but be sure I shall return, and woe betide you if I come as a foe!"

His retreat was unmolested, and, with all his force, he met Radetzky beneath the walls of Verona. "You come to tell me all is lost," said the Marshal. "I come to tell you all is saved," was the reply. "All, indeed, *was* saved," continues the writer from whom these facts are obtained: "and the resolution and activity of these three commanders—Radetzky, Gorzkowsky, and D'Aspre—went far to retrieve the honor of the Austrian arms, stained by an act of pusillanimity so flagrant as the capitulation of Venice. Three battalions were instantly dispatched to the relief of Mantua; and, from that moment, the fate of Lombardy was decided."*

* London Quarterly Review.

That this was the fact the event proves. Yet, far otherwise seemed "the fate of Lombardy decided" on that 4th day of April, 1848, to those who were actors and spectators of its events—far otherwise than to their subsequent chronicler. The following passage from a Parisian journal, bearing date April 15th, may serve as a pendant to the quotation above, and indicate the spirit which then prevailed:—"Enthusiasm seems at its height. Priests, monks, women, children, old men, the ill, the well, all offer most zealous devotion to the Italian cause. With their white and delicate hands, Milanese ladies prepare cartridges and military equipments. The celebrated Princess of Belgiojoso has disembarked at Genoa with two hundred Neapolitan and Calabrian volunteers, equipped from her own purse, and to be paid by herself during the whole campaign. It is a Holy War, a new crusade, which, blessed by Pius IX., rouses from its profoundest depths that old land of Italy, so long unused to such emotions. The only apprehension which now modifies the triumph of the victors is that their foe may escape them. The tocsin pealed by towns and cities deafens Radetzky, and stupefies and demoralizes his soldiers. They find in this lovely land, so long oppressed by them and so recently devastated, not one friend to call on, not one refuge to fly to! Even their retreat is already cut off: for, while Italy precipitates itself like a torrent towards the base of the Julian Alps, the Tyrol and the Friul rise before the broken bands and part them forever from their base of operation."

CHAPTER VII.

DIPLOMACY.

Return we to Venice. One of the earliest duties to which the Provisional Government addressed itself was the announcement of the new republic to foreign powers. The preparation of these documents devolved, probably, on Tommaseo, as acting Secretary of Foreign Affairs, one of the most distinguished authors of modern Italy. As early, indeed as the 26th of March, the following note was despatched to Milan :—" We hailed with infinite joy the account of the emancipation of our generous sister of Lombardy. On the very day you shook off the Austrian yoke, a Provisional Government of the Venetian Republic was proclaimed here under the glorious banner of St. Mark. We are influenced by no local prejudice ; we are, above all, *Italians*, and the insignia of St. Mark figures on the tri-colored banner. We are united to you, Lombards, not only by the tie of affection, but, also, by community of misfortunes and hopes. When the hallowed soil of the country shall have ceased to be sullied by the feet of the foreign oppressor, we shall join you in discussing the form of government most conducive to our common glory. We intended, at first, to send you a special deputation ; but the important and multifarious labors with which we are overwhelmed, do not admit of our dispensing with the services of any of our distinguished citizens. We impatiently await your direct communications. *Viva l'Italia, Viva Milano, Viva liberta, fratellanza!*"

To the monarchical powers of Russia, Prussia, Turkey, Holland, Belgium, Denmark, Sweden, Spain, Portugal, Brazil, Bavaria, Hanover, &c., was addressed a brief circular, which commences thus cavalierly:—"A part of the old Venetian States has constituted itself a republic. In communicating to you this fact we do not feel ourselves called upon the justify or to explain it. Upon history will devolve this task." To France and England are tendered assurances of friendship. To the Papal See is given a pledge never to disturb order in the adjacent states. A joint note to Sardinia, Naples, and Tuscany, expresses a wish for intimate relations of friendship conducing to common advantage. Greece is reminded of the period when the standard of the Morea floated from a mast of St. Mark. To America is recalled the fact, that, to a native of Genoa she owed her discovery, and to a native of Florence her name; yet, that a third Italian republic owed to her sister beyond the ocean an exemplar, and would yet owe to her much that she had to learn.

These addresses to foreign powers were transmitted in all instances through their Consular representatives at Venice; and only to France and England were despatched special envoys. To the former power were sent three—Zanardini, Nani, and Caotorta.

The effect at Vienna of late events in North Italy seems to have been profound. The Imperial cause was viewed as little less than desperate. In a single week, Austria had been stripped of all her Italian provinces; and their recovery, against the combined arms of the whole peninsula, seemed utterly hopeless. And, could they be recovered, it was doubtful if they could be retained, except by the sword ever unsheathed, and the bayonet ever fixed. Besides, England, although she had expressed through her minister at Turin, Mr. Abercromby, formal disapprobation of Charles Albert's violation of the Treaty of Vienna, sympathized, no doubt, to a certain extent, with the Italian struggle; while Lord Palmerston himself, as late as the 20th of the ensuing month, could see "no reasonable ground for expecting that any attempts by Austria to reconquer Italy could be attended with success." As for France, there could be no doubt of her designs and wishes, if the express words of Lamartine, her ruler, meant anything at all. Of Italy he said—"Should an armed hand contest the right of those states to consolidate themselves into one Italian country, the French Republic will deem it her duty to give armed protection to the legitimate movements of the nationality of the peoples." That this sentiment was not mere words, seemed proven by the fact that a French army of 62,000 men was hovering for months on the frontier of Sardinia, ready to cross the Alps at the earliest intimation. He, also, assured Gen. Pepé in March, that "France was disposed to send 100,000 men to Italy to favor her independence." But the fears of Charles Albert, quickened by the recent silly invasion of Savoy by a few thousand idle operatives of Lyons, were hardly less of an army of Republican French allies in his rear, than of an army of Absolute Austrian foes in his front; while the people were clear-sighted enough to know, that France, whether Republic or Kingdom, could never desire a united and independent Italy, any more than she could a united and independent Germany.

In view of all these facts and circumstances, it is not so surprising as it might otherwise seem, that, as early as April 5th, almost the very day that Radetzky concentrated his retreating forces on Verona, Count de Hartig, who was familiar with the Italian character from previous official residence in that country, should have been dispatched from Vienna, leaving finally on the 10th, at the head of a commission to offer terms to the revolted kingdom. Accompanying the army of 30,000 men—constantly and greatly augmented by fugitives—led by General Count Nugent down through the passes of the Friuli into the Venetian provinces, he issued a proclamation promising the Italians recognition of their nationality, a free press, every species of liberty, and all the advantages and privileges claimed by them through the revolution—if they would only remain connected with Austria. Subsequently the proposition assumed the form of two plans which were laid before Lord Palmerston, for the mediation of England, by M. Hummelaüer, Austrian Envoy at London. The first proposal was the complete independence of the Lombardo-Veneto kingdom, though still attached to the Empire, with a distinct administration under a Viceroy, an Archduke of the House of Hapsburg, and with its own army. The second proposal was the absolute independence and cession of Lombardy, with full power to choose her own government and to govern herself, or, to unite herself with Sardinia—Austria retaining the line of the Adige and the Venetian territory under a liberal government, with her forces concentrated at Verona.

But, liberal as were these proposals—liberal beyond all peradventure or possibility prior to March, '48, yet, which were not finally withdrawn before July—they were rejected by Lord Palmerston as not liberal enough to satisfy one of the parties!

To give up Venice—Venice to which she had not one *scintilla* of title, Austria would not for an instant listen; while Milan, "which had been a fief of the German Empire for a thousand years," she yielded without a struggle! To give up Venice, she said, would be to give up the Italian Tyrol, causing thereby a dismemberment of the empire, to which she could never consent. The tenacity with which Austria clung to Venice is, indeed, remarkable—even admitting its value to her commerce and to all Germany. The Milanese, that fertile territory, which, without dispute, had been hers ever since the battle of Pavia, in 1520, and the defeat of Francis by Charles, she was ready to resign: but Venice, a city which she had held for less than half a century, and to which her right was even less than that of the freebooter—

> " That they should take who have the power,
> And they should keep who can—"

—Venice, she viewed as the brightest gem in her Imperial diadem, and only with existence itself would she consent to yield it. But this would be yet more incomprehensible did we not behold elsewhere similar national phenomena. England deems the Rock of Gibraltar —which she acquired by questionable stratagem, and which, while it has already cost her fifty millions sterling, costs her, annually, yet, forty thousand more, although of not the slightest possible benefit to her—on confession of her own statesmen—as the proudest trophy of her prowess and the mightiest symbol of her power: and so a fond mother often prizes most the most worthless, unattractive, and troublesome of her progeny.

But, while Austria was thus tenacious, Venice, on the other hand, with the full consciousness of her undoubted rights to independence, with the proud memory of her old republic of fourteen hundred years, with the indignant recollection of the baseness and perfidy by which her freedom had been stolen, and with the glorious fact, not to be denied, that she had once more achieved her liberties, and was, *de facto*, free, might well laugh to scorn any diplomacy which should attempt to make her again an appendage to the empire of the hated Teuton—a propitiatory *holocaust* offered up on the shrine of Italy for the freedom of only a part. But the magnanimous Milanese seem never, for one moment, to have entertained the idea of availing themselves of the liberal offer of the Emperor at the expense of Venice; albeit, Charles Albert, months later, when it was too late, under date of July 7th, addressed a confidential letter to Mr. Abercromby, declaring his personal willingness that Austria should retain Venice.*

The fact is, flushed with the wonderful success which had attended their movements, nothing less than the absolute cession of all Northern Italy, from the base of the Julian Alps to the banks of the Po, and from the Adriatic Sea to the Mediterranean, with Trieste, Venice, and Genoa for seaports, would, at this early date, begin to satisfy either Venice, Lombardy or Charles Albert. Indeed, so utter and so irremediable was deemed the rout of "the barbarians," that, when the Milanese deputies, Borromeo and Beretta, met the king at Pavia, April 29th, they urged him to carry the war even into Istria and Dalmatia, old provinces of Venice over the Adriatic before '97; while the Venice Gazette irritated the British Consul Dawkins, by allusion to the Ionian Isles—also Venetian territory before the invasion of Napoleon! Yet, a splendid realm would that "United Kingdom of Northern Italy" have formed; and no wonder that the ambitious king of Sardinia valued his life lightly in the comparison with its crown. The laws of nature and of nature's God—language, geography, affinities of feeling and sentiment—all proclaim that such a nation of right should exist; yet, from immemorial time has it been split up into separate and hostile states, and is now, perhaps, farther from that desired and deserved consummation of centuries, than ever before

* At Milan and Venice, early in April, Charles Albert was suspected of a purpose of sacrificing Venice to Austria, even as did Bonaparte at Campo Formio, and was fiercely denounced.

—unless, indeed, as some declare—the greater the oppression the nearer the consummation.

But, to resume our chronicle of events at Venice:—Our record had come down to the 5th day of April, the day that Count de Hartig left Vienna to join the army of General Nugent in Friuli, on his mission of conciliation, and two days after Marshal Radetzky's arrival at Verona, which he had at once declared in a state of siege, and from which point, as a basis, he had resolved to attempt the recovery of Venice and Lombardy by force of arms.

To name all those events of interest by which this first month of the Venetian Republic—this month of April, was noted, would be out of the question, except by assuming for the narrative the form of a diary. Event pressed on event, both at home and abroad; and, hardly an event of them all was there, which was not, more or less, intimately associated with the ultimate weal or woe of the republic. A hasty summary of these events in the order of their occurrence, with but little of comment, detail, or attempt at grouping, is all that the limits or design of this work permit.

On the 4th of April, all the property of the Imperial Viceroy lying within the Republic of Venice was sequestrated to the use of the state; and, on the 14th, all property of Francis V., Duke of Modena, was, in like manner, sequestrated, provisionally, for the use of the State of Modena—though never sold. The property of the Dukes of Modena lying in Venice seems, by the bye, to have been, at all times, peculiarly unsafe. In 1797, when Napoleon took Venice, he appropriated to French benefit a sum of not less than 1,800,000 francs, belonging to this same unfortunate Duke of Modena—or rather to his father*—which chanced to be lying on deposite for safe-keeping in the public treasury of that republic.

* Francis IV.

On the 9th, there was a tumultuous assemblage on the Place St. Mark, and the 13th number of a daily paper, called "*Il Libero Italiano*," issued for that day, was committed to the flames for having expressed doubts respecting Charles Albert and the Roman General Durando, because of their tardy prosecution of the war. The policy of expressing such "doubts" at Venice, at that time, was, no doubt, very questionable: but, beyond all doubt, the time wasted by the king of Sardinia in front of the position of Radetzky, and in the siege of Peschiera, during the month of April, was the cause of his ultimate disastrous defeat. By a few forced marches with a portion of his troops—a strong reserve being left to defend Lombardy against incursions from Mantua and Verona—he might, with or without Durando, even as Durando with or without him—have forbidden the junction of Gen. Nugent descending from the Friul with 30,000 men, and Gen. Welden descending from the Tyrol with 10,000 more—forbidden absolutely their junction with Radetzky's 50,000 men at Verona.

As it was, however, the conflagration of a splendid bridge over the Tagliamento, and of another lesser one over the Piave, and the unsuccessful resistance of Ferrari with his 8,000 troops at Cornuda, seem the only impediment offered. Even Radetzky was amazed—none more than he, doubtless, and rejoiced, also, at this incomprehensible inaction—this strange neglect, to cut in pieces the detached wings of the Austrian army in detail, instead of suffering them to become invincible by union; and the veteran seems to have attributed it in his despatches "either to the want of courage or of power to act on the offensive."

How widely different was the policy and conduct of Napoleon, whom the Sardinian king professed to imitate, when, in June of 1796, fifty years before, the veterans Wurmser and Melas, under somewhat similar circumstances, descended the Alps, augmenting the Austrian force in Italy to 100,000 men against a French army of less than one-third that number! Too weak to match the two armies united, Napoleon flying from point to point assailed them singly; and defeating each with utter rout and ruin, in five days the campaign was over! But Napoleon was in pursuit of no "Italic Crown"—he left no unprotected capital in his rear—he sought no conciliation of peasantry at cost of a starving army—his troops were well appointed, well commanded, well disciplined, well fed—he had three out of the four fortresses of the formidable quadrangle—his mind was undistracted by conflicting hopes, and doubts, and fears—flushed with success and confident of victory he pressed straight onward with a single end, aim, object—the expulsion of Austria from Italy; while, finally, he never ordered a general, situated as was Durando with his 20,000 men, to suffer himself to be driven out of a country which had presumptuously made itself free,—either through superstitious reverence for a Papal interdict, or in order that to himself might subsequently accrue the glory of its re-capture—as Charles Albert *possibly* did!

On the 11th of April, the Sardinian Consul at Venice officially recognized the Republic in behalf of his king; and, on the following day, Signor Lazzaro Rebizzo was received as the accredited Envoy from that government. On the 13th, twenty-two naval officers, mostly Venetians by birth, arrived at Venice, having escaped from the Austrian fleet in the harbor of Pola, whither it had been long before wisely sent, for greater safety, by Colonel Marinovich, the late Commandant of the Arsenal.

And yet, but for a strange lack of forecast, every vessel of that fleet could have been secured, and Venice, by it, would have been infallibly saved. The spirit pervading the officers of the Imperial

Navy, the officers and men being mostly Venetians, was clearly that of the Bandieri. On first intelligence of the revolution, the tricolor superseded the red and white on an Austrian frigate at Naples and on two brigs in the Adriatic, which, at once, crowded all sail for the Lagune. But, the despatches for the fleet at Pola were ill-advisedly committed to the captain of the steamer which bore Palffy and his officers to Trieste. Forced by his passengers to land at the latter place first, his despatches were seized by the authorities, and the half-mutinous fleet was at once placed beneath the heavy batteries of Pola, where its crews were re-organized and exchanged.

On the 14th, the Provisional Government appropriated the sum of 300,000 Lire—$50,000—for the purpose of redeeming from the *Mont-de-Pieté*, or Pawning Establishment, all articles lying there in pledge not exceeding in value 75 cents each. On the same day arrived Gen. La Marmora, Director of the Marine School of Genoa, commissioned by Charles Albert to superintend the defence and fortification of Venice; and a more efficient arming of the forts was at once decreed. Venice was designed to present the aspect, not of a fortified place merely, but of a fortified province, by means of her double zone of batteries, 70 in number, circling an extent of seventy miles, and rendering her in some respects the most stragetic military point in all Italy. The Provisional Government also assumed the direction of the Lombardo-Veneto Railroad designed to unite Venice, Verona, and Milan, and claimed its revenues. Postage on newspapers was fixed at five *centessimi* each, which is equivalent to a *carantino*, or about one cent—the correspondence of Bishops and the Pope being declared free. A corps, composed of two hundred citizens, proposed to the Provisional Government to serve gratuitously in defence of the city and forts. A telegraph system was devised, connecting all parts of Venice with the National Palace, near the centre of the city, on the Place St. Mark—an arrangement calculated to be exceedingly serviceable in a place like Venice cut up by canals, and especially at a crisis like the present, though it was never carried out into actual use.

On the 21st, Paleocapa, Minister of Public Works, departed for the camp of Charles Albert, in order to implore immediate defence for Friuli, menaced by the army of Gen. Nugent; and, on the 22nd, Udine, the capital of that province capitulated, though on liberal terms, after a two hours' bombardment. But the people of Friuli, says Consul Dawkins, were never very zealous in the cause.

Considerable feeling was, about this time, roused in Venice, by the appearance in the Milanese journals of severe censure on the Venetians for having selfishly declared a republican form of government, independent of the rest of Italy, and before her soil was freed from the barbarians. It was, probably, as before remarked, easier for Milan to censure Venice for the course she had taken, than it would have been for her to resist pursuing herself a course identically the same under the same peculiar circumstances. But Venice had already officially declared to Milan that her Republic was only "provisional."

On the 26th, quite a sensation was created by intelligence from Padua of a revolt of the convicts in the prisons of that city, some eight hundred in number; and that it had been only quelled by the Civic Guard firing on the mutineers, by which three of them were slain. The Spirit of Revolution seems to have been contagious. Even convicts could not resist its influence! Many, doubtless, imprisoned under the old *regimè*, and by the old and corrupt tribunals, were unjustly confined.

CHAPTER VIII.

"LA SPADA D' ITALIA."

THE month of May opened with increased activity on every side. The Barnabite monks, Alessandro Gavazzi and Ugo Bassi, Chaplains of the Papal Crociati, who, like "Peter the Hermit," and "Walter the Penniless," of the 11th century, had wandered all over Italy, preaching a crusade—a crusade of Freedom, had now reached Venice; and, daily, in the Place St. Mark, did they harangue the multitudes, receiving contributions for the cause of the republic. At the close of a single exhortation, 24,000 Lire, or $4,000, in money was contributed, and vast quantities of plate, provisions, arms, and clothing. Ladies resigned their jewels, and even the lower classes tore off their ear-rings and bracelets, and those fine Venetian chains called *jasseron*, manufactured and sold by the yard by the goldsmiths of the Rialto Bridge for ages, characteristic of the Sea-city—and gave up even the large silver pins, which the poorest possess, and which serve to confine and ornament their masses of night-black hair. Superfluous, and even indispensable articles of household and domestic utility, under the patriotic fervor of the hour and the eloquent adjurations of the monks, were also thrown into the military

PATRIOTIC CONTRIBUTIONS.

Page 127

chest beneath the arcades of St. Mark; while the water-carriers of Friuli offered even the metallic vessels of their vocation! Never in all the long chronicle of Venice—never in her proudest and palmiest day—numberless and signal as were her exhibitions of generosity and devotion—not even in the dark hour of the War of Chioggia and the League of Cambray, was there exhibited liberality and patriotism like this! Every one offered something. Manin contributed his silver snuff-box, "the only article of exchangeable value he possessed!" The brothers Bevaliqua contributed their castle!

At Padua, the preaching of these monks was wonderfully effective, and the proceeds were 194,000 Austrian Lire, equivalent to nearly $33,000! Even the fishermen of Chioggia, an old village of 24,000 inhabitants on the Adriatic shore, twenty miles from Venice, contributed its mite of 600 Lire, under the exhortation of Father Tornielli; and the good father had opportunity one day to prove, that he was as zealous to fight as to preach, if need there might be, when an Austrian frigate, towed by a steamer, approached the coast. Instantly the *generale* was beaten calling to arms; and the entire population—old men, women and children not excepted, poured forth in a mass along the coast of Pelestrina, led by Priest Tornielli and Deacon Arrigoni, to dispute the advance of a foe, which had adopted this method of discovering the preparations for defence and the inclination to employ them.

On the 5th of May, the Festa of Pius V. was solemnized with great pomp, at Venice, Ercole Mastäi-Ferretti, nephew of the Pope, with a hundred and fifty pontifical crusaders, participating. Father Gavazzi, chaplain of the corps, harangued the multitudes in St. Mark's Place on the occasion, with his usual wild and thrilling eloquence; and the simultaneous intelligence of the repulse of Charles Albert at Santa Lucia and Croce-Bianca had but little effect to dampen the enthusiasm. Indeed, the words of this fanatic, yet eloquent monk, as he daily harangued the excited masses in the square of St. Mark, seem to have been equalled in effect only by those of Pope Urban II., when, in the Market-place of Clermont, he was interrupted by the clamorous shouts of ten thousand men, who with one voice, exclaimed—*Deus vult! Deus vult!* "It is the will of God! It is the will of God!"

The name of this eloquent monk, Alessandro Gavazzi, together with that of his friend and companion, the yet more eloquent Ugo Bassi, have more than once occurred, and deserve more particular mention. Both were natives of Bologna, and the former, of distinguished parentage, born in 1809, was the second of twenty children. In person he is tall, well-formed, with dark hair, eyes, and complexion, a full and oval face, and a thoroughly Italian countenance. At sixteen he entered the Order of St. Barnabas, and at twenty was Professor of Rhetoric at Naples, until his ordination at Arpino, when he became a teacher of *belles lettres* at Leghorn. Driven thence at the age of twenty-five for liberalism, he repaired to Piedmont, where he preached two years with great effect, until driven by the Jesuits to Parma. Here he preached four years, and often ten times in a single day, when he was silenced and imprisoned by Gregory XVI. Subsequently he preached at Perugia and Ancona, and in 1845 was silenced at the College of St. Severino, until the advent of Pius IX., when he was called to Rome. But his burning eloquence was again deemed perilous. He denounced Gregory XVI. —he denounced Austria at the anniversary of the massacre of the Paduan students—he was rebuked, silenced, consigned to the convents of Polveriera and Gonzario. But he was soon released. Revolution had begun. Milan had triumphed. Borne on the shoulders of students to the Pantheon, Gavazzi eulogized the martyrs of the five days. He it was who first called the contest a "Holy War." He it was who first assumed the tri-color cross on his breast and shoulder, which he has worn ever since. For weeks he harangued immense multitudes in the vast and classic ruin of the Coloseum. The enthusiasm roused was overwhelming. Thousands from his hands received the Cross of Liberty. Durando and Ferrari, with 17,000 Swiss and Crociati, marched for Lombardy; and Gavazzi, appointed by Pius chief chaplain, accompanied the fiery host,* and throughout the whole of the disastrous campaign which followed with the cross in one hand and the sword in the other, led them onward—roused enthusiasm—consoled the sick—shrived the dying—buried the dead—supplied every want by his eloquent appeals to the people—braved the horrors of Vicenza, and won a medal on that red field, "where 10,000 Italians with 40 guns fought 49,000 Austrians, led by Radetzky, with 112 guns:" roused excitable Venice by his thrilling appeals day after day, and night after night, to such a pitch of frenzy, that he was desired to withdraw by the prudent Manin—was driven from Tuscany by her Archduke for his insur-

* In one of Gavazzi's Lectures at Metropolitan Hall occurs the following remarkable development:—"I shall narrate to you a conversation which took place between me and Pius IX., previous to the war in Lombardy. I was on very intimate and friendly terms with the Pope, through my preaching in Italy, and by the influence of friends:—'Holy Father,' I said, 'all Italy calls you her saviour.' 'Gavazzi,' answered the Pope, 'do not speak to me of Italy, but only of the Roman States.' 'But, Holy Father, the Italians admire your reform, and you must obtain the same for all.' 'Gavazzi,' replied Pius IX., 'beware, in your preaching, to speak of Italy.' Before I left for Lombardy I went to see the Pontiff once more to obtain his blessing, and he inquired from me where I was going. 'To Bologna, Holy Father.' 'And thence,' added the Pope, where shall you go?' 'To Ferrara: and from that city shall cross the river at Po.' 'You shall not,' vehemently replied Pius IX. 'I shall,' I answered, 'in order to re-conquer for your Holiness the State of Polesina, which was taken away from the dominions of the Papal See at the Congress of Vienna.' The Pope appeared more easy, but ordered me not to say nor do any thing in the name of Italy."

rectionary harangues at Leghorn and Florence—was called to Bologna to quell the revolt of that city against the Pope—repaired to Rome on the flight of Pius, and, as Chaplain-general, organized military hospitals and superintended the surgical ambulances, aided by the Princess Belgiojoso and the Countesses Pallavicino and Piascane, throughout the whole desperate struggle and siege—was at Velletri with Garibaldi at the rout of 20,000 Neapolitans by 14,000 Romans*—braved peril on the bastions until the entry of the French—was saved from destruction by the American artist and consul, Freeman—escaped to London, and gained his bread as a teacher—assailed the Papacy in that capital in a series of lectures; and, finally crossed the Atlantic, landed at New York on the 22d of March, '53, and at once entered on a series of lectures on the same subject, repeated in various other cities with wonderful effect.

The story of Ugo Bassi, companion of Gavazzi for twelve years, is much that of his friend if we except his repeated wounds in battle, and his melancholy doom. Repairing to his native Bologna, after the defeat of Custozza, it was through his exhortations on the 8th of August that the Austrians were driven out of the city by a populace armed only with knives. Subsequently, at Rome, he was chaplain to Garibaldi's Legion; he embarked, when all was lost, with that chief and Ciceroacchio at Cesenatico, for flight—was seized August 4th, 1849, by Croats near Ravenna—was conducted to Bologna, and sentenced to be shot—was demanded on the 7th, by the priests for dis-consecration by scalping the crown of his head, the centre of his forehead, the palms of his hands—all parts once touched

* "On the field of Velletri," says Gavazzi, "I saw the difference between the death of the patriot and that of the myrmidons of despots. I confessed the dying soldiers of both armies: the dying Neapolitan cursed his king, and died in the agonies of despair—the patriot soldiers died calm and happy, with '*Viva L'Italia! Viva la Liberta! Viva Jesu!*' upon their lips."

by holy oil; and, on the morning of the 8th, exactly forty-three years, almost to an hour, from his birth, and almost on the very spot, was shot by Croats—seven balls entering his bosom, and the populace rushing to the spot to dip their handkerchiefs in the streaming blood of their saint and martyr—UGO BASSI! And night after night, for weeks subsequent, despite all the anathemas of the Cardinal-Legate Bedini—

"Unseen hands strewed flowers upon his grave."

A more perfect, pure, and beautiful career and character than his, biography does not present. He might be deemed, indeed, almost the original of the sainted Gabriel of the "Wandering Jew." A liberal and eloquent preacher at Bologna, in the month of July, 1847, when the cholera was raging in Sicily, he at once sought its horrors at Palermo and Syracuse, administering all the physical comfort and spiritual consolation which his angelic nature could suggest. On the opening of the great drama of 1848, he took the field with his friend Gavazzi, and visited every camp and city of the Lombardo-Veneto. At Treviso he was severely wounded.

"My poor, dear friend Ugo Bassi!" exclaims the eloquent Gavazzi. "He was a man of the most varied acquirements; gifted by God and nature with a beautiful form; nobly endowed in mind; master of the dead and many of the living languages; a good musician; one of the best of the modern poets of Italy; and, as a pulpit orator, the very first—he followed the fortunes of the national army, was wounded in battle, and was everywhere with the legions of the hero Garibaldi. Poor Bassi! so young, so kind, so beloved, so talented, so dear to Italy—after six hours of secret trial amongst those scenes where he had so often preached the freedom of Italy, and amidst the tears of the Austrian soldiers who were ordered to shoot him, Ugo Bassi fell, exclaiming, "Long live Jesus —long live Italy!"

The excitement and enthusiasm roused by the preaching of Bassi and Gavazzi, early in May, in the Square of St. Mark, is indescribable. "Never did I witness," says the latter, "such a scene as that presented on the night of my arrival at Venice, when, from the balcony of Manin, in the National Palace, I addressed 40,000 people swarming that magnificent square, beneath the beams of the moon!" Some idea of this excitement and the sanguine hopes it inspired, may be inferred from the fact, that, a few days later, when the French war-steamer *L'Asmodée* entered the port, and two of her officers came on shore, they were received with a perfect ovation of triumph, as if the messengers of immediate aid from France! Two days afterwards, Gen. Antonini, commander of the Italian Legion organized at Paris, which left that city amid such boundless enthusiasm, was appointed Commandant of the city and fortifications of Venice; and the command of the navy was committed to Rear-Admiral Giorgio Bua. The Italian Legion was composed of Italian, French, and Polish adventurers to the number of five hundred and fifty, and Gen. Antonini was a veteran of the Polish and French wars. Embarked at Marseilles, they reached Genoa April 24th, but so cool was their reception both there and at Milan, in consequence of the late invasion of Savoy by the operatives of Lyons, that they at once passed on to Venice.

On the day of their arrival, a corps of volunteers, sent by the Provisional Government of Sicily, under command of Col. La Massa, also reached Venice. The same day, Duke Philip Lante Montefeltro was named Commandant of Treviso, then besieged, in place of Gen. Guidotti slain in a sortie; and a loan of ten millions of Lire—less than two millions of dollars—bearing interest five per cent. per annum, was imposed by the Provisional Government, payable in six years, and secured by the pledge of Railroad stock. Next morning, the Neapolitan fleet of two frigates, seven war-steamers, and a brig-of-war, which the day before had been seen from the Campanile, entered the port; and their officers received a cordial and imposing official welcome on the Piazetta of St. Mark.

On the 13th, the birth-day of Pius IX. was celebrated with great pomp at the Cathedral, the Holy Father having attained his 56th year. The day before, the monk Ugo Bassi was severely wounded in a sortie from Treviso; and a few days afterwards Priest Tornielli organized a band of crusaders he had been commissioned to enroll. The part played by ecclesiastics in the Italian Revolution was, as is observed, by no means unconspicuous.

Meantime, intelligence arrived daily—almost hourly from the theatre of war. At the Alpine passes of Cadore, the mountaineers had, for weeks, disputed the advance of the Austrians; but, finally, the passes were forced, and thus a new route to the Tyrol was opened to Radetzky. At the pass of the Froscon mountain, twelve shepherds headed by Augusto Navasa, resisted the progress of 150 Croats—a second Thermopylæ—a second Leonidas and his Spartans, with a happier fate—for, strange to say, not one was slain! Vicenza was, also, assailed by Nugent, but without result.

On the 21st of May Gen. Durando reached the neighborhood of Vicenza with 6,000 men and twelve pieces of artillery. Here he was met by Manin and Tommaseo, President and Minister of the Provisional Government at Venice, escorted by a thousand men, among whom was the Italian Legion of Gen. Antonini. Subsequently this daring corps, joined by others, boldly assailed the Austrians under Gen. Nugent, following them on their route to Verona—General Antonini losing his left arm in the conflict. The limb was amputated and he returned to Venice, but was unable to resume command of the city until the 25th of the ensuing month.

Meantime various minor decrees of interest were issued by the government. Resistance to the Civic Guard was declared to be "Public Violence," equivalent in its enormity and penalty to treason. A commissariat commission was created to superintend everything relating to the price and appropriation of provisions. Persons accused of crime were suffered to select two able counsellors for their defence; and persons receiving marks of distinction from foreign states were permitted to wear them. The public archives were thrown open to all persons of good character. An enrolment of militia was decreed, the duration of service being three years for infantry, and six for cavalry and artillery. The commission in charge of charitable institutions, for which, as has been mentioned, Venice has been distinguished from her earliest history, was reorganized. On the 24th of May, the birthday of the Queen of England, was honored by a royal salute. On the previous night a second assault had been made on Vicenza, held by Col. Belluzzi with 10,000 men, by Prince Taxis, sent by Radetzky, from Verona with 18,000 men and forty heavy guns. Commencing at sunset, it was suspended at midnight, and recommenced at dawn: but, baffled by an enthusiastic defence, in which even ladies mingled, the foe was driven from the city, and before night was *en route* for Verona, leaving 2,000 dead behind. There was, no doubt, brave fighting in this affair. A company of eighty Venetian crusaders, led by Francesco Zerman, assailed two hundred Austrians who had shut themselves up in an outpost, and took one hundred and seven prisoners. It was on this same 23rd of May, that Gen. Pepé refused, at Bologna, to obey the royal order recalling him to Naples.

On the day previous, the Sardinian squadron appeared off the

Lido, and having been joined by the Neapolitan and Venetian squadrons, bore away for Trieste, and drove the Austrian fleet within the Mole of the Lantern, which protects that port. Trieste was thus, *de facto*, in a state of blockade from the sea. It is a little amusing, that the Imperial Minister of Marine at that place had, just three weeks before, declared on paper that Venice was blockaded by sea, when not a single Austrian ship had approached her harbor, save only that towed towards the coast of Chioggia by a steamer, and scared off by a squad of fishermen led by a priest! On the day after the arrival of the Sardinian fleet arrived a proclamation from the king of Sardinia, addressed to the people of Venice, declaring that his intervention had but one object—the expulsion of the barbarians from the soil of Italy. Already, on the 12th instant, the immediate junction of Lombardy with Piedmont had been commended in a proclamation from the Provisional Government of Milan, "under the constitutional sceptre of the house of Savoy;" and lists had been ordered to be opened for recording the votes of the people for or against it—the lists, very appropriately, to be closed on the anniversary of the defeat of Barbarossa on the field of Legnano, seven centuries before—"Legnano, that Morat—that Morgarten—of Lombardy," on the 29th of May, 1176: whilst, on the 30th, deputations from Padua, Treviso, Rovigo, and Vicenza intimated to the Government of Venice their purpose of seceding from the Venetian Republic and uniting themselves with the kingdom of Piedmont; desiring, also, her own decision on the same subject within three days.

At this time, and for some time previous, as we learn from cotemporary publications, two distinct parties had existed at Venice, one for an independent republic, and one for fusion with Piedmont. Many obstacles to Italian unity arose in the minds of those opposed to this, among which not the least was the anticipated difficulty of fixing the capital of the ideal "Kingdom of Upper Italy." Milan, sanguine in the hope of being the fortunate city, was zealous for immediate annexation; but Venice, which had less cause for such hope, was less zealous. Nevertheless, a strong party in the city, subsidized, perhaps, for the purpose, wrote and shouted without ceasing—"*Viva Carlo Alberto, la Spada d'Italia!*"* Urged by these demonstrations, and in response to the declaration of the province, the government put forth a decree on the 3d of June, convoking, on the 18th of that month, the assemblage in the Ducal Palace of deputies chosen by the citizens of the Republic—the voters to be, at least, twenty-one years of age and the deputies twenty-seven; the ratio of representation being one deputy for every two thousand inhabitants, or thereabouts:—the purpose of which convocation should be—first, to deliberate on the present state of affairs, and to decide whether immediate action relative to government was advisable, or, whether it should be deferred to the close of the war: second, to decide, in event of the declared expediency of immediate action, whether Venice ought to be a distinct state, or annexed to Piedmont: third, to confirm the existing Administration of Government, or to substitute another.

The popular interest in this movement was, doubtless, quickened by recent successes of the Austrian arms, and the extreme probability, that, despite the army of Charles Albert, all the towns and cities of the province of Venice would once more, and very shortly, be under a foreign yoke.

We left Radetzky early in April with forty-five or fifty thousand men beneath the walls of Verona, and Charles Albert with nearly 70,000 men pressing towards him. On the 8th, 10th, and 11th, the king carried the bridges of Goito, Monzanbano, and Borghetto,

* The sword of Italy.

crossed the Mincio, entered the formidable quadrangle of the four fortresses of Verona, Mantua, Legnano and Peschiera, each half a night's march from the other, and occupied Valleggio. One of the bridges had been blown up by the Wohlgemuth Brigade, but the Sardinians crossed on a parapet left standing, though under a sharp fire. At Goito, Radetzky lost 27 Italians by desertion, 38 more as prisoners, and also a field-piece. On the other side 50 men and two officers were slain. On the 12th the small town of Castelnovo was burned by 3,000 Austrians and Italians; and 400 of the inhabitants were slain; and all because it had received Manara and his brave band, which had fought well but had been defeated! Only five houses in the town remained standing! "The streets were full," says an eye-witness, "of the half-roasted bodies of men, women, and children, on which hungry dogs were feeding!" The town had 2,000 inhabitants, and lies on the road to Verona. The Taxis Brigade, composed of Italians from the Veronese garrison, seconded the Croats in their atrocities! On the 13th, Charles opened a useless fire of field-pieces on Peschiera, and vainly summoned it to surrender; and, on the 19th, approaching Mantua, equally in vain gave her citizens a chance to revolt. At Pastrenogo, again approaching Peschiera, Sunday, April 30th, at the hour of noon, after hearing mass, the Sardinian army of 25,000 men attacked Radetzky with 20,000; and, after five hours' fighting, drove the Austrians into Verona with a loss of 1,200 killed and 500 prisoners. Great gallantry was exhibited by the Piedmontese and Parmesans. On the 5th of May, there was skirmishing near Rivoli and Pontone, and on the 6th, again approaching Verona, with all his forces, Charles unwisely attempted to storm the heights of Croce-Bianca and Santa Lucia, near Verona. Defection of 5,000 Italians and 4,000 semi-mutinous Hungarians was vainly hoped; as well as co-operation of the 60,000 inhabitants of Verona, whom the crafty Radetzky had effectually disarmed. The Piedmontese were defeated with a loss of 1,500 dead and wounded; but there were no prisoners; while Radetzky lost but 900 and had 100 taken. The Duke of Savoy and the Archduke Francis Joseph—so soon to become sovereigns of the respective realms now at war—are said to have "played a most brilliant part in this fight." The moral effect of Santa Lucia was paralyzing. A single regiment lost 200 men by desertion shortly after.

Radetzky now concentrated his troops in and around Verona, while Charles Albert carrying his head-quarters to Somma-Campagna, covered the vast plain of the Veronese, and seemed almost to envelope his foe. And here, strange to relate, with two hostile armies face to face, one of them vastly superior to the other, ceased all warlike movements for well-nigh a month! Meantime Charles was indulging dreams of his Kingdom of Upper Italy and "gathering votes;" and Father Radetzky was strengthening Verona and "gathering bayonets,"—awaiting Baron Welden with his 10,000 men from the Tyrol, and Count Nugent with his 30,000 from the Friul—numbers augmenting with every day's and every mile's advance. Meantime, also, Count de Hartig had descended from Vienna on his mission of peace, and had begun proclaiming conciliation; and, meantime, Count Nugent, collecting all the stragglers on his route, was fighting his way down through the mountain-passes already mentioned. This army consisted almost entirely of Croats and Hungarians,—all the Italians who had been disbanded by capitulation, like those who had deserted, having repaired to their homes. Many of these, especially those of three battalions which deserted at Cremona and one at Brescia, went to Milan; but not being enlisted by the insurgents, or not choosing to enlist, went home, where they remained during all the contest. It has been said, that, had Charles Albert, instead of his absurd jealousy of Lombard, Tuscan, Roman, Neapolitan aid, in his anxiety to owe his "Italic Crown" only to Piedmontese arms, sent a courier to every town and village of the Lombardo-Veneto, like Malise with the fiery cross of the Scottish Highlands, proclaiming a *levée en masse*, and then paralyzed the Croats with the tocsin in every town, and drowned them by cutting the dikes of the rivers, Radetzky would have been annihilated and Lombardy been freed almost without a blow! Of the German troops very few deserted. At a subsequent period, when Kossuth called home his countrymen to fight for Hungary, despite a liberal distribution of secret circulars in the Magyar tongue at Mantua and Verona, but few if any responded to the appeal. The stern injunctions sent by the Ban Jellachich to his 35,000 Croats to be true to their colors and country, seem to have been, on the contrary, very effective.

To oppose the passage of the forces of Nugent and Welden, which furnished a nucleus for the rendezvous of all the scattered troops which had composed the garrisons of Udine, Treviso, Venice, and the neighboring places in the revolt—the whole country rose *en masse*; and, so fierce was the resistance, that nine villages were committed to the flames in order to strike terror into the residue. Cadore and Udine were crushed by superior numbers. The eight artillery and rocket batteries of Gen. Nugent are said to have done dreadful execution. On the 12th of May, he invested Treviso, a town of 15,000 inhabitants, protected by battlements and marshes, when operations were suddenly suspended in order to hasten the junction with Radetzky. Another cause for this sudden suspension is, also, assigned. The daughter of Gen. Nugent was a prisoner in Treviso, and her execution, it is asserted, had been threatened by the Provisional Government in event the town was bombarded by her father's order. On the 22d, on plea of ill-health, Gen. Nugent committed his command to Prince Taxis* at Olmo and retired to Görtz. On the same day, Radetzky sallied from Verona and received his long-promised reinforcements at San Bonifacio; and, as we have already seen, ordered Prince Taxis to turn back the very next day to Vicenza, with 18,000 men and a heavy siege-train, to take the city.

Meantime, since the affair of Santa Lucia on the 6th of May, no collision had taken place between the armies of the king and the Marshal. On the advance of Austrian reinforcements, Charles seems hardly to have bestowed a serious thought. He had undertaken Lombardy, Radetzky and the four fortresses, for his part of the war; and had left Durando, Ferrari, and Pepé, with their Romans, Neapolitans and Lombards, to oppose Nugent and Welden, and protect Venetia. About the middle of May, the heavy batteries of the king having reached his camp, he commenced a regular bombardment of Peschiera. On the 26th, he summoned the place and granted twenty-four hours for consideration. On the 29th, Radetzky, hastening from Verona to the rescue with 40,000 men, fell on 6000 Tuscans and Neapolitans under Gen. De Laugier at Curtatone; and, after a bloody conflict from ten until four o'clock, overwhelmed and routed them with his superior numbers, though with a loss of 800 dead or wounded. The intrepidity of the Tuscans, especially of the Students' Legion, merited all the eulogy which will ever distinguish the name of Curtatone. Yet they were said to have been needlessly sacrificed to the disorder of the Sardinian reserve under Gen. Bava. This severe engagement was fought

* Prince Thurn and Taxis was this noble's full title, and his was the Italian "Taxis Brigade."

on the anniversary of the victory of the Lombard League over Barbarossa, nearly seven centuries before, and was worthy the occasion. The same day, it will be remembered, had been appointed for the closing of the registers of the votes of the Milanese on the question of fusion with Piedmont. Two days later, the king, warned of the Marshal's approach by the 500 fugitives to his camp, survivors of Curtatone,* crossed the Mincio, and, on the 1st of June, Radetzky was defeated at the Bridge of Goito with a loss of 3,000 men to 1,000 on the other side. Charles Albert received a contusion on the ear by the near flight of a cannon ball, and his elder son, the Duke of Savoy, to whom with the flying artillery, the victory was chiefly due—was wounded in the thigh by a musket-ball. Prince Felix Schwartzenberg, subsequently Premier of Austria, was, also, wounded, and Prince Hohenloe-Ruthein was taken prisoner. Schwartzenberg was, also, wounded in the arm, May 6th, at Santa Lucia, but soon recovered and continued in the service. Three Austrian Archdukes were personally engaged—among them the young Francis Joseph, so soon to be Emperor. It has been said that the leaders of the Italian movement themselves were rarely in the field. This is a mistake. Mazzini himself, at one time, bore a musket; and several were at Goito.

On the evening of the battle of Goito, capitulated the fortress of Peschiera. This place had been blockaded and besieged by the Duke of Genoa for nearly two months, more or less closely, during which period, 4,000 bombs had been thrown into the town, reducing it almost to ruins. The fortress, however, which is amazingly strong, was uninjured. It is a regular pentagon situated at the out-

* Of the 6,000 under De Laugier, there were 2,000 prisoners, including one entire battalion of Neapolitans, with 60 officers and five guns. Six hundred fled to Goito and 1,200 retreated in order on Macaria: leaving about 3,000 slain and missing.

let of the Lago di Garda into the Mincio, and surrounded by water. Its garrison consisted of 2,000 Croats, and its Commandant, Baron Rath, also a Croat, had been there more than twenty years. Repeated attempts to relieve, or to supply the place, had been made by Radetzky. On the 28th and 29th, Col. Zobel, with a convoy of munitions, and 5,000 men from Rivoli, had been driven back, after severe skirmishing. Famine, disease, and destitution of every necessary of life, alone, it is stated, reduced this impregnable fortilace; and 2,000 rations of food were furnished the starving garrison, by the victors, immediately on entering the place. But, though food was scarce, ammunition was plenty, and the number of cannon taken was one hundred and eighty. The garrison, reduced to 1,600, marched out of the fortress next morning with all the honors of war, led by old Baron Rath, and laid down their arms a mile distant. They then marched to Ancona and embarked for Trieste, under pledge not to take up arms again during the war.

Austria was now reduced to Verona, Mantua, and Legnano. But the reduction of Peschiera, though deemed a triumph by the victors, is said to have been more injurious than beneficial in its results. The preposterous importance attached to the fall of this fortress may be inferred from the subjoined extract from a bulletin of the Provisional Government of Lombardy at Milan, June 2nd :—" The fall of Peschiera and the victories of the last week in May, guarantee the result of the war of independence."

Had Charles Albert, after his victory at Goito and the fall of Peschiera, " made a rush on the Adige," say military critics, Radetzky might never again have beheld the walls of Verona. But one day was wasted in visiting Peschiera, and another day in a *Te Deum* for his victories of the 1st, and several days in waiting for fair weather; while Radetzky, with three corps of his army, joined by

Welden with 16,000 troops, making 43,000 men with heavy batteries, had, on the 9th, silently enveloped the walls of doomed Vicenza. This city was held by Durando with only 12,000 Swiss, Roman, Neapolitan, Lombard, French, and Venetian troops, regular and irregular, of all arms: while the inhabitants numbered about 30,000. Among the officers was the celebrated author and statesman, the Marquis Massimo d'Azeglio of Turin, the late Premier of Sardinia, who was wounded at Vicenza—like Napoleon, some where else—in the foot. At day-break on the 10th, the attack began with sixty-two guns and a simultaneous assault at all the gates. Gen. Culoz, late of the garrison of Venice, was, with his brigade, at the head of the assault. The outposts were carried by storm. All day and all night, raged the fight. The authorities and citizens resolved to perish under the ruins of the place. Thrice the white flag was run up, and twice shot down. At 6 o'clock on the morning of the 11th, Durando obtained a capitulation—the lives and property of the citizens to be respected, and the garrison to march out with the honors of war, on *parole* to serve no more against Austria within three months; and at 3 o'clock Radetzky entered the city. "The city of Palladio was thus saved;" albeit, it is lamented by an able Italian writer, that it had not been taken by storm—that the moral effect of a Moscow—a Saragossa—a Milan destroyed by Barbarossa, was lost to Italy, and thus was put off her hour of redemption for years. "It was good for Italy that Vicenza should cease to be." Thousands fell on both sides, among them many officers. The Swiss lost 600. Radetzky admits 600 men and 40 officers killed, among the latter being Prince Taxis. Vicenza ranks with Curtatone for Italian courage in 1848.

And Charles Albert—assured of Radetzky's march on Vicenza

on the 9th, it was not until the 13th that he approached defenceless Verona; and then the Marshal, with the whole of his first corps had returned! Thus Vicenza was lost and Verona not won.

The fall of Vicenza, although inevitable, and although the town was defended with such desperate intrepidity against such overwhelming odds, aggravated suspicions already strong at Venice against Gen. Durando. This officer was most unfortunate, to say the least, from the very beginning to the very end. He was first suspected, because detained on the right bank of the Po, by the orders of Pius; he was next suspected because detained beneath the walls of Mantua, by the orders of the king; he was afterwards suspected because, in obedience to orders from the same source, as he declared in reply to a remonstrance from Venice, he suffered the junction of Nugent with Radetzky, and retreated from Treviso; and, finally, he was suspected because of the fall of Vicenza!

But in all these suspicions, whether well-founded or ill, Venice was only true to her ancient instincts; and Durando may, possibly, be viewed as only another Carmagnola, with a less terrible doom.

Ancient Venice never forgave defeat under a foreigner; and she never forgave victory! Either event was almost equally fatal to the chief actor! And, as with foreigners, even so with her own sons; and as with her army, so with her navy. Pisani in the 14th century, Grimani in the 15th, and Morosini in the 17th, were disgraced for misfortunes; and yet each one was subsequently invoked, even in chains, to defend an ungrateful country against its foes! Not to succeed was perfidy, and the penalty death; while to succeed was perfidy, also; for it implied the possession of powers, or the attainment of glory, which might at some future day, imperil her own! Her army she never committed to a citizen, who might acquire in war too much glory for her safety; and her navy she never entrusted to a foreigner, who might betray her; while two Procurators were always sent to watch the general in his camp, a custom imitated by the French Republic. She never trusted "the man who sold his blood:" if successful, she suspected him—if unfortunate, she destroyed him. She rarely rewarded. Her Lagune was her defence, and her islands were never desecrated or endangered by the tread of armed men.

The capitulation of Vicenza, the most disastrous event of the campaign, caused the Central Committee of War at Venice, at once to resolve to concentrate all the forces then at Padua and Treviso, on the capital, for its defence. On the night of the 12th, therefore, about 6,000 troops with their arms and baggage retired from Padua, and marched for Venice, followed by all the civil officers of the place and many of the inhabitants. The Austrians under Gen. D'Aspre, after some hesitation, in apprehension of mines or an ambuscade, entered the abandoned place and took undisturbed possession. But the little city of Treviso, with the same rash and obstinate bravery which caused her, almost alone of Lombard cities, to resist Louis XII., and Maximilian I., and the allies of Cambray, more than three centuries before, now disobeyed the order of Venice and held out an ill-advised and hopeless resistance against Baron Welden, who, on the 31st of May, had resumed the siege abandoned by Gen. Nugent, some weeks before. Twelve hours of bombardment, on the 14th, however, brought her to reason, and with reluctance she was allowed the same terms of capitulation as Vicenza; thus causing by her obstinacy, the loss to Venice of the service of her garrison of 3,500 troops for a period of three months, and the entire disarming of her citizens. The desperate valor of Treviso may, perhaps, be attributed, however, in some degree, to the fact of a proclamation of Baron Welden to his army to give no quarter to any of the Crusaders—by which troops it was largely garrisoned —upon the charge that they had perpetrated atrocious outrages in a hospital at Villa Franca. Despite, therefore, the entreaties of some of the inhabitants, their city was in ruins around them, before capitulation caused the bombardment to cease. At first, Baron Welden accorded only to the Papal Grenadiers the honors of war and the retention of their arms; and the same condition being refused the Crociati, they refused to submit. Welden was resolute, and the chief of the Crociati ordered the drums to beat the *generale*. At this crisis, which menaced a conflict of utter extermination, the Podesta Olivieri rushed to the enemy's camp, and, with great difficulty, persuaded the Marshal to accord the terms required. The Italian troops, therefore, all marched out of the city with their arms and baggage and the honors of war, pledging themselves to retire into the Papal States, and not to bear arms against Austria for a period of three months. As for the city, she pledged herself to disarm her citizens.

The capitulation of Treviso had taken place on the 14th of June. On the 18th, Prince Lichtenstein occupied Mestre, a town of 5,000 inhabitants, which lies in full view of the towers of Venice, without resistance; and, establishing a strong *cordon militaire* of 7,000 men along the borders of the Lagune, cut off all communication of the city with the main land. One week later, and the surrender of Fort Cavanella, on the Adige, brought once more under the Austrian yoke the entire province of Venetia—"the Alpine stronghold of Osopo," the town of Palma Nuova in the Friul, and the capital itself, alone excepted.

As for Venice, she was now effectually blockaded by land. A blockade by sea had existed on paper for six weeks; but the combined Neapolitan, Sardinian, and Venetian fleet had not only prevented that manifesto from being executed, but had driven the Austrian fleet under the guns of Trieste for protection. There was a menace of placing that port in blockade, but the intervention of the foreign Consuls and of the captain of an English frigate then in the harbor caused the purpose to be suspended. Shortly afterwards, the same disturbances at Naples which had caused the recall of the Neapolitan troops from the banks of the Po, caused that, also, of the Neapolitan fleet, under Admiral De Cosa, from the shores of the Adriatic; and the Venetian and Sardinian fleets then sailed for Venice. On the 6th of June, the Sardinian fleet coming back within reach of the batteries of Trieste, two of its ships were struck by their balls, when the whole fleet moved off without returning the fire! On the morning of the 7th, the combined fleet again appeared off Trieste; and, on the following day, the blockade of that city was formally declared by the Sardinian Admiral Albini and the Venetian Admiral Bua, in behalf of their respective governments—to commence, for Austrian vessels, June 15th, and, for the vessels of all other powers, one month later.* But this blockade was merely nominal; nor was it ever designed to be otherwise. In the existing condition of the Austrian Navy, disordered and demoralized to the last degree, a blockade of the whole Adriatic could have been easily maintained; but then it would have commercially isolated Austria and Hungary, and would have been felt by the commerce of Germany, Russia, all Central Europe, and by that even of England, France, and the United States. It was not, therefore, to be thought off; and so, as early as March 29th, all maritime contest was waived by Sardinia, and the war confined to

* The blockade of Trieste by nineteen vessels commenced nominally May 23d. A loyal address was made on the occasion by the citizens to Count Gyulai, Military Governor.

the land! The Sardinian squadron, therefore, ready for sea at Genoa, March 27th, did not put to sea until just a month later, and on the same day that the Neapolitan fleet left Naples. Austria, however, declared a blockade of Venice, April 30th, which she subsequently maintained, and her fleet appeared off the Lido on the 6th of May. Still, on the 23d, when the Sardinian and Neapolitan squadrons, numbering nineteen vessels, appeared before Trieste, it was merely for "observation and protection," without the slightest purpose of "bombardment or blockade," as was declared at the time by the Sardinian Premier—all the terrors of the inhabitants, and the protests of consuls, and the discharge of batteries, to the contrary nevertheless! Thus, without even lifting a finger, Germany, it has well been said—"paralyzed the strongest arm of Sardinia." Virtually, the war in the Peninsula of '48–49 was of North Italy—not against Austria alone, but against all Germany. For, Styria, Croatia, Hungary, the Tyrol—all Central Europe was roused by the revolt of the "vassal" Lombards,—and was ready to rush down the Alps to crush them. The Teuton of every nationality led her foes. Berlin and Frankfort rejoiced with Prague and Vienna in Radetzky's triumphs. The German Diet claimed even the Adige as the Austrian frontier; and united in feeling, if not in fact, with Bavaria and Prussia in protesting against the blockade of Trieste. Had Austria, therefore, succumbed, Germany, it has been fairly inferred, would have taken up the quarrel; and had France crossed the Ticino, Russia and Prussia would have crossed the Isonzo, once more to make Lombardy the battle-field of Europe. Russia and Prussia opposed the Italian constitutions to the very last.*

The naval force of Venice, it may be remarked, had been very recently called into existence. The Arsenal, immediately upon the

* Mariotti.

evacuation of the Austrians, had assumed that ancient activity immortalized by Dante's "Inferno;" and, within the period of two months, two brigs and three corvettes, bearing the appropriate names—*San Marco*, *Il Crociato*, *La Civica*, *La Lombardia*, and *L'Indépendenza*, had issued from its water-gates; not to mention numerous *trabaccoli*, or small schooners, and gun-boats; whilst numerous other *trabaccoli* and gun-boats, with several steamers, remained on the stocks.

www.ingramcontent.com/pod-product-compliance
Lightning Source LLC
LaVergne TN
LVHW021132110826
845150LV00005B/1008

* 9 7 8 1 4 2 5 5 5 1 6 4 3 *